ROMAN FREEDMEN
DURING THE
LATE REPUBLIC

ROMAN FREEDMEN
DURING THE LATE REPUBLIC

———

SUSAN TREGGIARI

OXFORD
AT THE CLARENDON PRESS

OXFORD
UNIVERSITY PRESS

Great Clarendon Street, Oxford OX2 6DP

Oxford University Press is a department of the University of Oxford.
It furthers the University's objective of excellence in research, scholarship,
and education by publishing worldwide in

Oxford New York

Athens Auckland Bangkok Bogotá Buenos Aires Calcutta
Cape Town Chennai Dar es Salaam Delhi Florence Hong Kong Istanbul
Karachi Kuala Lumpur Madrid Melbourne Mexico City Mumbai
Nairobi Paris São Paulo Singapore Taipei Tokyo Toronto Warsaw

and associated companies in Berlin Ibadan

Oxford is a registered trade mark of Oxford University Press
in the UK and in certain other countries

Published in the United States
by Oxford University Press Inc., New York

© Oxford University Press 1969

The moral rights of the author have been asserted

Database right Oxford University Press (maker)

Reprinted 2000

All rights reserved. No part of this publication may be reproduced,
stored in a retrieval system, or transmitted, in any form or by any means,
without the prior permission in writing of Oxford University Press,
or as expressly permitted by law, or under terms agreed with the appropriate
reprographics rights organizations. Enquiries concerning reproduction
outside the scope of the above should be sent to the Rights Department,
Oxford University Press, at the address above

You must not circulate this book in any other binding or cover
and you must impose this same condition on any acquirer

ISBN 0–19–814280–3

Printed in Great Britain
on acid-free paper by
Biddles Short Run Books
King's Lynn

Oxford Scholarly Classics

This new series brings together a number of great academic works from the archives of Oxford University Press. Reissued in Spring 2000 in a uniform series design, Oxford Scholarly Classics will enable libraries, scholars and students to gain fresh access to some of the finest scholarship of the last century.

FOR ARNALDO

PREFACE

THIS book was originally planned to cover the period left largely undiscussed in A. M. Duff's *Freedmen in the Early Roman Empire*. No attempt is made to emulate Duff's thorough treatment of the Augustan legislation, and the approximate terminal date of my discussion is 27 B.C. But, although the treatment of legal developments may fairly be broken off there, it has not seemed appropriate to draw a sharp line between the republican, triumviral, and imperial periods when discussing social history, especially as the careers of republican freedmen often continued significant into Augustus' principate. The scanty and patchy sources for the Republic have also imposed a more schematic treatment than that of Duff. The main emphasis falls on the last century B.C., for Cicero, as ever, gives the most generous literary evidence. Our information on the second and earlier centuries is so sporadic that I have not claimed to discuss the period in detail, although the position of freedmen in the tribes may be traced fairly adequately.

My debts to many friends and scholars are great. The subject was originally suggested to me by Professor Sir Ronald Syme, to whose guidance and inspiration I owe much. Over a number of years I have enjoyed the constant help and encouragement of Mr. P. A. Brunt, who saved me from innumerable errors and whose ungrudged ideas appear on almost every page. Professor David Daube with infinite patience and kindness introduced me to the complexities of Roman private law, and Professor Alan Watson has also give me generous help in solving many difficulties. Mr. Russell Meiggs and Mr. J. A. Crook, who examined the book in its earlier form as a B.Litt. thesis, made useful corrections and suggestions. What I owe to earlier published work will be clear from the bibliography. I regret that A. W. Lintott's *Violence in Republican Rome* appeared too late for me to refer to it in Chapter IV.

The Craven Committee and the Director of the British School at Rome, who enabled me to spend two terms in Italy when I was beginning my research, and the Librarians and staff of the

Ashmolean, the Bodleian, and the Joint Library of the Hellenic and Roman Societies, who have been invariably helpful, all deserve my sincere thanks. I am grateful also to the Delegates of the Oxford University Press for the honour they have done me in accepting my book for publication, and to all their staff for their courtesy, care, and skill. Finally, for encouraging me to undertake this work I must thank Dr. L. H. Jeffrey and Mr. D. L. Stockton, for helping me to carry it through, Mr. and Mrs. Nicholas Milford, Mr. and Mrs. John Frith, Dr. and Mrs. Michael Pratelli, and Miss Brenda Bolton, and lastly but most of all my husband and daughters without whose generous support and exhortation it would not have been finished.

S. M. T.

London, March 1969

CONTENTS

LIST OF ABBREVIATIONS — xi

I. INTRODUCTION — 1
  (i) The Origins of Freedmen — 1
  (ii) Motives for Manumission — 11
  (iii) Forms of Manumission — 20
  (iv) Numbers of Freedmen — 31

II. THE LEGAL EFFECTS OF *LIBERTINITAS* — 37
  (i) *Libertini* in Public Law — 37
    (a) Voting Rights — 37
    (b) Eligibility for Office in State and Municipality — 52
    (c) Eligibility for Equestrian Rank — 64
    (d) Military and Naval Service — 67
  (ii) The Legal Position of *Libertini* in relation to their Patrons — 68
  (iii) The Legal Position of *Libertini* in relation to *Ingenui* other than their Patrons — 81

III. CAREERS — 87
  (i) Trade and Industry — 91
  (ii) Agriculture — 106
  (iii) The Learned Professions and the Fine Arts — 110
    (a) Scholars, Teachers, and Writers — 110
    (b) Doctors — 129
    (c) Architects — 132
    (d) Painters and Sculptors — 135
    (e) On the Stage and in the Circus and Arena — 138
  (iv) Private Service — 142
  (v) The Public Service — 153
  Conclusions — 160

IV. POLITICS — 162
  (i) The '*Ordo Libertinus*' — 162
  (ii) The *Collegia* — 168
  (iii) *Liberti* as Political Agents — 177
  Conclusions — 193

CONTENTS

V. RELIGION — 194
  (i) The State Religion — 194
  (ii) Other religious *Collegia* — 200
  (iii) Foreign Cults — 204
  Conclusions — 207

VI. FAMILY AND SOCIAL LIFE — 208
  (i) The Family — 208
  (ii) Social Relationships — 215
  Conclusions — 227

VII. THE SONS OF FREEDMEN — 229
  Conclusions — 235

VIII. CONCLUSIONS — 237

APPENDICES
  1. Freedmen whose Origin is Attested — 246
  2. Nomenclature of Freedmen — 250
  3. The Freedmen of M. Cicero — 252
  4. The Application of the word 'servus' to a Freedman — 265
  5. Lutatius Paccius — 267
  6. Tigellius and Phamea — 269
  7. Sarmentus — 271
  8. The Position of Freedmen in the Italian Communities which had not obtained the Roman Franchise — 273

BIBLIOGRAPHY — 274

INDEX I. GENERAL INDEX — 281

INDEX II. FREEDMAN AND PROBABLE FREEDMEN

ABBREVIATIONS

AE	*L'Année épigraphique*
AHR	*American Historical Review*
AJP	*American Journal of Philology*
Ant. Class.	*L'Antiquité classique*
Athen.	*Athenaeum*
BCH	*Bulletin de correspondance hellénique*
Bruns, *Fontes*	C. Bruns, *Fontes iuris Romani antiqui* (Seventh Edition)
CAH	*Cambridge Ancient History*
Camb. Hist. Journ.	*Cambridge Historical Journal*
CIG	*Corpus Inscriptionum Graecarum*
CIL	*Corpus Inscriptionum Latinarum* (References to vol. i are to the Second Edition)
CP	*Classical Philology*
CQ	*Classical Quarterly*
CR	*Classical Review*
Degr.	A. Degrassi, *Inscriptiones Latinae Liberae Rei Publicae* (1963)
Dittenberger, *Sylloge*	Dittenberger, *Sylloge Inscriptionum Graecarum* (Third Edition)
EJ	Ehrenberg and Jones, *Documents illustrating the Reigns of Augustus and Tiberius* (Second Edition, 1955)
ESAR	T. Frank and others, *An Economic Survey of Ancient Rome*, vol. i, 1933
FGH	Jacoby, *Die Fragmente der griechischen Historiker*
FIRA	Riccobono, Baviera, Ferrini, Furlani, and Arangio-Ruiz, *Fontes iuris Romani anteiustiniani* (vol. i in Second Edition)
Hist.	*Historia*
IG	*Inscriptiones Graecae*
IGR	*Inscriptiones Graecae ad Res Romanas Pertinentes*
ILS	Dessau, *Inscriptiones Latinae selectae*
JRS	*Journal of Roman Studies*

ABBREVIATIONS

MRR	T. R. S. Broughton, *Magistrates of the Roman Republic* (1951)
PBSR	*Papers of the British School at Rome*
Philol.	*Philologus*
Proc. Camb. Phil. Soc.	*Proceedings of the Cambridge Philological Society*
PIR	*Prosopographia Imperii Romani* (*PIR²* referring to available volumes of the Second Edition)
RE	Pauly–Wissowa–Kroll, *Real-Encyclopädie*
Rev. Phil.	*Revue philologique*
Rhein. Mus.	*Rheinisches Museum für Philologie*
Röm. Mitt.	*Mitteilungen des Deutschen Archäologischen Instituts, Römische Abteilung.*
TAPA	*Transactions of the American Philological Association*
ZSS	*Zeitschrift der Savigny-Stiftung für Rechtsgeschichte, Romanistische Abteilung*

I

INTRODUCTION

ROME in the last century of the Republic was a society in which race, class, culture, and religion were in the melting-pot. In this society the part played by freed slaves is generally held to have been no insignificant one. Before we can discuss what effect the freedmen had on society and society on them, the question of their original provenance, their background, how they won *libertas* and *civitas*, and what numerical relation they bore to the population at large, needs to be considered.

(i) *The Origins of Freedmen*

The origins of a freedman differ from those of a free-born man who has not passed through slavery in that the circumstances of his birth and nationality may be less relevant than those of his slavery and manumission. Race and heredity are clearly important factors in shaping his life and character, but stronger forces may be at work in the powerful compulsions of slavery and the pressures affecting ex-slaves in a class-conscious society. It is, however, the racial characteristics of freedmen on which it seems natural to concentrate in the first place when considering what marked them off from the Roman-born. ' "Roma est", civitas ex nationum conventu constituta'[1]: the racial mixture of the urban population was a vital factor in politics. By the time of Cicero, the *Urbs* had become a microcosm of the Empire, and for this situation it was freed and enfranchised slaves, and not resident foreigners, who were mainly responsible. The urban plebs was dominated by ex-prisoners-of-war, said Aemilianus,[2] to whom Italy was but a step-mother.

[1] *Comm. Pet.* 54. Though the authorship of this work is still in doubt, I use it, with caution, as a well-informed source on the Ciceronian age. For a recent discussion see Balsdon, *CQ* N.S. 13 (1963), 242 ff., with references at n. 1 and in the note on 249.

[2] Vell. ii. 14. 4; cf. Val. Max. vi. 2. 3.

It is war-prisoners who are normally stressed in our sources. We can distinguish various classes of slaves, first of all *nati* and *facti*. Those who are born into slavery[1] may be kept by the mother's master, in which case they are *vernae*, or they may be sold to new owners. In the second class, that of *ingenui* who become slaves, we have *alumni*, abandoned infants who became[2] the property of those who brought them up; children sold by their parents; men who sold themselves to pay their debts; war-captives, and victims of kidnapping and piracy. Roman law[3] forbade the sale of child or self: poverty, however, must often have made such expedients attractive and we cannot rule it out for this period.[4]

In the provinces, such sale certainly occurred: Sulla's exactions in Asia in 85–84 B.C. compelled many parents to sell their children and resulted in a glut of Asian slaves.[5] Kidnapping was notoriously rife, especially in Asia and Syria, which had been for centuries the happy hunting-ground of slave-traders, so that *Syri* were famous as slaves well before the Empire had spread to the East.[6] Cilician pirates were the most famed entrepreneurs in this trade, but they had their land-based colleagues too. When Roman rule moved east it merely gave an additional impetus to the slave-trade, and the newly prosperous Delos became the great slave-mart of the eastern Mediterranean, capable, according to Strabo,[7] of a day's turnover of tens of thousands. Such figures are always suspect,[8] but we have no reason to disbelieve that a number in the region of a myriad could be handled on an exceptional day. The flourishing state of the slave-trade in the East is reflected in the fact that the leaders

---

[1] Whether of two slave parents or of a liaison between *ancilla* and *dominus*.
[2] Illegally. See A. Watson, *The Law of Persons in the Later Roman Republic* (Oxford, 1967) p. 171. Comedy (Plautus, *Cist.* 124, *Cas.* 41 f.; Terence, *Heaut.* 627) shows that audiences were at least familiar with the idea.
[3] On the law of enslavement in general see Watson, ibid. pp. 159 ff.
[4] See W. L. Westermann, *The Slave Systems of Greek and Roman Antiquity* (Philadelphia, 1955), p. 59, and the review by Brunt, *JRS* 48 (1958), 167 f.
[5] Plut. *Lucullus* 20.
[6] Cf. Plaut. *Trinum.* 542: 'Suri, genus quod patientissimumst hominum.' M. Rostovtzeff, *Social and Economic History of the Hellenistic World* (Oxford, 1926), pp. 781 ff. Evidence for later opinion: Cic. *Prov. Cons.* 10: 'Judaeis et Syris, nationibus natis servituti'; Livy, xxxv. 49. 8: 'Syros . . . haud paullo mancipiorum melius propter servilia ingenia quam militum genus'; xxxvi. 17. 5.: 'Syri et Asiatici Graeci . . . vilissima genera hominum et servituti nata'.   [7] xiv. 668.
[8] Westermann, op. cit. p. 65, regards it as 'gross exaggeration'.

THE ORIGINS OF FREEDMEN

of the slave-revolt in Sicily in 135 B.C. were a Syrian and a Cilician, and that Eunus was able to call most of his followers Syrians.[1] The illicit trade was so efficient and widespread that in 104 B.C. a *senatus consultum* was passed, at the instance of Nicomedes II of Bithynia, ordering Roman pro-magistrates to rescue from slavery subjects of allied states wrongfully enslaved.[2] Kidnapping by pirates[3] and during the Civil and Social[4] Wars occurred in Italy itself in the first century B.C.

But kidnapping took second place to war as a large-scale source of slaves. The evidence on the selling of *captivi* is set out by M. E. Park.[5] It is worth noting that to sell prisoners was an extreme measure, not usually resorted to in the case of civilized foes, unless they were obstinate opponents (like the Carthaginians sold in 146 B.C.) or rebels (some Greek cities were so penalized in 84 B.C.). Dangerous barbarians were automatically treated as undeserving of any such forbearance: Park's list gives 60,000 Cimbri, 90,000 Teutones, a million Gauls killed or captured by Caesar.[6] The Sardinians in 177 yielded large numbers of slaves; the estimates for the Punic captives vary from 36,000 to 55,000.

It is clear that we can draw a rough distinction that westerners were sold *sub hasta*, while in the East slaves were made by the slave-trader more often than by the general. The rule is subject to exceptions, especially in Sulla's campaigns, and the Roman conquest was followed by an increase in slave-trading, thanks to the impositions of the tax-collector.

A useful list of slaves and freedmen, groups and individuals, whose nationality is mentioned in the sources, was compiled by Bang[7] and has since been expanded by Park.[8] It substantiates what

---

[1] It may not have been true of all of them, but it indicates the national loyalty of the majority. Eunus' wife was his συμπολῖτις (Diod. xxxiv. 2. 24). Cf. J. Vogt, *Sklaverei und Humanität* (supplement to *Hist.* vol. 8, 1965), pp. 44 ff. for details on nationality of rebel slaves. *Contra* Westermann, op. cit., p. 65.

[2] Diod. xxxvi. 3. 1.   [3] Cic. *de Imp.* 23.

[4] e.g. Cic. *Cluent.* 21; 162. cf. Suet. *D.A.* 32. 1.

[5] *The Plebs in Cicero's Day* (diss. Cambridge, Mass., 1918), pp. 32 f.

[6] Park, *Plebs*, p. 31. Cf. Köser, *De Captivis Romanorum* (Giessen, 1904), pp. 93 ff. Westermann, op. cit., p. 63, estimates *c.* 150,000 as the total of slaves taken.

[7] 'Die Herkunft d. römischen Sklaven.' *Röm. Mitt.* (1910), pp. 225 ff., (1912), pp. 189 ff.   [8] op. cit., pp. 35 f.

we should in any case guess, that slaves were drawn from every available source in the Roman world. A list of freedmen alone, based on this list, will be found in Appendix 1.

Our knowledge of the provenance of freedmen will be seen to be patchy. Whether or not we are told the nationality of a *libertinus* is largely a matter of chance. A biographical note in a historian or monographer is the most likely source. Thus, we tend to know the nationality of freedmen of importance, as, for that matter, we know more about their lives in other respects. From the outset, our sources are fuller on freedmen who were notable in the fields of scholarship, literature, and politics. Funerary inscriptions, on the other hand, to which we owe much of our information on the poorer *libertini*, rarely (for reasons of space) give such details. Besides, a freedman ordering his tomb was usually more interested in his career after manumission. If his origin was of importance to him in his profession, a freedman might mention it on his memorial,[1] as would a *verna* for reasons of sentiment or prestige.[2] In the literary sources, we may know the origin of a freedman because he was enslaved late in life: Tyrannio the elder, for instance, had been an eminent professor at the time of his capture, and this information is unlikely to be forgotten. Another point that emerges is that the origin of *libertini*, or alleged *libertini*, was often disputed even during their lifetime, as in the cases of Lenaeus,[3] Hyginus,[4] and Valerius Cato.[5] If this happened to famous men, the origin of less eminent freedmen was likely to be obscured still more rapidly.

Most of those of whose enslavement we are told or can guess[6] were war-captives: Alexander Polyhistor of Miletus, Tyrannio of

---

[1] The Greek doctor Manneius, who seems libertine, not peregrine, stresses his origin in Tralles, where there was a noted medical school (*CIL* i. 1684= Degr. 799).

[2] *Vernae* from Minturnae: J. Johnson, *Excavations at Minturnae* (Philadelphia, 1933), ii, Inscriptions, part i: no. 11, 6; possibly no. 3, 1 (but see Degr. 724, n. 1).

[3] Suet. *Gram.* 15 has a romantic tale that he was kidnapped (from where a textual corruption prevents us from knowing with certainty); Schol. ad Juvenal, i. 20 believes 'Lenius' to be native of Aurunca. For details, see Appendix 1.

[4] Suet. ibid. 20: a Caesarian prisoner, but not known whether from Alexandria or Spain.

[5] He claimed to be an *ingenuus* wrongfully enslaved (Suet. ibid. 11).

[6] For references, see Appendix 1.

Amisus, Timagenes of Alexandria, Julius Hyginus from Alexandria or Spain, Julius Licinus from Comata, and perhaps the Athenian Ateius Philologus, the Syrians Publilius the mime writer, Staberius Eros and Manilius the astrologer, Pompeius Demetrius of Gadara. The only one, so far as we know, who may have been a victim of kidnapping is Pompeius Lenaeus. Valerius Cato claimed to have been wrongfully enslaved; Cilnius Melissus from Spoletium and Antonius Gnipho from Gaul were *alumni*. Greeks, Syrians, and 'Italians' predominate, but this was to be expected as we are dealing with men of Hellenistic culture, since the major source is Suetonius, *De Grammaticis*. Caution is needed when dealing with alleged Italians, however, as these appear to have often been *vernae* of foreign stock, although in the civil and social wars it was easy enough for *ingenui* to be enslaved.

It has often been held that Greeks and Hellenized 'Orientals' were in the majority among freed slaves. This belief has been made the basis of important generalizations about the dilution of the Roman character. From the evidence set out above, we should *a priori* expect westerners to outnumber easterners among freedmen as well. We shall take up this point again later. From the lists of known *freedmen*, conversely, we might conjecture a numerical superiority of orientals. But our list is biased in favour of men of culture. Such men tended to be of Greek stock, from Greece, Asia, Syria, or Egypt. But with the spread of Roman power, Greek culture followed in its train, and the freedmen from the western provinces of whom we hear, since they drew the attention of scholars and writers, are, necessarily, often men of Greek culture too. Antonius Gnipho, perhaps from Transalpina, will have been as 'Hellenized' as Tyrannio of Amisus or Publilius the Syrian. The spread of Graeco-Roman ideas meant precisely this levelling and fusion of culture which in the late Republic was already beginning, for certain favoured men, to obliterate racial handicaps. We have to beware of dismissing all Gauls as trousered barbarians or all easterners as effete, thus taking over the prejudices of Cicero's audiences or the sneers of Juvenal.

As for freedmen of a humbler type, craftsmen or traders, their origin is nowhere directly revealed. Their inscriptions, as already mentioned, are often brief. The poor, buried in mass graves, or *columbaria* with fellow freedmen and slaves, tell us still less. A method which suggests itself is the examination of *cognomina*, which in fact often appear to be determined by nationality.[1] Tenney Frank held[2] that possession of a Greek *cognomen* suggested that a freedman came from the Hellenized half of the empire, while a Latin *cognomen* was not enough to show western origin, since these, he believed, were preferred and could be given to easterners too. His interpretation of the inscriptional evidence led him to suppose that of the ordinary population of the city of Rome in imperial times about ninety per cent had foreign blood in its veins, and since Rome was not enough of an industrial centre to attract many resident aliens, this foreign element was largely of libertine origin. Furthermore, these *libertini* were mostly from the Greek East. A sample of slaves and *libertini* yielded seventy per cent with Greek names, that is, for Tenney Frank, of eastern provenance.

If we make a similar division of the Greek and Roman *cognomina* to be found in republican and Augustan inscriptions in *CIL* i. 969–1422, 291 freedmen in all, we find 224 Greek to 67 Roman names. On Frank's criteria, this would indicate a strong predominance of 'Graeco-Oriental' freedmen.

However, M. L. Gordon in a valuable article[3] discredited this method of attack. She shows that it is not true that Greek names were never borne by westerners: one has only to look at the names of the imperial German guard.[4] For the Republic, we could cite Antonius Gnipho or Cilnius Melissus, the latter from a Latin colony.[5] Factors other than the race of the slave controlled his name, for instance the familiarity of Romans with Greek culture, a natural reluctance to use unfamiliar barbarian names (though some Celtic names might be Latinized easily), and the extreme poverty of the Latin language in the matter of names.[6] *Libertini* in fact stand out among the *plebs* because they possess a *cognomen*, since the name by which they had been known as slaves remained

---

[1] Aegypta, Cilix, Syrus, etc.   [2] *AHR* 21 (1916), 689 ff.
[3] *JRS* 14 (1924), 93 ff., reprinted by M. I. Finley in *Slavery in Classical Antiquity* (Cambridge, 1960), pp. 171 ff. Cf. Westermann, op. cit., p. 96.
[4] *JRS* 14 (1924), 103.   [5] Suet. *Gram.* 21.
[6] Cf. B. Doer, *Die römische Namengebung*, Stuttgart (1926), pp. 46 ff.

as surname when, on manumission, they took the *nomen gentile* and (usually) *praenomen* of their patron. *Cognomina*, except for the aristocracy, were of comparatively recent introduction, and although for the upper classes they were regular by the first century B.C., there are several instances of well-known men, such as Marius or Sertorius, who lack a surname. The lower classes seem to have been slow to follow the fashion: among their inscriptions mention of a third name is the exception.[1] *Libertini* also appear often enough without *cognomen*, for instance Cicero's scribe, M. Tullius, is never given another name in Cicero's allusions to him.[2] Compared with the rich variety of Greek names held by freedmen, only a handful of Latin names exist in our inscriptions: the primitive type of Olipor, Gaipor, Marpor;[3] the equally dull Primus, Tertius; racial names such as Laudica (Laodicean) or Syrus; nicknames like Baro[4] or Cerdo;[5] even names common to the aristocracy like Rutilius, Spinther, Libo. Even the names which seem to denote nationality do not always do so:[6] we cannot therefore tell whether Cicero's Aegypta or Ap. Claudius' Cilix were really natives of Egypt and Cilicia.[7] Names like Sabinus or Graecus might be used to indicate moral or intellectual qualities. Similarly, allusions to history in such names as Antiochus or Seleucus or to localized cults in Menophilus, which refers to the Phrygian deity Men Tyrannus, may indicate the personal taste of the slave-owner or dealer rather than of the slave.

Therefore, even though Greek names predominate among republican as among imperial inscriptions of freedmen, this should not

[1] Cf. the Coptos inscription (*ILS* 2483 = *EJ* 261). In the inscriptions from tombs of the poor in *CIL* i. 969–1014 and 1202–1422, there are about 15 definite *ingenui* with *cognomina*, as against about 44 without. Tribe is generally mentioned instead (e.g. 1259, 1314 = Degr. 802 and 792). A son may adopt a *cognomen* when his father had none (*CIL* i. 1294, 1328—both common nicknames, Rufus and Capito, held also in noble families).
[2] Possibly *honoris causa*. For inscriptions cf. *CIL* i. 1227, 1268 = Degr. 919, 822. On *ollae* it is natural that *cognomen* should be omitted (*CIL* i. 1015–1201 = Degr. 873–94).
[3] Slave of Aulus, Gaius, Marcus.   [4] Blockhead.   [5] Craftsman.
[6] Gordon, *JRS* 14 (1924), 98 f.
[7] For such names from the Republic cf. Cilix (Cic. *Fam.* iii. 1. 2), Aegypta (Cic. *Att.* viii. 15. 1), Laudica (*CIL* i. 1324), Lyde (ibid. 1364), Syrus (ibid. 1351, 1360), Asia (ibid. 1263), Macedo (ibid. 1398), Macedonius (ibid. 1289), Galla (ibid. 1069), Sabinus (ibid. 1371).

lead us to conclude necessarily that their bearers came from the Greek-speaking half of the Empire.[1] The distinction is facile and inaccurate and tends to rest on the Juvenalian idea[2] that Rome was corrupted by the presence of Greeks and Syrians, that these were generally freedmen, so Greek and Syrian *libertini* were both influential and in the majority. The confusion is made worse by the common 'short-hand' description of provincials from the lands east of Italy as 'orientals'. To divide the Empire in this way begs too many questions: it might lead us to think of Semitic Carthaginians as westerners or of the Thracian gladiator as over-civilized and effete. Now the Romans had very little idea of statistics and Juvenal is picking on types which happened to meet with his disapproval. A similar prominence is and has been ascribed to the Jews in many modern societies: they are a people who make themselves felt. Other Romans, when arguing a case, accuse various other races of predominance in Rome. Thus Scipio Aemilianus in 131 B.C., rebuking the Roman mob as being made up of men whom he himself had brought to the city as prisoners of war,[3] implies, if we take him literally, that most freedmen and new citizens were Spaniards or Carthaginians; Cicero refers to the large numbers of Greeks, Asians, and Jews who took part in *contiones*[4] (and these too would mostly be freedmen). Thus it seems that we cannot lay down a hard-and-fast rule as to which national groups prevailed among freedmen. They, like Rome, will have been made up 'ex nationum conventu'.[5]

If we are to categorize freedmen at all, the dividing-line should be drawn, not between West and East, for this distinction turns out to have little value, but between civilized and uncivilized peoples and cultured and uneducated individuals. The factor which interested the dealer and prospective client in the sale of a slave was whether he was an educated and intelligent man (which meant, for the Roman world, a man with a smattering at least of Graeco-Roman culture) or suited to manual work. Captives from the

---

[1] But cf. Johnson, *Minturnae* i. 113 for cautious statistics for a limited group.
[2] Juvenal, *Sat.* iii. 62-6, 76-8. See too Tac. *Ann.* xv. 44. 3.
[3] According to the version of Val. Max. vi. 2. 3. Cf. A. E. Astin, *Scipio Aemilianus* (Oxford, 1967), p. 234.
[4] Cic. *Flacc.* 17, 66.   [5] *Comm. Pet.* 54.

THE ORIGINS OF FREEDMEN

eastern provinces might belong to the second class just as easily as did the Gaul or Briton.[1] 'Eastern' origin did not automatically carry with it those allegedly Greek qualities most conducive to the success of a slave or freedman. Cicero's grandfather is made to remark in the *De Oratore* that the better a Syrian knew Greek, the worse he was:[2] many Syrians, then, had little knowledge of the language. Other 'oriental' nations were noted for qualities the reverse of Attic: the Cappadocian was 'sine sensu, sine sapore, elinguem, tardum, inhumanum negotium'[3]; the Phrygian would respond only to blows[4]; Cilicians and Syrians were largely employed on the great Sicilian estates of the second century B.C.[5], while Thracians were the most noted gladiators.[6] According to Varro,[7] Gauls and Spaniards were especially adapted to stock-farming. Ethiopians are found as *venatores*.[8] The Cimbri and Teutones were probably mostly drafted to the *latifundia*, and these included women and children, who would have been fit for little else:[9] some of the boys and younger men survived to take part in Spartacus' revolt.[10]

Barbarian slaves, unskilled or savage, could expect nothing better than the mines[11] or the *latifundia*, where life was notoriously hard, men were expendable, and there was little hope of manumission.[12] They have left little record of their existence. Some may have been luckier than their comrades: Caesar, for instance, made a practice of giving Gallic prisoners to his troops[13] and for these there was a possibility that they might remain as batmen and perhaps please their masters, or at least be sold singly to slave-dealers, in which case they might have a chance better than that of war-prisoners sold

[1] On whom see Cic. *Att.* iv. 17. 6.
[2] Cic. *de Or.* ii. 265. Cf. A. H. M. Jones, *The Greek City from Alexander to Justinian* (Oxford, 1926), pp. 288 f.
[3] Cic. *Post Red. in Sen.* 14.
[4] Cic. *Flacc.* 65.
[5] Diod. xxxiv. 2. 24, xxxvi. 5. 1.
[6] Plut. *Crassus* 8.
[7] *RR.* ii. 10. 4.
[8] Pliny, *NH* viii. 131.
[9] Gordon, *JRS* 14 (1924), 103. For women and children on farms with *pastores*, cf. Varro, *RR* ii. 1. 26.
[10] Livy, *Ep.* xcvii, cf. Oros. v. 24.
[11] Strabo, iii. 147, xii. 562.
[12] Below, p. 106 f.
[13] Suet. *DJ* 26. 3.

en bloc. We know of one such captive, one from the thousands enslaved, who entered the service of Julius himself and was freed by him or his heir, C. Julius Licinus.[1] Unfortunately, we are not told anything of Licinus' background, whether he had been a complete barbarian, or whether he had belonged to the ruling class: our sources concentrate on his 'barbaric' vices of greed and insolence. Caesar perhaps perceived in him some of the ability which later gave him an important post under Augustus, but it is not certain that it was he who freed him.

It was, however, the Hellenized, or at least Romanized, races which normally provided Rome with her slave craftsmen, teachers, administrators, personal servants. Not all, obviously, were of a high standard of Greek culture: the Roman shopkeeper and his wife, when choosing an assistant or a maid, would look for a strong, healthy, and not too stupid slave, able to understand Latin. For such jobs, Gallic tribesmen were obviously not adapted; a Syrian, Asian, or Greek filled the bill, one of the races born to slavery. A Sardinian or a Gaul from Cisalpina or Narbonensis would have to do at a pinch, but the former were famous for their obstinacy.[2] The freedmen we know tended to belong to a very limited class: scholars, confidential servants of the governing class, certain of the more prosperous tradesmen and craftsmen, merchants, workers in a few well-documented industries such as pottery. Of these, fewer still have left traces of their original nationality. We meet, in fact, the cream of the *libertini*, and these tend to be men with a high degree of skill or learning, men who had not only the qualities to recommend them to their masters, but who also made their mark in society after manumission. It is scarcely surprising that such men tend to come from the most civilized backgrounds, and not merely Greece, Syria, Asia, or Italy itself, but from towns like Gadara, Athens, Amisus, Alexandria.[3] As regards the freedmen on whom we have no definite information, craftsmen and shopkeepers and lower servants, we can guess that perfumers, jewellers, metal-workers, chefs, dancing-girls, would come from a Hellenized background.

[1] Dio, liv. 21. 2 f., Suet. *DA* 67.
[2] Cic. *Fam.* vii. 24. 2; Auct. *Vir. Ill.* iii. 57. 2. [3] Appendix 1.

We hear little specifically of *vernae*, but no doubt many of the freedmen of whose origin we are not informed will have been home-born slaves. Such men were well placed to receive a good training: scholars and professional men were often specially educated from boyhood in a rich household, and a master might take a kindlier interest in a *verna*. Atticus specialized in home-born slaves,[1] and the *grammaticus* Epirota, born at Tusculum,[2] was one of them. The origins of one of the best documented of all freedmen, Tullius Tiro, are not precisely known: Gellius[3] calls him 'alumnus' of Cicero, but in the context this appears to mean pupil and not a child Cicero had reared, so it remains an open question whether Tiro was home-born, a foundling, or a bought slave. The main point about *vernae* is that their race is of less importance than the circumstances of their birth, in slavery and in a Roman family.[4] Such slaves were often, it seems, inexactly but significantly regarded as Italians.[5]

Thus, while Roman conquest and the activities of dealers brought slaves from the whole Mediterranean world to Rome, the proportions of slaves from the various nations will not correspond with those of freedmen. While uneducated peasants and rough tribesmen were those who most easily fell victims to slavery, they were at the same time those least likely to be freed. The educated or skilled man, less likely to fall into the hands of the slave-trader, and, except in particularly brutal wars, not often sold out of hand on capture, had the best chances of manumission.

(ii) *Motives for Manumission*

It has been said[6] that slaves of a certain type, for instance those working on the great estates or in the mines, seem to have had little chance of being freed. Others, employed in less brutish work, and especially those who came into close contact with their masters, had a fair chance of manumission. We will now consider briefly

---

[1] Varro, *RR* ii. 1. 26; Nepos, *Att.* 13. 3 f.
[2] Suet. *Gram.* 16. It would be interesting to know if the event took place at Cicero's villa.
[3] xiii. 9.   [4] Cf. Gordon, *JRS* 14 (1924), 110.
[5] Appendix 1.   [6] p. 9.

what slaves could hope for manumission and what motives might lie behind their manumission.[1]

Public opinion in Rome accepted the freeing of slaves as normal and even desirable. Cicero apropos of the punishment of crucifixion could say:[2]

> Nisi forte hanc condicionem vobis esse voltis quam servi, si libertatis spem propositam non haberent, ferre nullo modo possent.... An vero servos nostros horum suppliciorum omnium metu dominorum benignitas vindicta una liberat, nos a verberibus, ab unco, a crucis denique terrore, neque res gestae neque acta aetas neque vestri honores vindicabunt?

With some twisting of fact to suit his context, the orator again observed in the *Philippics*,[3]

> Etenim, patres conscripti, cum in spem libertatis sexennio post sumus ingressi diutiusque servitutem perpessi quam captivi frugi et diligentes solent...

It is admitted, then, that slaves can, and do, hope for freedom, and that after enslavement in war a man might hope by working well and saving his *peculium* to win or buy his liberty in a relatively short time.

The motives and causes which led to manumission naturally varied considerably. Even among the pragmatic Romans, a philosophic idea cannot be discounted entirely. Though the Roman might sometimes justify his position of power by telling himself that other races were morally inferior and born to servitude, both as subjects of a foreign domination and as individuals actually enslaved,[4] he was also open to more generous ideas. The Stoic view that slaves could be the moral equals of their masters was fashionable in the late Republic: it is discussed by Cicero.[5] Horace, *libertino patre natus*, brings the concept out of the field of metaphor and looks at it from the slave's angle: Davus tells his master:[6]

---

[1] Both questions will be considered again later with reference to particular *métiers* in which freedmen are found.
[2] *Rab. Perd.* 15–16.   [3] viii. 32.
[4] The idea of course goes back to Aristotle, *Pol.* 1253[b] ff. Cic. *Prov. Cons.* 10, cf. *Har. Resp.* 19; Livy, xxxv. 49. 8; xxxvi. 17. 5.
[5] *Parad.* v. (33 ff.). Cf. Publilius Syrus, *Sententiae* (ed. Bickford-Smith), 219: 'Famulatur dominus, ubi timet quibus imperat'; 356: 'Minus est quam servus dominus, qui servos timet;' Phaedrus, 42. 1 ff.: 'Aesopi ingenio statuam posuere Attici Servomque collocarunt aeterna in basi, Patere honoris scirent ut cuncti viam Nec generi tribui sed virtuti gloriam'.
[6] Hor. *Sat.* ii. 7. 75 ff. Horace concludes that the *sapiens* is free (83 ff.).

MOTIVES FOR MANUMISSION

Tune mihi dominus, rerum imperiis hominumque
tot tantisque minor, quem ter vindicta quaterque
imposita haud umquam misera formidine privet?
adde super, dictis quod non levius valeat: nam
sive vicarius est qui servo paret, uti mos
vester ait, seu conservus, tibi quid sum ego? nempe
tu mihi qui imperitas alii servis miser atque
duceris ut nervis alienis mobile lignum.

Such considerations might act on a Horace or a Cicero, making them treat their slaves as human beings and think it almost a duty to reward good service with freedom, but it could also induce acquiescence in the institution of slavery.[1] Moral doubts trouble few: often those who had been slaves themselves were the cruellest masters.[2] The freedman Isidorus had no compunction about owning, in his less palmy days, 4,116 slaves,[3] and it was a freedman's son, Vedius Pollio, whose treatment of his slaves outraged the commonest human rights and shocked even contemporaries.[4]

In practice, it was recognition of individual merit, rather than doubts on the validity of the master–slave relationship, which provided the highest motives for manumission. Cicero refers to the class of *libertini* as 'sua virtute fortunam huius civitatis consecuti'.[5] Q. Cicero remarks that Tiro was too good to be a slave, 'indignum illa fortuna'.[6] Lucullus took a similar view about the distinguished prisoner Tyrannio of Amisus: his manumission by Murena was an insult because it acknowledged an enslavement that could otherwise have been denied.[7]

Such high-thinking was a luxury. But recognition of talent was a motive in many cases. The *grammaticus* Lutatius Daphnis, for instance, though purchased by Catulus for the vast sum of 700,000 sesterces, remained his slave only a short time.[8]

---

[1] Aristotle was at least troubled by doubts. The question of whether slavery was justifiable in itself was scarcely put in republican Rome. Below, pp. 241 ff.
[2] Sen. *Clem.* i. 18. 2.   [3] Pliny, *NH* xxxiii. 135.
[4] Dio, liv. 23.   [5] *Cat.* iv. 16.
[6] *Fam.* xvi. 16.
[7] Plut. *Lucullus* 19. 7.
[8] Suet. *Gram.* 3: DCC milibus nummum . . . emptum ac brevi manumissum. P. Fraccaro, *Opuscula* (Pavia, 1957). ii. pp. 45 ff. thinks Daphnis was freed *testamento*, but this is only conjecture.

Staberius Eros[1] and Voltacilius Plotus[2] were freed for their scholastic attainments. Not only could such men be more useful to their patrons after manumission, but their intellectual talents were thought to demand recognition. The same motive may have operated in the case of other valuable slaves—the skilled Arretine potters for example—but it must have been confined to masters rich enough to afford such gestures.

Altruism tempered by caution or vanity may be discerned in the common practice of *manumissio testamento*. A master who freed by will could reward his deserving slave without incurring any inconvenience himself. On the contrary, if he published his intention before his death he might reap the reward of more devoted service (the possibility of being murdered for his pains was remote, given the severity of Roman law towards slaves whose master was murdered[3]); he might also enjoy the prospect of a fine funeral, his corpse attended by grateful freedmen with caps of liberty on their heads, witnesses to their patron's munificence.[4] It is, however, uncharitable to suppose that these were the only motives. The perfumer of Venusia, himself a freedman, Philargyrus, who freed his whole *familia* and probably left his fortune to the new *liberti*, may have lacked a family and friends whom he could benefit, but he showed a spirit worthy of an ingenuous Roman.[5]

Manumission during the master's life also did him credit because it swelled the train of his clients. Dionysius rightly attacks the motive here as ostentation,[6] but at least it aped the virtue it did not possess. *Liberalitas* was supposedly part of the character of the Roman gentleman: the noble, the rich bourgeois, even the more successful ex-slave might pretend to it. The behaviour dictated by fashion or the canons of taste sometimes did duty for that dictated by morals—one of the saving graces of a class-conscious society.

---

[1] Suet. *Gram.* 13: 'propter litterarum studium'.
[2] Suet. *Rhet.* 3: 'ob ingenium ac studium litterarum'.
[3] Auct. *Rhet. ad Herenn.* i. 14. 24 (murder of *dominus* by slave freed in his will); cf. Tac. *Ann.* xiv. 42 ff.; Pliny, *Epp.* iii. 14, viii. 14. 12 ff.; *Hist. Aug. Hadr.* 18. 11. *Dig.* xxix. 5. 1. 28.
[4] Dion. Hal. iv. 24. cf. Petr. *Cena* 71.
[5] *CIL* i. 1703 = Degr. 825: '. . . C. l. Philargyro unguentario, isque familiam suam manumisit pecuniamqu(e) . . .'.
[6] Dion. Hal. iv. 24.

MOTIVES FOR MANUMISSION

A commoner motive for manumission, shared by the poorer slave-owners without social pretensions, was recognition of good service.[1] Cicero writes to Terentia in the emergency of 58 B.C., when the threat of confiscation was hanging over them, that they will manumit any of her slaves who deserve it.[2] Fidelity and trustworthiness,[3] the qualities valued also in a *libertus*,[4] devotion to the patron even in a bad cause,[5] complicity in murder and sharp practice according to the still more jaundiced view of Dionysius, might win a slave his freedom.[6] 'Officium' would describe this quality, if regarded in a favourable light.[7]

The warmer personal feeling, which was no doubt Cicero's main motive for freeing Tiro, or at any rate for timing the manumission as he did,[8] is to be found in other cases, for example in the inscriptions put up by patron to *libertus* or *libertus* to patron.[9] Still stronger ties of affection also operated. The *Lex Aelia Sentia*, while restricting the power of a master under twenty years old to manumit, allowed him to free blood-relations or a slave-girl he wished to marry.[10] Such situations seem to have arisen frequently in the republican period. Although slave-marriage was not recognized by law, it was often respected: a newly-freed slave might therefore have a *contubernalis*, parent, or child still in slavery, whom he would try to redeem by the normal process of purchase and manumission. A situation might thus easily arise in which a father was technically the freedman of his own son, or the wife *liberta* of her husband.[11] Other married couples are *conliberti*,[12] both freed by the master, and

---

[1] On the *servus bonus* see Vogt, *Sklaverei*, pp. 84 ff., 93 ff.
[2] *Fam.* xiv. 4. 4: 'tuis (servis) ita promissum est te facturam esse ut quisque esset meritus. Est autem in officio adhuc Orpheus, praeterea magnopere nemo'. (We hear no more of Orpheus.)
[3] Vogt, *Sklaverei*, pp. 83 ff.
[4] Cic. *Fam.* iv. 9. 1; xiii. 23; xiii. 70.
[5] Cic. *Rosc. Am.* 130—the stock excuse for criminal activity by freedmen. Cf. for slaves, Plaut. *Capt.* 200; Publilius, *Sent.* 525; Petron. *Cena* 75.
[6] iv. 24.
[7] Cic. *Fam.* xiv. 4. 4. Below, p. 80.
[8] Appendix 3, p. 261.
[9] e.g. *CIL* i. 1547 = Degr. 565; *CIL* i. 1332 = Degr. 928.
[10] Gaius, i. 19; *Dig.* xl. 2. 13.
[11] e.g. Quint. vii. 7. 9. *CIL* i. 1223; 1248; 2135 = Degr. 946.
[12] e.g. *CIL* i. 1221 = Degr. 793; *CIL* i. 2527 = Degr. 795. Other pairs with the same *nomen* may be either *conliberti* or *patronus* and *liberta*, e.g. *CIL* i. 1401 = Degr. 939.

we might guess that patrons were sometimes so considerate of a *contubernium* as to arrange a double manumission so as not to break up the marriage. *Concubinae*[1]—and probably, for that matter, *concubini*[2]—might also be rewarded with their freedom. Manumission for the express purpose of marriage is described in the funerary inscriptions of Larcia Horaea,[3] who married the son of her patrons, themselves *libertini*, and of Caninia,[4] who married her patron and probably one-time *conservus*.

Economic motives were naturally important, indeed probably uppermost, in the minds of poorer slave-owners, and in the case of slaves who lacked close contact with their masters, for instance the lower domestic servants of large houses, who were freed in large numbers. It was expensive to keep a slave, and when he grew old or ill it became uneconomic.[5] He might be virtually unsaleable, but if freed he could be made to render various benefits to the patron: *operae* if the latter stipulated them, and, in certain cases, a share in the freedman's property on his death. (Both advantages would of course be nullified if the slave was completely past work.) Further, the freedman would usually support himself, taking the burden of finding food and lodging from the shoulders of his patron.[6] The institution of the corn dole encouraged poorer masters to turn their slaves into *cives Romani* and so transfer the obligation of feeding them to the state: this practice became so common that in 56 B.C. it was recognized to be a public nuisance, and later Augustus had to take measures to exclude recently manumitted slaves from taking a share in the *congiaria*.[7] When a slave was manumitted informally,[8] any capital his talents might earn was returned to his master at his death, since at law he was still a slave. But this mode of manumission did not allow the patron various benefits obtained through formal manumission. A short-term financial advantage could also be secured by the patron when the slave bought his own freedom, though as in this case the slave was not receiving a

---

[1] *CIL* i. 1227 = Degr. 919; *CIL* i. 2527 = Degr. 952.
[2] For sexual relationships of masters with male slaves, cf. Auct. *Bell. Hisp.* 33.
[3] *CIL* i. 1570 = Degr. 977 (dating to the time of Caesar).
[4] *CIL* i. 1216.   [5] Cato, *RR* 2. 7.   [6] Below, pp. 77 f.
[7] Dion. Hal. iv. 24; Dio, xxxix. 24; Suet. *DA* 42.
[8] Below, pp. 29 ff.

MOTIVES FOR MANUMISSION

beneficium, he may have been exempt from the obligation to render *operae*. On the debit side was the fact that when a slave was freed, a tax of five per cent of his value was owed to the state. This *vicesima libertatis* had been instituted in 357 B.C., we are told,[1] and in the first century B.C. remained one of the few sources of revenue from Italy. Cicero,[2] sarcastically, hints that it was felt by slaves to be an obstacle to their manumission, but it would be true only in extreme cases. Duff[3] suggests, logically but without evidence, that the *vicesima* was paid by the master when he had taken the initiative in manumitting, by the slave when he bought his freedom. There may have been a greater variety of arrangements than this.

We can only conjecture how often the initiative was taken by the slave, who offered his *peculium*,[4] or part of it, in return for liberty. This was the pocket-money normally allowed to slaves, and the frugal,[5] instead of spending it on transitory gratification, saved it up to buy their liberty: 'ille unciatim vix de demenso suo Suom defrudans genium conpersit miser . . .'[6] The anxieties of Tityrus, whose freedom was so long delayed by the fecklessness of Galatea, come easily to mind.[7] Slaves who were in business as their masters' agents, the slaves of important men who could collect perquisites or bribes, slaves of public bodies, had a chance of amassing a large *peculium* and of obtaining their liberty rapidly. For the *servus callidus* of Plautus, payment by the slave is more normal than manumission gratis by the master.[8] Others, especially, one would think, rustic slaves, probably took the best part of their lifetime before saving enough to buy freedom.[9] The amount paid presumably varied with the value of the slave.[10] The *peculium* gave the slave hope, however distant, and was thus of value to the master in keeping the slave contented with his lot.

---

[1] Livy, vii. 16. 7.   [2] Cic. *Att.* ii. 16. 1.
[3] A. M. Duff, *Freedmen in the Early Roman Empire* (Oxford, 1928), p. 29.
[4] For the legal aspects of *peculium*, Watson, *Law of Persons*, pp. 178 ff.
[5] Cic. *Phil.* viii. 32.
[6] Ter. *Phorm.* 43 ff.; cf. Cic. *Parad.* v. 39, Sen. *Ep.* 80. 4. For the slaves who did not care to save, Plaut. *Capt.* 120.
[7] Verg. *Ecl.* i. 27. The *motif* of purchasing *libertas* is inextricably tangled with the free grant of freedom by Octavian.
[8] Payment: *Aul.* 310, *Capt.* 120; Gratis manumission: *Capt.* 408, 948.
[9] They were given *peculium*, but hardly ever seem to have been freed. Below, pp. 106 f.   [10] Duff, *Freedmen*, pp. 17 f.

The hope of manumission for good service was also held out to slaves by their owners in order to keep them docile. In a large household especially, the master would be compelled to free deserving slaves in order to encourage the rest to imitate their good service. If not, the efficiency of the whole establishment would suffer. Manumission thus would be used in order to maintain morale.

Finally, negative reasons on the master's side might decide the manumission of a particular slave. Free men could not be examined under torture. Therefore, to avoid being incriminated by slave-evidence, masters might hurriedly manumit possible witnesses. This was done, for example, by Clodia[1] and Milo.[2] When there was a possibility in 58 B.C. that Cicero's entire property might be confiscated, he decided to insure himself against total loss by manumitting his *familia* rather than allowing it to fall into the hands of others, but the manumission was to take effect only if the property was confiscated, and Cicero anticipated that his slaves would have difficulty in maintaining their claim to be free.[3]

The manumitter was sometimes not a private individual but some public body or limited company. The state, *municipia*, *coloniae*, temples, and *societates* could manumit the slaves they owned.[4] The *collegia* or guilds, however, lacked the right until the time of Marcus Aurelius.[5] The qualification of manumission of *servi publici* was no doubt good work,[6] but many will have bought their freedom, since they had excellent opportunities for collecting a fat *peculium*. We know of few public *liberti* from the late Republic, but this is due mainly to the sketchiness of the sources.[7]

But the Roman state might also figure as the manumitter of slaves other than *servi publici*. 'Servos denique, quorum ius, fortuna, condicio infima est, bene de re publica meritos, persaepe

---

[1] Cic. *Cael.* 68.
[2] Cic. *Mil.* 57 ff., Asconius (ed. Clark), *Mil.* 35. Cf. also Livy, viii. 15. 7.
[3] Cic. *Fam.* xiv. 4. 4. Presumably the manumission would have been informal.
[4] Varro, *LL* viii. 83.
[5] *Dig.* xi. 3. 1.
[6] L. Halkin, *Ant. Class.* 1935, 137.
[7] On public slaves and freedmen in general, Halkin, *Ant. Class.* 1935, 125 ff. Republican instances of *liberti* of the state or public bodies are Publicius Menander, a particularly favoured Greek interpreter in the service of promagistrates (Cic. *Balb.* 28; *Dig.* xlix. 15. 5. 3, cf. Watson, *Law of Persons*, pp. 240 ff.). and Pompey's double, Publicius (Val. Max. ix. 4. 1, Pliny, *NH* vii. 53).

MOTIVES FOR MANUMISSION

libertate, id est civitate, publice donari videmus.'[1] Such manumissions were often performed over the heads of the legal owners. Slave-informers were often given freedom, in many cases for the betrayal of their masters.[2] A Volscian slave who betrayed Artena became a freedman with the name Romanus,[3] which implies that Roman citizenship was part of the reward, and indeed Rome regarded liberty and citizenship as inseparable: 'libertate, id est civitate'. The Volscian slave here was not given Volscian citizenship, for obvious reasons. Other slaves owned by foreigners probably did not receive Roman citizenship, but that of their masters.[4] Sometimes a price was paid to the slave-owners: the *volones* who fought for Rome in the Second Punic War were bought and later freed by the state.[5] The custom persisted in the last century of the Republic. The slave who betrayed Sulpicius Rufus in 88 B.C. was freed—and hurled from the Tarpeian Rock.[6] During the Second Triumvirate, a slave who killed a proscribed man was to be given his freedom, ten thousand drachmas, and the *civitas* enjoyed by his master.[7] Similarly, C. Cassius freed slave-informers on Rhodes,[8] but these will have gained Rhodian citizenship, not Roman (unless perhaps their masters were Roman). The state also intervened to free *ingenui* unjustly enslaved,[9] but this is not an instance of manumission but of an act of justice which would restore the victim to his free condition and not make him *libertinus*.

The majority of slaves were doubtless freed for the economic motives described, to provide an incentive to other slaves, to free the master from economic burdens while giving him the right or option to exploit his new freedman often to more advantage than before. Employing slaves often of higher culture or skill than themselves, the Romans were impelled to adopt an attitude to

---

[1] Cic. *Balb.* 24.
[2] Livy, ii. 2, iv. 45, xxii. 33, xxvi. 27.
[3] Livy, iv. 61. 10.
[4] e.g. Capuans, Livy, xxviii. 3. 5.
[5] Livy, xxiii. 35, xxiv. 11. 3, xxiv. 18. 12, xxv. 20. 4, xviii. 38, xxviii. 46. 13; Macrob. *Sat.* 1. 2. 31.
[6] Livy, *Ep.* lxxvii.   [7] App. *BC* iv. 7. 11, cf. 29.
[8] App. *BC.* iv. 73.
[9] Livy, xlii. 22. 5, xliii. 8. 7, *Per. Ox.* xlix; Diod. xxxvi. 3. 2. All are examples of *senatus consulta* ordering the freeing of enslaved allies or enemies who had surrendered and been enslaved by Roman generals.

manumission which seems remarkably liberal when compared, for example, with that of the American Southerners in a Christian civilization. In the southern states, as long as slaves were trained only for agriculture, they were dependent on their masters, and the incentive of manumission did not need to be provided. Freeing negroes could be prohibited by the legislature or ruled out by society.[1] A parallel situation perhaps existed for Roman rural slaves.[2] But the educated slave with a will of his own in a state with vast numbers of slaves and without a police-force, could not be held by mere compulsion.

(iii) *Forms of Manumission*

To the master who wished to free a slave in the late Republic various courses of action, of varying degrees of convenience and with varying effects, were open. Three formal modes were possible, all of which conferred *libertas* and *civitas*. But, as the number of manumissions grew, the formal modes were found cumbersome, and an easy informal method developed, which was capable of conferring only a partial and permissive liberty, and did not carry with it the Roman citizenship. The formal modes, *manumissio censu*, *vindicta*, and *testamento*, originated in the earliest times: tradition connected *manumissio censu* with Servius Tullius[3] and *manumissio vindicta* with the infancy of the Republic,[4] while *manumissio testamento* was treated in the Twelve Tables.[5] In fact, all three seem genuinely ancient, though precise dating is not to be relied upon. The important point is that at Rome (and probably in Latin cities generally) the state concerned itself at an early period with the freeing of slaves, and that all the formal modes of manumission soon, if not originally, conferred the franchise. In their earliest forms, all three methods demonstrate the necessity of the state's participation: it appears in *manumissio vindicta* as ratification by the magistrate, in *testamento* in the authorization of the will by the *Comitia Calata*, and in *censu* as action by the censor.

[1] Cf. K. M. Stampp, *The Peculiar Institution. Negro Slavery in the American South* (New York, 1956), *passim*.
[2] pp. 106 f.
[3] Dion. Hal. iv. 22. 4.
[4] Livy, ii. 5. 9.
[5] Ulp. *fr.* 2. 4.

FORMS OF MANUMISSION

Manumissio vindicta was the least restricted of the three modes, since, while manumission at a census would usually be possible only during eighteen months every five years, and testamentary manumission came into effect only on the death of the master, the *vindicta* ceremony could be carried out at almost any time,[1] before one of a number of different magistrates.[2] Qualified magistrates, we may deduce, were a dictator, consul, *interrex* or praetor, that is, probably, anyone with *imperium*. Certainly by the late Republic proconsuls and propraetors were also competent, since in imperial times provincial governors, including, from the time of the institution of the office by Augustus, the *praefectus Aegypti*,[3] were allowed to ratify manumissions, and this power will have been necessary in republican times as soon as Romans and their slaves came to be based abroad. Q. Cicero, for instance, seems to have freed Statius in his capacity of proconsul of Asia in 59 B.C.[4]

Master and slave came before one of these magistrates. So much is clear. The exact procedure that followed has caused considerable discussion. The traditional view of *manumissio vindicta* is that it was a judicial process. Buckland describes it succinctly as follows:

This is a fictitious application of the procedure in a *causa liberalis*. If a claim of liberty was made on behalf of a man alleged to be wrongfully detained as a slave, the claim took the form of an action brought by an *adsertor libertatis*, claiming him as a free man, the form being, at this time, that of *sacramentum*,[5] Used as a mode of manumission, it was evidently a case of *cessio in jure*. The *adsertor libertatis*, who at least in

---

[1] Not, strictly, on *dies nefasti* (Varro, *LL* vi. 30), but a *Lex Hortensia* permitted manumission on *nundinae* (Trebatius *apud* Macrob. *Sat*. i. 16. 28).

[2] Livy, xli. 9. 11: 'ad legem (sc. Claudiam of 177 B.C.) et edictum consulis senatus consultum adiectum est, ut dictator, consul, interrex, censor, praetor, qui nunc esset *quive postea futurus esset*, apud eorum quem *qui* manu mitteretur, in libertatem vindicaretur, ut ius iurandum daret, qui eum manu mitteret, civitatis mutandae causa manu non mittere'. The censor is mentioned because he was responsible for *manumissio censu*. Provincial governors, if qualified at this date to ratify manumissions, were irrelevant to this *senatus consultum*, which dealt with Latins, presumably in Italy, trying to obtain the citizenship.

[3] *Dig.* xl. 2. 7. 17. 21.

[4] Cic. *Att*. ii. 18. 4. There were some doubts on the legality of the magistrate manumitting *apud se* when master: Cic. *Att*. vii. 2. 8. Cf. W. W. Buckland, *The Roman Law of Slavery: the condition of the slave in private law from Augustus to Justinian* (Cambridge, 1908), p. 454 (citing *Dig*. i. 10. 1. 2, 18. 2; xl. 2. 5; xl. 20. 4).

[5] Cf. Watson, *Law of Persons*, pp. 218 ff.

later times was often a lictor, claimed him before a magistrate as free, touching him with a wand which appears in *sacramentum* and which gives its name to this mode of manumission. The *dominus* made no defence and the magistrate declared the man free.[1]

A novel interpretation was propounded by Lévy-Bruhl,[2] who held that there was no *adsertor*, no judicial process, no fiction, but that *manumissio vindicta* was merely a declaration by the master followed by ratification from the public authority. He argues that none of the references[3] adduced to prove the existence of the *adsertor* is reliable or decisive and so the theory that *manumissio vindicta* was a collusive process in which magistrate, master, and a third party agreed to pretend that the slave was rightfully a free man, collapses.[4] But Lévy-Bruhl cannot remove the basic similarity between *manumissio vindicta* and the process for freeing a man unjustly enslaved. The rod has an important part in both ceremonies and the words of the magistrate in adjudging the object claimed are the same as in *in jure cessio*.[5] The texts which show the presence of the *adsertor* are indeed difficult, but not as inconclusive as Lévy-Bruhl held:

Cicero, *Ad Atticum*, vii. 2. 8. Itaque usurpavi vetus illud Drusi, ut ferunt, praetoris, in eo qui eadem liber non iuraret, me istos liberos non addixisse, praesertim cum adesset nemo a quo recte vindicarentur.

Cicero in this letter has described to Atticus the dereliction of two freedmen, who had left his son without permission. This probably meant that they had broken the oath to perform *operae*.[6] Cicero, wanting to punish his freedmen, hopes that this will be enough to allow him to invalidate the manumission. He therefore takes over the decision ascribed to Drusus[7] to deny the manumission of a slave who had refused to take after manumission the oath which he

[1] *Roman Law of Slavery*, p. 441.
[2] H. Lévy-Bruhl, 'L'affranchissement par la vindicte', in *Quelques problèmes du très ancien droit romain* (Paris, 1934), pp. 56 ff.
[3] Cic. *Att.* vii. 2. 8; Livy xli. 9. 11 (quoted above, p. 21, n. 2); Festus, s.v. *sertor*. There is no mention of an *adsertor* in classical discussions of *manumissio vindicta* (*Code* vii. 6. 16; *Dig.* xl. 2; Ulpian, *Reg.* i. 17; *Fr. Dos.* 5; Gaius, i. 17).
[4] Lévy-Bruhl, *Quelques problèmes*, p. 73.
[5] F. Schulz, *Classical Roman Law* (Oxford, 1951), p. 348; Watson, *Law of Persons*, pp. 169 f., 191 ff.   [6] Below, p. 75.
[7] Probably M. Livius Drusus cos. 112, praetor between 120 and 115 B.C. Cf. *MRR* ii. 581. It appears that 'ut ferunt' modifies 'praetoris'; that is, Cicero was sure of the attribution to Drusus, but not sure that the decision belonged (as was likely) to his praetorship.

FORMS OF MANUMISSION

had promised before. But in the present case the oath presumably had been taken, but was broken afterwards.[1] Cicero backs his weak analogy with the decision of Drusus, therefore, by adding[2] that the ceremony of manumission could be attacked on the grounds that, as he had been the presiding magistrate, the master had not been represented,[3] so there had been no one present from whom[4] the slaves could properly be claimed. It is clear that there must, in the correct ceremony, have been a third person present to claim the slave, presumably the *adsertor libertatis*.

The text of Livy which deals with *manumissio vindicta* is corrupt, but this does not affect the phrase 'in libertatem vindicaretur', which naturally suggests the presence of an *adsertor* who claimed the slave from his owner. Probably, therefore, the process of *manumissio vindicta* in the late Republic retained all the characteristics of *in iure cessio*.

Master and slave[5] came before the magistrate, not necessarily, perhaps, *pro tribunali*, and the *adsertor* claimed[6] the slave as free, touching him with the *festuca* or rod.[7] The master made no defence,

---

[1] It is not exactly clear how long afterwards. The slaves had been freed during one of Cicero's tenures of *imperium*, in 66, 63, or May 51 onwards, probably the latter, and Cicero was writing in December of 50 B.C. The defection may have taken place while young Marcus and Quintus were visiting Deiotarus between August and December 51 B.C. (Cic. *Att.* v. 17. 3; 18. 2. 4; 20. 9).

[2] 'Praesertim' shows that this is a second view, in my opinion. But Watson, *Law of Persons*, pp. 191 f., holds that the only similarity between Cicero's argument and that of Drusus is that both denied that they had (validly) declared the slave free.

[3] Such a ceremony had not been declared invalid, but there were doubts, which Cicero wished to exploit. See p. 75, n. 1, and Arangio-Ruiz, *Scritti Mancaleoni* (*Studi Sassaresi* xvi), p. 29.

[4] Not 'by whom' which makes nonsense of the argument (though it would be a clearer indication of the presence of the *adsertor*). The whole text runs: 'So I have taken over the old decision made by Drusus, as they say in his praetorship, in the case of the man who did not repeat the same oath after his manumission, that I did not declare them free, especially as no one was present from whom they could properly be claimed.'

[5] Livy xli. 9. 11, quoted above, p. 22, n. 2. It is uncertain, because of the corruption whether it was the master or the slave who was required to swear that the manumission was genuine, but it is more likely that it was the former, a *civis* (Watson, *Law of Persons*, p. 192).

[6] Lévy-Bruhl thinks the master made the claim, *Quelques problèmes*, pp. 60 f. In imperial times, the magistrate could ratify manumissions when *in transitu* and even in private houses (*Dig.* xl. 2. 7. 8).

[7] Plaut. *Mil.* 961; Gaius, iv. 16. Also called *vindicta*, e.g. Plaut. *Curc.* 212, Hor. *Sat.* ii. 7. 76. On the symbolism see S. Tondo, *Aspetti simbolici e magici nella struttura giurìdica della manumissio vindicta* (Milan 1967).

but it is not certain whether he pronounced a formula or kept silent. It would be consonant with the collusive nature of the process, and with the fact that the master was sometimes also the presiding magistrate, if he said nothing.[1] The slave was then adjudged free, the magistrate pronouncing the *addictio*, probably in the words 'Eum liberum addico.'[2] The slap, 'alapa', which the master in classical law gave to the slave, probably did not occur in the republican ceremony.[3]

How ancient was *manumissio vindicta*? It is likely that it was the oldest form of manumission. *A priori*, we should expect a form of manumission which took effect at once to precede manumission by will; *manumissio censu* is said to have been introduced when freedmen already existed,[4] so we might guess them to have been freed *vindicta*. The tradition regarding the manumission of Vindicius in the first year of the Republic, however, is in apparent conflict with this view. According to Livy, the slave informer against the conspiracy to restore the Tarquins was rewarded immediately after the execution of the guilty:

praemium indici pecunia ex aerario, libertas et civitas data. Ille primum dicitur vindicta liberatus; quidam vindictae quoque nomen tractum ab illo putant; Vindicio ipsi nomen fuisse. Post illum observatum ut qui ita liberati essent in civitatem accepti viderentur.[5]

No certainty can be reached on this period, but an attractive case has been made[6] for holding that Livy has here confused a genuine

[1] M. Wlassak, *ZSS* 28 (1907), 18, 22. *Contra*, Lévy-Bruhl, *Quelques problèmes*, p. 65. Cf. *Dig.* xl. 2. 23: 'Manumissio per lictores hodie domino tacente expediri solet et verba sollemnia licet non dicantur ut dicta accipiuntur.' But in the classic period the original nature of the process had been so overlaid that this is not conclusive for a formula pronounced by the master in republican times. Paul, *Sent.* iv. 12. 2, says that deaf-and-dumb masters could not manumit *vindicta*, presumably because silence in their case implied nothing (Buckland, *A Textbook of Roman Law from Augustus to Justinian* (Cambridge, 1921), p. 452).

[2] Or 'dico' or 'do'. Varro, *LL* vi. 30: 'Contrarii horum vocantur dies nefasti, per quos dies nefas fari praetorem "do," "dico", "addico" ...' (see Watson, *Law of Persons*, p. 193); Cic. *Att.* vii. 2. 8: 'me istos liberos non addixisse'.

[3] Watson, *Law of Persons*, p. 193.

[4] Dion. iv. 22. 4. If the *vindicta* process goes back to the regal period, it will have taken place before the king or his deputy (e.g. the *praefectus urbis*).

[5] Livy, ii. 5. 9 f.; cf. Dion. v. 13. 1 (who gives the name Vindicius but does not mention the method of manumission); Plut. *Popl.* 7. 5. (who also mentions the name, but says the manumission was decreed by the people).

[6] D. Daube, *JRS* 36 (1946), 74 f.

FORMS OF MANUMISSION

tradition that this was the first time that *manumissio vindicta* conferred the citizenship, with a romantic story that the whole process was introduced at this time and named after the first slave so freed.[1] Livy, the only author who mentions *vindicta* in this connection, seems at least to have got hold of an old version of the legend, for in historic times public benefactors were manumitted by magistrates in a simple administrative act, resembling *manumissio censu* rather than *vindicta*.[2]

Manumissio censu was a less convenient method, since it could be used only when the census was being taken, theoretically quinquennially, but in practice, in the last century of the Republic, irregularly. There was also some doubt as to whether a slave freed by the censor became free at once or when the *lustrum* was completed, up to eighteen months later.[3] In an age when censors frequently failed to complete the *lustrum*,[4] *manumissio censu* must have been extremely unattractive. Why, given these doubts and disadvantages, did it exist at all? Daube suggests[5] that it originally had the advantage of conferring the franchise, while the other modes did not. This is strongly backed by the tradition reported by Dionysius[6] that when he introduced the census, Servius Tullius also allowed manumitted slaves who wished to stay in Rome rather than returning home, to participate in the citizenship. That is, Servius enfranchised slaves already freed by other modes, even against the wishes of their patrons.[7] It is natural that state action about slaves should have been preceded by private manumission, so Dionysius

[1] The *nomen* 'Vindicius' itself is strange. It appears to be cognate with 'Publicius', the name usually given to slaves freed by the state, and may be genuinely ancient, connected with 'vindex', 'vindico', rather than with 'vindicta'.

[2] Buckland, *Roman Law of Slavery*, pp. 589 f.

[3] Cic. *de Or.* i. 183: 'Quid? de libertate, quo iudicium gravius esse nullum potest, nonne ex iure civili potest esse contentio, cum quaeritur, is, qui domini voluntate census sit, continuone, an, ubi lustrum sit conditum, liber sit?' (Cf. *fr. Dos.* 17: there was a great 'dissensio' (clearly not in the second century A.D. though he uses the present tense: he is referring to republican times) as to whether everything took effect ('vires accipiant omnia') immediately or at the end of the *lustrum*). The debate seems never to have been resolved (Watson, *Law of Persons*, pp. 185 ff). [4] As in 89, 65, 64, 55, 42 B.C. [5] *JRS* 36 (1946), 173.

[6] iv. 22. E. Gabba has demonstrated that Dionysius' source here is probably an aristocratic history of the Sullan period (*Athen.* 39 (1961), 114 ff.). But there is nothing to show that the fact of Servius' enfranchisement of freedmen was not a genuine part of the tradition.

[7] And justified his action (Dion. iv. 23).

is at least logical. He does not mention *manumissio censu* itself, but it can be assumed that it too was traditionally of Servian origin.

Manumissio censu was always essentially unilateral action by the state, although the master's consent or *iussum* to the slave to present himself before the censor was normally a condition of such enfranchisement. The opinion of Mommsen[1] was that the action of the censor, like that of the praetor (on his view) in *manumissio vindicta*, was collusive: the magistrate pretended that the slave was already a free citizen when he entered his name on the list. But, whatever was the case in regard to *manumissio vindicta*, there is no reason to suppose that entry on the census list did not, at least in early times, constitute in itself a valid claim to citizenship, or that the censor was not competent to confer citizenship. Later, admittedly, the work of the censors became so complicated that the lists ceased to be reliable, 'quoniam census non ius civitatis confirmat et tantum modo indicat eum qui sit census ita se tum gessisse, pro cive'.[2] But Cicero is here arguing that the citizenship of Archias rested on a more valid proof than entry on the census-list (in fact, he had not been so entered, because when a census had been completed he had been abroad), and this is not to say that deliberate enfranchisement by the censor (as opposed to the mere entry of one who claimed to be a citizen already) was not as valid as the grants of citizenship so often made by consuls and proconsuls.[3] The lists might include non-citizens or omit citizens, but, in spite of errors due to carelessness or fraud and incompleteness caused by the absence of citizens on campaign or failure to register, inclusion would constitute a presumption, which could be scrutinized, that a man was a citizen.

The slave, authorized by his owner,[4] presented himself before the censors. Presumably, he gave some evidence of his status and his

---

[1] *Staatsrecht Römisches* (Leipzig, 1887), ii, p. 374, n. 4.

[2] Cic. *Arch.* 11. Cf. the lax census of 197–196 B.C., which admitted Italians to the citizenship and was frustrated by the *Lex Licinia Mucia* of 95 B.C. (E. Badian, *Foreign Clientelae* 264–70 B.C. (Oxford, 1958), p. 213).

[3] Cf. H. Last, *JRS* 35 (1945), 35 ff.; D. Daube, *JRS* 36 (1946), 58, 60 ff., and most recently, Watson, *Law of Persons*, pp. 186 f.

[4] Cic. *de Or.* i. 183: 'qui domini voluntate census sit . . .'; Ulp. *Reg.* i. 8: 'Censu manumittebantur olim qui iussu dominorum . . . censum profitebantur.' Boeth. *ad Cic. Top.* 10: 'Si quis ergo consentiente vel iubente domino nomen detulisset in censum civis Romanus fiebat et servitutis vinculo solvebatur.' See for full discussion, Daube, *JRS* 36 (1946), 63 ff.

FORMS OF MANUMISSION

master's consent and status as a citizen, especially if the master's presence was not essential, and, if required, satisfied the censor that he was a suitable person to receive the citizenship. Registration as a *civis Romanus* produced the result that he could no longer be a slave, since liberty and citizenship were inseparable.[1] Theoretically, at least, the censor could probably act to free a slave even without the master's consent, as he did in the case of bondsmen[2] and other magistrates did in the case of slaves who performed a public service.

How long did *manumissio censu* remain in use? After Sulla, the census was held only at irregular intervals. The usefulness of this mode of manumission had probably been impaired early, when other modes also began to confer the franchise. *Manumissio censu* was still alive in 177, when the *senatus consultum* to prevent Latins fraudulently enslaving themselves to Romans on the understanding that they would be manumitted and thus gain the citizenship, was passed, for censors are there mentioned as magistrates responsible for manumission.[3] Again, Cicero put it at the head of his list of the formal modes of manumission,[4] although this does not necessarily mean that it was used or common in his time. Probably it survived in the Ciceronian age for use in certain circumstances, for example, a master who could not conveniently reach a magistrate with *imperium* could probably send his slave alone to Rome to go before the censor.

Manumissio testamento was always a popular method of manumission, since such generosity was gratuitous for the testator, who gained an escort of mourning 'pilleati' at his funeral,[5] while all disadvantages, such as the loss of his slaves' services and payment of the *vicesima libertatis*, fell on his heirs. But it may be doubted if the widely held view that this was the commonest mode of manumission[6] is the true one: the rush on manumissions in the late

---

[1] Cic. *Balb.* 24.
[2] Daube, *JRS* 36 (1946), 67.   [3] Livy, xli. 9. 11.
[4] Cic. *Top.* 10: '. . . Si neque censu nec vindicta nec testamento liber factus est, non est liber; . . .'
[5] Dion. iv. 24. 6.
[6] e.g. Buckland, *Roman Law of Slavery*, p. 460; Watson, *Law of Persons*, p. 194.

Republic was triggered off partly by the fact that poor masters found it cheaper and more convenient to manumit than to feed and lodge slaves, since freedmen could receive cheap corn with other citizens and perform *operae* for their patrons.[1]

Testamentary manumission was dealt with in detail in the Twelve Tables,[2] and so probably goes back further still, though it would naturally be later than forms of manumission which took effect in the master's lifetime. Originally, wills had to be ratified in the *Comitia Calata*, which met every six months; once the will had been passed manumission took effect immediately on the master's death. In early times, the element of public control was thus present in this as in the other modes of manumission, but later the *Comitia Calata* no longer functioned and the state lost its part in testamentary manumission, since not even the witnesses knew the contents of the will.[3]

The essential in *manumissio testamento* was that the order to manumit should be properly worded. The classic formula was 'Stichum, servum meum, liberum esse iubeo' or 'Stichus, servus meus, liber esto', that is, a *jussum* had to be expressed or implied. A clause of the form 'Stichum, servum meum, liberum esse volo' was not legally binding, though the heir might, if he chose, treat it as a *fideicommissum*.[4] An inexactitude in the formulation could have bitter consequences for the slave who expected freedom, and whose master had intended to give it to him.[5] Slaves were often freed *testamento* on certain conditions,[6] for example that they paid a fixed sum to the heir or to a third party,[7] or that they performed certain services either before or after manumission.[8] On the other hand, they were often given a bequest or made sole heir.[9] It has been held that in cases where there was doubt whether a slave had been legally freed *testamento* or not, the jurist would rule by *favor*

[1] Dion. iv. 24; Dio, xxxix. 24; P. A. Brunt, *JRS* 48 (1958), 165.
[2] Cf. Ulp. *fr.* 2. 4.
[3] Daube, *JRS* 36 (1946), 59.
[4] Gaius, ii. 267. Cf. Watson, *Law of Persons*, pp. 195 f., on *fideicommissa*.
[5] e.g. *Dig.* xxxii. 29. 4.
[6] Watson, *Law of Persons*, pp. 201 ff.
[7] *Dig.* xl. 7. 3. 11–12 (Ulp., citing Labeo, Trebatius).
[8] *Dig.* xxxii. 30. 2 (Labeo).
[9] *Dig.* xxxiii. 5. 21, pr. i (Pomp., citing Labeo, Trebatius). Below, pp. 216 f.

FORMS OF MANUMISSION

libertatis to uphold his freedom,[1] but it has recently been shown that there are no grounds for maintaining the existence of *favor libertatis* as a legal principle in republican times.[2]

Circumstances could easily arise in which any of the three informal modes of manumission was inconvenient or impossible, for instance if there were no magistrate available or if the master or slave[3] were dying. So, by the end of the Republic, an informal mode had grown up, in which the state had no part. This was *manumissio inter amicos*,[4] as contrasted with *manumissio iusta ac legitima*[5] or *iusta libertas*.[6] The name meant that it was performed informally, as between friends, not that it took place before the patron's friends as witnesses.[7] In fact, it seems that often no witness was present, though in such cases some evidence of manumission, presumably written, would need to be available. In republican times, the manumission perhaps usually took the form of a verbal declaration to the slave, as happens in comedy.[8] The formula normally used was 'liber esto'.[9]

The status of slaves so freed was not one of full liberty, and was probably never regulated by law during the republican period, but only by the praetor. Gaius explains as follows:

> Admonendi sumus . . . eos qui nunc Latini Juniani dicuntur olim ex iure Quiritium servos fuisse, sed auxilio praetoris in libertatis forma servari solitos, unde etiam res eorum peculii iure ad patronos pertinere solita est; postea vero per legem Juniam eos omnes, quos praetor in libertate tuebatur, liberos esse coepisse et appellatos esse Latinos Junianos.[10]

The liberty enjoyed by informally manumitted slaves before the *Lex Junia* was conditional: they were said to enjoy liberty by their masters' consent, although the praetor might intervene to protect

---

[1] e.g. F. Schulz, *Principles of Roman Law* (Oxford, 1936), pp. 220 ff.
[2] Watson, *Law of Persons*, pp. 207, 214 f., 217; *Tulane Law Review* 42 (1968), 302 f.
[3] Not unexampled: Mart. i. 101.
[4] Gaius, i. 44.   [5] Sen. *Dial.* vii. 24. 3.   [6] Gaius, i. 17.
[7] Schulz, *Classical Roman Law* (Oxford, 1951), p. 84; A. Biscardi, *Manumissio per mensam e affrancazioni pretorie* (Florence, 1939), p. 13.
[8] Where informal manumission is dramatically necessary: Plaut. *Epid.* 730; *Men.* 1093; Ter. *Ad.* 970.
[9] Ibid. and Plaut. *Men.* 1029.   [10] iii. 56.

them.¹ The *dominus* retained his rights over their *peculium* and any children would remain his slaves. The chief benefit obtained from this state of semi-liberty seems to have been that the master could no longer compel his slave to work for him full-time.² *A fortiori*, the informally freed slave was not a Roman citizen. It was the *Lex Junia* which regularized the position, changing the *de jure* slaves into freedmen and Latins. The date of this enactment has been disputed, but cannot in any case have been republican, since Cicero in 44 B.C. declared that only the three formal modes conferred *libertas*,³ and he held that true liberty was not possible without citizenship.⁴ It is most likely to be put[5] among Augustus' measures for controlling manumission and regulating the position of freedmen, and may perhaps be dated to 17 B.C. The *princeps* saw clearly the dangers of facile and undiscriminating manumission; and the damage done by the type of emancipation which the master had some chance of revoking,⁶ and which, consequently, he might carry out without due thought, must have been proportionately greater than that done by formal manumission. But it may be doubted if the class of semi-freedmen was ever very numerous. It is ignored by republican sources, except the comic writers. We hear of vast numbers of *manumissiones iustae*, calculated to exploit the corn-dole, but informal manumission had no such attractions.⁷ One suspects, therefore, that informal manumission was not common until after the *Lex Junia*. It may have been resorted to as a temporary or emergency measure, when a magistrate was not available to perform a *manumissio vindicta*, and perhaps by the poorer class of

¹ *fr. Dos.* 5: 'Antea enim una libertas erat et manumissio fiebat vindicta vel testamento vel censu et civitas Romana competebat manumissis: quae appellatur iusta manumissio. Hi autem, qui domini voluntate in libertate erant, manebant servi: sed si manumissores ausi erant in servitutem denuo eos per vim ducere, interveniebat praetor et non patiebatur manumissum servire.'
² For what the evidence of comedy is worth, Plaut. *Men.* 1034 makes the informally manumitted Messenio offer to work for and live with Menaechmus (whom he takes to be his legal patron).
³ *Top.* 10.   ⁴ e.g. *Caec.* 96; *Balb.* 24.
⁵ Duff, *Freedmen*, pp. 210 ff.
⁶ In practice, the praetor would be slow to intervene.
⁷ Evasion of the *vicesima* will hardly have been important. A state of semi-freedom might encourage a slave to increase his *peculium* to the advantage of his master and the burden of providing board and lodging might be lifted in some cases but no other motive suggests itself.

FORMS OF MANUMISSION 31

masters. For instance, it is possible that Tiro was freed in this way, because of his illness.[1]

A few rare methods of manumission need a passing mention. *Manumissio sacrorum causa*, which is mentioned only by Festus,[2] a type of *vindicta*[3] or of informal manumission,[4] is clearly a late form and does not concern us here. A form of manumission *apud IIviros*, found in the Latin colony of Salpensa in the time of Domitian, which consisted in a declaration before the magistrates, is interesting as a possible parallel to *manumissio vindicta*.[5] Finally, the elder Cato testified to the possibility of a master adopting his slave and so making him a free man.[6]

It seems likely that slaves of particular merit or those who would be more useful to their master as freedmen, were freed *vindicta*, as also most of those who were freed to relieve their owner from the trouble of supporting them. *Manumissio censu* cannot have been much used in the first century B.C. The frequency of *manumissio testamento*, perhaps most common in the richer and more ostentatious households, is hard to determine, but I should incline to put it in second place, not in the first, as is often done.[7]

(iv) *Numbers of Freedmen*

It would be useful to know how many *libertini* there were in the citizen-body, or at least in what proportion they stood to the *ingenui*. Tenney Frank has suggested two possible lines of approach. One method[8] seeks to calculate numbers of freedmen in the late Republic by utilizing information on the five per cent tax on manumission, the *vicesima libertatis*. Theoretically, if we knew how much money

[1] See Appendix 3, p. 261.
[2] s.v. 'manumitti'. Cf. Buckland, *Roman Law of Slavery*, pp. 447 f.
[3] Lévy-Bruhl, *Quelques problèmes*, p. 66.
[4] M. Wlassak *ZSS* 287 (1907) 22 ff. Cf. Tondo, *Aspetti simbolici* pp. 123 ff.
[5] *Lex Salpensana* 28; cf. Daube, *JRS* 36 (1946), 60. For a recent suggestion that the same form of manumission was found at Urso and that it was *vindicta*, A. d'Ors, *Epigrafía jurídica d. España romana* (Madrid, 1953), pp. 241 f.
[6] Justinian, *Inst.* i. 11. 12: 'Apud Catonem bene scriptum refert antiquitas, servi, si a domino adoptati sint, ex hoc ipso posse liberari. unde et nos eruditi in nostra constitutione etiam eum servum, quem dominus actis intervenientibus filium suum nominaverit, liberum esse constituimus, licet hoc ad ius filii accipiendum ei non sufficiat.' Cf. Gell. v. 19. 13; Watson, *Law of Persons*, p. 87, n. 1, 90 ff.
[7] Above, pp. 27 f. [8] *AJP* 53 (1932), 360 ff.

had been accumulated from this tax over a definite number of years, and the average price of slaves in the same period, a simple division of the money in the fund by five per cent of the average price of slaves would give an approximate figure for the number of slaves freed during that time. Unfortunately, Frank did not possess such data. He assumes that the money taken by Caesar from the treasury in 49 B.C. (which he reckons to have been 12,000,000 *denarii*) was the revenue accumulated from the *vicesima* alone and had been mounting up since 82 B.C., when, he conjectures, Sulla had emptied the *aerarium*. But neither of these hypotheses can be proved. The average manumission-value of Greek slaves at Delphi, even if, as Frank says, controlled by the existence of the Roman market at Delos, 400 *drachmae*, is not a strong basis for his estimate of 500 *denarii* for Rome. Unhappily, therefore, his neat estimate of about 16,000 manumissions each year in the period from 82 to 49 B.C. cannot be used.

Tenney Frank also attempted[1] to gauge the proportion of men of foreign, that is, largely libertine, extraction in the body of ordinary citizens of imperial Rome.[2] The figures he gives are not those of *libertini* alone, but include those whom he would reckon as of recent libertine descent. For the *Urbs*, Frank arrives at a proportion of about ninety per cent. Although minor criticisms may be made about his criteria,[3] it is impossible to deny that extant inscriptions show a city population made up predominantly of freedmen and their families. The same is true of republican inscriptions, more limited in scope though they are, where the ratio of *libertini* to freeborn is roughly three to one.[4] What is to be made of these figures?

---

[1] *AHR* 21 (1916), 689 ff. [2] *CIL* VI, ii and iii.
[3] E.g. since *conubium* between *ingenui* and *libertini* was possible, not all families where one member with a foreign name suggests libertinity will have consisted entirely of *libertini*.
[4] In *CIL* i. 1202–1422 a group consisting mainly of monuments of the well-to-do and *collegia*, there are approximately 380 *libertini* to 90 *ingenui*. (Roman names without filiation are omitted from these totals and amount to about 20.) The only other large group of inscriptions from the City consists of the names from the *ollae* discovered in a burial chamber in the vineyard of S. Cesareo (*CIL* i: 970–1201). The occupants were very poor and include slaves. The small jars did not leave room for a long inscription: most have just *nomen* and *praenomen*, so that only 8 can be identified certainly as *ingenui*, 31/2 as *libertini*; 115/8 are of dubious status.

Taken at their face-value, they suggest that freedmen far outnumbered native Romans in their own city. But this, though conceivable to Frank for the period of the principate, does not seem likely for the first century B.C. Lily Ross Taylor[1] explains the phenomenon by the conjecture that *libertini* were so proud of their citizenship that they were more inclined than *ingenui* to commemorate themselves. But, although it is no doubt true that *libertini* liked to put up monuments listing the *tria nomina* of a citizen, there is no reason to think that the native Romans who opposed the enfranchisement of the Italians or listened to the patriotic speeches of Cicero were any less proud of their status. It seems more probable that the division was an economic one. Poor *ingenui* are found with freedmen in mass tombs, where one small bone in a jar was all that was left of their bodies (the rest being buried in the *puticuli*) and a brief note of their family and personal names, usually without *cognomen*, filiation, or tribe, all that survived of their personalities.[2] Others will not even have secured this slight immortality. Poor free-born Romans, who worked as dockers or builders' labourers,[3] could not afford to set up inscriptions. The comparatively well-off shopkeepers and craftsmen were, as we shall see, mainly freedmen, and it is this class which set up most of the inscriptions which give us information on individuals in Rome. Men who were in neither of these two classes, wealthier and more leisured, although they might live in Rome for much of their active life, would often have a home in the country to which they retired, and so, unless they were members of guilds, leave little trace in inscriptions. As Cicero said, 'We are all from the *municipia*'.[4]

As *ingenui* who lived in Rome for a large part of their lives might leave relatively little evidence of their existence, so the circumstances of the lives of freedmen tended to exaggerate their predominance. As was long ago pointed out by Duff, those freedmen whose funerary inscriptions we have may have been free only a small part of their lives, so that we can never arrive at a true percentage of the

---

[1] *AJP* 82 (1961), 113 ff. [2] p. 32, n. 4, above.
[3] P. A. Brunt, *JRS* 52 (1962), 69 f.
[4] Cf. such connoisseurs of Roman life as Horace and Martial (although the former was buried in Rome). Few inhabitants of modern Rome can claim to be *romani di Roma* and loyalty to the village is still strong.

proportion of freeborn to freedmen at any point of time. The nature of the inscriptional sources distorts the picture.[1]

But, even if we could calculate a ratio of freedmen to freeborn, we should then want to apply it to obtain total population figures for both groups. As the population of the city fluctuated considerably under the late Republic and the total at any one time is a matter of conjecture,[2] to hope to establish a figure for the libertine population is an idle dream.

We have to fall back on a less exact account. References to the number and influence of freedmen in political gatherings are frequent. According to Cicero, the transference in 169–168 B.C. of the *libertini* from country to urban tribes, where their vote had less weight, had saved the state.[3] Aemilianus had protested at the articulate new citizens, who had, he alleged scornfully, recently been his own war-prisoners.[4] The *Commentariolum Petitionis*,[5] Appian,[6] and Cicero himself[7] refer to the influence of foreigners,

---

[1] *Freedmen*, pp. 197 f.

[2] 320,000 members of the *plebs urbana* were given a donative by Augustus in 5 B.C. (*Res Gestae* 15. 2), while the *plebs frumentaria* in 46 B.C. was again 320,000, reduced to 150,000 by Caesar (Suet. *DJ* 41. 3), and in 2 B.C. numbered just over 200,000 (*Res Gestae* 15. 4; cf. D. van Berchem, *Les Distributions de blé et d'argent à la plèbe romaine sous l'empire* (Geneva, 1939), pp. 21 f.). The *plebs frumentaria* consisted of adult male citizens; the number of their dependants and of slaves and *peregrini* is not determined. Modern authorities differ in their interpretation of the sources and their estimate of the total citizen population. J. Beloch (*Die Bevölkerung der griechisch-römischen Welt* (Leipzig, 1886), pp. 392 ff.) guessed the population of the city, citizens and their families, to have been at most 550,000 in 5 B.C., perhaps 400,000 in Sullan times. Including non-citizens, he would put the Augustan figure at 800,000. J. Carcopino (*La vie quotidienne à Rome à l'apogée de l'empire* (Paris, 1939), pp. 32 ff.), estimates 1,000,000 at the same date. But even if we take, for instance, Beloch's figures for 80 B.C. and 5 B.C., they are no sure guide to the population in between. A census of 46 found depopulation (Dio, xliii. 25. 2) and Appian says the population had been reduced by half (*BC* ii. 102). Caesar, besides cutting down the numbers of those eligible for the corn dole, decreased the city population by his colonization programme, which removed many freedmen (Suet. *DJ* 42; Strabo, 381; Bruns, *Fontes* 28. 105). In these circumstances, the question of determining the proportion of *libertini* to *ingenui* in a city where the numbers of male citizens were continually shifting is bound to fail. See now Brunt, *Past and Present* 35 (1966), 8 ff.

[3] *De Or*. i. 38: Scaevola speaking of the reform made by the Elder Gracchus as censor, 'libertinos in urbanas tribus transtulit, quod nisi fecisset, rem publicam quam nunc vix tenemus, iam diu nullam haberemus.' (The dramatic date is 91 B.C.) Below, p. 47.

[4] Vell. ii. 4. 4; p. 8, above
[5] 54.
[6] *BC* ii. 120.
[7] *Flacc*. 17; 66.

NUMBERS OF FREEDMEN

clearly in the main freedmen, not free-born immigrants. From influence, numbers might be deduced. Trade in Rome seems to have been largely in the hands of freedmen,[1] but many ex-slaves were among the *plebs frumentaria*, the discontented poor, and they appear to have joined Clodius' bands of armed thugs,[2] who are often referred to by Cicero as 'servi', a word commonly used in insults for ex-slaves.[3] Large numbers of freedmen were among Caesar's colonists when he drew off the 'sentina urbis'.[4]

We know of occasional large accretions to the libertine population, for example the manumission of the ten thousand Cornelii by Sulla,[5] and the increase produced by Pompey's corn commission of 56 B.C.[6] and the corn-distributions in general.[7] On the other side of the picture, there is ample evidence for the decline in the numbers of *ingenui* through a low birth-rate (or high infant mortality)[8] and war casualties.[9] However, there is no evidence that *libertini* were not as responsible as *ingenui* for the low birth-rate: war-service, supposed to be a factor conducive to small families for free-born citizens, had its counterpart for freedmen in the probability that they would not be manumitted very young,[10] while the sons of *libertini* had the same chance of being killed in war as had *ingenui*, except that if they lived in Rome they were normally left in peace by the recruiting-officer.[11] If the number of manumissions was startlingly high, therefore, it did not necessarily have a proportionate effect on the population, since, firstly, many freedmen were probably old on manumission and did not live long as free citizens, and secondly, they were as likely as *ingenui* to have small families or none at all.[12]

---

[1] Below, pp. 91 ff.   [2] Below, pp. 172 ff.   [3] Appendix 4.
[4] Suet. *DJ* 42; Strabo, 381; Bruns, *Fontes* 28. 105.
[5] App. *BC* i. 100; 104.
[6] Dio, xxxix, 24; cf. Livy, vii. 25. 9.
[7] Dion. Hal. iv. 24.
[8] App. *BC* i. 10; Livy, *Ep.* lix; Cic. *Marcell.* 23; Dio, xxix. 24. Park, *Plebs*, pp. 6 ff., discusses the decline in native stock.
[9] e.g. Hor. *Odes*, i. 2. 23 f.
[10] A controlling factor for freedwomen; children of older parents might also be weaker and less likely to survive infancy. Below, pp. 212 ff.
[11] P. A. Brunt, *JRS* 52 (1962), 74.
[12] M. K. Hopkins (*Comparative Studies in Society and History* 8 (1965), 124 ff.) has recently shown that the effective family-planning methods of Rome were infanticide or abortion rather than contraception. However, there is little

Libertine numbers were relatively high in Rome, where there was little room for *ingenui* in trade or professions. *Libertini* and their descendants seem to have dominated the Roman *petite bourgeoisie*, while residents of native stock belonged mainly to the upper-classes and the proletariat. Again, freedmen are found in large numbers among shopkeepers and dealers and country towns, and in trading-centres such as Capua they played a vital part. But this pattern did not apply to country districts, where farming was in the hands of *ingenui* and slave-workers. We shall probably be right in assuming that only in Rome itself and a few major cities did freedmen dominate. The idea behind their confinement to the urban tribes seems to have been that freedmen resident in Rome but enrolled in the country tribes would easily have out-voted their few fellow tribesmen who were able to journey from their country homes for elections or legislative assemblies. It was Rome, if we may trust Juvenal, which naturally drew the foreigner, in fact the freedman.

mention of either exposure of children (Suet. *DA* 65. 4; *Claud.* 27) or abortion (Juv. vi. 366 ff., 595 ff.) and, although an *ex silentio* argument is admittedly weak in this context, I cannot believe that either was important in keeping the population down, compared with mortality of infants and mothers and infertility due to malnutrition and ignorance.

II

THE LEGAL EFFECTS OF *LIBERTINITAS*

(i) *Libertini in Public Law*

THE *libertus* of a Roman citizen was himself *ipso facto* a Roman citizen.[1] This state of affairs was a source of surprise to foreign onlookers in republican times,[2] and a matter of congratulation to later writers.[3] But were the freedmen full citizens, and, if they were so in law, to what extent did *mos* modify *lex*? The ex-slaves in Rome were *cives Romani*, but they could also be described, though infrequently, as *cives Romani libertini ordinis*.[4] What was the kind of social and political life to which that label limited its owner? One has only to glance at almost any speech of Cicero in order to see the powerful effect of class-consciousness on Roman life: call a man an Insubrian or an auctioneer and you have gone a long way towards discrediting him as a politician. The stigma of slavery will of course be dragged in at every opportunity, and this is a stigma that not only the Senate and the rich, but the ingenuous *plebs* also, would recognize as such. In the field of law too, the position of freedmen was affected, not only by praetorian precedent, but by decisions of executive magistrates, notably the censors, and by the interpretation of the *mos maiorum*, so that it is often hard to tell whether it was law or practice and prejudice that put freedmen at a disadvantage *vis-à-vis* their ingenuous fellow citizens in public life or their patrons in private.[5]

(*a*) *Voting Rights*

There were several forms of limited citizen-rights in the Republic, but there is no evidence that the status of freedmen resembled

[1] Unless the manumission had been informal, in which case he was legally a slave. Above, p. 30.
[2] Dittenberger, *Sylloge*, 543 (the reaction of Philip of Macedon in 214 B.C.).
[3] e.g. Dion. Hal. iv. 22 f.; App. *BC* ii. 120.
[4] Livy, xlii. 27. 3; xliii. 12. 9; xlv. 44. 19; Auct. *Vir. Ill.* 73. See also C Nicolet, *L'Ordre équestre à l'époque républicaine* i (Paris, 1966), p. 168.
[5] 'Libertus' means the freedman in relation to his patron, 'libertinus' in relation to everyone else and to the state.

any of them. There is an ancient tradition that Servius Tullius first gave the franchise to ex-slaves, putting them in the urban tribes and apparently in the centuries as well, and assessing them on capital other than land.[1] The king's motive was, we are told, πολυανθρωπία.[2] The story at least indicates that there was a tradition that *libertini* held the full rights of citizens at an early period. Livy, too, puts the gift of the franchise through *manumissio vindicta* very early.[3]

Not much reliance can be put on reports from historians of the first century B.C. on the traditions of Rome's early history. Until the late fourth century we are in the dark. Evidence for the increased number of manumissions is then given by the institution of the *vicesima libertatis*, ascribed to 357 B.C.[4] With the end of the Struggle of the Orders, the way was open for freedmen to take their place in society. The background to this advance is the rise of a new class, the city craftsmen, and impending conflict, no longer between patrician and plebeian, but between *nobiles*, the new aristocracy of office, and those who had no share in administration, but to whom increased wealth had brought an incipient political awareness.[5] It is in this context that the policies of Appius Claudius Caecus are to be viewed. He appears to have opposed the new plebeian *nobiles*, but supported the under-privileged people: to have been neither a stern unbending aristocrat, looking for support to the clients of the patricians, nor a demagogue and Caesar *manqué*, but a faction-leader with the usual interlocking aims of the type, power, and *clientela* for himself, benefits for his clients.[6] Who exactly were these clients?

Claudius took a noticeable interest in the advancement of *libertini* and their sons. His censorship in 312 B.C. was remarkable for an attempt to adlect, among others, the sons of freedmen to the

---

[1] Dion. Hal. iv. 24, perhaps following a Sullan source. Above, p. 25, n. 6.

[2] For a similar idea of the advantage of manumission to the state, Plaut. *Persa* 474.

[3] Above, p. 24.

[4] Livy, vii. 16. 7. Cf. L. R. Taylor, *The Voting Districts of the Roman Republic* (Rome, 1960), p. 133.

[5] See P. Lejay, *Rev. Phil.* 44 (1920), 92 ff.

[6] Cf. A. Garzetti, *Athen.* 25 (1947), 175 ff., especially 202; E. S. Staveley, *Hist.* 8 (1959), 410 ff.

LIBERTINI IN PUBLIC LAW

Senate.[1] When this failed, he took what both Livy and Diodorus consider to have been an alternative course of action with the same end in view. According to Livy:

posteaquam eam lectionem nemo ratam habuit nec in curia adeptus erat quas petierat opes urbanas, humilibus (Gronovius corrects to 'opes, urbanis humilibus') per omnes tribus divisis forum et campum corrupit, tantumque Flavi[2] comitia indignitatis habuerunt ut plerique nobilium anulos aureos et phaleras deponerent. Ex eo tempore in duas partes discessit civitas; alius integer populus, fautor et cultor bonorum, aliud forensis factio tenebat, donec Q. Fabius et P. Decius censores facti et Fabius simul concordiae causa, simul ne humillimorum in manu comitia essent, omnem forensem turbam excretam in quattuor tribus coniecit urbanasque eas appellavit. Adeoque eam rem acceptam gratis animis ferunt ut Maximi cognomen, quod tot victoriis non pepererat hac ordinum temperatione pareret.[3]

Diodorus[4] says that Claudius gave the citizens permission to be enrolled in whatever tribe they wished. This reform is connected explicitly with the freedmen only by Plutarch,[5] but Livy's use of expressions such as 'humiles' and, in contrast, 'integer populus' suggests that he too was thinking of that class, as does his statement that Claudius was following up his attempt to adlect the sons of freedmen to the Senate. But what form did the redistribution take? According to Taylor, a man's tribe was presumably decided by domicile, and a change of one would mean a change of the other.[6] But in the context under discussion, she assumes[7] that an anomaly had arisen in the case of *libertini*, since many of them were now resident in the country, in the *oppida* or on their own or their patrons' estates, but were still enrolled in the urban tribes. We are to suppose, then, that some *libertini* resident in the country were members of urban tribes. Now, a difficulty arises over the text of Livy. Taylor follows the manuscripts in reading 'opes urbanas': 'obviously Claudius won *opes urbanae* by his distribution of the *humiles*'.[8] Claudius was seeking supporters in the city, which he had

[1] Below, pp. 54 ff.
[2] On this supporter of Claudius and son of a freedman, below, pp. 56 f.
[3] ix. 46; cf. Val. Max. ii. 2. 9.   [4] xx. 36.
[5] *Popl.* 7. Taylor, *Vot. Dist.*, p. 135; cf. Diod. xx. 36.
[6] *Vot. Dist.*, p. 8.   [7] *Vot. Dist.*, p. 135.
[8] *Vot. Dist.*, p. 135, n. 13.

not gained by his adlection of new senators. But what could be meant by 'opes urbanae' in the context of support in the Senate? 'Nec in curia adeptus erat quas petierat opes urbanas' will not make sense. Moreover, as Badian has pointed out,[1] the reading 'urbanas' does not offer the needed contrast with 'forum et campum'. The emendation 'urbanis' gives a better sense. 'Humilibus' needs to be further defined.

If 'urban' is to describe the 'humiles', does it mean members of the urban tribes or city-dwellers? The latter fits easily with 'forensis factio', for, although country-dwellers could form a pressure-group in the forum, they could not usually attend the assemblies regularly, especially if they were banausic tradesmen in country towns, or farmers, and the term does not suit them. These 'humiles' were apparently able to attend legislative assemblies[2] regularly and threatened to swamp the 'integer populus' at the elections. The former sense, 'urbani' meaning 'urbani tribules', seems unparalleled, so we should probably not translate 'humble citizens from urban tribes'. Country-dwellers would indeed have some influence on the 'campus', but only sporadically on the 'forum'. Taylor herself, while arguing that Claudius allowed 'humiles' with property in the country (and she seems to be thinking of men who worked and lived there) to enrol themselves in the country tribes, says that city-dwellers too were included in the redistribution. This appears inconsistent.[3]

The reaction of the censors of 304 against Claudius, and the stern judgement of Livy suggest that Claudius was doing something more radical than merely putting men into the tribe, to which, by right of holding property or living in its territory, they logically belonged. While Claudius cannot have allowed the 'humiles' to choose any tribe which seemed good to them, as a literal acceptance of Diodorus or Plutarch[4] would lead us to suppose, he was apparently adopting a bold plan to increase his *clientela* by a strong

[1] *JRS* 52 (1962), 207.
[2] 'Forum et campum', i.e. legislative as well as elective *comitia*. Taylor, *Vot. Dist.*, p. 136; Fraccaro, *Opuscula* ii, 'Tribules ed Aerarii', pp. 161 ff.
[3] Unless Taylor is thinking of wealthy freedmen who lived in Rome, but had country estates. This can hardly have been a large class in the fourth century and Livy's words do not suggest rich men, but rather a rabble.
[4] Plut. *Popl.* 7; Diod. xx. 36. 4.

party capable of out-voting the 'integer populus'. I would therefore adopt the emendation 'urbanis', and take it to mean men resident in the city, not urban *tribules*. This is not to exclude Taylor's convincing conjecture that even at this date many freedmen were resident in the country and still on the lists of the urban tribes, but Livy's text, even apart from the disputed word, suggests that the people in whom Claudius was chiefly interested were living in Rome itself.

It is necessary to clarify the position in which a freedman found himself with regard to registration. If he was freed *censu*, he was, no doubt, assigned at once to a tribe, when put on the census-list as a citizen. But if he was freed by one of the other modes, what happened? Did he wait for the next census before being entered on a tribal list? Taylor shows[1] that individual foreigners when enfranchised by magistrates probably took the tribe of the magistrate or even *privatus* whose *nomen* they also took. Did freedmen in the same way take the tribe of their patron, as they took his *nomen* on manumission? Apparently this was not the case, as such a system would have distributed freedmen among all the tribes, whereas they appear to have been mostly in the urban tribes. The enrolment, then, was perhaps carried out by the magistrate in charge of the *vindicta* manumission. But this would not apply to *testamento* (where no magistrate was responsible and the role of the *Comitia Calata* had dropped out) and would lead to a confused organization, so it is likely that a newly enfranchised slave had at this date to wait for his enrolment in the tribe at the next census. The censors acted in accordance with a *lex* passed by the people in cases such as the creation of new tribes and the enrolment of individuals from allied states which acquired the Roman franchise.[2] But they exercised their own discretion in enrolling individuals who already held the citizenship. In the case of *libertini*, the exercise of censorial power is often seen. It seems probable that Claudius' predecessors had generally assigned freedmen to the urban tribes—no doubt the bulk of them on grounds of residence there.[3] The increase in

---
[1] *Vot. Dist.*, pp. 19 ff.   [2] Taylor, *Vot. Dist.*, pp. 17, 23.
[3] For although many *libertini* lived in country *oppida*, these are the well-to-do and well-documented traders, while Rome had a high proportion of 'humiles' too poor to leave much evidence.

manumissions, which was beginning even at this date, might lead to overcrowding of the city tribes and a consequent drop in the value of the vote to the 'humiles' concentrated there. The majority of the 'humiles' in Rome will probably have been freedmen, as most of the city *ingenui* were drawn off to colonies at this time. One solution to the problem of the imbalance caused by the urban tribes might have been to increase their number; the other was to redistribute men from the overcrowded tribes, even if they lived in the city. This was apparently what Claudius did. It could be conjectured that, as Plutarch's suggestion that he allowed freedmen to choose arbitrarily which tribe they wanted to join can hardly be right, they were enrolled in that of their patrons.[1] This would give opportunities for organized 'forensis factio'.

Whatever the exact nature of the reform, it clearly resulted in a marked, but perhaps gradual, increase in the power of the 'humiles' —gradual, that is, unless the lack of opposition till 304 B.C. is taken as a sign of the impotence of Appius Claudius' *inimici* rather than their acquiescence. Between 312 and 304 B.C., Claudius' protégé, the freedman's son, Cn. Flavius, held several offices, and this indicates influence over the voters. The next pair of censors, who held office in 307 B.C., when Claudius himself was consul, C. Junius Bubulcus and M. Valerius Maximus, followed his example.[2] But the election of Cn. Flavius to the curule aedileship shocked the censors of 304 B.C. into confining the freedmen to the urban tribes, thus regularizing a situation which had probably been only *de facto* before. Possibly the custom of putting discredited *ingenui* too into the urban tribes dates back to this censorship of P. Decius Mus and Q. Fabius Rullianus.[3] But later censors were not bound to follow suit, and some at least seem to have emulated Claudius, for in one of the *censurae* between 234 and 219 B.C., 'Libertini in quattuor tribus redacti sunt, cum antea dispersi per omnes fuissent, Esquilinam, Palatinam, Suburanam, Collinam.'[4] Taylor convincingly suggests that the censor responsible for this tightening-up was Q. Fabius Maximus in 230–229 B.C.[5] The situation may have

---

[1] As was later proposed by Manilius. Below, p. 50.
[2] Cf. Garzetti, *Athen.* 25 (1947), 208.
[3] Taylor, *Vot. Dist.*, p. 138. [4] Livy, *Ep.* 20.
[5] *Vot. Dist.*, p. 138. *Censurae* were held in 234/3, 230/29, 225/4, 220/19 B.C.

changed on other occasions during the third and second centuries, on which our evidence is extremely scanty.

Little can be gleaned about the second century. A law of 189 or 188 B.C., taken by Taylor to refer to the sons of *libertini*, is more likely to have dealt with the illegitimate sons of *ingenui*.[1] We are told merely that the censors enrolled as citizens everyone who had free parents. This is surely not to be interpreted as a distribution of the sons of freedmen to the country tribes. When freedmen themselves were placed in rustic tribes by some pairs of censors, one imagines that their sons might well be left undisturbed even if their fathers were confined to the city tribes again at the next census. The explanation that a grant of *civitas* to *spurii* is meant, is more convincing.[2]

Concessions to freedmen with certain qualifications were made by a pair of censors whose date is unknown, but who preceded Ti. Sempronius Gracchus and C. Claudius Pulcher in 169 B.C. Livy's text here is so corrupt and fragmentary that a certain interpretation is impossible. A break in the manuscripts precedes the remark:

In quattuor urbanas tribus discripti erant libertini praeter eos, quibus filius quinquenni maior ex se natus esset,—eos, ubi proxumo lustro censi essent, censeri iusserunt—et eos, qui praedium praediave rustica pluris sestertium triginta milium haberent, * * * * censendi ius factum est.[3]

In the preceding chapters, Livy had been discussing foreign policy. He then went on to give a backward glance at a previous censorship, before describing the disagreement which took place between the censors of 169 B.C. about the placing of freedmen in the tribes. The names of the censors here described appeared in the lacuna. The text as we have it appears to give an account of a censorship in which *libertini* owning a country estate of a fixed minimum value or fathers of a son over five were placed in the

[1] Plut. *Flam.* 18. 1: προσεδέξαντο δὲ πολίτας ἀπογραφομένους πάντας ὅσοι γονέων ἐλευθέρων ἦσαν, ἀναγκασθέντες ὑπὸ τοῦ δημάρχου Τερεντίου Κουλέωνος, ὃς ἐπηρεάζων τοῖς ἀριστοκρατικοῖς ἔπεισε τὸν δῆμον ταῦτα ψηφίσασθαι. Cf. Badian, *JRS* 52 (1962), 207.
[2] This, like the suggestion about sons of *libertini*, was a hypothesis propounded by Mommsen (*StR* iii, pp. 436 ff.).
[3] Livy, xlv. 15. 1 f.

country tribes. There is also a reference to the previous census ('proxumo lustro'), when *libertini* with a child[1] had presumably been put in the country tribes. In the later census, these were allowed to keep their position (as long as the child which had allowed them to obtain the privilege was still alive), but the precedent was not followed and no new fathers were re-assigned to the rustic tribes. In the lacuna, it has been suggested that something like 'iis, sicut antea factum erat, in tribubus rusticis',[2] appeared so that the complete sentence would run:

> In quattuor urbanas tribus discripti erant libertini praeter eos, quibus filius quinquenni maior ex se natus esset,—eos, ubi proxumo lustro censi essent, censeri iusserunt—et eos, qui praedium praediave rustica pluris sesetertium triginta milium haberent, *iis, sicut antea factum erat, in tribubus rusticis* censendi ius factum est.

Thus, the sense would be that one pair of censors gave *libertini*, who owned estates worth 30,000 sesterces, or had a child,[3] the right to be assigned to a rustic tribe, while their immediate successors allowed those who had obtained the privilege through paternity to retain it, but did not maintain the precedent to benefit those who had become fathers since the last *lustrum*, and retained the idea that ownership of property should give the right to enter a country tribe.

A. H. McDonald[4] connects these concessions with the liberal ideas of the period, of which the grants of citizenship in 188 B.C. to Arpinum, Formiae, and Fundi are an example. G. W. Botsford[5] had previously connected this passage with Livy's comment on the censorship of M. Aemilius Lepidus and M. Fulvius Nobilior in 179 B.C.: 'mutarunt suffragia, regionatim generibus hominum causisque et quaestibus tribus discripserunt'.[6] He translates, 'they changed the arrangements for voting and drew up the tribal list on a local basis according to the social orders, the conditions and the

---

[1] 'Filius' does not definitely imply a son.
[2] A. H. McDonald, *Camb. Hist. Journ.* 6 (1939), 138, n. 96.
[3] Of approximately one year old—a sensible precaution, given the high mortality rate in the first months.
[4] *Camb. Hist. Journ.* 6 (1939), 130.
[5] *The Roman Assemblies* (New York, 1909), p. 85 n. 3. Cf. also H. Scullard, *Roman Politics 220–150 B.C.* (Oxford, 1951), pp. 182 ff.
[6] xl. 51. 9.

LIBERTINI IN PUBLIC LAW

callings of men'. He refers the measure particularly to *libertini*, and interprets 'genera' as referring to freed or free-born status; 'causae' as covering qualifications such as the possession of a child over five; 'quaestus' as a man's occupation, especially whether he was a landowner or a tradesman—a reference to the *praedium* qualification. McDonald[1] held, unlike Botsford, that the *Comitia Centuriata* was affected by the change. Taylor[2] holds that probably only a few freedmen were put in the centuries, so that it was the *Comitia Tributa* which was affected, and, though I do not wholly agree with her reasons, I too would guess that, as the census classes are not explicitly mentioned, it was primarily the tribal assembly which was altered by the regional reorganization of 179 B.C.

But the evidence is insufficient to allow a decision that Livy in the preface to his account of the census of 169 B.C. referred to the same censors who reorganized the assembly, though a presumable innovation about the allocation of freedmen would suit the character, as far as we know it, of the census of 179 B.C.[3] Thus the second pair of censors in question would most naturally be those of 174 B.C., the immediate predecessors of Gracchus and Pulcher.[4] The corrupt passage of Livy is then giving a complete list of censuses.

In 169 B.C., as Livy goes on to describe, Ti. Sempronius Gracchus wished to disfranchise the freedman entirely, in reaction to the policy of his predecessors, which had not indeed, compared with the earlier attempts of Ap. Claudius Caecus, been very radical. Gracchus' idea was the most extreme threat which the *libertini* ever faced: an outright attack on the political rights which Rome had, unlike other ancient states, conferred on her ex-slaves. The text reads, continuing from the passage quoted above:

---

[1] *Camb. Hist. Journ.* 6, (1939), 134 and n. 64.
[2] Because, she thinks, few had the property qualification, and fewer still the age to be admitted to the ranks of *iuniores* (*Vot. Dist.*, p. 140).
[3] It is hard to put it earlier, for the census of 184, that of Cato, was renowned for its strictness.
[4] McDonald's argument (*Camb. Hist. Journ.* 6 (1939), 138) that the privilege to freedmen who had children was not continued in the later census because of the conquest of Sardinia in 177–6 B.C. and consequent flood of freedmen, is unattractive, since it supposes a very rapid manumission of prisoners and an extraordinarily rapid reaction by the censors. *Sardi* were noted less for the ease with which they were freed than for the fact that they were always on the market because unsatisfactory—*Sardi venales* (Cic. *Fam.* vii. 24. 2).

46   LEGAL EFFECTS OF *LIBERTINITAS*

Hoc cum ita servatum esset, negabat Claudius suffragii lationem iniussu populi censorem cuiquam homini, nedum ordini universo adimere posse. neque enim, si tribu movere possit, quod sit nihil aliud quam mutare iubere tribum, ideo omnibus quinque et triginta tribubus emovere posse, id esse civitatem libertatemque eripere, non, ubi censeatur, finire, sed censu excludere. Haec inter ipsos disceptata; postremo eo descensum est, ut ex quattuor urbanis tribubus unam palam in atrio Libertatis sortirentur, in quam omnes, qui servitutem servissent, conicerent. Esquilinae sors exiit: in ea Ti. Gracchus pronuntiavit libertinos omnes censeri placere. Magno ea res honori censoribus apud senatum fuit. Gratiae actae et Sempronio, qui in bene coepto perseverasset, et Claudio, qui non impedisset.[1]

The major difficulty which arises here is in the interpretation of 'hoc cum ita servatum esset'. If the words after the lacuna in the preceding sentence have been rightly connected with the action of predecessors of Gracchus and Pulcher, we may conjecture that the rendering of sections 3–4 above should run:

> Since this (sc. right) was kept, Claudius denied that the censor could, without a mandate from the people, deprive any individual, let alone a whole order, of the franchise. For his capacity to move a man from a particular tribe (which only meant that he ordered him to change his tribe) did not imply that he could remove him completely from all thirty-five tribes, which was equivalent to depriving him of citizenship and liberty, and was not to define where a man should appear on the census-list, but to exclude him from it.

The account of Gracchus' sweeping plan to exclude the *libertini* from the franchise will have appeared in the first of the two lacunae, before the flashback to previous censorships. In my view, 'hoc cum ita servatum esset' cannot mean that the concessions about land-owning *libertini* were removed—for the measure on which the censors eventually agreed was clearly severe, if Gracchus had originally wanted to deprive freedmen of the vote entirely—but that those individuals already assigned to rustic tribes were not moved. Thus, I take 'libertinos omnes' as meaning *libertini* not already placed in a tribe. To change with a stroke of the pen the status of men admitted to rural tribes by preceding censors would

[1] xlv. 15. 3–7.

LIBERTINI IN PUBLIC LAW

have been an extreme measure unless warranted by a 'forensis factio' like that quashed in 304 B.C. This view is supported by the fact that Cicero praised the Gracchan solution highly:

saepe alias et maxime censor saluti rei publicae fuit: atque is non accurata quadam orationis copia, sed nutu atque verbo libertinos in urbanas tribus transtulit, quod nisi fecisset, rem publicam, quam nunc vix tenemus, iam diu nullam haberemus.[1]

I would not insist on the interpretation I have given above of the concession which was allowed to stand in 169 B.C.—Cicero's use of the expression 'transtulit' may suggest that some freedmen who had been privileged in previous *lustra* were transferred—but some at least maintained their position in country tribes. Possibly those with land stayed, those with children were returned to city tribes. If, indeed, 'censendi ius factum est' refers to landowning freedmen and 'hoc' picks up 'ius', the guess that freedmen with farms worth over 30,000 sesterces were excepted from the ruling of 169 B.C. will gain support. But it must be stressed that we have not enough facts for certainty to be possible.

In any case, the important point is that from 169 B.C. onwards freedmen were regularly confined to the city tribes. It is likely that Gracchus and Pulcher meant succeeding censors to draw lots to establish which of the four tribes should take freedmen in their *lustrum*. Our two witnesses to later practice are agreed that the effect of the 169 B.C. precedent was to keep *libertini* in the four urban tribes, and not just in *Esquilina*.[2] It is to be assumed that this situation continued into the first century, since Cicero makes Scaevola speak of it in 91 B.C.

The next reference we have to the status of *libertini* in the assemblies is the statement of the *De Viris Illustribus*[3] on Scaurus' consulship in 115 B.C.: 'legem de sumptibus et libertinorum suffragiis tulit'. This is normally taken to have been another tightening-up measure—possibly connected with the introduction of secret ballot and the consequent emancipation of freedmen from

---

[1] *de Or*. i. 38.
[2] Cic. *de Or*. i. 38. Auct. *Vir. Ill*. 57: 'censor libertinos qui rusticas tribus occuparant in quattuor urbanas divisit'.
[3] 72.

the influence of their patrons.[1] Taylor,[2] however, has connected this with a passage in the *De Oratore*,[3] where Caesar is discussing wit. A text which is again corrupt reads:

> Saepe etiam versus facete interponitur, vel ut est vel paululum immutatus, aut aliqua pars versus, ut satius Scauro stomachanti; ex quo sunt non nulli, qui tuam legem de civitate natam, Crasse, dicant:
> st, tacete, quid hoc clamoris? Quibus nec mater nec pater, tanta confidentia? Auferte istam enim superbiam.

The trochaic *septenarii* presumably come from some well-known play and 'satius' is usually emended to a reference to Statius and the following words corrected to give 'ut Stati a Scauro stomachante'. Orelli, however, suggested 'ut Stati Scauro stomachanti', which involves fewer changes and is the alteration adopted by Taylor. The comic reference to men without father or mother is to slaves or freedmen, who had no recognized parents,[4] so Taylor conjectured that freedmen were here addressed and that Scaurus in 115 B.C. had made concessions to certain freedmen (perhaps for services rendered to the Senate against C. Gracchus in 121 B.C.) and that in 109 B.C. at the trial of M. Calpurnius Bestia before the Mamilian court of inquiry, at which Scaurus was counsel for the defence, he was supported by grateful freedmen, at which his opponent, Memmius or another prosecutor, produced this taunt. The theory is open to two objections.[5] Orelli's text does not give the name of the speaker, which in a literary discussion is odd, or rather, unthinkable. The people addressed, on the other hand, are sufficiently indicated by the quotation, on the usually accepted text. It neither makes sense for the speaker to taunt Scaurus, but actually address others, nor for the person feeling anger to be other than the speaker. Secondly, in Taylor's reconstruction, the time-lag between the contretemps in 109 B.C. and the law of Crassus, the *Lex Licinia Mucia* of 95 B.C. (and, for that matter, between the murder of C. Gracchus and the alleged reward to the freedmen

---

[1] This would not necessarily mean a swing against the aristocrats. Not all freedmen had aristocratic patrons, nor would all ex-slaves be *populares* when allowed to vote secretly.
[2] *Vot. Dist.*, pp. 142 f.   [3] ii. 257.
[4] Patron substitutes 'pater' for the freedman. Cf. Mart. ix. 12 for the jibe.
[5] Both made by Badian, *JRS* 52 (1962), 207 f.

in 115 B.C.) is extraordinary. The earlier view of Fraccaro[1] that we have here a reference to a quotation levelled by Scaurus at Italians in Rome at the trial of Norbanus, which probably took place in 95 B.C., fits all the known facts much better. Taylor did not offer any argument against this view except the textual one, which she supports by the very unconvincing corroboration that Scaurus had influence in the tribes, and especially 'apud rusticos'.[2] So the evidence of the *De Oratore* is out of court as a proof that Scaurus' law of 115 B.C. was in favour of the freedmen. Much more likely, it was a repressive law.[3] The *De Oratore* passage, however, remains interesting for us in that it reflects too the prejudice against freedmen. The original lines were addressed to slaves or freedmen, and when they were quoted in polemic 'the sting in the tail', as Badian put it, 'is precisely that Scaurus equates these respectable Italians with ex-slaves'.[4]

When we next hear of the position of the freedmen, they are in the urban tribes. Their distribution through all the tribes was a cause dear to the hearts of the *populares* in the last years of the Republic. Sulpicius Rufus brought in a law to distribute *libertini*, perhaps at the end of his career when he was desperate for support, and not as part of the bill for the distribution of the allies.[5] It is mentioned only by the Epitomator,[6] 'Cum P. Sulpicius tribunus plebis auctore C. Mario perniciosas leges promulgasset ut exsules revocarentur, et novi cives libertinique (in tribus xxxv) distribuerentur . . .', and by Asconius,[7] who says that he brought the bill 'cum per vim rem publicam possedisset et ab initiis bonarum actionum ad perditas progressus esset: quod et initium bellorum civilium fuit et propter quod ipse Sulpicius consulum armis iure oppressus esse visus est'.

Sulla annulled this law with the rest of Sulpicius' legislation. It

---

[1] *Opuscula* ii 'Scauriana', pp. 132 ff. E. Gabba (*Athen.* N.S. 31 (1953), 263) and Badian (*Hist.* 6 (1957), 334, n. 139) agree.
[2] *Vot. Dist.*, p. 143.
[3] Fraccaro, *Opuscula* ii, p. 132.
[4] Compare the arrogance of a proconsul in 91 B.C., who is said to have treated the Italians not as free men and allies, but as slaves (Diod. xxxvii. 13. 2).
[5] Taylor, *Vot. Dist.* pp. 143 f.
[6] Livy, *Ep.* lxxvii.
[7] *Corn.* 64C.

was possibly revived by Cinna in 87 B.C.,[1] but more probably had to wait until 84 B.C., when the Cinnans, in their search for support, carried out the distribution, if we may trust our one source.[2] If the law was passed, it was abolished by Sulla. For in 66 B.C. Manilius revived the bill, taking it over from Cornelius, and it was, according to Asconius,[3] once more the old Sulpician law. According to Dio, the terms of the Manilian law, and therefore presumably of the earlier laws too, were that *libertini* should vote in the tribe of their patron.[4] Manilius' bill was carried by violence: 'Nam eo tempore cum C. Manilius tribunus plebis subnixus libertinorum et servorum manu perditissimam legem ferret ut libertinis in omnibus tribubus suffragium esset, idque per tumultum ageret et clivum Capitolinum obsideret, discusserat perruperatque coetum Domitius ita ut multi Manilianorum occiderentur.'[5] For this reason, it was invalidated by the Senate.[6]

Finally, Clodius took over the law, and was preparing to promulgate it at the time of his death. Cicero in the *Pro Milone*[7] claims that laws to put free Romans in the power of their slaves[8] were all ready for submission to the people and Asconius[9] in his note explains that *libertini* were to be allowed into the rustic tribes. The bill was not necessarily the same as that of Sulpicius, but it seems likely that it too arranged to enrol freedmen in the same tribes as their patrons, since Cicero complained that people like himself would have been controlled, which probably means outvoted by their own freedmen.

After the death of Clodius, the bill was never revived. Power in

[1] Cf. Schol. Gronov. p. 286 St.: 'Coepit Cinna de libertinorum suffragiis agere, Octavium cum senatu contra ipsum habuit; ortum est bellum civile.' If this was an omnibus law with that on the allies attested by more reliable sources, provision may have been made for the freedmen.

[2] Livy, *Ep.* lxxxiv. [3] *Corn.* 64C.

[4] xxxvi. 42. 2: τῷ γὰρ ἔθνει τῷ τῶν ἀπελευθέρων ... ψηφίσασθαι μετὰ τῶν ἐξελευθερωσάντων σφᾶς ἔδωκεν, Cf. Mommsen, *StR.* iii, p. 439.

[5] Asc. *Mil.* 45B.

[6] Dio, xxxvi. 42. 2.

[7] *Mil.* 87: 'Incidebantur iam domi leges quae nos servis nostris addicerent.' Cf. 89.

[8] Cf. Appendix 4.

[9] *Mil.* 52C: 'Significasse iam puto nos fuisse inter leges P. Clodii quas ferre proposuerat eam quoque qua libertini, qui non plus quam in iiii tribubus suffragium ferebant, possent in rusticis quoque tribubus, quae propriae ingenuorum sunt, ferre.'

the voting-districts from now onwards was unnecessary to the politician. Caesar was able to dissolve the *collegia* which had served as the basis for Clodius' organization, and in which *libertini* had played an important part, and he did not need to conciliate them by changing the tribal system.

The position of freedmen with regard to the *Comitia Centuriata* presents a problem which is baffling because of lack of evidence. One passage that has been referred to the centuriate assembly I have followed Taylor in connecting rather with the *Comitia Tributa*,[1] although effects on the *Centuriata* would of course have followed if *libertini* were members of that body too. Freedmen were excluded from the *equites equo publico* and were not normally called up to serve in the infantry either, but we do not know of any statutory prohibition.[2] There is a possibility that in early times they were placed with the *capite censi*,[3] who formed one century in the *Comitia Centuriata*. But later the *Centuriata* was primarily an organization for voting and, till 107 B.C., the tax assessment of citizens. Freedmen could hardly be deprived of a substantial part of the franchise, nor the state of revenue from the richer freedmen. There is no evidence that freedmen were not registered in the appropriate classes for these purposes.[4]

On the other hand, there is some affirmative evidence. The *Commentariolum Petitionis*[5] mentions the importance to the consular candidate of the support of freedmen who are 'gratiosi navique in foro'. As the consular elections are in question, these men must have influence in the centuriate assembly and influence in the assembly is not very likely to exist where there was no membership.

The census lists of the *Centuriata* were not merely for the guidance of the recruiting-officer, and there is no need to suppose that physically incapacitated youths were excluded from the *iuniores*

---

[1] Above, p. 45.
[2] Mommsen, *StR*. iii, pp. 448 ff.; P.Fraccaro, *Studi P. Bonfante* i (Milan, 1930), p. 119.
[3] Plut. *Popl*. 7. Cf. P. Willems, *Le Droit public romain* (Louvain, 1883), pp. 108 f.
[4] A. Rosenberg (*Untersuchungen zur römischen Zenturienverfassung* (Berlin, 1911), pp. 87 ff.) indeed held that the reform of the *Centuriata* was inspired partly by the need to check the power of rich freedmen in the urban classes.
[5] 29.

because they would not be called up, or that *libertini* were debarred from the urban classes of either age group on the score of unsuitability for the army.

To sum up, although from time to time freedmen with certain qualifications might be admitted to rustic tribes, the normal practice throughout republican history was for the censors to allot newly freed slaves to an urban tribe. This was the standard system in the whole of the late republican period. Sons of freedmen with property in country districts could sometimes secure a transfer. Rich freedmen, though confined generally to the urban tribes, may have enjoyed more power through their membership of the richer and more powerful classes of the urban *centuriae*, which would otherwise have been thinly manned by *ingenui*. In assessing the freedmen's position in the tribes it is relevant to remember that free-born Italians, after a long struggle to obtain the franchise in the first place, suffered for a time under a similar restriction as to tribe. The position of favoured individual provincials who obtained the citizenship might be better. Criticism was aimed at Balbus because he succeeded in changing to a better tribe;[1] privileges might be conferred by magistrates.[2] Such concessions, however, may perhaps have been made to influential freedmen as well as to provincials who had served their patrons well.

(b) *Eligibility for Office in State and Municipality*

It is dogmatically asserted by many modern authorities[3] that neither the freedman nor his son was ever, in strict law, eligible for the Senate or the magistracies, and that the freedman himself was also debarred from the *equites equo publico*. Although the sons of *libertini* in the social context are separately discussed, it will be well to consider their political rights here.

As a preliminary, a possible source of confusion needs mention. This is the application of the term *libertinus*. In classical usage it

---

[1] Cic. *Balb.* 57. See L. R. Taylor, *Party Politics in the Age of Caesar* (California, 1961), pp. 54, 114. Technically, he was rewarded for a successful prosecution, but favouritism was clearly suspected.

[2] Cf. *FIRA* i. 55 (= *EJ* 301) 11. 2: the tribe Cornelia was assigned to the newly enfranchised *nauarchos* Seleucus, son of Theodotus of Rhosus, and his family for services rendered during the triumviral period to Octavian.

[3] e.g. Mommsen, *StR.* iii, pp. 451 ff.; Schulz, *Principles*, p. 122.

means the freedman in relation to society, while *libertus* is used of a freedman in relation to his *patronus*, his ex-master. But Suetonius, discussing the adlection of freedmen's sons to the Senate by Claudius and the emperor's argument that he was imitating his ancestor Appius Claudius Caecus, who in 312 B.C. had also adlected 'libertinorum filios', claims that Claudius had made a slip, 'ignarus temporibus Appi et deinceps aliquamdiu libertinos dictos non ipsos, qui manu emitterentur, sed ingenuos ex his procreatos.'[1] Suetonius does not support this piece of historical erudition in any way. But our other sources are all in agreement with Claudius.[2] Nor can they be using 'libertinorum filii' in the alleged archaic sense to mean 'grandsons of freedmen',[3] without explanation that they were going against the clear normal usage of the word.[4] Even Livy does not appear to use 'libertini' in this sense.[5] Mommsen saved Suetonius from complete inaccuracy by arguing that 'libertinus' applied to both freedmen and their sons, but this involves inserting 'solum' in the text so as to read 'non solum ipsos'.[6] So, even if Appius Claudius had used the word 'libertini' to mean both the fathers and the sons, the authorities whom we have on his actions would not. Suetonius' theory thus becomes irrelevant, even on Mommsen's view. Probably the text should be allowed to stand and Suetonius, not the antiquarian Claudius, was misled.

To take the Senate first, the argument that freedmen's sons were ineligible is *a priori*, and so many exceptions are known that if there was a rule, it must have been laxly kept in the last century of the Republic. In fact, the argument rests on a *petitio principii*. A direct statement on the matter is given in the speech which Tacitus puts into the mouth of Claudius in connection with

---

[1] *Claud.* 24. 1; cf. Isid. *Orig.* ix. 4. 47: 'libertorum filii apud antiquos libertini appellabantur, quasi de libertis nati. Nunc vero libertinus aut a liberto factus aut possessus.'
[2] Tac. *Ann.* xi. 24; Plut. *Pomp.* 13; Diod. xx. 36; Livy, ix. 46. 1.
[3] *Pace* Mommsen, *StR.* iii, pp. 420 ff., with whom Taylor (*Vot. Dist.*, p. 132) agrees.
[4] Cf. Duff, *Freedmen*, pp. 50 ff.; Quint. v. 10. 60: 'qui servus est, si manumittatur, fit libertinus'. Gaius, i. 10–11, etc.
[5] There are clear instances of the normal usage: xxxiv. 9–13; xlv. 15.
[6] *StR.* iii, p. 422.

the adlection of Gauls in A.D. 48:[1] 'Advenae in nos regnaverunt: libertinorum filiis magistratus mandare non, ut plerique falluntur, repens, sed priori populo factitatum est.'[2] Tacitus *in propria persona* makes a similar statement in the same context: 'cunctisque civium, si bonis artibus fiderent, licitum petere magistratus, ac ne aetas quidem distinguebatur'.[3] Claudius, then, suggests that the practice of making freedmen's sons magistrates was common, and he and Tacitus (if we may distinguish the two voices) both exclude the existence of any statutory bar. Tacitus' own statement, taken literally, would allow even freedmen a legal right to stand.

It had been *mos* which had, until enabling laws were passed, kept plebeians out of office. It continued to exclude ex-slaves. Livy makes Canuleius say in his speech on the legalization of *conubium* between patrician and plebeian, 'Et perinde hoc valet, plebeiusne consul fiat, tamquam servum aut libertinum aliquis consulem futurum dicat?'[4] There is no suggestion[5] that *mos* would exclude the sons of freedmen.

There are a number of examples to exclude any such *mos*. The *terminus post quem* is of course the admission of *plebeii* to office. The end of the struggle of the orders opened the door first of all to the old plebeian families, and we should naturally expect the less wealthy and distinguished plebeians to achieve office only after a considerable time-lag.[6]

In his *censura* of 312 B.C. Appius Claudius adlected to the Senate, presumably among others, the sons of *libertini*: 'senatum primus libertinorum filiis lectis inquinaverat et, posteaquam eam lectionem nemo ratam habuit, nec in curia adeptus est quas petierat opes, urbanis humilibus per omnes tribus divisis forum et campum

---

[1] *Ann.* xi. 24. The reference does not appear in the actual speech as we have it from the Lyons inscription (where the reference to 'advenae' is more fully developed than in Tacitus. Note especially Servius Tullius, 'captiva natus'.) It has been suggested that the reference to the sons of freedmen came from another Claudian speech (R. Syme, *Tacitus* (Oxford, 1958), p. 707).
[2] The idea was probably taken from Canuleius. Cf. Livy, iv. 3. 7.
[3] *Ann.* xi. 22.   [4] Livy, iv. 3. 7.
[5] Unless, which I do not believe, Livy used 'libertinus' in the sense given it by Suetonius.
[6] See Lejay, *Rev. Phil.* 44 (1920), 118.

corrupit.'[1] Livy and Claudius in Suetonius' account are in agreement[2] that this was the first occasion on which sons of freedmen were put on the senatorial roll. We are told that Appius Claudius did not remove any existing senators—although it was claimed that he passed over some who were worthier[3]—and probably the proportion of freedmen's sons on his list was quite small. Propaganda, as in the case of Sulla and Caesar later, always exaggerated the 'disreputable' element in new adlections. In any case, the consuls declined to adopt the list. This was permissible and may be partly accounted for by conjecturing that they preferred to use the list they had had while colleagues before, in 317 B.C. Garzetti[4] indeed has argued that contemporaries would not have been as shocked by the adlection of the sons of freedmen as were Livy and later writers. He backs this view by reference to a theory[5] that private law grew progressively stricter in its attitude to freedmen. But in public law, a gradual tightening-up cannot be shown. The Emperor Claudius remarks that it was generally held that the sons of freedmen had held office in recent times, so to his contemporaries it appeared that practice had, if anything, grown more, not less, liberal. Claudius himself held that it had always been liberal. In social life too, *libertini* were probably more readily accepted in the late Republic than earlier.[6] But it is surely relevant to the climate of opinion in Appius Claudius' day to remember that freedmen were still almost invariably of similar Italian stock to their patrons, and that, as later many freedmen owed much of their position to the fact that they belonged to the same Greek culture as their patrons, so, in the fourth century they may have been well treated because they were fellow Italians, who chose to remain in Rome enjoying the benefits of its citizenship although they could have returned to their original homes by *postliminium*. So Garzetti may well be right in arguing that there was no moral prejudice against freedmen in

---

[1] Livy, ix. 46. 10 ff. Cf. above, pp. 38 ff. See also Livy, ix. 29. 7, 30. 1 f.; Diod. xx. 36. 4; Val. Max. ii. 2. 9; Suet. *Claud.* 24; Plut. *Pomp.* 13; Auct. *Vir. Ill.* 34. 1: 'Appius Claudius Caecus censor libertinos quoque in senatum legit': 'libertinos' is probably a slip, for if the author agreed with Suetonius, he should have written 'libertinorum filios'.
[2] Unsurprising as they were tutor and pupil.
[3] Diod. xx. 36. 4.   [4] *Athen.* 25 (1947), 201 f.
[5] Below, p. 69 ff.   [6] Below, pp. 224 f.

this period: but there was of course social prejudice on the part of aristocrats against the *humiles*, who included freedmen's sons, taking office.

Baulked in his attempt to liberalize the Senate, Appius Claudius turned to indirect methods: he increased the power of the *humiles*,[1] and the result was the election to the aedileship of a freedman's son, Cn. Flavius, for 304 B.C.[2] According to Licinius Macer, Flavius had already held office, the tribunate and two triumvirates.[3] Possibly his tenure of the tribunate was in 305 B.C. The sources are unanimous that he was 'patre libertino',[4] and there is no suggestion that this means grandson of a freedman.[5] It appears to have been more relevant to Flavius' career that he was a scribe than that he was the son of a freedman, for nothing is said about his father's patron, but the fact that he was *scriba* to Appius Claudius was of great importance.[6] According to certain annalists he was not allowed to be declared elected to the aedileship before he had laid down his appointment as *scriba*.[7] Flavius' famous *coup* of publishing the civil law is dated by good authority to his days as a secretary, although others put it in 304 B.C.[8] He also had the Fasti displayed.[9] Appius Claudius supported him in this action, which was designed to give the common people more understanding of public events. It is also

---

[1] Above, pp. 39 ff.
[2] Livy, ix. 46. 1: 'Cn. Flavius Cn. filius scriba, patre libertino humili fortuna ortus, ceterum callidus vir et facundus, aedilis curulis fuit.... (10) Ceterum Flavium dixerat aedilem forensis factio, Appi Claudi censura vires nacta.'
[3] Macer *apud* Livy, ix. 46. 3. *MRR* i, p. 168. These offices would fill the gap between 312 and 304 B.C., and are not inconsistent with the other annalists, who say Flavius was the first freedman's son to be aedile (Diod. xxii. 36. 6), not the first to hold a magistracy. Pliny (*NH* xxxiii. 17) says the tribunate was held concurrently with the aedileship.
[4] Gell. vii. 9; Val. Max. ii. 5. 2, cf. ix. 3. 3: 'humillimae sortis'; Pliny, *NH* xxxiii. 17; Diod. xxii. 36. 6: υἱὸν ἀπελευθέρου is quite unambiguous, though he could have been misled by Latin sources if Suet. *Claud.* 24 were right.
[5] The father's name appears to have been, not Gnaeus as Livy has it, but Annius. Cf. Cic. *Att.* vi. 1. 8; Pliny, *NH* xxxiii. 17; Gell. vii. 9.
[6] Pliny, *NH* xxxiii. 17.
[7] Livy, ix. 46. 2; Gell. vii. 9, reporting Piso. Flavius had been aedilician scribe. Macer, reported by Livy, held that Flavius had resigned when he was elected to earlier offices.
[8] Cic. *Mur.* 25; *Att.* vi. 1. 8; Macrob. *Sat.* i. 15. 9; *Dig.* i. 2. 2. 7. *Contra*, Livy, ix. 46. 5; Val. Max. ii. 5. 2.
[9] *Fasti Capitolini*, ed. A. Degrassi (Turin, 1954), p. 16. Cf. Livy, ix. 46, etc.

significant that Flavius' colleague as curule aedile[1] was a new citizen from Praeneste, 'qui paucis ante annis hostis fuisset', and that two sons of consuls were passed over in their favour.[2] Flavius had an unusually active term of office: the nobles, though not the entire Senate, opposed him in disgust at his election, but he kept his head and succeeded in asserting his position,[3] turning the tables on his opponents, when they ostentatiously went into mourning, by dedicating a temple to *Concordia*.[4] Livy, with justification, as far as we can see, called him 'humili fortuna ortus, cetera callidus vir atque facundus', and he obviously had ability as well as backing. His measures were democratic but not outrageous, in spite of the horror of Appius Claudius' die-hard opponents, and his political career appears to have survived the censorship of Fabius, which destroyed Appius' other great liberal undertakings.

The next piece of evidence on the subject is dubious. We are told by Suetonius and the Epitomator[5] of a curious incident in 249 B.C., when the consul, Claudius Pulcher, was recalled and compelled to appoint a dictator. With deliberate malice, he selected a dependant of his own, one Claudius Glycias. The Epitomator calls him 'sortis ultimae homo'; Suetonius says he was a minor civil servant, a *viator*. According to the *Fasti Capitolini*, however, he had, like Flavius, been a *scriba*. It may be that this man was the son of a freedman, rather than a poor relation of the consul. It is clear that he was meant to be a man of straw, and the remark of Suetonius is not inconsistent with servile origins. His full name, as given in the *Fasti*, was M. Claudius C. f. Glicia,[6] and the *cognomen*, with the spelling undecided between Greek and Latin, might suggest foreign origin, and hence libertine parentage.[7] Claudius was

[1] It is remarkable that a freedman's son could rank as a *patricius*.
[2] Pliny, *NH* xxxiii. 17.
[3] When certain *nobiles* did not offer him a seat, he sent for his curule chair (Livy, ix. 46. 9, etc.).
[4] Pliny, *NH* xxxiii. 17, following old annals, etc.
[5] Suet. *Tib.* 2; Livy, *Ep.* xviii.
[6] s. 249 B.C. It was not at this early date the regular custom that a freedman should take his patron's *praenomen*, so the fact that Pulcher was 'Publius Claudius Appi filius Gai nepos' is not against this view.
[7] This argument is never conclusive; cf. the Romans with *cognomina* such as Sophos or Philippus.

thought to be mocking the state in its extremity and his protégé was hastily forced to abdicate.[1]

We are not on much firmer ground with A. Gabinius, the tribune of 139 B.C., who carried the *Lex Tabellaria*. He seems to have been descended from a family of slave-potters at Cales, but it is likely that his closest freedman ascendant was a grandfather, not his father.[2] Or hostile tradition may have invented even the slave grandfather. The success-story of Gabinius is remarkable, for he founded a line of senators, which few *populares* managed to do.

The status of P. Furius, tribune in 99 B.C.,[3] is not in doubt: Appian tells us that he was son, not of a free-born citizen, but of a freedman.[4] He was a faction-leader with powerful *inimici*, for he took the part of Marius against Metellus Pius. Though, like Marius, he was at one time allied with Saturninus and Glaucia, he turned against them in the end.[5] This cost him dear after his tribunate, when he was brought to trial on an unknown charge, and lynched by the mob.[6] Here, too, a freedman's son with powerful patronage gained an influential position, but he was probably no mere subordinate of Marius, for we are told that he had his own followers[7] and he had private *inimicitiae* with Metellus, who had deprived him of the public horse in 102 B.C.[8]

The ally of Saturninus who was tribune for 100–99 B.C. and was killed on the first day of his office in December 100 B.C., L. Equitius, was of mysterious origins. According to the Optimate

[1] Suet. *Tib.* 2.
[2] Cicero (*Legg.* iii. 35) calls him 'homo ignotus et sordidus'. Livy, *Per. Ox.* liv, col. viii, has been restored to read:
A. (G)abinius, verna(e nepos legem tulit ut)
suffragium per ta(bellam ferretur.)
Conceivably 'filius' might be the right restoration, but Badian has shown (*Philol.* 103 (1959), 87) that the tribune was probably son of a certain *praefectus*. For Gabinius' earlier career, see Polyb. xxxviii. 10. 1 ff., 11.
[3] Date disputed. See E. Gabba on App. *BC* i. 33. 2; E. Gruen, *Hist.* 15 (1966), 32 f. It may have been 100 B.C.
[4] *BC* i. 33. 2: οὐδ' ἐλευθέρου πατρὸς ἀλλ' ἐξελευθέρου.
[5] Dio, *fr.* 95. 2; App. *BC* i. 33. 2; Oros. v. 17. 11: 'quae (sc. the recall of Metellus) ne perficeretur Marii consulis et Furii tr. pl. factionibus intercessum est'.
[6] Dio, *fr.* 95. 3; Cic. *Rab. Perd.* 20, 24; App. *BC* i. 33. 3; Val. Max. viii. i, *Damn.* 2; Oros. v. 17. Cf. Gruen, *Hist.* 15 (1966), 34 f. Probably there were two accusers and one trial.
[7] Oros. v. 17.
[8] Dio, *fr.* 95. 2.

tradition, he came 'ex infimo loco'.[1] Cicero called him 'ille ex compedibus atque ergastulo Gracchus',[2] and Appian explicitly says that there was a belief that he was a runaway-slave.[3] But according to the *De Viris Illustribus*[4] he was 'libertini ordinis'. Valerius Maximus[5] indeed holds that his candidature was illegal, and if the false Gracchus was in fact a freedman, this would be the only direct statement we have on the illegality of freedmen standing for office.[6] But it seems much more likely that 'libertini ordinis' is to be taken as meaning that Equitius was the son of a freedman, on the analogy of the later senatorial and equestrian orders, to which sons belonged. The tradition about the false Gracchus rapidly became vague, and his true origins were further distorted by the patent slander of political enemies. Libertine parentage, which would account for the accusations that he was a runaway-slave, seems likely for him.

Neither Flavius nor Furius was, as far as we know, attacked as a magistrate because of his birth, on a point of law. Flavius probably was ineligible, or was considered so, by the presiding aedile, because of his civil-service appointment, and his election caused scandal, but it was not attacked as illegal. Furius was removed from the ranks of the *equites equo publico*, perhaps on the ground of low birth, but possibly on the pretext of immorality.[7] We do not know if any of these men were senators as well as magistrates, but probably none of them was. This is implied for Furius at least, in the fact that he had been *eques*.

But during the forty years which followed, until the barriers broke down in the chaos of civil war, the sons of freedmen apparently gained ground in the Senate. One Popilius was removed from the list by the censors of 70 B.C. The reasons given were two: Gellius accused him of having accepted a bribe when *iudex* at the trial of Oppianicus in 74 B.C., while his colleague, Lentulus, denied the truth of the charge, but agreed that Popilius should be removed

[1] Valerius Maximus puts him in a section dedicated to such men, ix. 15. 1.
[2] *Rab. Perd.* 20.   [3] *BC.* i. 32. 1.   [4] 73.   [5] ix. 7. 1.
[6] Unless it were illegal because Equitius' claim to be the son of Ti. Gracchus had been rejected by the censors.
[7] Cf. Cic. *Rab. Perd.* 24: 'hominem omnibus insignem notis turpitudinis'. Val. Max. viii. 1, *Damn.* 2: 'inquinatissimae vitae'.

because he was the son of a freedman, leaving him, however, the right to sit with senators at the games, and the other privileges of the order.[1] Cicero accepts Lentulus' account of the parentage of Popilius and it seems from his expressions that it depended on the individual senator whether or not he chose to accept the sons of *libertini* as senators.[2] Popilius had entered the Senate legally, presumably by election as a magistrate or adlection by Sulla,[3] but Lentulus chose to make an issue of his birth, much as some censors might be stricter than others in removing men of irregular life.[4] Nevertheless, his concessions about *ornamenta* are an indication that the omission of Popilius from the list was not intended as a disgrace. His colleague Gellius' attack on Popilius had nothing to do with his libertine origins.[5] He was able to stand for office again, although in the event he was disqualified because of a charge of corruption.[6]

Horace's lines show that there was nothing to stop a freedman's son getting into the Senate, but that an unusually severe censor might throw him out again:

> esto populus Laevino mallet honorem
> quam Decio mandare novo, censorque moveret
> Appius, ingenuo si non essem patre natus:
> vel merito, quoniam in propria non pelle quiessem.[7]

The aim of Appius Claudius as censor in 50 B.C., according to Dio, was to expel Caesarian partisans, and his colleague, Caesar's father-in-law, Piso, tried to please both sides, and, in his efforts to be conciliatory, allowed Claudius to remove all the sons of freedmen

---

[1] Cic. *Cluent.* 131 f.
[2] 'Negat hoc (sc. the bribery charge) Lentulus, nam Popilium, quod erat libertini filius, in senatum non legit, locum quidem senatorium ludis et cetera ornamenta relinquit' (132).
[3] Sulla is said to have adlected ἐκ τῶν ἐπιτυχόντων ἀνθρώπων (Dion. Hal. v. 77) *equites* (App. *BC* i. 100; Livy, *Ep.* lxxxix); *gregarii milites* Sall. *BC* 37). Afterwards, censorial adlection gave place to election to magistracies as the qualification for the senate (Cic. *Legg.* iii. 27). See Syme, *PBSR* N.S. 1 (1938), 22 ff.; Gabba, *Athen.* 29 (1951), 262 ff. (listing Popilius as a possible Sullan senator).
[4] In 50 B.C. the strictness of Ap. Claudius was a matter for sarcasm (Cic. *Fam.* viii. 14. 4).
[5] The censors of 70 B.C., as befitted them after a decade without censorship, were noted for their strictness. Cf. Cic. *Div. in Caec.* 8; Livy, *Ep.* xcviii: sixty-four senators were removed.
[6] Cic. *Cluent.* 132.
[7] *Sat.* i. 6. 19 ff.

LIBERTINI IN PUBLIC LAW

from the senate, as well as many better-born men, including Sallust.[1]

The objection to the son of a freedman father is similar to the neglect suffered by even the ablest *novus homo*: Horace would be breaking no law by going into politics, but he would be going out of his proper métier. The feeling that politics were the rightful business of the rich and leisured *nobiles* was as strong in Rome as most of the laws, and even the humane Cicero, *novus* himself, often conformed in his public utterances with the fashionable scorn for any man who did not belong to the inner circle of the ruling-class.

In the revolutionary period, the Senate became contaminated with people of doubtful antecedents. Caesar in 47 B.C. admitted *equites*, centurions, and 'lesser men';[2] in 45 B.C. we are told that soldiers and the sons of freedmen were among the new senators.[3] It is entirely possible that men who started out as soldiers or freedmen's sons had since acquired qualifications which would have justified their adlection to the Senate.[4] War and intrigue threw up a number of capable men.[5]

The triumvirs admitted a number of sons of *libertini* to the Senate.[6] Worse, it is agreed by a number of authorities that slaves became magistrates under their rule. According to Dio,[6] a certain Maximus, when about to become quaestor, was recognized by his

---

[1] xl. 63. 4. See P. Willems, *Le Sénat de la République romaine*, vol. i (Louvain, 1878), pp. 187 f., 561 ff. Plut. *Cic.* 27.3 mentions a senator M. Gellius who was reputedly not of free parentage.

[2] Dio, xlii. 51. 5.   [3] Dio, xliii. 47. 3.

[4] Cf. Syme, *PBSR* N.S. 1 (1938), 1 ff.

[5] e.g. P. Ventidius, captured at Asculum during the Social War and led in triumph, but later *consul suffectus* (43 B.C.) and himself a *triumphator*. Did he pass through a period of slavery? The sources (Gell. xv. 4; Dio, xliii. 51. 4 f.) are not explicit. Dio's ἀφεθείς is the nearest we get to a suggestion of libertinity, but it is consistent with his having been released as a war-prisoner or from illegal slavery, rather than with manumission. Syme (*Roman Revolution*, p. 71) seems to imply that he had been a slave, but in a later article (*Latomus* 17 (1958), 73 ff.) showed that the *nomen* belonged to a Picentine family of high standing, which means that Ventidius bore his own family name and did not acquire Roman citizenship through slavery. The scribe who became quaestor under Caesar (Cic. *Off.* ii. 29) may have been the 'Cornelius scriba' known as a profiteer earlier (Sall. *Or. Lep.* 17). It has been conjectured that he was a freedman of Sulla. See Willems, *Sénat*, i, pp. 593 f. But as his *praenomen* was Q. not L. he is not particularly likely to have been freed by Sulla (Syme, *PBSR* N.S. 1 (1938), 13).

[6] Dio, xlviii. 34. 4.

owner and dragged off, and another slave was discovered while actually praetor and first freed, then hurled from the Tarpeian Rock. These events are put in 39 B.C. The slave who became praetor was a protégé of Antony, Barbarius Philippus, we are told elsewhere.[1] Ulpian,[2] mentioning this occurrence, adds that if the people had known that he was a slave, election would have made him a freedman, for slavery was inconsistent with office,[3] but this idea was clearly not accepted by Barbarius' contemporaries. Freedmen's sons in the Senate were small fry compared with Maximus and Barbarius, even if the latter were deprived of office. Oddities such as this could not be expected to survive the disturbances of the civil wars, when the status of free men was so often imperilled or questioned, and origins were easily obscured.[4] But the sons of freedmen continued to hold magistracies. We hear of a certain C. Thoranius, who, as tribune in 25 B.C., took his father to sit in the seats reserved for tribunes at the games,[5] thus sharing the honour of his position with an ex-slave. The father may have been freed by C. Toranius,[6] a tutor of Augustus commemorated on an inscription,[7] which makes it possible to conjecture that he was a nominee of the *princeps*.

I conclude therefore that there is ample evidence that the sons of freedmen held magistracies and became senators, and no evidence that this infringed any rule, though some censors might reverse the decision of their predecessors or the vote of the people and eject a freedman's son from the Senate. But there is no suggestion that they were ever ejected from office. Moreover, there is no conclusive proof that *libertini* themselves were debarred by law from holding office, but we find no mention of any certain freedmen holding office: the lowest legitimate magistrates mentioned are their sons. *Mos*, which was strong against the sons of freedmen, was

---

[1] *Suda s.* Barbios Philippikos. He is to be distinguished from M. Barbatius Pollio. See Syme, *Hist.* 4 (1955), 57; *Roman Revolution*, p. 196; *PIR*² B50.
[2] *Dig.* i. 14. 3.
[3] Some corroboration for the view that any free citizen was technically eligible for office.
[4] Cf. Ventidius (above, p. 61, n. 5); M. Aurius (Cic. *Cluent.* 21 ff.); Valerius Cato (Suet. *Gram.* 11).
[5] Dio, liii. 27. 6.
[6] The more correct spelling.
[7] *CIL* i. 29; cf. *PIR* T216.

stronger still against freedmen themselves. It seems conclusive against the existence of any idea that freedmen would stand for office at Rome that, where rules were laid down by law, they were often debarred. Thus, C. Gracchus' *Lex Iudiciaria* indirectly excluded them from jury-service.[1] It is also likely that they could not normally hold magistracies in Roman colonies. It would, of course, be a reasonable practice that aliens recently enfranchised, often of different cultural backgrounds from that of their adopted country, should not immediately stand for office. Free-born individuals did not normally hold office soon after their family or area had obtained the citizenship, although there was no explicit legal ban.[2] The qualifications for office were not legal, but social and economic: prestige, wealth, education, and support.[3] Similarly, there was probably no ban on freedmen in office or in the Senate: the prohibition was not explicit and legal, but *libertini* lacked many of the prerequisites of political advancement. If they had powerful patronage their sons were in roughly the same position as the kin of recently enfranchised foreigners, men like the Younger Balbus, when they sought office.[4]

In Italian towns and in Roman colonies, *libertini* were normally kept out of office as at Rome. At Minturnae, for instance, with its mixed Roman and Oscan population, we find ingenuous *duoviri*,[5] and this appears to have been normal practice, though, I would suggest, probably not laid down by law. In new foundations, a written constitution might make hard-and-fast rules. Caesar in his colonies allowed freedmen to hold office, a necessary step since many of the colonists were freedmen.[6] But the *Lex Julia Municipalis* does not specifically exclude freedmen from office.[7] Augustus, with his restrictive policy as regarded freedmen, seems to have explicitly

---

[1] Below, p. 67.
[2] I accept the view that no *ius honorum* existed separately from the *civitas*, although under the Principate careers might be accelerated by adlection to the Senate by the *princeps*. See Syme, *Tacitus*, i. p. 459 and n. 9; ii. p. 590.
[3] Syme, *Tacitus*, ii, pp. 587 ff.
[4] Syme, *Roman Revolution*, pp. 80 f.
[5] J. Johnson, *Excavations at Minturnae*, ii, inscription 25 = Degr. 742.
[6] Bruns, *Fontes* 28. 105: *libertini* eligible for the decurionate at Urso. Cf. Strabo 381.
[7] Bruns, *Fontes* 18. 89 ff.

prohibited their election,[1] but I would regard this, not as a return to the usual legal position after the innovations of Caesar, so much as a consolidation by the law of what seemed a desirable practice. The Augustan sevirate became a consolation to freedmen debarred from office, and a municipal career was wide open to their sons, who, if rich, acquired honours easily.[2]

(c) *Eligibility for Equestrian Rank*

Mommsen[3] claimed that the sons of *libertini* were excluded from the *equites equo publico*, along with their fathers. This view needs modification. The term *equites* was used to describe several distinct or sometimes overlapping categories, as has been shown by Mrs. Henderson in a recent article.[4] It is not possible to restrict it to the eighteen centuries of *equites equo publico*,[5] for the Gracchan jurors and men who possessed a certain census qualification also arrogated to themselves the title of *equites*. But the complexity of the situation with regard to the *equites* does not greatly affect discussion of the status of freedmen and their sons in this connection.

First, there are clear instances of the sons of freedmen enrolled in the eighteen centuries or holding military commands that imply that they were *equites equo publico*. P. Furius, the tribune of 99 B.C., had held the public horse until 102, and there is no suggestion in the extremely brief notice of his demotion by the censor Metellus that it had been illegal for him to be *eques equo publico*, though his libertine origin may have been the pretext for Metellus' action.[6] Julius Rufio, son of a freedman of Caesar, is said to have been left in command of three legions at Alexandria,[7] which, if the story is not mere hostile propaganda, should mean that he was an *eques*. The poet Horace is another instance: in this case the freedman's son was *tribunus militum*.[8] Later, we find M. Aurelius Cottanus, son of a freedman of Cotta Maximus, another *tribunus militum*.[9]

[1] See *Lex Malacitana*, Bruns, *Fontes*, 30. 53 ff.
[2] J. S. Reid, *The Municipalities of the Roman Empire* (Cambridge, 1913), pp. 233, 510; Gordon, *JRS* 21 (1931), 65 ff.
[3] *StR*. iii, pp. 451 ff.   [4] *JRS* 53 (1963), 61 ff.
[5] Pace C. Nicolet, *L'Ordre équestre à l'époque républicaine* i (Paris, 1967) passim.
[6] Dio, *fr*. 95. 2.   [7] Suet. *DJ*. 76.
[8] Hor. *Sat*. i. 6. 48; Suet. *Vit. Hor*.; L. R. Taylor, *AJP* 46 (1925), 161 ff.
[9] *CIL* xiv. 2298 = *EJ* 358.

LIBERTINI IN PUBLIC LAW

Horace's words about the dislike he incurred as a *parvenu*, and the unusual emergencies in which he and Rufio served, show that there was social difficulty about the employment of freedmen's sons as *equites equo publico*, but suggest no legal bar.

More, we hear of an ex-slave holding the position of *tribunus militum*: the victim of Horace's fourth epode. This man, whose servile origins are indicated by the jibe that he had been 'sectus flagellis . . . triumviralibus',[1] aroused the indignation of freeborn Romans just as Horace himself had done, because of his office. He is probably a special case, who gained office in a turbulent period.[2] Other freedmen in the triumviral period or immediately after held offices that were regularly equestrian under the Principate. Pompeius Menas is cited as *legatus* or *praefectus* at various times under Sex. Pompeius and Octavian.[3] A certain freedman of Caesar, Demetrius, was allegedly put in command of Cyprus by M. Antonius *circa* 39 B.C.[4] Menas held Sardinia for Sex. Pompeius in 40 B.C.[5] Julius Licinus, freedman of Caesar or Augustus, was for years, before Augustus' visit in 16–15 B.C., financial procurator of Gaul, or at least of Lugdunensis.[6] Others have been conjectured. It seems to me, however, that just because a freedman held a post which was often equestrian, we do not necessarily have to assume that he ranked as *eques equo publico*. Menas, for instance, held an important military command under Sex. Pompeius before he received privileges appropriate to an *eques* from Octavian.[7] The civil wars caused the leaders to use as agents men who were private rather than public servants and it will have been hard to draw a firm line between the procurator of a triumvir and his personal

---

[1] Hor. *Epod.* iv. 11.
[2] The Scholia identify him with Pompeius Menas, which seems unlikely, though it would add to the point of the last four lines (cf. E. C. Wickham ad loc.) Menas had been given the *anulus aureus* by Octavian and was thus exempt from normal rules. M. I. Henderson (*JRS* 53 (1963), 70) appears to accept the identification.
[3] *MRR*, ii p. 603: legate, lieutenant or *praefectus classis* under Sex. Pompeius before 39–38 B.C.; *praefectus classis* under Octavian, 38–37, under Pompeius, 37–36, under Octavian, 36–35. He is formally termed *praefectus* by Velleius (ii. 73. 3) and Florus (ii. 18. 2); cf. Porph. on Hor. *Epod.* iv.
[4] Dio, xlviii. 40. 6. Below, p. 189.
[5] Dio, xlviii. 45. 5. Below, pp. 188 f.
[6] Dio, liv. 21. 2 ff. Below, pp. 190 f.
[7] Below, p. 66.

agent.[1] Some of these agents perhaps approximated closely to *equites* in fictitious rank.

In the case of some freedmen, we have evidence of intervention by high authority to improve their status. The right to wear the gold ring[2] was until A.D. 23 confined to senators and *equites equo publico*. At that date, it was extended also to equestrian *iudices*, and the qualifications were *ingenuitas* and the census of 100,000 sesterces through three generations and the right to sit in the fourteen rows (which belonged to *iudices* and the *equites equo publico*).[3] But freedmen obtained the gold ring or usurped it and the privileges which were accorded to its wearer. Pompeius Menas received the *anulus aureus* from Octavian and was admitted to equestrian rank;[4] T. Vinius Philopoemen, who had saved his patron during the proscriptions, was also, we are told, enrolled among the *equites*;[5] Antonius Musa received the gold ring.[6] The effect of the grant is to increase the social standing of the recipient. It had during the Republic been given to *ingenui* by *imperatores*,[7] and Octavian as triumvir and later as *princeps* is the major example of a general making such grants to freedmen. The privilege, in the examples we have seen, marks a special service to the ruler, or a special merit. It may be accompanied by a gift of money[8] to establish an equestrian census qualification. But it did not make the freedman the equal of an *eques Romanus*: it merely reduced the barrier. The grant came to be used to bestow a fictitious *ingenuitas*,[9] yet it did not cancel a freedman's obligations to his *patronus*.[10]

Freedmen who enjoyed the rights of the *anulus aureus* might receive promotion in the hierarchy of administration from the same

[1] Compare Theophilus, Antony's steward at Corinth, below, p. 190.
[2] Duff, *Freedmen*, Appendix ii; Nicolet, *L'Ordre équestre*, pp. 139 ff.; Henderson, *JRS* 53 (1963), 67 ff.
[3] Henderson, *JRS* 53 (1963), 69 f.
[4] Dio, xlviii. 45. 7: δακτυλίοις τε χρυσοῖς ἐκόσμησε καὶ ἐς τὸ τῶν ἱππέων τέλος ἐσέγραψε. Cf. Suet. *DA* 74; App. *BC* v. 338.
[5] Suet. *DA* 27. 2 'T. Vinium Philipoemenem... equestri dignitate honoravit.' Dio, xlvii. 7. 5: ἐς τὴν ἱππάδα κατατάξαι.
[6] Dio, liii. 30. 3: τὸ χρυσοῖς δακτυλίοις (ἀπελεύθερος γὰρ ἦν) χρῆσθαι... ἔλαβεν.
[7] Duff, *Freedmen*, p. 215 f. To his examples of freeborn persons receiving the *anulus aureus* in republican times, add Cic. *Verr.* iii. 185 ff.
[8] As to Musa, Dio, liii. 30.
[9] App. *BC* v. 338 (Menas); *Code*, vi. 8.
[10] Nicolet, *L'Ordre équestre*, p. 141.

despot who had broken the usual rules to confer the ring. But they do not seem to have succeeded in gaining the coveted privilege of the fourteen rows. The freedmen who are attested as having pushed themselves into the reserved seats outraged public opinion.[1] It is an indication of the wealth and ambition of freedmen that they were inclined and able to usurp such rights, and their pretensions led to the regulations of A.D. 23.

Libertini were excluded from service as *iudices* under the Gracchan law.[2] They are naturally never given the vague title of *equites* which Cicero applies to *iudices*, the wealthier *publicani*, or men with the proper census.[3] Only in exceptional circumstances do they obtain the *ius anuli aurei*, which removed some of the stigma of slavery and opened the door to advancement, or hold offices in the army or administration which were normally the preserve of *equites equo publico*.

Freedmen's sons would have been eligible for jury service under the Gracchan law, if they possessed the necessary capital, and there is no reason to doubt that they performed this task, disliked as it was by ingenuous Romans.[4] They were not excluded by law from the *equites equo publico*. Freedmen themselves were not legally eligible for equestrian rank in any sense of the term.

(d) Military and Naval Service

What was the position of *libertini* with regard to the army? According to Mommsen,[5] they were at first ineligible because they did not normally own land; later, in the mid third century, when other non-landowners were made eligible, they were excluded. But it has been shown above that some will have been in the classes and the poorer freedmen in the *capite censi*.[6]

---

[1] Hor. *Epod.* iv. 15 f.: 'sedilibusque magnus in primis eques | Othone contempto sedet'; Sarmentus, a freedman and protégé of Maecenas, caused an outcry by usurping equestrian privileges and sitting in the xiv rows (Schol. Juv. ad *Sat.* v. 3). Porphyrio credits him with genuine equestrian status (ad Hor. *Sat.* i. 5. 51). Appendix 7.
[2] If identical with Bruns, *Fontes* 10, which has a clause demanding that jurors should name their fathers: 'Quos legerit, eos patrem, tribum, cognomenque indicet' (15). Freedmen had no legal fathers.
[3] Cf. Henderson, *JRS* 53 (1963), 62.
[4] Henderson, *JRS* 53 (1963), 66.
[5] *StR.* iii. pp. 448 ff.
[6] pp. 51 f.

In emergencies *libertini* served in the army, though it seems to have been thought exceptional: 'seniorum etiam cohortes factae libertinique centuriati',[1] says Livy on one occasion. They were called up in 217 B.C.[2] and again in 90 B.C.[3] They also formed the bulk of the marines in the Roman navy,[4] but *imperatores* seem to have fought shy of recruiting them for the legions. *Mos* was a strong factor in deciding recruiting policy: not till 107 B.C. did a general break decisively from custom to enrol the *capite censi*. One criterion in choosing troops seems to have been the stake a man had in the country—hence, no doubt, the excellence of 'rusticorum mascula militum proles'.[5] For this reason, perhaps, it was *libertini* with children who were enrolled in 217.[6] Ex-slaves might be lacking in loyalty to the country of their adoption, so Rome might be running a risk in trusting to them for defence. The occupations of *libertini* often unfitted them for campaigning: *opifices* and *sellularii* were not the stuff of which the legions were made. Roman generals, even after Marius, rarely levied men in the *Urbs*; when they did, the results tended to be disappointing.[7] Sons of *libertini*, of course, were not debarred from serving with the legions, admitted as they were to the ranks of equestrian officers. They indeed in the late Republic enjoyed full legal parity[8] with men who boasted an ingenuous grandfather.

(ii) *The Legal Position of* Libertini *in Relation to their Patrons*

'Maiores nostri . . . (libertis suis) non multo secus ac servis imperabant.'[9] Torn from its context, this remark of Cicero's has

[1] x. 21.
[2] Livy, xxii. 11. 8. Even slaves fought in the Hannibalic War: the *volones*, who were bought by the state and later freed (Livy, xxiii. 35; xxiv. 11. 3; 14; 18. 12; xxv. 24; xxvii. 38; xxviii. 36. 14). [3] App. *BC* i. 49.
[4] Livy, xxxvi. 2. 15; xl. 18. 7; xlii. 27. 3; J. H. Thiel, *Studies on the History of Roman Sea-Power in Republican Times* (Amsterdam, 1946), p. 12 and *passim*. The *remiges* were usually slaves (Livy, xxiv. 11 ff.; xxvi. 35. 5, etc.).
[5] Hor. *Od.* iii. 6. 37 f.
[6] Similarly, such freedmen obtained voting privileges more readily. Mommsen (*StR.* iii, p. 449) suggested that *libertini* allowed into rustic tribes in the second century may have been eligible for the army.
[7] P. A. Brunt, *JRS* 52 (1962), 74.
[8] The *Lex Terentia* of 189 B.C. had given children of freedmen citizenship *optimo iure Quiritium*. Cf. Berger, *Encyclopedic Dictionary of Roman Law* (Philadelphia, 1953), p. 560. Certain concessions had been made during the Hannibalic War (Macrob. *Sat.* 16. 14). [9] Cic. *QF* i. 1. 13.

been supposed to represent the actual position of freedmen in early times, and not only their position *de facto*, but that sanctioned by law.[1] They were, according to this view, in a state of subjection to their patrons, a legally enforced *obsequium* backed by various patronal rights and powers, and finding its most usual and oppressive expression in the imposition of an unusual burden of *operae*. Later, the praetor Rutilius Rufus improved the condition of *liberti* to some extent, but in practice they remained under the firm control of their patrons. A more moderate school of thought[2] holds that *obsequium* was not enforced by law in the republican period, and that it was first sanctioned by the introduction of the *accusatio ingrati liberti* in the *Lex Aelia Sentia*. Finally, the extreme radical view of Cosentini[3] is that *obsequium* in the technical sense of the 'duty owed by a *libertus*' does not appear in law until post-classical times, when it became a 'blanket-word' to cover all the separate, specific obligations previously evolved. The problem, therefore, is whether the theoretical *obsequium* of the freedman to the patron existed in republican times; if it did exist, what it involved, or, if it did not, what were the obligations and duties which existed. The existence or non-existence of the *obsequium* may not be of vital practical importance for the existence of specific duties and ties between patron and freedman, but the question is at least of interest in relation to the climate of opinion.

The major text on the rights of patrons and freedmen in republican times is:

Ulpian, *Dig.* xxxviii. 2. 1. Hoc edictum a praetore propositum est honoris, quem liberti patronis habere debent, moderandi gratia. Namque, ut Servius scribit, antea soliti fuerunt a libertis durissimas res exigere, scilicet ad remunerandum tam grande beneficium, quod in libertos confertur, cum ex servitute ad civitatem Romanam perducuntur. Et quidem primus praetor Rutilius[4] edixit se amplius non daturum patrono quam operarum et societatis actionem, videlicet si hoc pepigisset, ut, nisi ei obsequium praestaret libertus, in societatem admitteretur

---

[1] See, for example, Jacques Lambert, *Les Operae Liberti* (diss. Paris, 1934), pp. 8 ff.
[2] e.g. Duff, *Freedmen*, p. 37; Arangio-Ruiz, *Istituzioni di diritto romano* (9th ed. Naples, 1947) ii, p. 488.
[3] C. Cosentini, *Studi sui liberti*, i (Catania, 1948), pp. 72 ff.
[4] Presumably Rutilius Rufus, praetor not later than 118 B.C. (*MRR* ii, 613).

patronus. Posteriores praetores certae partis bonorum possessionem pollicebantur: videlicet enim imago societatis induxit eiusdem partis praestationem, ut, quod vivus solebat societatis nomine praestare, id post mortem praestaret.

The mention of *societas* and of *obsequium* has been bracketed as an insertion by E. Albertario,[1] and this is accepted by Cosentini,[2] who is thus enabled to consider the reference to *obsequium* late. But other authorities accept the whole passage as genuine and I see no reason to doubt it. The word 'obsequium' may, then, have appeared in the original edict, though not, it seems, in any more technical sense than 'not transgressing, showing reverence'.[3]

The *societas* was entered into at the time of the manumission, the patron's contribution to it being the gift of freedom, and the *libertus*, for his part, agreeing to show *obsequium*. The *actio societatis*, in the event of the freedman's failure to obey, would give the patron certain rights over the property of his *libertus*. Now, the *obsequium* was a duty arising from a *stipulatio* which the patron might make, as the obligation to perform *operae* arose from an oath by the freedman at the time of manumission.[4] *Obsequium*, then, if it was a technical legal concept at all in the late Republic, was not demanded from all freedmen, but only from those who had made a specific agreement with their patrons.

Another passage from Ulpian is also held by Cosentini[5] to refer to Rutilius:

Dig. xliv. 5. 1. 5: Quae onerandae libertatis causa stipulatus sum, a liberto exigere non possum. Onerandae autem libertatis causa facta bellissime ita definiuntur, quae ita imponuntur, ut si patronum libertus offenderit, petantur ab eo semperque sit metu exactionis ei subiectus, propter quem metum quodvis sustineat patrono praecipiente.

Cosentini suggests that Rutilius may have made this ruling in 114 B.C.[6] If so, he was protecting *liberti* further by refusing to uphold the pact of *societas* if it reduced the *libertus* to a state of

---

[1] *Studi di diritto romano* i. *Persone e famiglia* (Milan, 1933), pp. 397 f., bracketing 'et societatis' and 'videlicet' et seq. to 'admitteretur patronus'
[2] *Liberti*, i, pp. 80 ff.; 190 ff.
[3] Cf. *Dig.* xliv. 5. 1. 5, and the use of 'honoris' in *Dig.* xxxviii. 2. 1.
[4] See Watson, *Law of Persons*, pp. 228 f.
[5] *Liberti*, i, p. 95. Cf. Lambert, *Operae*, pp. 240 ff.
[6] *Liberti*, i, pp. 95, 181.

LIBERTINI IN RELATION TO PATRONS

subjection. (Cosentini himself, bracketing the mention of *societas*, would disagree.) Three views are thus open: that of Cosentini, that Rutilius in 118 B.C. allowed only action to compel performance of *operae*, and in 114 refused to allow the validity of *stipulationes onerandae libertatis causa*; secondly, that Rutilius in 118 allowed actions to be brought to secure obedience from the *libertus*, if a *pactio* had been made (and also to secure *operae*); or thirdly, that Rutilius in 118 allowed such actions, but later he or another praetor severely limited them. It seems to me that, while we may be fairly sure of the second, the third view is also tenable, for measures to limit the power of the patron to burden his freedman unjustly seem characteristic of the late Republic, as we shall see in connection with *operae*.[1]

So far, it does not seem that *obsequium* was regularly demanded or that it meant anything other than a general attitude of respect. When it was due because of a *stipulatio*, it was enforced by court action, with the threat of confiscation of *bona*. Various other texts are quoted to enlarge this picture of the *obsequium* as assimilating freedmen to slaves, but they are hardly relevant.[2]

Lambert[3] held that the *obsequium* was supported by specific patronal powers.[4] He postulated a 'potestas patronalis', which gave the patron *manus iniectio*, *ius vitae necisque* and the right to compel the freedman to continue to live in the household. There is no obvious reason to think that this last could be enforced, although it was a frequent practice for the freedman to live in his patron's house.[5] The texts cited on *manus iniectio*, which would have allowed the patron to compel obedience from his freedman,[6] are:

Valerius Maximus, v. 4. 5.

[1] Below, pp. 74 ff.
[2] Cic. *QF* i. 1. 13 (quoted p. 68), which has no legal bearing. The assimilation of *libertini* to slaves by a contemptuous society is sufficiently familiar (Appendix 4), and a patron might, even kindly, think of his freedman as in a way his slave, because of his moral and sometimes physical dependence. *Vat. fr.* 307 (Paul), the application of which is wholly obscure.
[3] *Operae*, pp. 34 ff.; 73 ff.
[4] All dismissed by Cosentini, *Liberti*, pp. 82 ff.
[5] e.g. Plaut. *Men.* 1034 (where the slave offers to do so); *Code* vi. 3. 12; cf. *Dig.* vii. 8. 2. 1.
[6] Lambert, *Operae*, pp. 86 f. Others, e.g. Kaser, *ZSS* 68 (1951), 582, take it to mean power to re-enslave.

This is a case of *manus iniectio* exercised over a son and is therefore out of court.

Quintilian, vii. 7. 9. Patri in filium, patrono in libertum manus iniectio sit . . .

The premiss of a rhetorical exercise of this kind is not necessarily founded on actual or Roman law. Lambert,[1] in fact, shows convincingly that this particular situation is not based on Roman law. No other texts are cited. Lambert nevertheless insisted on postulating *manus iniectio*.[2]

The evidence for the *ius vitae necisque* over freedmen is also ambiguous. The cases cited are:

Valerius Maximus, vi. 1. 4.

This is the story of P. Maenius, probably late republican,[3] who killed a freedman for kissing his daughter. But Valerius Maximus was not interested in legal matters and he does not tell us that the father was not tried for murder.[4] We may compare the *delitto di onore* of Sicily and southern Italy today, which is accepted and often praised by local society, but which nevertheless comes under the murder laws.

Suetonius, *Divus Julius* 48. Domesticam disciplinam in parvis ac maioribus rebus adeo severeque rexit, ut pistorem alium quam sibi panem convivis subicientem compedibus vinxerit, libertum gratissimum ob adulteratam equitis Romani uxorem, quamvis nullo querente, capitali poena adfecerit.

'Capitali poena', despite the context of domestic discipline, could mean that Caesar acted either himself as *praefectus morum* and dictator,[5] if the incident belongs to that era, or through the courts, to remedy a situation which might have appeared private. But, even if Caesar acted privately as patron, it seems from Suetonius' words that his severity, though admirable, was unusual. It is

---

[1] *Operae*, pp. 85 ff.; cf. Watson, *Law of Persons*, p. 228, n. 2.
[2] A procedure which is rigorously scorned by Cosentini, *Liberti*, i. p. 85.
[3] Münzer, *RE* xiv. 251.
[4] Cosentini *Liberti*, i, pp. 91 ff.; Watson, *Law of Persons*, p. 227. *Contra* Kaser, *ZSS* 68 (1951), p. 582.
[5] See Cosentini, *Liberti*, i, p. 93, who thinks that either Caesar acted as dictator or the freedman had been informally manumitted and was legally a slave.

LIBERTINI IN RELATION TO PATRONS 73

possible to hold that it was illegal also,[1] but we may have evidence here for an obsolescent patronal right, which Caesar could invoke for propaganda reasons.[2]

Suetonius, *Divus Augustus*, 67. Polum ex acceptissimis libertis mori coegit compertum adulterare matronas.

This is clearly out of court, for it is a case of compelled suicide.

None of the special powers adduced as backing up the *obsequium* can thus be certainly proved. The word 'obsequium' in the Republic does not seem to be used in a technical sense to mean the obedience owed by *liberti* in particular, even if Rutilius used it in his edict. It is a normal word for 'compliance' or 'allegiance', and is used most frequently to denote political adhesion.[3] The only instance of its use with reference to a freedman in the whole of Cicero's correspondence is to describe the attitude of Cicero to Atticus' *libertus* Dionysius, not that of a freedman to his patron.[4] This silence is probably significant, since there are several letters in which we might expect a reference to *obsequium* demanded by a *stipulatio*, or even merely sanctioned by *fas*. Thus, when Cicero wanted to get his freedman Hilarus to leave Macedonia, where he was apparently doing his best to ruin his patron's reputation, he could think of no more effective method than to appeal to Atticus' influence or guile,[5] and when two other *liberti* abandoned their charge, he was hard put to it to find any compulsion which might be brought to bear on them, unless by denying the validity of the manumission, on the grounds of a flaw in the ceremony.[6]

Despite the *Lex Aelia Sentia* and the *accusatio ingrati liberti*[7] which it introduced,[8] the patron's hand was not effectively strengthened under the early Principate. The law, as we learn from Tacitus,[9] allowed ungrateful freedmen to be relegated *ultra*

---

[1] Watson, *Law of Persons*, p. 127.
[2] Cf. the prosecution of Rabirius in 63 B.C.
[3] e.g. Cic. *Fam.* x. 15. 1; x. 11. 3; *QF* i. 3. 3. 3.   [4] Id., *Att.* viii. 4. 1.
[5] Ibid. i. 12.
[6] Ibid. vii. 2. 8. Above, pp. 22 f. It is possible that Cicero could also have charged the freedman with violation of *obsequium*, but that it was easier to make the other argument effective. See Watson, *Law of Persons*, p. 229, n. 3.
[7] For the idea of ingratitude in the Republic, see Plaut. *Persa* 799 ff., discussed by Watson, *Law of Persons*, p. 229, n. 3.
[8] Duff, *Freedmen*, p. 37; Barrow, *Slavery*, p. 191.   [9] *Ann.* xiii. 26 f.

centesimum lapidem, which, as indignant patrons in Nero's reign complained, meant that they were driven to the resorts of Campania. The grounds of the complaints against *liberti* are described in a corrupt and much-emended passage, but the gist is that they were said to be insolent and occasionally violent. It was suggested in the Senate that the gift of liberty might be made revocable by the patron in such cases, 'nec grave manumissis per idem obsequium retinendi libertatem per quod adsecuti sint: at criminum manifestos merito ad servitutem retrahi, ut metu coerceantur quos beneficia non mutavissent'.[1] But the reform was defeated on the ground that it would be unjust to put all *liberti* in a state of subjection, and that the Augustan legislation making manumission more difficult should encourage patrons to be more prudent in granting freedom.

It appears that the laws of Augustus increased the patron's rights against freedmen who did not show a proper respect, by allowing *relegatio*. Kaser[2] held that this means, not that the patron had until then had no redress against an ungrateful and undutiful *libertus*, but that his extensive rights were vanishing in the late Republic, and so had to be revived by Augustus. He was able to believe this because he held that the patron had *manus iniectio* and *ius vitae necisque*. But Augustus apparently did nothing to revive these alleged powers. It seems likely that if the *ius vitae necisque* had ever been possessed by patrons over their freedmen, it was not relevant to the society of the late Republic. *Manus iniectio* could have existed at an early date, as it was part of the *patria potestas* over sons, but there is no evidence for its exercise over freedmen. I therefore think that the only power a patron had over his *libertus* was that which might be conferred by *stipulatio*, a partnership demanding *obsequium* in return for liberty, or an oath promising to perform *operae*, taken at the time of the manumission. The right to keep *liberti* in a state of submission by means of the *stipulatio*, however, was probably revoked by praetorian edict some time after 118 B.C., on the grounds that it was *onerandae libertatis causa*.[3] Augustus

---

[1] Tac. *Ann.* xiii. 26.   [2] *ZSS* 68 (1951), 582.
[3] Above, p. 70. Labeo held that such *societates* were void (*Dig.* xxxviii. 1. 36). See Watson, *Law of Persons*, pp. 228 f.

LIBERTINI IN RELATION TO PATRONS

subsequently, because of this, gave patrons the modified right of *relegatio*. It seems to me, then, that the only effective control exercised by patrons in the late Republic was through the *operae*.

The privilege of imposing *operae* was one of the most valuable enjoyed by the patron. The obligation to work for the patron after manumission sprang, not from the status of *libertus*, but from an oath which the freedman took after manumission. This is made clear by *Digest*, xxxviii 1. 31 (Modestinus): 'Operis non promissis manumissus etiamsi ex sua voluntate aliquo tempore praestiterit, compelli ad praestandas non potest,' and for republican times by the mention of Cicero of the revocation by Drusus of the manumission of the freedman 'qui eadem liber non iuraret'.[1]

The concept that *operae* were naturally owed to the patron in gratitude for the supreme gift of freedom was probably late in becoming law,[2] but it seems to have formed part of the current of thought long before, if *liberti* often performed *operae* when not legally bound to do so. This would be very natural if the *promissio iurata liberti* were ancient. Arangio-Ruiz has conjectured that it was as old as manumission itself.[3]

The oath was normally taken at the time of the manumission. Since oaths sworn by slaves were not legally valid, it was usual to exact a promise first from the slave, which he was then bound by *fas* to repeat after the manumission.[4] We have already seen how the obligation of *fas* might be maintained by the praetor.[5]

That the oath to perform *operae* was the rule rather than the exception[6] is shown by the practice of *redemptio operarum*, by which a *libertus* could buy himself off from the performance of the *operae*

---

[1] 'Itaque usurpavi vetus illud Drusi, ut ferunt, praetoris, in eo, qui eadem liber non iuraret, me istos liberos non addixisse, praesertim cum adesset nemo a quo recte vindicarentur' (*Att.* vii. 2. 8). It is not clear whether Chrysippus, like the *libertinus* in Drusus' case, had refused to confirm by oath the promise previously made, or whether the similarity to the earlier case lies solely in the fact that Cicero will deny the validity of the manumission, but on the grounds of a flaw in the *vindicta* ceremony. The 'praesertim' seems to support the former view; Cicero can attack on two counts. See pp. 22 f., and 73.

[2] Cf. Cosentini, *Liberti*, pp. 105 ff.

[3] *Istituzioni*, p. 322.

[4] *Dig.* xxxviii. 1. 7 (Ulp.): 'Ut iusiurandi obligatio contrahatur, libertum esse oportet qui iuret et libertatis causa iurare.' Cf. Cic. *Att.* vii. 2. 8.

[5] Drusus in Cic. *Att.* vii. 2. 8.

[6] Except in the case of *manumissio testamento*.

which he had promised (or, perhaps, of some of the *operae* when others had been performed already). The *Lex Aelia Sentia* prevented the patron from binding the freedman to pay money instead of the *operae*, but allowed the bargain if the *libertus* took the initiative.[1] It would appear from this that previously the patron had been free to put pressure on the freedman to pay, *onerandae libertatis gratia*.[2] On the other hand, if the patron agreed to remit the *operae* without exacting compensation money, the transaction was null, at least in classical law, and did not confer the normal additional benefit of *libera testamenti factio*.[3] There were also other methods of acquiring exemption from *operae*, but probably all these were introduced by the detailed Augustan legislation on the subject.[4]

In classical law, transference of the *operae* to a third party was allowed only in special cases, if the patron was in financial straits, or if he could not use the *operae* to advantage himself, for example, if the freedman were a doctor or a pantomime, 'neque enim oportet patronum, ut operis liberti sui utatur, aut ludos semper facere aut aegrotare'.[5] Before the *Lex Aelia Sentia*, however, it appears that *locatio* was allowed exactly as it suited the patron, since the right to hire out the services of his freedman is connected with that of demanding a cash-payment instead of *operae*. The *operae*, then, might in the republican period be performed for the patron or for his *amici*, and on the patron's death they passed automatically to his children if they were heirs.[6]

The *operae* are traditionally held to have fallen into two classes, *officiales* and *fabriles*. The former were chiefly domestic, while the latter consisted of skilled labour, such as that of a physician, artist,

---

[1] *Dig.* xl. 9. 32. 1 f. (Teren. Clem.).   [2] *Dig.* xl. 9. 39 (Paul).
[3] Daube, *Studi Arangio-Ruiz*, i (Naples, 1953), pp. 192 f. on *Dig.* xviii. 1. 36.
[4] Exemption for a *libertus* with two or more children, allowed by the Lex Julia (*Code* vi. 3. 77, *Dig.* xxxviii. 1. 37); for a *liberta* married to her patron (*Code* vi. 39) or to anyone approved by her patron (*Dig.* xxxviii. 1. 28, 30), above the age of fifty (ibid. 35), or who reached a position of dignity inconsistent with the performance of *operae* (ibid. 34). But, though a *matrona*, she might continue to work for a *patrona* or female relatives of a *patronus* (ibid. 48). *Capitis deminutio* of the patron also cancelled *operae* (Cosentini, *Liberti*, ii, pp. 110 ff.)
[5] *Dig.* xxxviii. 1. 25, 27 (Jul.).
[6] Or, perhaps, in early times, only if the children were specifically mentioned in the *promissio iurata* (Cosentini, *Liberti*, ii, pp. 5 ff.).

LIBERTINI IN RELATION TO PATRONS

or architect, and of manufacturing work of all kinds.[1] As a further distinction, it is held that *operae officiales* were promised by oath and were not transferable, while *fabriles* were agreed by *stipulatio* and could pass to others.[2] Cosentini[3] argued at length against such a distinction and the use of such terms before post-classical times, but much of his case had already been anticipated by Lambert's admission that the terms were late.[4] A distinction between personal services, such as those hardly definable jobs carried out by Tiro (such as maintaining contact with his patron's friends, acting as family go-between, and keeping an eye on the political scene), and professional work to which a man might definitely bind himself, seems sensible, and was probably drawn even in republican practice. A *libertus* might reasonably promise to do a certain amount of secretarial work, or attend his master as his doctor, but many services would be too vague to be covered exactly in an oath, though we know that a job as imprecise as 'minding the house' could be promised.[5]

There were detailed rules in classical law about the services which might be demanded, rules dictated by the interests of both parties, the germ of which probably belongs to the praetorian law of republican times. The *operae* represented each one day's work: 'operae sunt diurnum officium'.[6] A thousand or a hundred *operae* are given as examples of the amount of work that might reasonably be required:[7] presumably these are both totals, in which case the extent of the *libertus*' liability was not always very great. They were performed when[8] and where[9] the patron ordered, but if the freedman was obliged to travel from Rome to the provinces or vice versa, the days spent on the journey counted as *operae*[9] and the patron bore the expense.[10] If the patron went globe-trotting beyond the imperial frontiers—and this, in particular, sounds like a republican provision, suiting the days when the Empire did not cover most of the civilized world—the freedman was not compelled to follow him.[11] The *libertus* was to be allowed enough time off to make his

---

[1] Lambert, *Operae*, pp. 181 ff.; Duff, *Freedmen*, pp. 44 f.
[2] Cf. *Dig.* xxxviii. 1. 6 (Ulp.); Gaius, iii. 83.
[3] *Liberti*, i, pp. 166 ff.   [4] *Operae*, p. 184.   [5] Cf. *Dig.* xxxviii. 1. 31; 49.
[6] Ibid. 1. 1.   [7] Ibid. 15, 24.   [8] Ibid. 22.
[9] Ibid. 20.   [10] Ibid. 21.   [11] Ibid. 20.

own living.[1] He normally provided his own food and clothing.[2] Time for recreation had to be allowed.[3] As for the type of work done, it was as a rule the *artificium* normally practised by the freedman,[4] including any learned after manumission.[5] However, it was laid down in the freedman's favour that he need not perform any *operae* which involved him in disgrace or peril of his life, even if he had been trained to them during slavery.[6] Not all these detailed rules will have been republican, but the attitude of equity on which they rest may well date back to praetorian rulings. Praetorian legislation also changed and developed the legal position with regard to the testatory rights of freedmen.

After the *operae*, the chief practical advantage enjoyed by the patron as the result of having manumitted a slave was the right, in some cases, to all or half of the freedman's estate. Originally, but in a period when the will had scarcely developed, this had not been so, but gradually the law and the praetor improved the patron's position.

Olim itaque licebat liberto patronum suum impune testamento praeterire. Nam ita demum Lex XII tabularum ad hereditatem liberti vocabat patronum, si intestatus mortuus esset libertus nullo suo herede relicto. Itaque intestato quoque mortuo liberto si is suum heredem reliquerat, nihil in bonis eius patrono iuris erat. Et siquidem ex naturalibus liberis aliquem suum heredem reliquisset, nulla videbatur esse querella, si vero vel adoptivus filius filiave vel uxor quae in manu esset sua heres esset, aperte iniquum erat nihil iuris patrono superesse.[7]

These rights were held also by the patron's sons and their male descendants[8] and, on the other side, by his daughter, son's daughter, or son's son's daughter.[9] A *patrona* had the same rights as her male counterpart.[10] The situation where intestacy occurred was thus regulated, but if the freedman chose to make a will naming as

---

[1] *Dig.* xxxviii. 1. 19: 'ita exigendae sunt ab eo operae, ut his quoque diebus, quibus operas edat, satis tempus ad quaestum faciendum, unde ali possit, habeat'.
[2] Ibid. 18.   [3] Ibid. 50.
[4] Ibid. 24.   [5] Ibid. 16.
[6] Ibid. 38, cf. 17. *Operae* specifically mentioned by the jurists are normally professional: *pictor* (ibid. 24); *librarius* (ibid. 7; 49); *medicus* (ibid. 27); *pantomimus* (ibid. 27); *vestiarius* (ibid. 45); *calculator* (ibid. 7); *nomenculator* (ibid. 7); *histrio* (ibid. 7).
[7] Gaius, iii. 40.   [8] Ibid. 45.
[9] Ibid. 46.   [10] Ibid. 49.

beneficiaries men who were not *sui heredes*, he was still able to exclude his patron.

However, both this freedom of choice and the preference given to a wife or adoptive children over the patron were in Roman eyes unjust.[1] The praetors therefore introduced new regulations to ensure that the patron should have a claim on half the estate of a freedman without natural heirs:

> Qua de causa postea praetoris edicto haec iuris iniquitas emendata est. Sive enim faciat testamentum libertus, iubetur ita testari ut patrono suo partem dimidiam bonorum suorum relinquat, et si nihil aut minus quam partem dimidiam reliquerit, datur patrono contra tabulas testamenti partis dimidiae bonorum possessio. Si vero intestatus moriatur suo herede relicto adoptivo filio vel uxore quae in manu ipsius esset vel nuru quae in manu filii eius fuerit, datur aeque patrono adversus hos suos heredes partis dimidiae bonorum possessio. Prosunt autem liberto ad excludendum patronum naturales liberi, non solum quos in potestate mortis tempore habet, sed etiam emancipati et in adoptionem dati, si modo aliqua ex parte heredes scripti sint aut praeteriti contra tabulas testamenti bonorum possessionem ex edicto petierint, nam exheredati nullo modo repellunt patronum.[2]

This privilege was not extended to *patronae*[3] under praetorian law: their position remained the same as before. Cosentini connected the praetorian reform with a general policy of safeguarding the *honor* due to the patron, at the expense of the freedman, and it was clearly a serious blow to the latter's independence. But from the Roman point of view it was an equitable recognition of the paternal relationship in which the patron stood to the freedman, and of the fact that he had founded the freedman's fortunes. The innovation is convincingly dated to between 118 and 74 B.C.[4]

The rights of *libertae* were naturally still more limited than those of *liberti*. Since the freedwoman was under the *tutela* of her patron,

---

[1] For if the patron freed a young man, it was fair that he should be deprived of his claim by children. But if he freed a man unlikely to have children of his own, it was unjust that the patron should be ousted by *adoptivi* or wife.

[2] Gaius, iii. 41.

[3] Or female descendants of *patronus*. Cf. Cic. ii *Verr.* i. 125, with Watson, *Law of Persons*, pp. 232 f.

[4] As indicated by the *termini post* and *ante quem* of *Dig.* xxxviii. 2. 1. and Cic. ii. *Verr.* i. 125. See Watson, *Law of Persons*, pp. 231 ff.; Lambert, *Operae*, pp. 244 ff.

any will she made required his consent, and if she did not make him an heir he had only himself to blame, while if she died intestate, he inherited automatically. The patron also had *tutela* over *liberti* who were under age (*impuberes*), and enjoyed similar advantages in their case.[1]

Other praetorian decisions intended to safeguard the relationship between patron and freedman also date back to the Republic. 'Praetor ait "parentem, patronum, liberos parentes patroni patronae in ius sine permissu meo ne quis vocet".'[2] This was a serious limitation, since the *libertus* was also debarred from taking action against his patron in many specific cases too, at least in later law.[3] Similarly, the *Lex Pompeia de parricidiis* considered a *libertus* who killed his patron as guilty of parricide.[4]

Although *obsequium* does not seem to have been a fully technical legal concept at this time, the concept of *fides* was relevant to the law's attitude to freedmen, as to clients in general. It was the basis of the right relationship between freedman and patron.[5] The freedman was bound to treat his patron well, as Cicero, distinguishing various types of rhetorical appeal to sympathy, points out: 'Tertius decimus, per quem cum indignatione conquerimur, quod ab eis a quibus minime conveniat, male tractemur, propinquis, amicis, quibus benigne fecerimus, quos adiutores fore putarimus, aut a quibus indignum est, ut servis, libertis, clientibus, supplicibus.'[6] The *fides*[7] and *officium*, which *liberti* showed or failed to show in crises such as the proscriptions and in normal circumstances, are familiar.[8] Similarly, the patron had obligations to protect and aid his freedman, less well defined, but sanctioned by the same extralegal principle of *fides*.[9]

[1] Gaius, iii. 43; Ulp. xxix. Cf. Schulz, *Principles*, pp. 145 f.; Buckland, *Textbook*, pp. 145 f. Further examples of the wills of *libertini* and disputes arising from them are Cic. *Att.* xv. 1. 1, 2. 4; *de Or.* i. 176; *Flacc.* 84.
[2] *Dig.* ii. 4. 4. 1, cf. ii. 7. 1. 2. See Watson, *Law of Persons*, p. 227.
[3] *Actiones famosae* (*Dig.* xxxvii. 15. 5. 1); *exceptio doli vis metusve causa* (*Dig.* xxxvii. 15. 7. 2; xliv. 44. 16); *interdictio unde vi et quod vi* (*Dig.* xliii. 16. 1. 43); *actiones* other than *famosae*, but containing the idea of *dolum* or *fraus* (*Dig.* xxxvii. 15. 5. 1, 7). Cf. Tac. *Ann.* xiii. 26: these laws, if in existence then, were evaded in Nero's reign. [4] *Dig.* xlviii. 9. 1.
[5] Cf. Schulz, *Principles*, pp. 231 f. [6] *Inv.* i. 109. [7] e.g. Cic. *Fam.* iv. 9. 1.
[8] e.g. Cic. *Scaur.* 23; App. *BC* iv. 101, 107, 109, 120, 187, 188, 198, 199. Below, p. 217.
[9] Schulz, *Principles*, pp. 231 f. Cf. Gell. v. 13 on *clientes* in general.

I conclude, then, that the whole structure of obligations and rights between patron and freedman rested on the moral concept of *fides* and that the law sought to strike a balance between conflicting interests. In the case of the praetorian rulings on attempts to keep the *libertus* in a state of unfair subjection by means of the *operae* or a *stipulatio* enforcing *obsequium*, the interests of the freedman were protected. It seems likely that the device of *stipulatio* was soon banned, even if allowed by Rutilius. Nor can I follow Cosentini in thinking that the Rutilian edict in fact reduced the liberty of the freedman by its regulation of the situation. Praetorian decisions on the law of testament, on the other hand, tended to safeguard the patron at the expense of the *libertus*. In republican times at least, *obsequium* does not seem to have been enforced by law, but only through an agreement between the parties, as was the performance of *operae*. But the idea of respect and dutifulness, *obsequium*, *honor*, *reverentia*, formed part of the moral obligation imposed by *fides*.

(iii) *The Legal Position of* Libertini *in relation to* Ingenui *other than their Patrons*

The legal relations of the *libertinus* with *ingenui* in general are less complex. Although, in public law, Rome might be concerned not to give freedmen all the rights of citizens without some limitations (though we have seen that these were perhaps extra-legal), and in private law saw to it that the rights of the patron to whom the *libertus* owed freedom and position were safeguarded, there seems to have been no reason why she should not have promoted the swift absorption of freedmen into the citizen-body by allowing parity, at law, with freeborn citizens. Society might be left to impose its own sanctions, ensuring that some were more equal than others.

The main field in which a legal bar to equality has been thought to have existed is that of marriage. In others, there were only minor handicaps under which *libertini* suffered. On manumission, the ex-slave became *sui iuris* and a *paterfamilias*.[1] He was not a member of his patron's or any other *gens*, according to the strict definition

[1] *Dig.* xxviii. 1. 14 (Paul).

of *gentiles* given by Cicero,[1] but this disability, shared with many *plebeii*, probably did not put the freedman at a juridical disadvantage.[2] There is no doubt that *libertini* possessed the *ius commercii*,[3] for they had the right to make wills[4] and could own land.

Freedmen's possession of the *ius conubii* was called into question by Mommsen,[5] but the consensus of modern opinion is against him.[6] It is worth citing Gaius' definition of *conubium*:

> Itaque liberos suos in potestate habent cives Romani si cives Romanas uxores duxerint, vel etiam Latinas peregrinasve cum quibus conubium habeant. Cum enim conubium id efficiat, ut liberi patris condicionem sequantur, evenit ut non solum cives Romani fiant sed etiam in potestate patris sint.[7]

Conubium made a marriage *iustum* and affected the status of the children, but it was not indispensable to legal marriage. Romans contracted valid marriages with Latin and peregrine women with whom Rome had no *conubium*. The scope of the alleged disability of freedmen to marry *ingenuae*[8] is therefore limited. But Mommsen held that mixed marriages of this kind were not only not fully *iusta*, until the legislation of Augustus, but null. There seems to be confusion in his argument here.

The main texts on Augustan legislation on libertine–ingenuous marriage are the following:

Dio, liv. 16. ἐπειδή τε πολὺ πλεῖον τὸ ἄρρεν τοῦ θήλεος τοῦ εὐγενοῦς ἦν, ἐπέτρεψε καὶ τὰς ἐξελευθέρας τοῖς ἐθέλουσι πλὴν τῶν βουλευόντων ἄγεσθαι, ἔννομον τὴν τεκνοποιίαν εἶναι κελεύσας.

---

[1] Cic. *Top.* vi. 29: 'Gentiles sunt inter se, qui eodem nomine sunt. Non est satis. Qui ab ingenuis oriundi sunt. Ne id quidem satis est. Quorum maiorum nemo servitutem servivit. Abest etiam nunc. Qui capite non sunt deminuti. Hoc fortasse satis est.' But in a looser sense, *libertini* seem to have had a *gens*: cf. Livy, xxxix. 19. 5 (grant of *gentis enuptio* to a freedwoman) and Cn. Flavius' tenure of the patrician office of curule aedile (p. 57).
[2] Cosentini, *Liberti*, i, p. 47.
[3] See Cosentini, *Liberti*, i, p. 47.
[4] *Testamenti factio*. Gaius, iii. 40.
[5] *StR.* iii. 1¹, pp. 429 ff.
[6] O. Karlowa, *Römische Rechtsgeschichte* ii. (Leipzig, 1901), p. 172; P. E. Corbett, *The Roman Law of Marriage* (Oxford, 1930), pp. 32 ff.; M. Kaser, *Das römische Privatrecht* (Munich, 1955–9), p. 269; Watson, *Law of Persons*, pp. 32 ff.
[7] i. 56.
[8] Or freedwomen to marry *ingenui*.

LIBERTINI IN RELATION TO INGENUI 83

Dio, lvi. 7. 2 (speech of Augustus)... . καὶ ἐξελευθέρας τοῖς γε ἔξω τοῦ βουλευτικοῦ οὖσιν ἄγεσθαι συνεχώρησα, ἵν' εἰ καί τις ἐξ ἔρωτος ἢ καὶ συνηθείας τινὸς ἐς τοῦθ' ὑπαχθείη, ἐννόμως αὐτὸ ποιοίη.

Dig. xxiii. 2. 23 (Celsus). Lege Papia cavetur omnibus ingenuis praeter senatores eorumque liberos libertinam uxorem habere licere.

Ulp. xiii. 1. Lege Julia prohibentur uxores ducere senatores quidem liberique eorum libertinas et quae ipsae quarumve pater materve artem ludicram fecerit.

Dig. xxiii. 2. 44 (Paul). Lege Julia ita cavetur: qui senator est quive filius neposve ex filio proneposve ex filio nato cuius eorum est erit, ne quis eorum sponsam uxoremve sciens dolo malo habeto libertinam aut eam quae ipsa cuiusve pater materve artem ludicram facit fecerit . . .[1]

Dio's "ἐπέτρεψε" in the first passage is far from precise and it is to be noted that he confines his remarks to the nobility, not the Senate. But the natural sense is that Dio regarded the Augustan law as a permission to non-*senatorii* to marry freedwomen, and that consequently he thought such marriages had been invalid previously.

The Celsus passage is distrusted because it ascribes the ruling to the Lex Papia of A.D. 9, instead of to the Lex Julia de Maritandis Ordinibus of 18 B.C. This, however, is not too discreditable, since the two laws are inextricably confused in the jurists and are generally referred to as the Lex Julia et Papia.[2] The ascription by Ulpian and Paul to the Lex Julia is of course to be accepted. Secondly, Celsus puts the general permission in the main clause and subordinates the specific prohibition to *senatorii*. The emphasis in the better jurists is precisely opposite.[3]

The Ulpian and Paul passages, the latter of which purports to quote the law exactly, suggest that mixed marriages of this type had so far been valid for all classes of society. Neither jurist mentions any clause conferring the right to marry *libertinae* on those outside the senatorial order, while the prohibition on senators implies that until then marriage with *libertini* or *libertinae* had been open to all.

---

[1] The ban extended also to female descendants of senators in the male line as far as great-granddaughters.

[2] Cf. P. Jors, *Über das Verhältniß der Lex Julia de mar. ord. zur Lex Papia Poppaea* (Bonn, 1882), pp. 4 ff. Code v. 4. 28 also ascribes the measure to the Lex Papia, but, being Justinianic, cannot stand against the consensus of Ulpian and Paul.

[3] It is possible that the passage has been worked over, and is not, in its present form, by Celsus.

It also implies permission to other orders in society to continue to marry *libertini*, which there was no need for Augustus to affirm, and it may be on this that Dio and Celsus base their remarks. The citation of the *Lex Julia*[1] shows that what Augustus did was to prohibit senators and their families from marrying freedwomen, knowing their status, and this implies that before such marriages had not been forbidden by law.

Mommsen held, however, that intermarriage was illegal, but took place in individual cases, either through a special concession, or through slackening of the law. Instances of marriage between *libertinae* and *ingenui* (and occasionally between *libertini* and *ingenuae*) are known from the Republic.[2] Literary references are not common, since the upper classes did not normally match with freedwomen, but the common people quite often intermarried with ex-slaves. Cicero in the *Pro Sestio* says of L. Gellius Poplicola, an *eques*, that he had married a freedwoman[3] to show that he was a true democrat.[4] The whole sentence is ironical and Cicero makes two points against Gellius, a dissolute character and an unworthy *popularis* policy. Had the marriage been invalid, he would surely have seized the chance to tax his victim with law-breaking or stupidity.[5]

The other *locus classicus* is the passage of Livy[6] where he describes concessions made by the Senate to reward the freedwoman and prostitute Fecenia Hispala in 186 B.C. This has been adduced to show that intermarriage was not normally allowed. It runs:

Utique Feceniae Hispalae datio, deminutio, gentis enuptio, tutoris optio item esset, quasi ei vir testamento dedisset; utique ei ingenuo

[1] In *Dig.* xxiii. 2. 44 and Ulp. xiii. 1.
[2] e.g. *CIL* i. 1528 = Degr. 949; *CIL* i 1289 = Degr. 796 (the latter *ingenua–libertinus*).
[3] It is not likely that *libertina* means daughter of a freedman. Above, pp. 53.
[4] 110: 'ut credo, non libidinis causa, sed ut plebicola videretur, libertinam duxit uxorem.' Cicero is making two jokes here: we are not really to believe that the marriage was not motivated by physical attraction, and a true Poplicola is above the tricks of a 'plebicola'.
[5] Watson, *Law of Persons*, p. 35, makes the very interesting suggestion that the freedwoman was possibly a *concubina*, in Gellius' intention, in which case Cicero is wise not to linger on the point. He also holds that the validity of the marriage, if it was a marriage, would not have been relevant to Cicero. I am inclined to believe that Cicero would have thrown any mud he thought might stick.
[6] xxxix. 19. 5 f.

nubere liceret, neu quid ei, qui eam duxisset, ob id fraudi ignominiaeve esset; utique consules praetoresque, qui nunc essent quive postea futuri essent, curarent, ne quid ei mulieri iniuriae fieret, utique tuto esset; id senatus velle et aequum censere ut ita fieret.

The crux here is whether a special dispensation was needed for Hispala to marry an *ingenuus*, or whether 'liceret' is to be taken so closely with what follows that we are to understand 'and that she should be allowed to marry a freeborn man without its involving his loss or disgrace'.[1] The case is further complicated by the fact that Hispala was a *meretrix*, and this might affect her husband's social standing, and lead to disgrace at the census. But the emphasis on 'ingenuo' seems to be against this, for even a freedman might surely suffer disgrace by marrying a prostitute. Now, Livy claims to be quoting the text of the decree. In the light of the legal texts on the legislation of Augustus, we cannot take the *senatusconsultum* to mean that marriages between *ingenui* and *libertinae* were invalid. But we can understand it to mean that they were discouraged by the censors, who might penalize freeborn men who married freedwomen, just as they might penalize senators who had freedman fathers. There was no law against the sons of freedmen taking part in political life, but they might be excluded from the Senate by the censors. Just so, the intermarriage of freeborn and freed might be perfectly valid, but the ingenuous partner might be penalized by a censorial *nota*. This would explain the language of Dio, "ἐπέτρεψε", and the *Digest*'s 'licere'. Augustus did not make valid marriages which had previously been invalid, but permitted marriages which had previously not been officially approved.[2] Confirmation of this view is provided by the probability that even the *Leges Julia et Papia* did not stop marriages between *libertinae* and *senatorii*.[3] It forbade them and penalized those who made them, but it did not make them void.

I conclude, then, that the law did not invalidate marriages between libertine and ingenuous in any class of society. But in aristocratic circles, the prejudice against such marriages was strong.

[1] See Karlowa, *Röm. Rechtsgeschichte*, ii, p. 172; Cosentini, *Liberti*, i, pp. 49 f.
[2] I accept fully here the argument and conclusion of Watson, *Law of Persons*, pp. 32 ff., especially p. 37.
[3] Corbett, *Marriage*, pp. 35 ff.; cf. *Code* v. 9. 1 f.; *Dig.* xxiii. 2. 48. 1, etc.

The major disadvantage for a noble who contracted an alliance with a freedwoman (an *ingenua* was apparently less likely to marry a freedman, but in her case the results would be different) was censorial *ignominia*. This would have very serious consequences. The censors could proceed against other *ingenui* who married *libertinae*, but they were unlikely to trouble about the lower classes, especially as many of the men who married freedwomen were themselves sons of freed parents. The change introduced by Augustus was to make a statutory prohibition of marriages between *senatorii* and freed persons, where before such marriages had not been specifically forbidden, only visited with penalties, and to encourage mixed marriages in other classes. The nobility outside the Senate was to be encouraged to marry freedwomen, if it would marry no one else. The threat of official sanctions against those who married *libertini* was removed, by implication, in order to boost the falling birth-rate.

III

CAREERS

WHEN it came to the choice of a career, the freedman's decision was modified by various factors which did not apply to the freeborn worker. In many cases, his choice must have been predetermined by his patron, either because he had been trained for some particular work,[1] or because his patron in freeing him had some specific job in mind. In the first case, it was often to the freedman's advantage to utilize his training, although he might in some circumstances reject it, for instance a slave gladiator might not wish to stay in the arena after his manumission.[2] In the second case, a tailor-made position in the patron's household or business must have been hard to refuse. Some freedmen, then, became the paid employees or managers of their patrons,[3] or even partners. Others might take a loan from their patrons, set up in business, and pay back a share of the profits. Others were quite independent, continuing in the *métier* learnt during slavery.[4] Others, again, learned a new *artificium* and made a new career, sometimes, no doubt, with useful backing from the patron.[5] In some circumstances, *libertinitas* might thus be of practical advantage: the slave might have received a useful training; possibly, too, he could rely on future help from his patron, who might take more interest in his freedman than in an ingenuous client. This last consideration applies mainly to the wealthier patron: lower down the social scale, the patron was often driven by his own financial difficulties

---

[1] Cf. C. A. Forbes, *TAPA* 86 (1955) 321 ff.; S. Mohler, *TAPA* 17 (1940), 262 ff.
[2] *Dig.* xxxviii. 1. 38.
[3] Pay has to be assumed. Some of the work done would count as *operae*; payment to *liberti* who lived in the household might be partly in the form of board and lodging. *Liberti* who were business-managers were perhaps paid on a commission basis.
[4] Cf. *Dig.* xxxviii. 1. 16. It is often hard to tell to which category a freedman belonged, especially in inscriptions. *Liberti* employed by their patrons are treated on pp. 142 ff.
[5] Cf. Cicero's freedman, the *scriba* Tullius.

to exploit his *libertus*,[1] while a freedman who had purchased his own freedom might find himself without capital. Besides lacking financial resources, the freedman of the poor or humble master might well find himself unprovided with the even more valuable resources of training and skill. The odd-job man or servant girl had little chance of finding good employment, and many of them must have swelled the idle *plebs frumentaria* or the casual labour-force of the city, while the *ancilla* continued her old work in the new role of a Roman *matrona*. In spite of the legends of 'libertinae opes',[2] many freedmen were very poor, as their burial in *columbaria* often indicates.

Another factor distinguishing *libertini* from *ingenui* in point of work was the climate of opinion regarding many forms of employment. Aristocratic prejudice saw agriculture,[3] war, and politics as the proper occupations for a gentleman. Trade was sordid unless conducted on a large and profitable scale. The learned professions were suitable for those of the right social standing, but for the gentleman literature was the indulgence of *otium*, and even the hard training and practice of law and oratory were not officially intended to be sources of livelihood. Such are the rigid views expressed by Cicero.[4] However, in practice things were different. Cicero certainly profited, even if indirectly, from his oratory; senators like Brutus often dabbled in usury; the irreproachable *eques*, Atticus, was involved in publishing, banking, and agricultural production. The 'flos equitum Romanorum'[5] consisted of the *publicani*; *negotiatores* (business-men) were often conceded a high social position—they were 'splendidi' and 'gratiosi'.[6] However, like the senatorial order, the more eminent *equites* resorted to some concealment about business ventures. They were engaged in *negotia* of one sort or another (especially, of course, tax-farming and money-lending), hardly ever overtly in trade, though it is likely that they engaged in, for instance, the slave-trade, on the quiet.

[1] Cf. Plaut. *Cas.* 293 and perhaps *Curc.* 548.
[2] Mart. v. 13. 6.
[3] Contrast Sall. *BC* 4. 1 for an unusual view.
[4] *Off.* i. 150 f.   [5] Cic. *Planc.* 23.
[6] e.g. Cn. Calidius, father of a senator (Cic. ii *Verr.* iv. 42 ff.); L. Raecius (ibid. v. 16 ff.); Appuleius Decianus, son of a tribune (Cic. *Flacc.* 70 ff., with Scholiast).

Mercatura was less respectable: the title 'mercator' is in fact generally avoided by traders in their funerary inscriptions, and it can be uncomplimentary in use by others.[1] Such was the position of the upper classes and of rich parvenus in Roman society: snobbery and nostalgia for an agricultural past curiously intermingled with an urge to make money, exploit new sources of wealth, and enjoy new opportunities for luxury.

Among the vulgar, contempt for so many forms of work was, as in all societies, impossible. However degrading in the eyes of a philosopher, retail trade and crafts had to be carried out. Cicero, influenced by Greek philosophical ideas about *banausia*, from Panaetius especially, condemned the wages of the craftsman as 'auctoramentum servitutis', because he was bound to his employer, 'neque quicquam ingenuum habere potest officina'.[2] It is clear from this that free men were employed in labouring jobs, but what does not appear is whether such *mercenarii* felt themselves disgraced. Some indication of the feelings of the common people is perhaps given by the contemptuous remark which Cicero once permitted himself in open court and before a hostile audience:[3] 'opifices et tabernarios et illam omnem faecem civitatum'.[4] The sneer is directed against the errors of Greek democracy, but it is general enough for his hearers to apply it to Rome and themselves. Not only political instability or domination by employer are adduced against the craftsman, retailer, and labourer: he and his work are closely linked, sometimes identified, with slavery. The 'opifices atque servitia'[5] of Rome were alike the material of agitators. Livy refers to the work of a butcher as 'servile ministerium'.[6] *Ingenui* in general, and especially those performing especially despised jobs, tended to conceal or apologize for them when they set up their funeral inscriptions. The prejudice against the more 'sordid' forms of employment seems to have existed among the poor *ingenui* as among aristocrats and philosophers.[7]

---

[1] See J. Hatzfeld, *Les Trafiquants italiens dans l'Orient hellénique* (Paris, 1919), pp. 195 f.; Cic. *Pis. fr.* 11.   [2] *Off.* i. 150.
[3] Unless it was inserted later, in the published version of the speech.
[4] *Flacc.* 18.   [5] Sall. *BC.* 50. 1.i   [6] xxii. 25. 19.
[7] Cf. F. M. De Robertis, *Lavoro e lavoratori nel mondo romano* (Bari, 1967), chs. 1 and 2, distinguishing the aristocratic and popular views, with impressive citation of sources.

The question presents itself: was this prejudice a consequence of the use of slave labour, or did it precede the great influx of slaves caused by imperial expansion? It is impossible to believe that in early times a freeborn Roman was despised for being a shopkeeper or a craftsman rather than a farmer.[1] But with the influx of foreign slaves after the Punic Wars, new standards of living became established, slaves began to steal employment hitherto performed by *ingenui*[2] and to create work for themselves and their successors. Gradually, they seem to have edged out the native Romans, leaving them two occupations only, farming and war.[3] In certain luxury trades, ingenuous and native competition was virtually non-existent from the start. Thus, certain jobs became tainted with slavery, *ingenui* tended to despise them, and prejudice gave slaves their opportunity. *Libertini* shared the opportunity, unless they grew too proud after manumission. But the prejudice against 'servile' work must not be exaggerated: displaced and unemployed freeborn citizens were often glad to undertake it, and it is the *conducticii*, whose employment was nearest that of slaves, of whom we have least record.[4]

Mention of luxury trades brings us to another point: apart from being prejudiced against certain forms of employment, native Romans were often ill-equipped to engage in them. This applies especially to the professions, in which the leading lights were usually Greeks or Hellenized easterners, based in such places as Athens, Cos, or Rhodes, while the practitioners to be found in Italy were mostly slaves or freedmen.

---

[1] Cf. Livy, 1. 43. 3: two centuries of *fabri* were with the first class; *ESAR* i. 31 (Guilds of Numa); G. Kühn, *De Opificum Romanorum Condicione Privata Quaestiones* (Halle, 1910), p. 16.   [2] e.g. Livy, xxxix. 7, 8 f.

[3] Dion. Hal. ii. 28: δύο δὲ μόνα τοῖς ἐλευθέροις ἐπιτηδεύματα κατέλιπε, τά τε κατὰ γεωργίαν καὶ τὰ κατὰ πολέμους.

[4] Especially, probably, in the building-trade and dock labour, in which it was more economic to employ free men. Cf. Suet. *Vesp.* 18; Brunt, *JRS* 52 (1962), n. 12. Crassus, who could keep his men fully employed and needed specialists, used slaves (Plut. *Crass.* 2. 3 f.). See De Robertis, *Lavoro*, pp. 60 ff., especially pp. 82 ff., who concludes that the aristocratic prejudice was mainly against paid labour which bound a man to fixed hours and stopped him enjoying *otium* and independence. This is true for the nobles. But we still have to explain the prejudice of poorer *ingenui* against some forms of wage-earning, and here a desire for independence may have been combined with dislike of 'servile' jobs. Cf. De Robertis, *Lavoro*, pp. 35 f.

Other factors too will have controlled the employment of *libertini*. If they were freed late, they often lacked the family ties which bound the *ingenuus*. They were normally exempt from military service. They were not able to undertake all the political activities open to a freeborn citizen. They will thus have tended to devote their energies to money-making with more concentration than *ingenui*, as did, for instance, the Quakers in England, or the Jews in many other countries, and for similar reasons.

(i) *Trade and Industry*

Apart from agriculture, the employment to which large numbers of slaves are best suited is work in a large factory. But Italy was not in this sense an industrial country: few articles were mass-produced. Most were made in a small work-room and sold by the maker in the shop in front. This is the type of 'opifex et sellularius'[1] envisaged by Cicero when he thinks of the workers of the *Urbs*. Some commodities, however, were produced on a larger scale: bricks, lamps, lead pipes, glass, Arretine ware. For the personnel involved in these industries, some sort of statistics are available. But there are drawbacks, in that only the more important members of the staff would attain the distinction of stamping the product with their own name. In many cases, this means that the name is that of the owner or contractor, in others it will be a foreman or designer whose name has come down to us. Arretine potters' marks provide the most useful information for our period, since their span, according to modern authorities, is from about 40 B.C. till the time of Tiberius,[2] and they therefore cast light back on the late Republic. The signatures are those of the designers of the original moulds from which the pots were cast; possibly, therefore, not the same men who afterwards made the pots. The information is arranged and analysed by Park,[3] following Oxé's chronological scheme of various 'firms'.

The earliest group of thirteen establishments, dated to about 40

[1] *Cat.* iv. 17. Just the same sort of shops may be found in the Campus Martius area today.
[2] Oxé, *Rhein. Mus.* 59 (1904), 108 ff.
[3] *The Plebs in Cicero's Day*, pp. 79 ff.

to 20 B.C., shows 123 slave workers, eight *libertini*, and one who may be a *libertinus*. One or two of the owners are themselves freedmen[1] and Park conjectures that the potteries they owned were not those where they had worked as slaves, since we do not possess their signatures as slaves. She considers that they perhaps set up their potteries after manumission. Other freedmen appear in positions of responsibility, possibly as foremen or branch-managers. One pottery[2] stands out because four out of its known staff were freedmen. Park suggests that they controlled the business after the death or withdrawal of the owner. In the later groups, a similar pattern prevails, complicated, however, by signatures of an ambivalent type, assignable to *libertini*, slaves, or *ingenui*.[3]

The second group, of five potteries, from about 30 B.C. onwards, contains signatures from sixty-eight slaves, four freedmen, and twelve of dubious status. Two of the owners or managers seem to be themselves freedmen.[4] The third group, from about 20 B.C. onwards, gives 154 slaves, ten freedmen, and seventy-two of doubtful status. One pottery appears to have been especially large, with fifty-eight slaves and one freedman, who was probably the overseer, since his name appears most often. In contrast is the small firm of T. Rufrenus, from which only four names are known: two or perhaps all four were freedmen.

[1] N. Naevius Hilarus and possibly L. Sauffeius Gaius or Gausa.
[2] That of Mesienus.
[3] e.g. 'Cn. Atei Hilarus' can be read as 'Cn. Atei s. Hilarus' (Hilarus, slave of Cn. Ateius), 'Cn. Atei l. Hilarus' (freedman of Cn. Ateius), or 'Cn. Atei(us) Hilarus' (an *ingenuus*). Dressel, with hesitation, assigns the form to freedmen (*CIL* xv, p. 703). Oxé (*Rhein. Mus.* 59 (1904), 136 ff.) held that on earlier vases it meant 'Cn. Ateius Hilarus' and was used by freedmen and *ingenui*; on later vases he read it as 'Cn. Atei Hilarus' and would regard it as libertine rather than servile. G. H. Chase, *Catalogue of Arretine Pottery* (Boston, 1916), p. 17, regarded it as servile. Park calculated the number of times each known freedmen signed as, on average, nine, while slaves average two or three, and the dubious class four. She seems to have been inclined to think they were not freedmen. It is conceivable that slaves in positions of unusual responsibility might sign more often, or that this class included both slaves and freedman, the distinction in signatures being obscured.
[4] L. Tettius Samia, employing nine slaves, one freedman, and one in the dubious class; M. Perennius Tigranus, with seventeen slaves, one freedman, and nine dubious. On Tigranus, cf. R. J. Charleston, *Roman Pottery* (London, 1955), p. 12. Park thinks that in the signatures 'M. Perenni', 'L. Tetti', we may have evidence for the ownership of the potteries before the freedmen took over, as managers or owners.

TRADE AND INDUSTRY

These statistics show clearly the predominance of slave over free labour, which means, in this context, over freedmen, since the only *ingenui* who made moulds in these potteries were owners who were also working-potters. The ratios, excluding the dubious figures, are, in the three groups, 1 : 19, 1 : 18, 1 : 16. A similar picture is obtained from other, less well documented, potteries.[1] Most libertine potters had probably worked in the same pottery before manumission, as can be seen in certain cases. The freedmen sign considerably more often than the slaves: as more responsible workers, they set up the moulds more often and they must often have been in a position of authority as foremen or branch-managers. Freedmen who were themselves pottery-owners might either have taken a firm over from their patrons (who retired and handed it over, or bequeathed it by will), or launched out on their own after manumission. Financial help, often at interest, must have been given by the patrons of many such freedmen. Some had large businesses,[2] others were themselves working-potters in their own firms.[3]

Charleston has suggested that the inspiration which led to the success of Arretium was Greek.[4] The method of production from moulds was an imitation of the so-called Megarian ware, and the apparently Greek origin[5] of many of the slaves and freedmen at Arretium, led him to conjecture that the bulk of the workers came from the East in the great influx of war-prisoners brought by Lucullus and Pompey. Another great impulse, Charleston held, was provided by Actium and the consequent shift of wealth and influence to Italy, which he surely puts a century too late. He appears to have regarded Perennius Tigranus as a key figure and conjectured boldly that he brought a 'team' of working-potters of eastern-Greek origin to Arretium at some time between 30 and 25 B.C. While this would of course, if proved, cast an interesting light on the possibility of deliberate encouragement of the Arretine industry by recruitment of Greeks, and on the artistic importance

---

[1] Park found, in eight firms in different parts of Italy, twenty-six slaves and only one freedman (*Plebs*, p. 84, n. 1).
[2] e.g. N. Naevius Hilarus, M. Perennius Tigranus.
[3] e.g. Philologus, Samia (Park, *Plebs*, p. 86, n. 4). [4] *Roman Pottery*, p. 12.
[5] *Roman Pottery*, pp. 7 ff., but it cannot be proved that they were really from the Greek lands.

of freedmen, it has to be admitted that the whole idea is entirely hypothetical, and there is hardly a step in the argument which is, or could be, proved. The wholesale transference of Greek potters from the East is striking but hardly credible, and the time-lag between the Mithridatic Wars and the first flowering of the patterned vases is too long. The working master-potters, at least, were Italians, so not all the inspiration was foreign. Moreover, the value set on the slave designers, in spite of the commercial usefulness of their signatures, does not, to judge from the low proportion of freedmen, seem to have been high. One in sixteen, or less, is a ratio lower than one would expect.

On the other hand, the Arretine works show the complete exclusion of *ingenui* in the industry from subordinate positions.[1] We can also see that *libertini* were able to succeed their patrons in control of a business, or find the capital to set up their own.

In other factory industries, we lack a *corpus* of inscriptions dated to our period. Imperial evidence bears out the conclusions drawn from Arretium. Analysis of inscriptions[2] on clay lamps and lead pipes gives fair evidence of the predominance of libertine workers in positions of responsibility in those industries. The lamps were stamped with the name of the factory-owner or contractor, and yet names which are probably to be ascribed to freedmen easily outnumber the apparently freeborn. In the case of pipes overseers, and sometimes the owner or foreman of the workshop, put their names on the product. In the former class, freedmen probably outnumbered both slaves and freeborn Romans, in the latter they were about equal to the *ingenui*. No doubt the ordinary workers, who are not commemorated by stamps, were slaves.

In industries of the type carried out in factories, therefore, we may conclude that the mass of the workers were slaves, the foremen and the more important craftsmen, for instance the designers, were mostly freedmen, who had usually worked their way up from slavery in the ranks of the workers, and that the owners were *ingenui*, or, occasionally, freedmen.

[1] For it is unlikely that they were employed on less skilled work of which we have no record.
[2] See Gummerus, *RE* ix. 2, 1500 ff.; Duff, *Freedmen*, pp. 109 ff.

TRADE AND INDUSTRY

Statistics on the artisans and tradesmen of imperial Rome will be found in Duff,[1] but evidence on this point may also be gleaned from the scantier republican inscriptions and literary sources. Here too freedmen had a strong hold. Many of the *opifices* were also *tabernarii*, craftsmen and shopkeepers, since many articles were made to order.[2] An example of the shopkeeper who produced some of his wares and bought others is given by the *purpurarii*, who may have imported some of their stuffs from Tyre, but were also dyers.[3] The testimony of Cicero on the financial standing, political motives, and social status of the *tabernarii* is unflattering. They were 'egentes'[4] 'inopes atque imperiti';[5] self-interest was, however, sufficiently enlightened to persuade them that *otium* was better than revolution and incendiarism.[6] The same class in society is referred to as 'opifices' by Sallust in close connection with 'servitia': it was to them that Lentulus naturally turned for help against the government in 63 B.C.[7] A similar connection between slaves, freedmen, and shopkeepers or craftsmen appears in the references to Clodius' followers.[8] It sounds as if freedmen fitted into a class of 'egentes', which formed a large part of the shopkeeping and artisan population of Rome.

The freedmen shopkeepers and craftsmen (*artifices*) of whom we have records naturally tend not to be of this poor and discontented class, since they were for the most part *magistri* of *collegia* or men wealthy enough to pay for a comparatively lengthy tomb-inscription. We thus tend to get from inscriptions a rather optimistic impression of the over-all situation, to which the discontents of the Clodians provide a useful corrective.

The epigraphical evidence is sketchy, but provides a picture which, when checked against other sources, appears reliable. *Libertini* easily excluded freeborn Romans in trades as diverse as those of butcher and perfumer. In the former trade, we hear of five

[1] *Freedmen*, pp. 114 f.
[2] e.g. Plaut. *Men.* 544 ff.
[3] See Loane, *Industry and Commerce*, pp. 63 ff., 75 ff.
[4] *Dom.* 89.
[5] *Dom.* 13.
[6] *Cat.* iv. 17: 'nulli sunt inventi tam aut fortuna miseri aut voluntate perditi qui non ipsum sellae atque operis et quaestus cotidiani locum, qui non cubile et lectulum suum, qui denique non cursum hunc otiosum vitae suae salvum esse velint.'
[7] *BC* 50.
[8] Below, pp. 112 ff.

freedmen[1] and one slave,[2] but, apart from the slanders on the father of M. Terentius Varro,[3] no ingenuous butcher. Some of these *libertini* might be employees of their patrons, but it seems unlikely for the two who give their trade addresses on the tombs, and it would be strange if the officials of a college were drawn wholly from butchers' assistants. Some might be set up in business by their patrons, who took a share of the profits. These butchers' businesses seem to have been on a small scale. Bakers, on the other hand, sometimes operated on a large scale, like Eurysaces, the great 'pistor redemptor',[4] who set up a flamboyant monument to himself and his trade at Porta Maggiore.[5] He does not give filiation and his *cognomen* may suggest libertinity. The interesting thing about him is his evident pride in his work, which is represented, sometimes grotesquely, on his tomb and that of his wife.[6] He will have been a contractor supplying bread to retailers or possibly to troops or public slaves.[7] Freedmen appear in other inscriptions as bakers, but there are no known *ingenui*.[8] The little we know of other tradesmen supplying food suggests that *libertini* were just as predominant there.[9]

In the production and sale of clothes, two freedmen *vestiarii* are known. Unsurprisingly, freedmen were much involved in the 'oriental' trade of *purpurarius*. We can trace here an interesting phenomenon, the spread of either subordinate branches or independent firms, controlled by *libertini* of the same *gens*. From the

[1] Two libertine magistri of the *Lanii Piscinenses* (*CIL* i. 978 = Degr. 97); one 'de colle Viminale' (*CIL* i. 1221 = Degr. 793); one 'de luco Lubentinae' (*CIL* vi. 33870 = Degr. 794); one other (*CIL* i. 979 = Degr. 98).
[2] *CIL* i. 979 = Degr. 98.   [3] Livy, xxii. 25. 19.
[4] *CIL* i. 1203 = Degr. 805.
[5] M. Rostovtzeff, *Social and Economic History of the Roman Empire*[2] (Oxford, 1957), i, table iv.
[6] The inscription runs 'Marcei Vergilei Eurysacis Pistoris Redemptoris Apparet'. If the last word means not that Eurysaces was an *apparitor* (which seems an inelegant introduction of a verb), but 'so it appears', parenthetically, meaning that anyone could tell from the monument that he was a baker, this too will be in keeping with the pride he took in his trade.
[7] Loane, *Industry and Commerce*, p. 66. Eight men kneading dough under the supervision of another, and also donkey-powered machinery, shown on the monument, suggest that the business was large and up to date.
[8] *CIL* i. 677 = Degr. 714; a *pistor candidarius*. C. Julius Aug. liberti l. Eros, who died in A.D. 11, who may have been private baker to his patron (cf. Cic. *Pis.* 67 for the rich man's habit of having bread baked at home). Another specialist, a *pistor similaginarius* (*CIL* i. 1207 = Degr. 807), is of unknown status.
[9] e.g. market-gardeners who were probably freedmen (Cic. *Fam.* xvi. 18).

Republic, we know of Veturia D. l. Fedra, a seller of purple from the area of the Marian monuments,[1] probably the Esquiline.[2] In the first century of the Empire, there was a D. Veturius D. l. Atticus, with a shop in the *Vicus Iugarius*.[3] An undated inscription commemorates a *purpurarius* named L. Plutius L. l. Eros from the *Vicus Tuscus*, with whom is mentioned a certain Veturia C. C. l. Attica,[4] so that this third firm too is to be connected with the Veturii. The earliest inscription introduces us to Fedra, her husband and *conlibertus*, Nicepor, their patron, D. Veturius D. l. Diogenes, and their freedman, D. Veturius D. l. Philargyrus. Only the woman is actually said to have been engaged in the trade: it remains possible that the others, or at least her patron, were also so employed. The second, Atticus, was commemorated by Veturia D. l. Tryphera, presumably his wife. Loane has conjectured[5] that Veturia C. C. l. Attica[6] was the wife of Plutius Eros; the monument was set up by a *liberta* or *conliberta*, Plutia L. l. Auge. She guessed that Diogenes' patron, D. Veturius, had founded a business of a considerable size, which either trained a large number of men and women who later set up their own shops, or controlled branches under the charge of *liberti*. At some stage there were two men named C. Veturius, at a guess partners of D. Veturius. We do not know anything of freeborn Veturii at this time. Nor do we know how many ingenuous or freed purple-sellers, who left no record, linked up those freedmen of whom traces happen to have reached us. The size of the interests of the Veturii in purple is thus not determinable. It is interesting, however, to note the importance of freedwomen in the trade.[7]

In other luxury trades, such as metalwork, freedmen were again important. They are found, for instance, in a business carried on by the Trebonii, who were *thurarii*. Three *ingenui*, probably cousins, Gaius, Publius, and Publius Trebonii, sons of Publius, Publius, and

---

[1] *CIL* i. 1413 = Degr. 809: 'purpuraria Marianeis'.
[2] On the location, S. B. Platner, *Ancient Rome* (Boston, 1911), p. 464.
[3] *CIL* vi. 37820.   [4] *CIL* xiv. 2433.
[5] *Industry and Commerce*, pp. 75 f.
[6] Attica might even be a daughter, born in slavery, of Atticus, but their patrons were different.
[7] Cf. Lydia (*Acts* xvi. 14). Another freedman *purpurarius*, at Capua (*AE* 1958, 267).

98   CAREERS

Gaius Trebonii respectively, are commemorated with five *liberti* and *libertae*, mostly freed by two of them, but C. Trebonius was patron in all ascertainable cases and so, presumably, was head of the firm.[1] We also know of a *libertus* and *liberta* of Sextus Trebonius, both *thurarii*.[2] Sextus was no doubt connected with Gaius, Publius, and Publius—possibly another cousin or a younger son of one of them, but conceivably a freedman, or freedman of another relative. We can thus picture a family using freedmen as managers of its shops or allowing them to set up in business on their own, as well as employing them as subordinates.[3] An interesting link also appears between the businesses of L. Lutatius Paccius,[4] *thurarius* and probably a freedman, and C. Quinctilius C. l. Pamphilus, *unguentarius*. Paccius commemorates[5] himself, Pamphilus, and several freedmen,[6] and as the two patrons had a freedwoman in common, it is likely that they were business partners, not merely friends. The other *liberti* are also likely to have been perfumers.

The luxury shops, then, tended to be run by freedmen. But *ingenui* often owned the business, although freedmen might eventually take over a family firm or found their own businesses. The wealth of the shopkeeper was not necessarily in accordance with the expensiveness of the goods he handled.[7]

We have little information on the *conducticii* and *mercenarii*, men who performed services for hire. The distinction which Kühn[8]

[1] *CIL* i. 1398 = Degr. 816.   [2] *CIL* i. 1399 = Degr. 818.
[3] Loane, *Industry and Commerce*, p. 143. Another example of the continuity of a trade in a family is given by the M'. Obellii. Both were goldsmiths, M'. Obellius M'. f. from the *Via Sacra* in republican times (*ILS* 3683d = Degr. 110), M'. Obellius Acastus, whose *cognomen* suggests libertinity, with a shop in the *horti* or *horrei Aureliani* later (*CIL* vi. 37780). The rare *praenomen* makes it almost certain that the two were connected. Another freedman goldsmith is attested by *CIL* 1307 = Degr. 770.
[4] See Appendix 5.
[5] *CIL* i. 1334a, b = Degr. 817, 823.
[6] Two of whom appear again in *CIL* vi. 21782.
[7] Cf., perhaps, the jeweller who specialized in pearls (*margaritarius*), C. Atilius Serrani l. Euhodus (*CIL* i. 1212 = Degr. 797), who claimed the title 'hominis boni, misericordis, amantis, pauperis' which, with the comma between the last two words (*CIL* would read 'amantis pauperis') would produce the information that Euhodus did not consider himself well-off.
[8] *De Opificum Romanorum Condicione*, p. 4: 'Quaestum conducticium habent qui locandis ex rebus suis (ex insulis, balneis, tabernis, servis) fructum capiunt. ... Mercenarii sunt quorum artes et operae, ut ait Cicero (*Off*. i. 150) emuntur.' But cf. Varro, *RR* i. 17. 2.

attempted to draw between *conducticii* as master-contractors and *mercenarii* as hired workmen, cannot be maintained. Nor does Latin often distinguish in particular jobs whether the owner of a business or a labourer is meant. We are often in doubt whether a *balneator*[1] is the owner of baths or an attendant, whether a *fullo* is the owner of a fullery or a malodorous labourer. Sometimes, a man might be both master-contractor or labourer, as happened, it seems, with Cillo, a slave responsible for an irrigation project at Q. Cicero's house at Bovianum.[2] He held the contract and was in charge of operations conducted by at least four subordinate slaves, and he worked with them. Whether he was a slave working independently on his master's behalf ($\chi\omega\rho\grave{\imath}\varsigma$ $o\mathring{\imath}\kappa\hat{\omega}\nu$) or one of Quintus' own slaves (which seems unlikely if a contract was necessary) we do not know. Similarly, when a man on his tomb styles himself *fullo*[3] or *cisiarius*,[4] it is not often clear whether he washed clothes and drove carriages, or gave orders to others who did so.

As an 'opifex mercenarius' a freedman might be employed as a fuller, linen-weaver,[5] surveyor,[6] auctioneer,[7] and in many other less-documented capacities. There must have been many *libertini* who were unskilled workers, employed on seasonal, dangerous, or unhealthy jobs, where slave-labour was too expensive, or competing against slaves. Such men as stevedores and builders left little record.[8] The system of firms, with freedmen as employees or independent operators branching out on their own after training and manumission, can be seen occasionally in the case of hired workers, for example a pair of freedmen weight-makers and surveyors are known from Naples.[9] There may have been a remote

---

[1] e.g. a freedman *balneator* at Capua (*CIL* i. 677 = Degr. 714).

[2] Cic. *QF* iii. 1. 3.   [3] e.g. *CIL* i. 2108 = Degr. 240.

[4] e.g. *CIL* i. 1446 = Degr. 103 add. *Cisiarii* drove and were not coach-builders. See M. Maxey, *Occupations of the Lower Classes in Roman Society* (Chicago, 1938), pp. 70 f.   [5] *lintio*: *CIL* i. 678 = Degr. 715.

[6] *mensor*: *CIL* i. 1423. Also an *ingenuus* (*CIL* i. 1573 = Degr. 168) and a slave (Johnson, *Minturnae*, ii, inscription 25 = Degr. 742.)

[7] *praeco*: *CIL* i. 1210 = Degr. 808; cf. Hor. *Ep.* i. 7. 50 ff. For other *praecones*, not freedmen, see Cic. *Planc.* 33; Quinct. 12; *CIL* i. 686 = Degr. 722.

[8] Two freedmen *tectores* (*CIL* i. 1734 = Degr. 815 and *AE* 1926, 54.) Often slaves (Cic. *Planc.* 62; Plut. *Crass.* 23 f.), but when freed they might continue as foremen or freelance builders. See p. 90, n. 4.

[9] *CIL* i. 1623 = Degr. 801. We do not know if they were employees, or had founded their own business or taken over that of their patrons.

connection between the auctioneer and wit praised by Lucilius and Cicero, Q. Granius,[1] and a freedman auctioneer, A. Granius M. l. Stabilio.[2] The latter may have been freedman of a family of auctioneers which included both his own patron Marcus and Quintus Granius. But he seems to have been his own master, either controlling a business of his own or having taken over that of his patron, for his credit was good and he took pride in a normally disreputable profession.[3] Other *praecones* were employees bound by their wage-packets[4] and selling cheap rubbish, like Philippus' protégé Vulteius Mena in Horace. The profession of auctioneering, then as now, was compatible with a wide range of social status. The auctioneer Sex. Naevius was perhaps a freedman's son,[5] and Horace mentions it as having been a possible choice for himself.[6]

While the owner of a business was often a freeborn citizen, and *ingenui* joined the ranks of *mercenarii* when hard-pressed, the freedmen in this field too increasingly arrogated to themselves the posts of foremen or managers, and often rose to be partners or owners. The social condition and way of life of the *opifices* and *tabernarii* of Rome must be seen through the eyes, not only of Cicero and Sallust, but of those who stood nearer to the life of the humble worker and freedman, of Horace and the fortunate freedman, Stabilio, and the baker, Eurysaces, who made a success of their jobs and were proud of them. Horace's character, Vulteius Mena, is true to type if not a real character:

> praeconem, tenui censu, sine crimine, notum
> et properare loco et cessare et quaerere et uti,
> gaudentem parvisque sodalibus et lare certo
> et ludis et post decisa negotia Campo.[7]

His *cognomen* suggests the freedman, as Philippus thinks possible before he knows his name.[8] He is of independent spirit, delighting

---

[1] Cic. *Planc.* 33, *Fam.* ix. 15. 2; Lucil. *apud* Gell. iv. 17. He was probably an *eques*.
[2] *CIL* i. 1210 = Degr. 808: 'Pudentis hominis, frugi, cum magna fide, praeconis, Oli Grani sunt ossa heic sita. Tantum est. Hoc voluit nescius ne esses. Vale.'
[3] Cf. *Lex Julia Municipalis* (Bruns, *Fontes* 18), 104. Cic. *Quinct.* 12.
[4] 'mercennaria vincla'. See Hor. *Ep.* i. 7. 50 ff.
[5] Cic. *Quinct.* 11, 55, 95, but Cicero is deliberately vague.
[6] *Sat.* i. 6. 86.   [7] *Ep.* i. 7. 56 ff.   [8] *Ep.* i. 7. 54.

in his familiar Rome in a way that recalls Horace himself, and taking life as he finds it, until the fateful meeting with his would-be patron. Thanks to Horace and Stabilio and Eurysaces, we can see that the workers and traders of Rome were not necessarily ashamed or discontented with what they were, and that the people of the *Urbs* were not all hopeless and ripe for revolt. The elder Horatius was not wealthy, but he earned enough from his job as a *coactor*[1] or from other sources, to have a small farm, keep several slaves, and obtain a good education for his son. The picture which Horace paints of his father[2] does not lead one to think that the freedman stock or the working classes constituted a rot in the state. In spite of Mena's vulgarity and ignorance, he and Horatius are patterns of the strongest type of Roman: simple, philosophical, hard-working, tolerant, independent.[3]

The aristocratic prejudice against *ingenui* engaging in crafts or trades does not seem to have been generally reflected in the lower orders of society. Freedmen sometimes stand out because of their ability, their pride in their work, or both. The native Roman was at a disadvantage in certain fields: luxury trades such as dealing in purple dyes and cloth or in perfume and unguents were mainly in the hands of freedmen, probably of Greek or eastern origin, much as jobs such as clothes-designing or cooking have until recently been connected with Frenchmen. Moreover, as we cannot tell how often the *libertini* of whom we hear were merely managers or agents for their patrons, the apparent predominance of that class may well be a distortion. A patron would naturally prefer his own *libertus* as manager to an *ingenuus* over whom he had less control, so that *libertini* had an advantage in finding jobs as subordinates. But the ingenuous owner may often have left no epigraphic trace that it was he, and not his freedman, who was the boss. We guess that the ingenuous *plebs frumentaria* found employment as *mercenarii*, often, perhaps, only temporarily, and that they were not wholly ousted by freedmen. But the freedmen formed a large, and hard-working

---

[1] Who held the position of go-between at auctions and received a commission. See E. Fraenkel, *Horace* (Oxford, 1957), pp. 4 f.; J. A. Crook, *Law and Life of Rome* (London, 1967), pp. 219 f.   [2] *Sat.* i. 6.
[3] See Cic. *Off.* ii. 70 on the qualities of poor clients; De Robertis, *Lavoro*, pp. 27 ff. on the artisans of the Empire and Italy at a later date.

part of the working class in the city. The more prosperous *ingenui* were probably concentrated outside Rome itself, working on their farms[1] and in the villages, and involved in military service.[2]

Moving up the social scale, we come to *mercatura* and *negotium*, commerce and business. The social status of men involved in trade varied widely, from that of the simple cattle-dealer of a *municipium* to the merchant of Delos, who preferred to call himself a 'negotiator'.[3] 'Negotium' included finance, banking, and money-lending, and also ownership of agricultural land in the provinces and the more profitable forms of trade. In Cicero's day, Roman businessmen and traders were everywhere, even in the as yet unconquered parts of Gaul, preparing the way for the legions, or gathering the spoils of conquest and empire.[4] This was the heyday of Roman and Italian trade, especially in the east, and it is interesting to see how freedmen fitted into the pattern.

Some of Rome's traders were of humble station and small capital, who trusted in the protection of their citizenship when they adventured into strange lands.[5] *Libertini* might well be among these citizens. Others belonged to the class of Optimate freedmen praised in the *Pro Sestio*.[6] These were 'homines locupletes atque honesti', like those who had testified against Verres, 'qui partim socios suos, partim libertos, partim conlibertos spoliatos, in vincla coniectos, partim in vinclis necatos, partim securi percussos esse dicunt.'[7] This latter passage is the best general statement we have on the employment of freedmen in commerce. Assessment of their position

---

[1] They might work on seasonal jobs on slave-run estates, if their own farms did not engage them fully.

[2] Freedmen were present of course in the country-towns as *opifices* and *tabernarii*, as has been seen from the above evidence. Cf. Duff, *Freedmen*, p. 115; *CIL* i. 2125 = Degr. 776.

[3] Hatzfeld, *Trafiquants*, pp. 193 ff. 'Negotiator' was especially applied to money-lenders, cf. Cic. *Att.* vi. 1. 4 ff., v. 21. 10 ff.

[4] Caes. *BG* i. 1; cf. for Narbonensis, Cic. *Font.* 11, the activities of Umbrenus (below p. 103 n. 5); Brunt, 2e *Conférence internationale d'histoire économique* (1962), 125.

[5] 'Homines tenues, obscuro loco nati, navigant, adeunt ad ea loca quae numquam antea viderunt, ubi neque noti esse iis quo venerunt, neque semper cum cognitoribus esse possunt. Hac una tamen fiducia civitatis non modo apud nostros magistratus . . . neque apud civis solum Romanos . . . fore se tutos arbitrantur, sed quocumque venerint, hanc sibi rem praesidio sperant futuram.' (Cic. ii. *Verr.* v. 167.) [6] Cic. *Sest.* 97. [7] Cic. ii. *Verr.* v. 154.

TRADE AND INDUSTRY

depends, however, on the degree of preciseness with which Cicero spoke. It goes without saying that some of the *liberti* mentioned were subordinates working for their patrons, the merchants of Puteoli.[1] Then Cicero mentions merchants who complained of the fate of their fellow freedmen: these men, then, were themselves freedmen, but what was their position as merchants? Were they independent *mercatores*, protesting on behalf of colleagues, subordinates, or partners? Or were they and their *conliberti* employees? If they were important witnesses, it is unlikely that they were mere employees or even *liberti* trading with funds entrusted to them by their patrons, although it would be natural for Cicero to exaggerate their status. They seem to have been independent *mercatores*. The case described in detail by Cicero, that of P. Granius, whose ship and merchandise were seized and whose *liberti* were beheaded by Verres, exemplifies what was probably the normal form of employment of freedmen in sea-trade: the freedmen were agents and employees of the patron.

'Negotiatores', as already mentioned, was a name often confined to the most respected of the business men. Those *equites* who were unable, through lack of capital, ability, opportunity, or inclination, to join the *societates* of the *publicani*, belonged to the upper echelons of the *negotiatores*.[2] They won adjectives such as 'splendidus' and 'gratiosus'.[3] But men of undistinguished social position could also be *negotiatores*[4] and hold important jobs, for instance as agents of the tax companies. *Libertini* even were not denied the title, and used it themselves to describe their activities.[5]

The largest number of *mercatores* and *negotiatores* known to us

[1] Theoretically, some might be independent *mercatores*, whose patrons came forward to accuse Verres even though their own financial interests were not involved. But it seems more likely that the *liberti* were either agents or men trading with their patrons' capital. Cf. M. Aurelius Maximi l. Zosimus, who probably started in this way (*EJ* 358. 10).

[2] See W. T. Arnold, *The Roman System of Provincial Administration to the Accession of Constantine the Great* (Oxford, 1914), pp. 90 f.

[3] e.g. Cic. ii. *Verr.* iv. 42 (*eques* whose son was a senator); *Flacc.* 70; *Fam.* i. 3; xiii. 74; cf. *Off.* i. 151.

[4] Cic. ii. *Verr.* v. 140; *Fam.* viii. 2. 2, etc.

[5] e.g. P. Umbrenus, the Catilinarian, 'libertinum hominem, a quo primum Gallos ad Gabinium perductos esse constabat' (Cic. *Cat.* iii. 14). He had been a businessman in Gaul: 'in Gallia negotiatus erat, plerisque principibus civitatis notus erat atque eos noverat' (Sall. *BC* 40).

comes from the Delian inscriptions, in which occupations are not specified. Of 221 'Romans' (which includes Italians) whose status is known, eighty-eight were freeborn, ninety-five freedmen, and forty-eight slaves. In other centres in the east, according to Hatzfeld, the proportion of freedmen was still higher. But he finds that they were usually grouped round an *ingenuus*, from which we can argue that they were nearly always subordinates.[1] However, freedmen also undertook ventures on their own account, as we know from the literary sources. One of Caesar's freedmen had lent money in Bithynia in 81 B.C.;[2] Philotimus, thesteward of Terentia, had *negotia* at Ephesus which led him into litigation in 47 B.C.;[3] Tiro was party to a contract in 44 B.C.[4] One would naturally explain the residence of many freedmen in the provinces, especially Asia, as dictated by involvement in business ventures of their own, though again many will have been acting for their patrons. Often, they will have been both *procuratores* (agents) and independent business men. Thus Cicero recommended C. Avianius Hammonius to Sulpicius, both as his patron's procurator at Sicyon, and 'suo nomine';[5] C. Curtius Mithres, who had been able to offer Cicero abundant hospitality at Ephesus, was in 46 B.C. involved in a lawsuit over a farm he owned at Colophon—presumably his business interests were wholly or partly agricultural.[6] Similarly, such freedmen as Cossinius Anchialus in Greece,[7] or (probably) Pompeius Vindullus at Laodicea,[8] would surely have been engaged in business of some sort.

The great public companies were run, of course, by the 'flos equitum Romanorum',[9] though freedmen were used as employees. The *decumani*, or tithe-collectors, were in a quite different class,[10] since this tax was farmed locally, and humble citizens or even public slaves were able to take the contract.[11] *Libertini* are likely to

[1] *Trafiquants*, pp. 24 ff. [2] Suet. *DJ* 2.
[3] Cic. *Att.* xi. 24. 4. [4] Cic. *Fam.* xvi. 23. 2.
[5] Ibid. xiii. 21. [6] Ibid. xiii. 69.
[7] Ibid. xiii. 23.
[8] Cic. *Att.* vi. 1. 25. He was probably a freedman of Pompey, not a client or relation, since when he died 'res ad Magnum Pompeium pertinere putabatur'. (The order emphasizes the fact that the *nomen* is the same.)
[9] Cic. *Planc.* 23.
[10] Brunt, *2ᵉ Conférence internationale d'histoire économique* (1962), 124.
[11] Nicolet, *Ordre équestre*, p. 325.

TRADE AND INDUSTRY

have been among them.[1] One public building contract is known to have gone to a freedman.[2] But the great public contracts of taxes and monopolies were outside the scope of *libertini*.

Freedmen are found among the humbler dealers, often, apparently, as their own bosses.[3] They were prominent in the cults of Capua and Minturnae, and although the inscriptions only occasionally attest a specific trade, we can guess from the location that these men were engaged in trade or manufacturing.[4] The breaking-down of the barriers between *ingenui* and *libertini* may be seen in these inscriptions and those of Delos, and is an *a priori* argument for parity of opportunity at work. This would not apply to trade in the east, when it needed capital as much as nerve and ability (except for freedmen aided by their patrons), but small businesses in Italian towns might well be controlled by freedmen. Evidence from the inscriptions of *collegia* is hard to assess, since we find slaves too dedicating with freedmen.[5] But when a man claims to be 'frumentarius' on his tomb, it is natural to think of him as a master corn-merchant.[6,7]

As one would expect, in trade and business ventures which required capital, *libertini* seem to have been employees rather than owners, except in favoured cases. The freedmen of the rich, like Philotimus, Curtius Mithres, Caesar's financier freedman, could afford to invest their money or that of their patron. They might hold shares in the public companies or go into partnership with their patrons[8] or *conliberti*; they might conduct a business

---

[1] Q. Apronius and P. Naevius Turpio, the two scoundrelly *decumani* of the *Verrines* are regarded by Nicolet (*Ordre équestre*, p. 325) as freedmen. It is intrinsically probable, and suggested by Cicero's description of them as 'servi homines' (ii. *Verr*. iii. 91), and of Apronius as 'vix liber' (ii. *Verr*. iii. 134).

[2] *CIL* i. 808 = Degr. 465: the paving of the *Via Caecilia* in the time of Sulla.

[3] *CIL* i. 1450 = Degr. 108: cattle merchants dedicating at Praeneste, one freeborn, one freedman *magister*; *CIL* i. 1618 = Degr. 231: a college of netmakers with a similar board.

[4] Johnson, *Minturnae, passim*; Frederiksen, *PBSR* N.S. 14 (1959), 80 ff.

[5] For instance, the slave employees of the *socii salinatores* and *socii picarii* at Minturnae (Johnson, *Minturnae*, i, inscriptions 1, 7, 14, 16, 19, 21, 26).

[6] *AE* 1959, 146 = Degr. 786a. Cf. Duff, *Freedmen*, p. 193 on imperial corn importers.

[7] Other possible *mercatores* of libertine status: Cic. *Quinct*. 24 (a slave-dealer); Cic. *Fam*. vii. 23. 2; Hor. *Sat*. ii. 3. 16 ff. (Damasippus the art-dealer).

[8] Cf. *CIL* i. 1596 = Degr. 938: a *libertus* who was *socius* with his patron, but we do not know in what business. The patron too was a freedman.

enterprise on money borrowed from the patron and pay interest or a fixed share of the profits. Where little capital was needed or boldness could be substituted for it, as in cattle-dealing or the Gallic slave-trade, *libertini* could compete.

(ii) *Agriculture*

In spite of the widespread use of slaves in agriculture,[1] at least on farms of any size, and notoriously on the great ranches, there is little evidence for the employment of freedmen. Manumission of rustic slaves is not mentioned by Cato or Varro. Cato foresaw only re-sale for old and worn-out slaves;[2] Varro, however, mentions *peculium*[3] and a stable family life[4] as a means of giving the slave a stake in the well-being of the estate. He also stresses the need to appoint as overseers men with expertise, who will be obeyed and respected.[5] These *praefecti* are to have special privileges and to be admitted to the master's confidence on matters of farm policy. It is strange in these circumstances that Varro neglects to mention manumission both as a possible incentive and as a reward to slaves of high value and capacity.[6]

Several reasons may be conjectured. First, as is always said, country slaves had less opportunity than members of the *familia urbana* for winning the favour of their master. This applies to the herdsmen on the ranches and to employees on any large estate where the master was generally absent—in fact to the sort of gentleman-farmer to whom Cato and Varro addressed themselves. But it was not true of the slaves of small farmers who lived, and sometimes worked, with their slaves, like Cato himself on occasion,[7] or Horace in holiday mood.[8] Moreover, even an absentee owner, like Cicero,

[1] Which Sallust called 'servile officium' (*BC* 4. 1), probably under the influence of the *latifundia*. Contrast Cic. *Off.* i. 151; *Sen.* 51 ff., etc.
[2] *RR* 2. 7.
[3] *RR* i. 2. 17; i. 17. 7; Cf. *CIL* ix. 3386; *Dig.* xv. 2. 3.
[4] *RR* ii. 1. 26; 10. 6 ff.
[5] *RR* i. 17. 4: 'aliqua . . . humanitate imbuti, frugi, aetate maiore quam operarios . . . periti rerum rusticarum'.
[6] Known *vilici* are almost invariably slaves. See *ILS* p. 743; Cicero (*Caec.* 55) assumes that a *vilicus* will be a slave. Elsewhere (*Planc.* 62) he suggests that any slave would do, as long as he was honest. Brunt, *JRS* 48 (1958), 168.
[7] Plut. *Cato Maj.* 1.
[8] Hor. *Ep.* i. 14. 39.

AGRICULTURE 107

kept an eye on the major operations of the farm and was well acquainted with the capabilities of his *vilicus* (bailiff).[1] Secondly, it may be conjectured that country slaves had little to gain from freedom. They were not trained for any other work; free agricultural *mercenarii* were already unemployed,[2] so they were not likely to be able to hire out their services if their own patrons did not keep them on, and their *peculium* would hardly suffice for a farm of their own. On the other hand, masters who did not have the cheeseparing mentality of Cato, might tolerate the presence of a few retired slave-workers on the farm. Horace's picture of country life, not usually sentimentalized, reflects an easy-going society in which technicalities of slave or free status might not be too important.[3]

But the negative evidence of Cato or Varro must not be over-emphasized. Evidence on farm-workers is in any case scanty. Virgil in the First Eclogue envisaged the manumission of Tityrus, and though the context is inextricably confused with the restoration of his lands to a free farmer, we have distinct references to *peculium*[4] saved up in order to buy freedom, although in the end the manumission seems to be *gratis*. A *vilicus* from a republican inscription[5] and the outspoken bailiff of Horace,[6] seem to have been slaves, but there is a possibility that the bailiff of Q. Cicero at Arpinum was a freedman, since he offered to make a contract to carry out a building project and it is hard to see how a slave could do so with his own master.[7] *A priori*, then, we should expect that the bailiff at least would sometimes be a freedman and that lesser slaves could occasionally save their *peculium* and buy freedom.

We hear of various freedmen employees on farms, but they often seem to be men employed originally in other capacities. A *vilicus* of Augustus was a freedman but had previously been a taster and was presumably freed before being given the job of farm-manager.[8] Some of Atticus' *liberti* who acted on his behalf in Greece were

---

[1] Cic. *QF* iii. 1. 5.
[2] Cf. Suet. *DJ* 42. 1.
[3] Cf. *Od.* iii. 17. 16; iii. 23; *Ep.* i. 14.
[4] Verg. *Ecl.* i. 32.   [5] *CIL* i. 1825 = Degr. 197 add.
[6] *Ep.* i. 14, especially 21 ff., 40, which indicate that he had been promoted from the *familia urbana*.
[7] Cic. *QF* iii. 1. 5. He was called Nicephorus.
[8] *CIL* vi. 9005 = *EJ* 157.

surely employed as managers of his Epirot estates.[1] A *libertus* normally employed as a civil servant was on hand to entertain the guests of Seius at a villa dedicated to birds and game, and had the facts about the farm at his finger-tips.[2] Such *liberti* seem mostly to have been confidential agents, whose employment on estates is comparable to their work in other fields of investment. It tells us nothing about the promotion of agricultural slaves to such positions of trust.

The interests of freedmen in agriculture were not limited to employment by their patrons. As early as the second century B.C., a large number of freedmen had landed property, since it was worth while to pass a law allowing those with estates valued at 30,000 sesterces or over to belong to the country tribes.[3] 'Back to the land' was an idea which attracted town-workers[4] like the *coactor* Horatius, while wealthier freedmen, like any other Roman of any pretensions, liked to have a country estate. Horace's home near Venusia is referred to as barely supporting his father and himself when they came to Rome for the boy's education.[5] But their manner of life was not too austere.[6] The cultured Tiro, on the other hand, will not have bought his farm just in order to make a living, although it was a good investment. His country house was situated near Puteoli, within easy reach of Cicero's villa, and in the middle of the fashionable holiday area. Young Marcus twitted him on his new-found rusticity:

Habes; deponendae tibi sunt urbanitates; rusticus Romanus factus es, quo modo ego mihi nunc ante oculos tuum iucundissimum conspectum propono; videor enim videre ementem te rusticas res, cum vilico loquentem, in lacinia servantem ex mensa secunda semina.[7]

[1] Eutychides, freed in 54 B.C. (Cic. *Att.* iv. 15. 1), in 51 B.C. welcomed Cicero at Corcyra (Cic. *Att.* v. 9. 1). He was perhaps not primarily an agricultural agent, as he had apparently been freed in compliment to Cicero, which would make him more likely to have been in some confidential job, for instance a secretary. Areus (Cic. *Att.* v. 9. 1) and Alexio (Cic. *Att.* vii. 2. 3, xiii. 25. 3, cf. ? xii. 53) were in Epirus as Atticus' agents, but it is not known that they were freedmen.
[2] Varro, *RR* iii. 2. 14.
[3] pp. 43 ff.
[4] He may have worked in Rome, not Venusia.
[5] Hor. *Sat.* i. 6. 71.
[6] Hor. *Sat.* i. 6. 78 ff.: 'vestem servosque sequentes | in magno ut populo, si qui vidisset, avita | ex re praeberi sumptus mihi crederet illos.'
[7] Cic. *Fam.* xvi. 21. 7. Note that Tiro is expected to employ a *vilicus*.

Other *libertini* enjoyed their country estates as sources of wealth and opportunities for ostentation. The rich Caecilius Isidorus, although he had suffered serious losses in the civil wars, died in 8 B.C. possessed of 4,116 slaves, 3,600 yoke of oxen, other stock to the number of 257,000.[1] His acreage will have been immense. Horace castigated an unidentified ex-slave, who in the thirties acquired a thousand *iugera* of valuable land:

> 'sectus flagellis hic triumviralibus
>   praeconis ad fastidium
> arat Falerni mille fundi iugera
>   et Appiam mannis terit...'[2]

Others were practical working farmers. A famous anecdote retold by Pliny illustrates the possibilities. A freedman named C. Furius Chresimus was indicted because with a small farm he made more profit than did his neighbours who owned more land. Chresimus chose an original method of demonstrating that his success was the result of good husbandry alone, not of witchcraft: he brought all his implements into the court, and regretted that he could not also bring his 'lucubrationes... vigiliasque et sudores'. He was naturally acquitted.[3] Curiously, all the other examples of land improvement adduced by Pliny also concern freedmen. Vetulenus Aegialus had taken over the estate at Liternum which had previously been owned by Africanus, and made a great success of vine-growing.[4] Recent years had seen the success of Acilius Sthenelus, a freedman or near descendant of a freedman, who improved his own holding and also that of the grammarian Remmius Palaemon.[5] We may also remember the unhappy auctioneer turned farmer in Horace, who was probably meant to be a freedman.[6]

Libertini were also concerned with market-gardening and horticulture. The three vegetable-growers mentioned by Cicero as

[1] He may have inherited from the Metelli, p. 239.
[2] *Epod.* iv. 11 ff.
[3] Pliny, *NH* xviii. 41 ff. The date of the trial cannot be fixed, but it is clearly early. The curule aedile named, Sp. Albinus, has not been identified.
[4] Pliny, *NH* xiv. 4. 9. No date is indicated, except the *terminus post quem* of Africanus' ownership.
[5] Pliny, *NH* xiv. 48. He was 'e plebe libertina'. He had improved a 60-*iugera* vineyard so much that he sold it for 400,000 sesterces. Remmius was active in the time of Tiberius (Suet. *Gram.* 23).   [6] Hor. *Ep.* i. 7; p. 100.

interested in renting a garden of his at Tusculum all had Greek names and were probably freedmen.[1] A maker of garlands, who may have grown the flowers he used, is attested.[2] The famous gardener in the *Georgics* may have been a freedman.[3] Important contributions to horticulture were made by other freedmen, mentioned by Pliny but not dated: one Corellius Tereus emulated his patron in introducing a new cross in chestnut-trees,[4] and a certain apple was named Sceptiana after its freedman creator.[5] There was a famous botanist and practised gardener named Antonius Castor, who reached the age of a hundred in Pliny's day and was presumably a freedman of M. Antonius or one of his children.[6] Innovations in the late Republic had also probably been made or encouraged by eastern freedmen imported in the wars of conquest.[7]

(iii) *The Learned Professions and the Fine Arts*
(a) *Scholars, Teachers, and Writers*

The prominence of freedmen in certain fields of literature and scholarship—in some fields, their predominance—is unsurprising, given the circumstances of Roman education and culture. 'Graecia capta ferum victorem cepit.' The Hellenization of Romans on their own soil was carried out largely by freedmen and slaves imported from Greek lands, first from Magna Graecia, later from Greece itself, and, to a still greater extent, from the Greek East. Practical training of the Roman type could be given by a Roman father,[8] but education as the first century knew it was a Greek import. Suetonius put the beginnings of real education in Rome in about 169 B.C.,[9] and it was a Greek slave who served as tutor in the household

---
[1] *Fam.* xvi. 18 (*holitores*).   [2] *CIL* i. 1566 = Degr. 783 (*coronarius*).
[3] Verg. *Georg.* iv. 125 ff. He is called 'Corycius senex' and Corycos in Cilicia was famous for pirates as well as gardening. Servius notes that he could have been one of the pirates transplanted by Pompey to Calabria, and cites Suetonius as his authority for the transplantation. As such, he could well have been technically a *libertus* of Pompey, as were Menas and Menecrates (p. 188), although never employed as a slave. Even if he was not a pirate, the presence of the Cilician would be hard to explain except on the hypothesis that he was a *libertinus*, but he seems more likely to have been imported as a pirate than as a rose-grower.
[4] *NH* xvii. 122.   [5] *NH* xv. 50.   [6] *NH* xviii. 41 ff.
[7] See L. Friedländer, *Darstellungen aus der Sittengeschichte Roms* (Leipzig, 1919–21), ii, p. 306 = Eng. ed. p. 167.
[8] Plut. *Cato Maj.* 20, but it was old-fashioned even in Cato's day.
[9] Suet. *Gram.* 2.

of Cato.[1] But recruits to teaching were not drawn only from Greek captives educated in the days of their freedom: once the pattern was set, promising slaves of any background were trained in Greek culture as future teachers and scholars.[2] Such education was the privilege of the ruling classes[3]—by the nature of society debarred from scholarship as a career[4]—and of slaves. The field was thus wide open to the latter. The offices of scholar, teacher, and writer, though in theory distinguishable, merge in many individuals. Creative writers might be half grammarians, schoolmasters, poets.

The beginnings of *grammatica* and poetry at Rome coincided, though literature itself made a better beginning than the study of it.[5] Livius Andronicus, according to Jerome,[6] had been slave tutor to the children of Livius Salinator and was freed 'ob ingenii meritum'. He was a Tarentine,[7] presumably a prisoner when the city fell in 272 B.C. The distinction of founding Roman drama[8] and of being the father of Roman literature[9] thus belongs to an ex-slave. In the first half of the second century, freedmen poets marched in the forefront of Roman literature while literary education lagged behind. Caecilius Statius,[10] perhaps to be considered Rome's greatest comic poet, according to a good authority,[11] is marked as a freedman by his *cognomen*, a common slave name,[12] but nothing is known of the circumstances of his enslavement and

---

[1] Plut. *Cato Maj.* 20. 3.
[2] Plut. *Cato Maj.* 20. 5 f. Cf. Orbilius' statement that a slave with some education was called 'litterator' when sold, a finished scholar 'litteratus'. He suggested that most of them were merely 'litteratores' (Suet. *Gram.* 4).
[3] And of a few of the poorer *ingenui*: Orbilius went to school at Beneventum (Suet. *Gram.* 9), Horace, exceptionally, did not go to the school 'quo pueri magnis e centurionibus orti' at Venusia, but to one frequented by the sons of senators and *equites*, that of Orbilius, in Rome (Hor. *Sat.* i. 6. 72 ff.).
[4] Cf. De Robertis, *Lavoro*, pp. 81 ff.
[5] Suet. *Gram.* 1: 'Initium (grammaticae) mediocre exstitit, siquidem antiquissimi doctorum qui iidem poetae et semigraeci erant (Livium et Ennium dico, quos utraque lingua domi forisque docuisse adnotatum est) nihil amplius quam Graecos interpretabantur aut, si quid ipsi Latine composuissent, praelegebant.'
[6] *Chron.* on 188 B.C.
[7] Accius *apud* Cic. *Brut.* 72. His date of 209 B.C. for Livius' arrival in Rome is, in my opinion, unacceptable. See H. B. Mattingley, *CQ* N.S. 7 (1957), 159 ff.
[8] In 240 B.C. (Cic. *Brut.* 71).
[9] Hor. *Ep.* ii. 1. 62.
[10] *Floruit* 179 B.C. (Jerome).
[11] Cic. *Opt. Gen. Or.* 2.
[12] Gell. iv. 20. 12 f.

liberation except that Jerome calls him an Insubrian from Milan.[1] Notwithstanding his non-Roman origins, Statius was noted for the *gravitas* of his works and in his day was the acknowledged leader of Roman drama.[2]

The *Andria* was produced in 166 B.C. and this time details of the author's life are not lacking. Suetonius states that P. Terentius Afer was born at Carthage and became the slave at Rome of a senator called Terentius Lucanus. He cannot have been a war-captive of the Romans, since his birth and death fell in the interval between the Second and Third Punic Wars, nor yet of the Numidians or Gaetulians, since there was no trade between them and the Romans before the fall of Carthage. Presumably, therefore, he was a slave at Carthage, before being transferred to Rome by sale or gift.[3] In any case, the transfer took place early in his life, for it was his Roman master who gave him a liberal education and his manumission also took place early. The production of his plays is dated to the years 166–160 B.C. and according to Suetonius, he was only twenty-four when he left Rome on the trip to Greece from which he never returned.[4] Terence was notoriously a protégé of the young Scipio Aemilianus, and it was rumoured that his familiarity with Scipio, Laelius, and Philus was not what it seemed on the surface. As in the case of Horace, jealousy was ready to assign discreditable motives to great men who courted a genius of low birth, and to the poet who accepted their friendship. Suetonius and other authorities rightly discount the stock charge of homosexuality;[5] the story that Scipio and Laelius had a hand in the writing of the plays died more slowly. Cicero and Nepos refer to the alleged authorship of Laelius.[6] Memmius to that of Scipio,[7] while other contemporary aristocrats, of greater age, were also canvassed.[8] Suetonius holds, more plausibly, that is was the noble, not the freedman, who was flattered, by the rumours of his collaboration. The career of Terence is interesting

---

[1] W. Beare, *The Roman Stage* (London, 1950), p. 76, doubts that he was a freedman, but gives no reasons. D. O. Robson (*AJP* 59 (1938)) argued for free, possibly Samnite, origin.   [2] Suet. *Vita Ter.* 2.
[3] Suet. *Vita Ter.* 1. See T. Frank, *AJP* 54 (1933) 268 ff.
[4] Suet. *Vita Ter.* 4. For the dating of the plays and a suggestion that his birth should be put c. 190 B.C. see Jachmann, *RE* v A i, 599 ff.
[5] *Vita Ter.* 1.   [6] Cic. *Att.* vii. 3. 10; Suet. *Vita Ter.* 3.
[7] Suet. *Vita Ter.* 3.   [8] Ibid. 4.

because for the first time we can see that brains and character could win a slave first a good education, then freedom, and finally the patronage of eminent men. Certain talents were capable of breaking down many barriers. Terence achieved also concrete success: the *Eunuchus* earned him the record fee of eight thousand sesterces,[1] and, *pace* the moralizing tradition that Terence died poor, he left twenty acres of gardens on the Via Appia, and his daughter was later in a position to marry an *eques*.[2] More lasting was his literary repute and the credit given to an African freedman by freeborn Romans, who considered him one of the greatest exponents of Latinity and Roman humour.[3]

Suetonius dates the introduction of the formal study of *grammatica* in Rome to the embassy of Crates of Mallos in about 169 B.C., in the era of Statius and Terence.[4] However, it was slow to gain ground, and the first teachers limited themselves to expounding specific works which interested them. Two of the early *grammatici* mentioned might have been freedmen,[5] but it was two *equites*, L. Aelius Praeconinus and Servius Clodius, who set the fashion. After them, education had a minor boom.[6] A slave teacher was sold for 700,000 sesterces, while another, apparently free, was hired for 400,000 sesterces a year to teach a large school. In spite of Suetonius' remarks about the respectability of scholarly writing,[7] very few of the professional teachers mentioned by him were *ingenui*, and those few often took up study and teaching *faute de mieux*. The famous L. Orbilius Pupillus, for example, when left alone in the world, tried the careers of *apparitor* and soldier before taking to teaching, which did not prove a financial success.[8] Later, M. Pomponius Marcellus, active under Tiberius, had formerly been a boxer,[9] while M. Valerius Probus wanted to be a centurion.[10]

[1] Suet. *Vita Ter.* 4.   [2] Ibid. 1; 5.
[3] e.g. Caes. *ap.* Suet. *Vita Ter.* 5: 'puri sermonis amator'; Vell. i. 17. 1: 'dulcesque Latini leporis facetiae per Caecilium Terentiumque et Afranium subpari aetate nituerunt.'   [4] Suet. *Gram.* 2.
[5] Ibid. 2: Laelius Archelaus and Vettius Philocomus. The Greek names would fit freedmen and the former could have been a freedman of the great Laelius.
[6] Ibid. 3. There were over twenty schools in Rome, and it was respectable to write works of criticism.
[7] Ibid. 3.   [8] Ibid. 9.
[9] Ibid. 22.   [10] Ibid. 24.

M. Saevius Nicanor, also called by the more native-sounding name of M. Saevius Postumius, was a freedman who was the first teacher to achieve recognition. Besides teaching, he wrote commentaries and a satire.[1] Little is known of the work of Lutatius Daphnis, freedman of Q. Catulus, whose transfers from one master to another involved immense fees. He was sold, it seems, first by Attius of Pisaurum,[2] presumably the poet Accius, to M. Scaurus, and later to Catulus,[3] each time for 700,000 sesterces. Only hypothesis is possible with regard to dating,[4] but the point of interest is that Daphnis was worth so much to two eminent men and that he was soon[5] manumitted, despite the high price paid. Daphnis was presumably used as a literary collaborator rather than a teacher of youth. Performance of a dual role, as teacher and collaborator, was, however, normal. Aurelius Opilius[6] taught first philosophy, then rhetoric, then grammar, but when Rutilius Rufus was banished, he gave up his school and accompanied him to Asia, where he wrote a number of books.[7] Cornelius Epicadus, by contrast, is not said to have ever been a teacher. He served his patron as a *calator*[8] and wrote a number of learned works which were of value to later commentators.[9] He also finished Sulla's uncompleted autobiography, 'de rebus suis'.[10]

The life of M. Antonius Gnipho[11] is related in some detail by Suetonius.[12] He was born in Gaul of free parents, but exposed,

---

[1] In which he joked about his libertinity and his double *cognomen*: 'Saevius Nicanor M. libertus negabit; Saevius Postumius vero idem ac Marcus docebit' (Suet. *Gram.* 5).

[2] Pliny, *NH* vii. 128.   [3] Suet. *Gram.* 3.

[4] Fraccaro (*Opuscula* ii, pp. 145 ff.) would put the first sale before 90/88 B.C., the second before 86 B.C. (for Catulus was murdered in 87/86) and guesses that Catulus freed him *testamento*.

[5] Suet. *Gram.* 3.

[6] Of whose manumitter we know only that he was an Epicurean (Suet. *Gram.* 6).

[7] They are cited by Gellius (i. 25. 17; iii. 3. 1).   [8] Suet. *Gram.* 12.

[9] e.g. *de sigillaribus*, cited by Macrobius (*Sat.* i. 11. 47).

[10] Goetz (*RE* iv. 1311) suggested that the librarian whom Tyrannio helped to arrange the library of Apellicon which had been captured in Athens (Strabo, xiii. 609) was Epicadus. Identification has also been suggested with 'Sulla litterator' who is scornfully mentioned by Catullus (xiv. 9). E. Ellis (ad loc.) thought that a freedman might by the indulgence or ignorance of society be referred to by his patron's *cognomen*. No evidence supports either of these hypotheses.

[11] Goetz (*RE* i. 2. 2618) dated him to ? 114–64 B.C.   [12] *Gram.* 7.

rescued, trained, and later manumitted by a Roman.[1] There is nothing to show whether he was a native of Cisalpina or Narbonensis, but his birth will have been outweighed by the fact that, like Terence, he had a Graeco-Roman education.[2] The identity of his patron remains obscure, but, as he was always closely connected with the Julii Caesares, the Antonius in question probably belongs to the branch related to that family. Gnipho's character and talent brought him great success.[3] When Caesar was a boy, Gnipho taught him in his house, probably taking other pupils too at the same time, as the slave Chilon had done at the house of Cato,[4] and as Verrius Flaccus did later at that of Augustus.[5] Later, he taught in his own home, giving lessons in rhetoric as well as grammar, and counting among his pupils orators as advanced in their studies as was Cicero in 66 B.C. His writings were exhaustive and learned.[6]

In 83 B.C., or thereabouts, an unusually interesting consignment of slaves arrived in Rome, probably from Antioch. The ship contained Staberius Eros, the grammarian, and two cousins later to become famous as the astronomer Manilius and the mimographer Publilius. The cousins were Syrians and presumably mere boys at the time. Very likely Staberius was a Syrian too, but was already a scholar.[7] The identity of his patron is not known—conceivably he was a miser Staberius, mentioned by Horace.[8] Among his pupils were Brutus and Cassius,[9] and he taught the children of the

---

[1] Such slavery was illegal: technically Gnipho was thus an *ingenuus*, but could not establish it. See Watson, *Law of Persons*, p. 171.

[2] On the culture of southern Gaul, see Suet. *Gram.* 3; Syme, *Tacitus*, ii, pp. 608 ff. Also A. Gwynn, *Roman Education from Cicero to Quintilian* (Oxford, 1926), p. 93.

[3] 'fuisse dicitur ingenii magni, memoriae singularis, nec minus Graece quam Latine doctus; praeterea comi facilique natura, nec umquam de mercede pactus, eoque plura ex liberalitate discentium consecutus' (Suet. *Gram.* 7).

[4] Plut. *Cato Maj.* 20. 3.   [5] Suet. *Gram.* 17.

[6] Ibid. 7. He is cited on a question of vocabulary by Quintilian (i. 6. 23) and Macrobius (iii. 12. 8), and credited with a commentary on the *Annales* of Ennius (Schol. Bern. *ad* Verg. *Georg.* ii. 119).

[7] Suet. *Gram.* 13. Staberius was '*suomet aere* emptus de catasta et propter litterarum studium manumissus'. Buckland, *Slavery*, p. 637, n. 2, explains this as meaning that he promised to pay for his liberty out of his future earnings and thus bought his manumission. But the text is corrupt and such a hypothesis should not be built on the two words which are insecure emendation.

[8] *Sat.* ii. 3. 84.

[9] The former born probably in 85 B.C. and the latter rather earlier.

proscribed free of charge. Either, therefore, he achieved success very soon after his arrival in Rome, or Suetonius is slightly inaccurate and Eros' concession to the sons of the proscribed belongs to any time in the considerable period after the proscriptions in which their effects continued to be felt.

L. Licinius Tyrannio was an eminent grammarian of Amisus before he was captured by Lucullus in 68-66 B.C. and transferred to Rome. For this reason, he stands out among the majority of his colleagues, with the possible exception of Eros. When Tyrannio was taken, Murena asked Lucullus to give him the prisoner, whom he at once freed, to the indignation of his chief, who thought that a man of such distinction should never have been regarded as a slave, 'for the giving of a seeming freedom was the taking away of an existing freedom'.[1] As *libertus* of Murena, Tyrannio was perhaps obliged to go to Rome, perhaps found it expedient; our evidence gives no trace of his ever performing *operae* for his patron. Rather, he appears as an independent scholar performing services for a number of Romans and making a large fortune in the process. He was engaged in arranging the books of Apellicon, including the manuscripts of Aristotle and Theophrastus.[2] He collected a vast number of books himself.[3] He helped the Cicerones with their libraries, arranging that of M. Cicero at Antium in 56 B.C.,[4] and in 54 B.C. supplying or selecting books for Q. Cicero's new collection.[5] Whether he himself acted as dealer is not certain, but he saw to the repair of Marcus' books, so it is likely that he organized the copying of manuscripts for Quintus. In 56 B.C. he was also tutor to Quintus' son.[6] Ten years later, M. Cicero was present when he gave a reading of one of his works, on accents.[7] His learning was wide: Cicero cites his authority on a matter of geography,[8] and Caesar suggested to him the subject of a monograph on metre.[9] It may also be remarked that, after starting with Lucullus and Murena, he continued to frequent the most cultured and aristocratic Roman society.

[1] Plut. *Lucull.* 19. 7.
[2] Plut. *Sulla* 26; Strabo, xiii. 609.
[3] *Suda*, s.v. Tyrannio, says more than 30,000, which sounds implausible.
[4] Cic. *Att.* iv. 4 a.
[5] Cic. *QF* iii. 4. 5; iii. 5. 6.
[6] Cic. *QF* ii. 4. 2.
[7] Cic. *Att.* xii. 2. 2; xii. 6. 2.
[8] Ibid. ii. 6. 1.
[9] *Suda*, s.v. scolion.

LEARNED PROFESSIONS AND FINE ARTS 117

The earliest Latin *rhetor* described by Suetonius was also probably a freedman. Rhetoric was, as we have seen, taught by some of the *grammatici*, but as an independent subject it had difficulty in establishing itself at Rome. When Rome acquired her empire, oratory came to be much in demand,[1] but, as the science of rhetoric was a Greek study, rhetoric at Rome too was taught in Greek. The Romans listened to Greek orators, and acquired technical knowledge from professors of rhetoric in Greek towns and *peregrini* in Rome, and also, no doubt, from Greek slaves and freedmen in their own households. The schools which Greeks established in Rome were banned in 161 B.C.,[2] but later Roman orators had the benefit of Greek teachers.[3] By the beginning of the first century, Latin *rhetores* had begun to open schools. They were expelled by the censors in 92 B.C., on the grounds that the innovation was undesirable.[4] Crassus, one of the censors, is pictured by Cicero as explaining his action by alleging that the new rhetoricians were not men of sufficient culture to carry out the delicate work of adapting Greek science to Latin.[5] Cicero himself, who here prophesied the future glory of Latin oratory, had in his youth wished to attend the classes of L. Plotius Gallus, one of these Latin teachers, but was dissuaded by learned men, who believed Greek to be a better mental discipline.[6] How well he succeeded in Greek oratory we know from his biographer.[7] The situation thus was that the most eminent rhetoricians taught in Greek and were Greeks, generally living in the east. When Cicero wanted advanced training, he naturally went to the provinces, to study under Xenocles of Adramyttium, Dionysius of Magnesia, and Apollonius of Rhodes (who knew no Latin).[8] Caesar, too, it will be remembered, was a pupil of

---

[1] Cic. *de Or.* i. 14.   [2] Suet. *Rhet.* 1; Gell. xv. 11.
[3] e.g. Diophanes of Mitylene, the tutor of Ti. Gracchus (Plut. *Ti. Gracch.* 8. 4).
[4] Suet. *Rhet.* 1.
[5] *de Or.* iii. 95: 'quamquam non haec ita statuo atque decerno, ut desperem Latine ea, de quibus disputavimus, tradi ac perpoliri *posse*, patitur enim et lingua nostra et natura rerum veterem illam excellentemque prudentiam Graecorum ad nostrum usum moremque transferri, sed hominibus opus est eruditis, qui adhuc in hoc quidem genere nostri nulli fuerunt; sin quando exstiterint, etiam Graecis erunt anteponendi'.
[6] Suet. *Rhet.* 2. Cf. Cic. *Opt. Gen. Or.* 18; *Part. Or.* 1 f.; *Brut.* 310; *Off.* i. 1.
[7] Plut. *Cic.* 4. 4 f.   [8] Ibid. 4. 4.

Apollonius.[1] Cicero, when he speaks of 'rhetorum principes', mentions freeborn Greeks, including the eminent teachers listed by Plutarch,[2] and makes it clear that their Latin-speaking opposite numbers were not professional rhetoricians in Rome, but the great advocates and orators, such as Cotta and Hortensius.[3] This explains why the professional teaching of rhetoric in Rome was connected with freedmen and despised: the best professional teachers were based on Greek lands, while the best-qualified Latin orators were nor professional rhetoricians.

Cur igitur ius civile docere semper pulchrum fuit hominumque clarissimorum discipulis floruerunt domus: ad dicendum si quis acuat aut adiuvet in eo iuventutem, vituperetur? Nam si vitiosum est dicere ornate, pellatur omnino e civitate eloquentia; sin ea non modo eos ornat penes quos est, sed etiam iuvat universam rem publicam, cur aut discere turpe est quod scire honestum est aut quod posse pulcherrimum est id non gloriosum est docere?[4]

Voltacilius Plotus is, however, the only certain freedman mentioned in Suetonius' damaged monograph.[5] The author does not vouch for the tradition that he had been a chained door-keeper as a slave, and then freed because of his scholastic ability and enthusiasm.[6] He is also said to have spoken in support of his patron in a case where the latter prosecuted, so he may have had experience of advocacy as well as theoretical oratory, which he then took up as a career. He taught Pompey, who became a second patron[7] to him, it seems, for he wrote the *Res Gestae* of Pompeius Strabo and of Magnus himself. From this special relationship seems to have arisen the statement of Jerome that Plotus was Pompey's own freedman, which the *nomen* shows to be erroneous.[8] According to

[1] Suet. *DJ* 4. 1.   [2] Cic. *Brut.* 316, cf. Plut. *Cic.* 4.
[3] *Brut.* 317. Cf. *Sen.* 29.
[4] Cic. *Orator*, 142. Cf. Sen. *Controv.* ii. *pr.* 5: 'Ante illum (sc. Rubellium Blandum) intra libertinos praeceptores pulcherrimae disciplinae continebantur et minime probabili more turpe erat docere quod honestum erat discere.'
On the introduction of rhetoric to Rome, see M. L. Clarke, *Rhetoric at Rome, A Historical Survey* (London, 1953), pp. 10 ff. On the distinction between noble orators and paid *rhetores* as teachers, see De Robertis, *Lavoro*, pp. 61 ff.
[5] Suet. *Rhet.* 3.   [6] 'ob ingenium ac studium litterarum'.
[7] Cf. pp. 223 f.
[8] At any rate it was not Pompeius. The form of the name is disputed. For the most recent discussion, see R. G. Lewis, *CR* N.S. 16 (1966), 271 ff., who is inclined to accept the identification of the rhetorician with the Pitholaus of Suet.

Nepos, Plotus was the first freedman to write history, previously the preserve of the ruling classes.[1] A better attested Pompeian literary freedman was Pompeius Lenaeus, who accompanied his patron on nearly all his campaigns and, after Pompey and his sons were dead, dedicated himself to teaching (in a school in the *Carinae* near the house of Pompey), and to the defence of his patron's memory. He avenged a criticism of Pompey by Sallust with a scathing attack on Sallust's character and literary style, but not, it seems, with a reasoned defence of Pompey.[2] The tradition is confused about his origin.[3]

In the cultured circles in which Cicero moved, freedmen appeared frequently as literary collaborators or as authors and scholars in their own right. The deliberate education of slaves for such positions may be seen in the case of Tiro, Cicero's secretary, research assistant, and later editor and anthologizer,[4] and the literary training of a slave-boy is mentioned for a freedman of Q. Cicero.[5] Another of Cicero's *liberti*, Laurea, was a poet.[6] Atticus, in connection with his publishing business, kept a staff of scholars, among whom the exceptionally learned M. Pomponius Dionysius is known to us in some detail. Cicero's estimates of his scholarship and character fluctuated. In 55 B.C., when he was manumitted, and

---

DJ 75 and Macrob. *Sat.* ii. 2. 13, who wrote lampoons against Caesar and whose name Lewis shows reason to think was M'. Otacilius, not M. Votacilius or Voltacilius. (He makes a curious slip in asserting that the pamphleteer's name was M'. Otacilius M'. Pitholaus, for he believes that Pitholaus was a freedman.) But, although the manuscripts of Macrobius and Suetonius *de Rhetoribus* may be corrupt, I still think that it is strange that Suetonius should not mention in the *de Rhetoribus* the attack on Caesar, if he knew that the *rhetor* and the pamphleteer were one and the same. I prefer not to accept the identification.

[1] Suet. *Rhet.* 3.

[2] Suet. *Gram.* 15. The scholiast on Juv. i. 20 mentions a 'Lenius' who wrote satires and is probably to be identified with Lenaeus. Perhaps, then, his attack on Sallust was not an isolated effort. Lenaeus is also known to have been given by Pompey the job of translating the works on poisons found in the collection of Mithridates (Pliny, *NH* xxxv. 5).

[3] Suet. *Gram.* 15 records a tale that Lenaeus was kidnapped and enslaved, but escaped to return to his native land (Athens, on the emendation of Heinsius) to study, and later offered his patron the price of his freedom, but was freed 'ob ingenium atque doctrinam'. Little reliance can be placed on this. Schol. Juv. i. 20 says Lenius was from Aurunca, which could easily be a mistake because it was the town of Lucilius.

[4] Appendix III, pp. 259 ff.

[5] Philologus, allegedly the betrayer of his patron (Plut. *Cic.* 48. 2).

[6] Appendix 3, p. 259.

given the *praenomen* of Marcus in compliment to Cicero, Dionysius was high in his favour.[1] He helped Cicero in his studies[2] and tutored young Marcus and Quintus.[3] In 50 B.C. the first signs of trouble appeared: his pupils complained of his bad temper, but Cicero disregarded them. He considered Dionysius 'doctum... sanctum, plenum officii, studiosum etiam meae laudis, frugi hominem, ac ne libertinum laudare videar, plane virum bonum'.[4] But at the outbreak of civil war, Dionysius became reluctant to perform his 'duties'. He parried Cicero's request that he accompany his pupils on the flight from Rome, when a learned man and a friend might have been expected to agree.[5] Cicero was so irritated that he told Atticus that Dionysius had been such a bad tutor that he himself had had to teach the boys in order to cover up the freedman's deficiencies.[6] 'Ego autem illum male sanum semper putavi, nunc etiam impurum et sceleratum puto, nec tamen mihi inimiciorem quam sibi.'[7] Through the smoke-screen set up by Cicero, we can see the difficult situation in which Dionysius found himself. He had to serve two masters, but also maintain cordial relations with both, sending polite greetings to one while working with the other.[8] Besides this, he had his own life to run.[9] The exact nature of his position as a dependent of Cicero is not clarified: possibly he was paid, but Cicero neglects such mundane details and concentrates on the bond of 'officium'. There seems to have been no question of Dionysius' being bound to work for his patron's friend as part of his *operae*. Cicero could exert no pressure on him,[10] nor did he ask Atticus to use his influence.[11] It appears that the work he did for Cicero was purely voluntary and depended on the convenience of both parties.[12] We might guess that compensation was casual[13] and took the form of keep, presents, books, money perhaps in lump sums.[14] It took the tact and devotion of a Tiro to manage such

[1] Cic. *Att.* iv. 15. 1.
[2] Ibid. iv. 8. 2.
[3] Ibid. iv. 18. 5; vi. 1. 12.
[4] Ibid. vii. 4. 1.
[5] 'doctus homo et amicus' (ibid. vii. 18. 3).
[6] Ibid. viii. 4. 1 f.
[7] Ibid. ix. 15. 5.
[8] Ibid. v. 9. 3; vii. 7. 1; vii. 4. 1; vii. 8. 1, etc.
[9] Ibid. viii. 10.
[10] Ibid. vii. 18. 3.
[11] Ibid. x. 2. 2.
[12] Ibid. xiii. 2, etc.
[13] As it seems to have been for Tiro (pp. 146 f.).
[14] Cf. Schulz, *Principles*, ch. xi *passim*, especially pp. 236 ff., on the informal guarantees provided by *amicitia* and *fides*.

a situation successfully with a patron as demanding and quick to take offence as Cicero—and Dionysius was as hasty as his employer: 'solet eum, cum aliquid furiose fecit, paenitere.'[1]

Licinius Apollonius, freedman of the younger P. Crassus, was apparently more successful as a literary hanger-on. Brought up from boyhood to study, he was an assiduous visitor at Cicero's house while the Stoic Diodotus lived there.[2] P. Crassus himself was highly cultivated,[3] and Apollonius, at least according to Cicero's skilful commendatory letter to Caesar, was devoted both to Crassus and to his patron's studious interests and so was much beloved by him.[4] After Crassus' death at Carrhae, Apollonius devoted himself to the cultivation of his patron's friends, among them Caesar and Cicero. He visited the latter in Cilicia, and Caesar actually during the Alexandrian campaign, making himself useful. Finally, he decided to write the *Res Gestae* of Caesar in Greek, and Cicero sent him off to Spain with a letter of recommendation. The way in which a freelance libertine scholar could work is clearly seen here. Cultivation—in some cases, toadying—of the right influential Romans secured employment, position, and financial rewards. The bestowal of immortality on Caesar would certainly merit more than another letter of commendation to carry back to Rome.[5]

The brothers C. and Ap. Claudius were, with other noble youths of the day, pupils of L. Ateius Philologus, alias Praetextatus, a grammarian and rhetorician.[6] He accompanied them to their provinces.[7] His own patron was probably L. Ateius L. f., son of a Sullan centurion and himself a *praetorius* and father of the jurist Capito,[8] who remarked, apparently as a compliment, that Philologus was a rhetorician among grammarians and a grammarian among rhetoricians. Suetonius says that he was born in Athens[9] and attended

---

[1] Cic. *Att.* viii. 5. 1.   [2] Till his death in 59 B.C.
[3] Cic. *Brut.* 282.
[4] Cic. *Fam.* xiii. 16. 1: 'erat enim et studiosus Crassi et ad eius optima studia vehementer aptus, itaque ab eo admodum diligebatur.'
[5] The same method of earning a living imposed itself on freeborn scholars too.
[6] Suet. *Gram.* 10.
[7] Asia in 55–53 B.C.; Cilicia in 53–51 B.C.   [8] *Cos. suff.* A.D. 5.
[9] Greek origin would account for the fact that, in a letter, Philologus put Latin literature as his 'second subject' after Greek (Suet. *Gram.* 10).

the classes of Antonius Gnipho. Perhaps he was a prisoner of the Sullan war. He was active at least until 29 B.C., for he was on familiar terms first with Sallust and then with Pollio, and is said to have supplied the former with a summary of Roman history,[1] from which to choose subjects. Pollio alleged that he collected old-fashioned words and expressions[2] for Sallust, but this Suetonius wisely rejects, as Philologus advised Pollio himself to avoid any obscure and unnatural locutions. But his anthology 'omnis generis', as he vaguely entitled it, was certainly a happy hunting-ground for anyone in search of archaisms.[3] If neither Suetonius nor his text is at fault, this 'Hyle' comprised eight hundred books. Such, no doubt, were the qualifications for adopting the surname Philologus.[4]

Valerius Cato, grammarian and poet of great repute, was said by some writers to be the freedman of a certain Bursenus from Gaul, and it seems that he was perhaps an *ingenuus*, illegally enslaved as a boy, as he claimed,[5] but who may not have succeeded in establishing his claim to freeborn, not freed status. Probably he was Italian[6] and Transpadana is meant. Cato taught and wrote books of grammar and poetry, his most-praised poems being the *Lydia* and the *Diana*. His circle included the poets Ticidas, Cinna, and Bibaculus,[7] and apparently also Memmius, Anser, and Cornificius.[8] Ovid lists him with Catullus and Calvus and the innovators.[9]

In a different field of literary endeavour, Publilius the Syrian,[10] whose arrival in Rome has already been mentioned,[11] flourished during the years of Caesar's dictatorship. According to Macrobius,[12] the young slave won the favour of his master's patron[13] by his ready wit and was consequently freed and carefully educated. He began

[1] 'breviarium rerum omnium Romanarum'.
[2] 'praecepta de ratione scribendi'.
[3] e.g. Festus, s.v. 'nuscitiosum'.
[4] 'quia multiplici variaque doctrina censebatur'.
[5] Suet. *Gram*. 11: 'ipse libello cui est titulus "Indignatio" ingenuum se natum ait et pupillum relictum eoque facilius licentia Sullani temporis exutum patrimonio.'
[6] Cf. M. Aurius (Cic. *Cluent*. 21); 'Cei uxor' (Cic. *Cluent*. 162).
[7] Suet. *Gram*. 11. [8] Ovid, *Trist*. ii. 437.
[9] See G. L. Hendrickson, *CP* 11 (1916), 249 ff.
[10] 'Syrus' was not, it seems, a *cognomen*.
[11] p. 115. [12] ii. 7. 6.
[13] Skutsch (*RE* xxiii. 2. 1920) suggested this could be Publilius, father of Cicero's second wife.

LEARNED PROFESSIONS AND FINE ARTS 123

to compose mimes, which he produced in the towns of Italy, until he made his début in the capital at the games of 46 or 45 B.C. Here even Cicero[1] saw his mimes, which were appreciated by the people and by Caesar himself more than those of the acknowledged master of the art, Laberius.[2] His influence remained strong enough for his moral effect to be discussed by Seneca[3] and for many of his brief, pithy, and often witty *sententiae* to survive.[4]

Q. Caecilius Epirota[5] was born at Tusculum, possibly even at Cicero's home there, for he was a slave of Atticus. His manumission occurred after Atticus' adoption by Caecilius in 58 B.C.,[6] but we do not know when. He taught Attica, apparently after her marriage to Agrippa in 30 or 29 B.C., but was suspected of unprofessional conduct. He then transferred himself to Cornelius Gallus and lived with him in such intimacy that he gave grounds for one of the most serious charges levelled at the former favourite by Augustus. After Gallus' death he opened a school, but, by contrast with many *grammatici*, took only young boys as pupils, and was responsible for the innovation of giving extempore Latin disputations and using contemporary poets such as Virgil as school texts. A contemporary, Timagenes of Alexandria, who had been captured by Gabinius in 55 B.C.[7] and was later freed,[8] became the friend of Antony[9] and Octavian,[10] taught rhetoric and wrote an account of Octavian's 'acta'. He later enjoyed the patronage of Pollio.[11]

The early part of Augustus' reign gave freedmen new opportunities in the deliberate encouragement of scholarship and literature by the *princeps*. Theodorus of Gadara, the freedman tutor of Tiberius,[12] enjoyed the patronage of Augustus and perhaps rose to the post of procurator in Sicily.[13] His scholarly works

[1] Cic. *Fam.* xii. 18. 2.
[2] Macrob. *Sat.* ii. 7. 6; Gell. xvii. 14.
[3] *Controv.* vii. 3. 8.
[4] Ed. Bickford-Smith.
[5] Suet. *Gram.* 16.
[6] Cic. *Att.* iii. 20. 1.
[7] *Suda* s.v. Timagenes.
[8] His *nomen* and patron are unknown, though he is said by *Suda* to have been sold to Faustus Sulla, who may have freed him.
[9] Plut. *Ant.* 72.
[10] Sen. *Controv.* x. 5. 22; *Ira*, iii. 23. 4 f.
[11] See G. W. Bowersock, *Augustus and the Greek World* (Oxford, 1965), pp. 109 f.
[12] *Suda* s.v. Theodorus.
[13] Cf. Bowersock, *Augustus and the Greek World*, p. 40.

included a monograph on Gadara, rhetoric, and history.[1] M. Verrius Flaccus, *libertus* of an unknown patron, attracted Augustus' attention by the success of his teaching methods and was appointed tutor to C. and L. Caesar. He took his old pupils with him to the Palatine, but was not allowed to admit new ones. His salary was 100,000 sesterces a year.[2]

The career of L. Crassicius Pasicles, a freedman from Tarentum who changed his name to Pansa, was very different. He began as an assistant to the writers of mimes, then set up a school and won fame by a commentary on the *Zmyrna*, thus gaining pupils of rank as high as Iullus Antonius, and bidding fair to rival Verrius Flaccus. But he abandoned his school in order to take up philosophy.[3]

An ex-slave and pupil of Orbilius and freedman of Scribonia the wife of Octavian was also a teacher and attacked Verrius Flaccus' book *De Orthographia*.[4] Hyginus,[5] a prisoner of war from one of Caesar's campaigns, who had been a pupil of Cornelius Alexander Polyhistor,[6] the historian, was freed by Augustus and put in charge of the Palatine library. He also taught and wrote many works, including one on bees which was used as a source by Virgil, commentaries on Virgil himself, and books on subjects as diverse as geography, the gods, Trojan families.[7] He was a great friend of Ovid and also of Clodius Licinus, the suffect consul of A.D. 4, and an historian. Hyginus had a freedman of his own trained in the same work.[8] Melissus,[9] a freeborn Italian, disowned by his parents and educated and given by his *nutritor* to Maecenas, was soon manumitted and enjoyed the patronage also of Augustus, who gave him the job of arranging the library in the Portico of Octavia. He compiled a collection of 'Ineptiae', and also wrote

---

[1] *F.G.H.* iii. c. 850.
[2] Suet. *Gram.* 17. For the salary compare the earnings of Remmius Palaemon (ibid. 23), 400,000 sesterces from a school and as much again from investment.
[3] Suet. *Gram.* 18.   [4] Ibid. 19.
[5] Ibid. 20. Sources differ as to whether he came from Spain or Alexandria.
[6] Ibid. 20. Alexander was a Greek *grammaticus*. According to *Suda*, s.v. Ἀλέξανδρος ὁ Μιλήσιος, he was a prisoner of the Mithridatic War and a slave tutor of Lentulus. The *nomen* Cornelius, which is attested also by Pliny, *NH* iii. 124, etc., shows that he was freed, presumably by Lentulus. For his historical and geographical works see Schwartz in *RE* 1. 2. 1449 ff.
[7] See Tolkiehn, *RE* xi. 628 ff.; Colum. *RR* i. 1. 13; Gell. 1. 21, vii. 6, etc.
[8] Suet. *Gram.* 20.   [9] Ibid. 21.

comedies, of a new type, called *trabeatae*. A freedman of Augustus himself was the poet Phaedrus, born in Thrace,[1] probably towards the end of the first century B.C., sent to Rome as a slave and freed by Augustus.[2] He wrote fables in imitation of Aesop, adapting and translating, and was exiled after offending Sejanus, because he introduced bold themes of his own.[3] In the same circles of imperial dependents, we may include the Younger Tyrannio,[4] a Phoenician slave, who took his name from his teacher Tyrannio the Elder, discarding his own name of Diocles. Captured in the wars of Antony and Octavian, he had been bought by a freedman of the latter, who gave him as a present to Terentia.[5] After his mistress had freed him, Tyrannio taught in Rome and wrote a large number of scholarly works.[6]

In the profession of philosophy, the position for freedmen was much the same as it was for rhetoric. The centre for philosophical studies was still Athens and it was there that a Roman went to pursue his education in this field.[7] At Rhodes, the great Stoic Posidonius taught Cicero and Caesar.[8] Greek philosophers from Panaetius the Stoic[9] onwards visited Italy and were teachers and sometimes clients of Roman nobles. In spite of the originally hostile attitude[10] to Greek philosophers in Rome, lectures had been given in 155 B.C. by Critolaus the Peripatetic, Carneades the Academic, and Diogenes the Stoic, sent as ambassadors.[11] Philo of Larisa,

[1] Phaedr. 44. 17 (ed. Alice Brenot, Budé).
[2] According to ancient manuscripts of his poems.
[3] Phaedr. 43. 7; 15 ff.
[4] *Suda* s.v. Tyrannio.
[5] Whom *Suda* identifies with the wife of Cicero. A. Hillscher, *Hominum Litteratorum Graecorum ante Tiberii mortem in urbe Roma commoratorum historia critica* (Leipzig, 1891), p. 315, suspects that this is a gloss and that the lady should be the wife of Maecenas, which is plausible. *Contra*, Wendel in *RE* viii. A. 2. 1819 f.
[6] Listed fully in *RE* viii. A. 2. 1819 f.
[7] e.g. Cicero studied in Athens under Antiochus of Ascalon, head of the Academy, in 79 B.C. (Plut. *Cic*. 4. 1); Cic. *Fam*. ix. 8. 1; *Acad*. i. 1; *Legg*. i. 54; *Brut*. 315); Brutus attended the lectures of Theomnestus the Academic (Plut. *Brut*. 24) and Cratippus the Peripatetic (ibid.) in 44 B.C. Young M. Cicero was with Cratippus (Cic. *Fam*. xii. 16. 2; xvi. 21. 3, 5).
[8] Plut. *Cic*. 4. 4; *Pomp*. 42. 5; Cic. *Acad*. i. 13.
[9] Cic. *de Or*. i. 45, etc.
[10] They had been expelled in 173 and 161 B.C. (Suet. *Rhet*. 1; Gell. xv. 11. 1).
[11] Cic. *de Or*. ii. 155, etc.

head of the Academy, visited Rome in 88 B.C. and Cicero was among his pupils.[1] Other, less eminent, philosophers established themselves at Rome, generally in the household or at least the circle of some Roman patron. Diodotus the Stoic was an inmate of Cicero's house, and received pupils there.[2] Philodemus the Epicurean, 'Graecus atque advena,' actually from Gadara, was a friend of Piso Caesoninus.[3] Cato was surrounded by Greek philosophers: Antipater of Tyre;[4] Apollonides, who was with him at Utica;[5] Athenodorus, whom he had visited in about 67 B.C. at Pergamum, and who was later in Rome and often with him[6]—all these were Stoics—and the Peripatetic Demetrius, who was also at Utica.[7] Augustus too had an impressive collection of philosophers in his circle, the Stoic Athenodorus, his tutor,[8] and later his friends ('contubernales'), Areius, Dionysius, and Nicanor.[9]

These men were free *peregrini*. The contribution of Italy to philosophy was small. There was a school at Naples, from which came Staseas, the first Peripatetic to take up residence at Rome, who lived with M. Pupius Piso,[10] and Aeschines, who went to the Academy.[11] But Naples was the centre of Greek culture in Italy.[12] Native Italian philosophers are represented only by such men as P. Nigidius Figulus, the Pythagorean,[13] C. Amafinius, a writer on Epicureanism,[14] and Catius the Insubrian, whose attempts to popularize Epicureanism were notably clumsy[15] These were not, of course, professional teachers.

[1] Plut. *Cic.* 3. 1. Cf. Cic. *Brut.* 306; *Acad.* i. 13; *Fam.* ix. 8. 1.
[2] Cic. *Att.* ii. 20. 6—his death in 59 B.C. Cf. *Fam.* xiii. 16. 4; *Acad.* i. 13, ii. 115; *Brut.* 309; *Tusc.* v. 113.
[3] Cic. *Pis.* 68 ff. Cf. R. G. M. Nisbet's edition, App. III; Bowersock, *Augustus and the Greek World*, pp. 32 ff., 39 f.
[4] Plut. *Cato Min.* 4.   [5] Ibid.. 65. 5; 66. 4; 69.
[6] Ibid. 10; 14. 1.   [7] Ibid. 65. 5; 69.
[8] Strabo, 675. Cf. Cic. *Fam.* iii. 7. 5; *Att.* xvi. 11. 4, 14. 4.
[9] Suet. *DA* 89. 1. Cf. Bowersock, *Augustus and the Greek World*, pp. 342 f.; 38 ff.; 123.
[10] (*cos.* 61 B.C.) Cic. *de Or.* i. 104.
[11] Cic. *de Or.* i. 45.   [12] Suet. *Vita Verg.* 11.
[13] *Praet.* 58 B.C., exiled, died in 45 B.C. He was thought the most learned Roman after Varro (Gell. iv. 9. 1).
[14] Cic. *Fam.* xv. 19. 2; *Tusc.* ii. 6 f.; iv. 7; *Fin.* iii. 40.
[15] Cic. *Fam.* xv. 16. 1, 19. Catius had translated εἴδωλα as 'spectra'. Cf. Quint. x. 1. 124 on his writings. Possibly he is the Catius of Hor. *Sat.* ii. 4 (cf. Wickham ad loc.).

Some freedmen were able to take an interest in philosophy: we are told that Aurelius Opilius, the freedman of an Epicurean, had taught it,[1] and L. Crassicus Pansa gave up his school to become a pupil of the Stoic Q. Sextius.[2] But Opilius gave up teaching philosophy in favour of rhetoric, and it is clear that this part of higher education was adequately catered for, as far as the aristocracy was concerned, by study abroad and with freeborn Greeks at home. At the same time, the demand was being met by Romans in books which adapted Greek philosophy for Rome, such attempts at popularization as those of Nigidius and Catius, and by other similar writers of other schools, at least 'rustici Stoici'.[3] The large contribution of Cicero himself was the most successful attempt to interpret Greek thought for the practical Roman; Varro and Lucretius too represent the best of this vogue.

The physical sciences at this time were largely neglected in favour of linguistic studies,[4] but philosophy of course covered much physical inquiry. P. Nigidius Figulus was interested in physics and astronomy. The latter was the most important science, as theories of the universe formed an important part of the dogmas of the schools, especially the Stoics, Epicureans, and Pythagoreans.[5] The Syrian freedman, Manilius, was an astronomer and probably the father or grandfather of the author of the *Astronomica*,[6] Caesar was able to gather a committee to work on the reform of the calendar.[7] Astronomy was generally confused with astrology, and this pseudoscience was very popular in the late Republic, despite the opposition of such sceptics as Cicero,[8] and became firmly entrenched under Augustus.[9] As on the higher plane it was the

[1] p. 114.
[2] Suet. *Gram.* 18. On Sextius, see von Arnim in *RE* ii A. 2. 2040 f., who shows that he was a freeborn Roman.
[3] Cic. *Fam.* xv. 19. 1.
[4] Cic. *Tusc.* i. 5: 'in summo apud illos (sc. Graecos) honore geometria fuit, itaque nihil mathematicis inlustrius; at nos metiendi ratiocinandique utilitate huius artis terminavimus modum'.
[5] Cf. Cramer, *Astrology in Roman Law and Politics* (Philadelphia, 1954), *passim*, especially pp. 3 ff., 44 ff.
[6] Pliny, *NH* xxxv. 199.
[7] The members were distinguished philosophers and mathematicians (Plut. *Caes.* 59. 3). Sosigenes was to be given the greatest share of the credit (Pliny, *NH* xviii. 210 ff.). He was presumably a *peregrinus*.
[8] Cic. *Div. passim*.
[9] See Cramer, *Astrology*, pp. 82 ff.

concern of philosophers, freedmen were almost excluded, although they could become soothsayers and *magi*. We hear of several in the latter class,[1] but there are no known freedmen practising as *astrologi* or *mathematici*, as they were called by post-Augustan writers. Geography also had an appeal in this period, and we know of several geographers besides Strabo, a freedman representative being the polymath Tyrannio of Amisus.[2]

In the lower stages of education, as elementary teachers, *litteratores*, and *grammatici*, freedmen played the most important part. But all *grammatici* were not 'illustres' like those treated by Suetonius. Most were poorly paid and not particularly respected.[3] *Rhetores* were often poor, and the most eminent of them were not the freedmen who taught in Italy, but free Greeks in the great centres of culture in the eastern empire, while much of the work which might have been done by freedmen in Rome was taken over by practising Roman orators, who took pupils into their households as Scaevola did Cicero,[4] and Cicero did Caelius,[5] and by treatises based on Greek teaching, such as the *ad Herennium* and the works of Cicero himself. Philosophy in the same way was taught by free Greeks, and dealt with in the writings of Romans. In literature, freedmen made their contribution in the persons of Andronicus, Statius, Terence, Publilius, Melissus, Phaedrus, and perhaps Valerius Cato, but once Greek culture had ceased to be the prerogative of foreigners, they were outshone by *ingenui*. This may have been to the advantage of literature, oratory, and thought, which were thus preserved from the dry-as-dust scholasticism evident in the methods of the rhetorical schools later and the linguistic studies of the *grammatici*, the atmosphere of an education far removed from everyday life and feeling, and even from the practical demands of Roman law.

---

[1] Including L. Tarutius of Firmum, on whom Cicero poured scorn (*Div.* ii. 98; cf. Plut. *Quaest. Rom.* 273 B.) and Theogenes at Apollonia, who astounded the young Octavius in 44 B.C. (Suet. *DA* 94. 12).
[2] Cic. *Att.* ii. 6. 1.
[3] Cf. H.-I. Marrou, *Histoire de l'éducation dans l'antiquité* (Paris, 1948), pp. 380 f.
[4] Plut. *Cic.* 3. 1. [5] Cic. *Cael.* 9.

(b) Doctors

Medicine in Rome relied on Greek science and almost all its practitioners were Greeks. In fact, the profession was held in contempt as being un-Roman.[1] The Elder Cato's views on the Greek doctor were notorious: 'nequissimum et indocile genus illorum et hoc puta vatem dixisse: quandoque ista gens suas litteras dabit, omnia corrumpet, tum etiam magis si medicos suos huc mittet.'[2] Cicero, however, mentions medicine, with architecture and teaching, as professions honourable to those of suitable rank.[3] He neither despised doctors nor objected to the practice of medicine by men of the proper station. Other Romans too favoured members of the profession: Crassus the orator,[4] Caesar,[5] and, of course, Augustus.[6]

But Roman *ingenui* did not normally practise medicine in republican and early imperial times, in spite of the change of opinion since the days of Cato the Censor. According to Pliny, this art alone, of those invented by Greece, had not as yet been practised by Romans.[7] Doctors such as Antistius,[8] A. Rupilius,[9] L. Tuccius,[10] are more likely therefore to have been enfranchised aliens or freedmen, not freeborn Romans.[11]

More than any other liberal profession, medicine attracted Greek *peregrini* to Rome and Italy.[12] The science was first put on its feet by a Greek doctor, Asclepiades,[13] much as visiting scholars had given the impetus to grammar and philosophy. He was the friend of Crassus[14] and teacher of Antonius Musa.[15] Octavian's doctor, M. Artorius Asclepiades, was another *peregrinus*, probably from Smyrna.[16] Ingenuous Greeks appear quite often as personal doctors

---

[1] Pliny, *NH* xxix. 17.
[2] Pliny, *NH* xxix. 14.
[3] *Off.* i. 151: 'iis quorum ordini conveniunt honestae'.
[4] Cic. *de Or.* i. 62.
[5] Suet. *DJ* 42.
[6] Suet. *DA* 59; Dio, liii. 30.
[7] *NH* xxix. 17: 'solam hanc artium Graecarum nondum exercet Romana gravitas.' Not to be taken *au pied de la lettre*.
[8] Suet. *DJ* 82.
[9] Cic. *Cluent.* 176.
[10] Pliny, *NH* vii. 183.
[11] See K. H. Below, *Der Arzt im römischen Recht* (Munich, 1953), p. 20.
[12] Below, *Der Arzt*, pp. 21 f.
[13] See T. C. Allbutt, *Greek Medicine in Rome* (London, 1921), pp. 177 ff.
[14] Cic. *de Or.* i. 62.
[15] Pliny, *NH* xxix. 6.
[16] Plut. *Brut.* 41; cf. *CIG* 3285; 2283.

in the service of Romans, for instance the doctors of Verres, Artemidorus of Perga,[1] and of M. Antonius' young son, Philotas of Amphissa.[2] But *peregrini* needed encouragement if they were to settle in Rome. Julius Caesar offered the franchise to any who would do so.[3] Augustus later, in gratitude to Musa, gave exemption from taxes to doctors in perpetuity, and this will have affected non-citizens in the provinces.[4]

Most doctors, therefore, like other 'professional' men, were probably slaves or freedmen rather than free foreigners. Slave doctors were employed both in the personal service of their owners and in public practice. Any Roman of standing[5] had his own doctor as part of his household staff, to attend on himself and the family, and this man would normally be a slave.[6] The second situation occurred when a master hired out the services of a slave doctor.[7] Such masters would usually have been doctors themselves. Some slaves were trained by their masters, who were doctors;[8] others were sent out for their medical education, as Musa had studied with Asclepiades.[9] Clearly there was a great diversity in the skill of *medici*: Pliny[10] and Galen[11] remarked on the sketchy training of many self-styled doctors, and such abuse was facilitated by the employment of slaves.

If, however, a slave was competent or, at least, gave satisfaction, he, like other specialists, might expect to win his freedom. *Libertini*, like slaves, are found in private service and public practice.[12] Cato's doctor and freedman, Cleanthes, was one of his most trusted followers.[13] Two brothers, both doctors, had a more important career. The famous Musa, a freedman,[14] doctor to Augustus and to

---

[1] Cic. ii. *Verr*. iii. 54, etc.
[2] Plut. *Ant*. 28. [3] Suet. *DJ* 42. 1.
[4] Dio, lxxx. 30. Cf. exemption for Cos in honour of its doctors under Claudius (Tac. *Ann*. xii. 61; cf. *CIG* 804, 805–6).
[5] e.g. Caesar (Suet. *DJ* 4); Piso (Cic. *Har. Resp*. 35; *Pis*. 83).
[6] Cf. Varro, *RR* ii. 16. 4; Plut. *DJ* 34. 3 f. Cicero's resident doctor Alexio was free, perhaps a freedman (p. 254).
[7] Cf. Cic. *Cluent*. 176 ff., where a slave of the doctor Rupilius is bought and set up in business by Sassia, who 'instructam ei continuo et ornatam Larini medicinae exercendae causa tabernam dedit'.
[8] *Dig*. xxxviii. 1. 26. Below, *Der Arzt*, pp. 7 f.   [9] p. 129.
[10] *NH* xxix. 17.   [11] i. 83; x. 5. 19.
[12] Cf., for imperial evidence, Below, *Der Arzt*, pp. 12 f.
[13] Plut. *Cato Min*. 70. 2 f.   [14] Dio, liii. 30.

LEARNED PROFESSIONS AND FINE ARTS

the high society of the age,[1] bore the *nomen* Antonius. His brother Euphorbus was under the patronage of Juba of Mauretania, who had been educated in Italy, fought for Octavian at Actium, and had been rewarded with the hand of Antony's daughter. Clearly, both Musa and Euphorbus had been slaves of Antony or his family, and Musa, at least, was freed by one of them. Euphorbus may have been freed by Antony, Cleopatra Selene, or her husband Juba. Musa and Euphorbus probably passed to their new patrons after the defeat of Antony, whether on their own initiative like the infamous Hipparchus, or under a certain degree of compulsion. Euphorbus at least might regard himself as having betrayed no loyalty, since he accompanied his master's daughter, and his new patron paid him the honour of naming a newly discovered herb after him,[2] so probably he found him congenial. Musa (who had trained under Asclepiades, as had, perhaps, his brother too) appears to have attached himself especially to Augustus, although, at least after his success in applying a cold cure to the *princeps* in 23 B.C., he enjoyed a large clientele, ready, as Horace humorously portrays himself,[3] to follow every prescription. A grateful Senate and emperor heaped rewards upon him, the *anulus aureus*,[4] a bronze statue, and the grant of exemption from taxes to his fellow doctors.[5] Nor does he seem to have suffered from the failure of his methods with Marcellus.[6] He revolutionized the school of Asclepiades;[7] his cures continued to be cited,[8] and works unreliably alleged to be his still survive.[9]

Several other freedmen doctors of much less eminence are known from our period.[10] Some have Greek names and are probably to be regarded as freedmen more often than free aliens.[11] One doctor, Menecrates,[10] who was probably a freedman, mentions his provenance

---

[1] Hor. *Ep.* i. 15. 3, etc.   [2] Pliny, *NH* xxv. 77.   [3] *Ep.* i. 15. 2 ff.
[4] p. 66.   [5] Suet. *DA* 59; Dio, liii. 30.   [6] Dio, liii. 30.
[7] Pliny, *NH* xxix. 6.   [8] Pliny, *NH* xxx. 117.   [9] *PIRA*² A 853.
[10] e.g. C. Hostius C. l. Pamphilus, who seems to have been a man of some means (*CIL* i. 1319 = Degr. 798 and *CIL* i. 1713 = Degr. 800); almost certainly L. Manneius Q. φύσει Menecrates (*CIL* i. 1684 = Degr. 799), after whose *nomen* we should probably understand 'Q. l.', not 'Q. f.' A free man, Menecrates will have been enslaved, and thus regarded his original name as his natural one.
[11] e.g. Cleophantus 'non ignobilis sed spectatus homo' (Cic. *Cluent.* 47), so perhaps *peregrinus*; Craterus, doctor to Atticus (Cic. *Att.* xiii. 13. 1, 14. 4; Hor.

and his father's name, which is rare.¹ This may be connected with the fact that in the Greek East medicine was in much greater repute than at Rome. There, as can be seen from inscriptions, whole families followed the profession, and they were given municipal office and other honours.² Menecrates might thus well have had professional reasons for giving his parentage. With the successes of Musa, and later of Xenophon of Cos and of Galen, which reflected on the whole profession, and, in the case of Cos, carried benefits to the doctor's place of origin,³ the status of the profession rose. The passing phase of the late Republic, which allowed men already trained and established in a profession to be enslaved, presents an artificially high level of attainment among freedmen. Later, the balance was redressed: imperial wars offered fewer and barbarous captives, to train *vernae* was expensive, and the opportunities of *peregrini* were consequently greater. The status of the profession of medicine would tend to go up to match the prestige it enjoyed in the Greek world, and its practitioners would tend to be free men rather than freed.

(c) *Architects*

Architecture, the art in which Rome excelled, nevertheless drew its recruits from foreigners and slaves as well as from freeborn Romans. The evidence of the *Corpus* as a whole, that is, mainly imperial inscriptions, suggests that numbers of freedmen and freeborn architects were about equal.⁴ Although most of the famous architects had Roman *nomina*, this is not always proof that they were not freedmen, and we are told that many architects came to Rome from the East,⁵ often, no doubt, as freedmen, not free aliens. It is reasonable to suppose that many of the subordinate architects at least will have been freedmen.

Sat. ii. 3. 161); Metrodorus, who attended Tiro at Tusculum (p. 245); Glyco, doctor to Pansa (Cic. *ad Brut.* i. 6. 2; Suet. *DA* 11); Herophilus, the oculist who claimed to be Marius' grandson (Val. Max. ix. 15. 1).

¹ Appendix 2.
² e.g. families of doctors: *IGR* iii. 374, cf. 364 f., 377, etc. (Adadae in Lycia); *IGR* iv. 300, 302, 482, 497, etc. (Pergamum); doctors in office: *IGR* iii. 534, 693; iv. 116, 1339; as benefactors: *IGR* iii. 737; iv. 182.
³ Coan inscriptions to Xenophon: *IGR* iv. 1053 ff., especially 1086.
⁴ A. Frova, *L'arte di Roma e del mondo romano* (*Storia universale dell'arte II*) (Turin, 1961), p. 10, found in *CIL* ix, 23 freedmen, 25 *ingenui*, 10 slaves. Cf. Duff, *Freedmen*, pp. 122 f.   ⁵ Pliny, *Epp.* x. 40.

LEARNED PROFESSIONS AND FINE ARTS 133

While other arts and sciences were transplanted from Greece, in architecture Rome could teach even Athens something at an early date, for it was a Roman D. Cossutius, who built the Olympieion for Antiochus Epiphanes in 174 B.C.,[1] and at the end of the century C. and M. Stallii[2] were also empoyed there. The traffic, however, was not one-way: in 138 B.C. the Roman temple of Mars was built to the design of a Greek, Hermodorus of Salamis.[3] Later, Trajan reminded Pliny that architects normally came to Rome from the Greek lands, and that all the provinces were well supplied with them.[4] Partly through its connection with public works, architecture was a respectable occupation for an *ingenuus* or *peregrinus* of the right social class,[5] and for the former, military surveying and building offered a wide field[6] to which *libertini* were not admitted. Thus we hear of many ingenuous architects active in the last century of the Republic.[7]

But the demand was great. Trajan mentioned a shortage of surveyors at Rome, when he was engaged in a heavy programme of public works,[8] and the building activity of the late Republic, and, even more, the age of Augustus, was also great. One has only to think of the probably Sullan temples at Praeneste and Tarracina, the Theatre of Pompey, the *basilica* and *forum* of Julius, Augustus' new *forum*, temples, and libraries. Private builders, among whom Cicero was only a moderate addict, erected town-houses and the sea-side palaces that Horace later attacked. For the expanding urban population, *insulae* were shooting up as fast as they fell, or were burned down. Aqueducts, drains, roads, bridges, were needed to serve the people. There was wide scope for all the architects Rome could get. Ingenuous architects naturally took slaves as assistants and pupils, and rich Romans would keep a slave or freed architect as part of their staff, or as employees in business.[9]

[1] Vitruv. vii. 15; cf. Hatzfeld, *Trafiquants*, p. 228.
[2] *IG* iii. 541.   [3] Prisc. viii. 792, *fr.* xi.
[4] Pliny, *Epp.* x. 18; 40.   [5] Cic. *Off.* i. 151.
[6] Cf. Vitruvius' colleagues as military surveyors to Octavian: they were called P. Mindius, Cn. Cornelius, M. Aurelius (Vitruv. i, pr. 2).
[7] For instance, P. Buxurius P. f. (*CIL* i. 1916 = Degr. 780); Valerius of Ostia (Pliny, *NH* xxxvi. 102 f.); and probably C. Mucius, who built Marius' temple of *Honos et Virtus* (Vitruv. iii. 2. 5; vii. pr. 17); Cluatius (Cic. *Att.* xii. 18. 1), and Numisius (Cic. *QF* ii. 2. 1).   [8] Pliny, *Epp.* x. 18.
[9] Thus Crassus had architects as well as slave builders (Plut. *Crass.* 2. 4);

The Cyrus who seems to have been a prominent architect in the 50s B.C.—he worked for Cicero on various occasions between 60 and 55[1] and when he died left Cicero and Clodius as his heirs,[2] which argued wealth and snobbishness,—may have been a freedman or an enfranchised alien. His *nomen gentile* was Vettius, since this was the name of his freedman Chrysippus. As this is rare as a magisterial *nomen* in the Republic, one would think that Cyrus was more likely to have been a freedman.[3] Chrysippus also worked for Cicero on several occasions between 59 and 44 B.C.,[4] but he had more important jobs. In 53 B.C., he was with Caesar in Gaul,[5] possibly engaged on the plans of the *Basilica Julia*.[6] In 45 B.C., he had on hand the arrangements for Caesar's triumph.[7] It is likely that Vettius remained in close touch with Caesar and his party and with Cicero and formed a link between the two during the years of civil war.[8] Cyrus, then, may have been important both as an architect and a go-between: if we knew that it was indeed he who was commissioned by Caesar to design some or all of his public works, a more emphatic judgement might be made.

In the Augustan or Tiberian period, we know of several freedmen who undertook public buildings. The arch of the Gavii at Verona, the temple of Augustus at Puteoli, and the large theatre at Pompeii were all designed by freedmen.[9]

Although architects inscribed their names on the buildings they built, as in the case of the three public works just mentioned, they are rarely named in literary sources. The names of the architects

---

Rufio seems to have been an architect and a freedman of C. Trebatius Testa (Cic. *Fam.* vii. 20. 1; *CIL* vi. 16120); Corumbus, slave of Balbus, is called 'bellus architectus' (Cic. *Att.* xiv. 3. 1). For professional architects cf. Cyrus and his freedman Vettius Chrysippus (above).

[1] Cic. *Att.* ii. 3. 2 (60 B.C.); *QF* ii. 2. 2 (56 B.C.); *Att.* iv. 10. 2 (55 B.C.).

[2] Cic. *Mil.* 46 ff. Clodius too had probably employed Cyrus: for his interest in building cf. Cic. *Mil.* 53; 74 f.

[3] If so, his patron must have predeceased him, for his property went to extraneous heirs.

[4] p. 254.   [5] Cic. *Fam.* vii. 14. 1 f.

[6] Park, *Plebs*, pp. 75 f.   [7] Quintil. vi. 3. 61.

[8] Cic. *Att.* xi. 2. 3. It is likely that the Chrysippus referred to here is Vettius. The other Chrysippus connected with Cicero, his own freedman is, in my opinion, to be ruled out (p. 258).

[9] Respectively, *CIL* v. 3464; x. 1614; x. 841. In the second case, the patron was also an architect (*CIL* x. 6339).

LEARNED PROFESSIONS AND FINE ARTS

and surveyors[1] who planned the Aqua Marcia or the temple of Fortune at Praeneste do not reach us. This is surely an index of the comparative neglect of the artist by Roman society. We know who built the Parthenon, but apart from a few *ingenui* with good connections, like Vitruvius himself, architects in Rome got less than their due. I suspect, therefore, that few were freeborn Romans—which is why those who were hit the headlines—and that, since at this date *peregrini* were not much tempted to try their luck in Rome, many architects were in fact freedmen, particularly the subordinate workers, who often later set themselves up in private practice, as did Chrysippus and the architect of the Puteoli temple.

(d) Painters and Sculptors

Painting, though a hobby of several Romans, of distant date, like Fabius Pictor, or physical disabilities, like the dumb boy, Q. Pedius, was, in the late republican and early imperial age a pursuit which brought ridicule on a Roman of any standing.[2] In Greece, by contrast, there was a prejudice against slaves engaging in painting and the plastic arts,[3] and this convention seems also to have affected Roman art, though hack-work was, no doubt, often carried out by slaves. Pliny stated categorically that there existed no famous work of art executed by a slave, and none of the artists whom he mentions is referred to as either slave or freedman. The artists listed were probably *peregrini* rather than slaves or freedmen.[4] Ascription to a town of origin often suggests the status of free alien, for slaves are usually identified by reference to their masters, and freedmen by their patrons. Thus artists like Iaia of Cyzicus, the portrait-painter contemporary with Varro,[5] or Timomachus of Byzantium, who painted the pictures for the temple of Venus Genetrix,[6] are to be thought of as *peregrini*. Some were enfranchised, for instance the Asian M. Plautius[7], the sculptor Pasiteles, contemporary with

---

[1] For some very minor surveyors cf. the two *mensores* (who were also weight-makers) from Naples (*CIL* i. 1623 = Degr. 801), and one from Ostia (*CIL* i. 1423), all freedmen, and probably one *ingenuus* from Teanum (*CIL* i. 1573 = Degr. 168).
[2] Cic. *Tusc.* i. 4; Pliny, *NH* xxxv. 19 ff.
[3] Pliny, *NH* xxxv. 77.
[4] Pace Frova, *Arte di Roma*, p. 372.
[5] Pliny, *NH* xxxv. 147 f.
[6] Pliny, *NH* xxxv. 136, 145.
[7] Pliny, *NH* xxxv. 115.

Pompey,[1] and the painter Tlepolemus of Cibyra, who was given citizenship by Verres.[2] Works of art being portable, they were not necessarily established in Italy or valued most for their artistic abilities.[3]

But, if freedmen did not produce great works of art, that is not to say that they were necessarily excluded from the practice of painting and sculpture. A painter, whether slave or freed is not known, formed part of the household staff of Livia,[4] and in an age when wall-paintings were a necessity of interior decoration, there must have been many slave practitioners of the art—especially as, in this case, the artist had to be on the spot. The demand of the Roman world was not so much for individual masterpieces as for tasteful variations on favourite themes, and slaves and freedmen in private employ or in commercial firms are to be expected here, as in the crafts of pottery and metalwork.

Cicero mentions Antiochus, an *accensus* and *libertus* of Gabinius, as being among the painters of Sopolis.[5] Sopolis was a famous painter,[6] and it appears that his studio housed pupils or assistants. The circumstances are obscure: the tit-bit about Sopolis is not (as far as we can tell) very relevant to Antiochus' prosecution, which was part of the political game being played in 54 B.C. against his patron, and we can only guess what an ex-civil servant could have been doing in the artist's studio. Perhaps he was a confidential freedman, who was primarily a painter, but capable of making himself useful in his patron's political work, as the architect Chrysippus and the painter Tlepolemus seem to have been for their employers Caesar and Verres.

The sort of work that a freedman artist did is better seen from the case of C. Avianius Evander, freedman of M. Aemilius Avianius. Cicero in 50 B.C. wrote to C. Memmius[7] (then in exile)

---

[1] Pliny, *NH* xxxvi. 39 f.
[2] Cic. ii. *Verr.* iii. 69; iv. 30 ff., 47, 52, 96. He had a brother, Hiero, who modelled in wax (ibid.).
[3] Tlepolemus and his brother, fleeing from their native city, attached themselves to Verres because his interest in art was known, but seem to have been employed as *recuperatores* and bullies rather than as artists in Sicily.
[4] *CIL* vi. 4008.
[5] 'nescioquis e Sopolidis pictoribus' (*Att.* iv. 18. 4).
[6] Pliny, *NH* xxxv. 148.
[7] *Fam.* xiii. 2.

asking him not to oust Evander from his (Memmius') *sacrarium* where he was working or living. Cicero is not explicit about the nature of Evander's 'operae', but from Pliny we learn that he was a sculptor,[1] and another letter of Cicero shows that he purchased statues from Avianius.[2] Hatzfeld conjectured[3] that Aemilius Avianius possessed a great factory turning out works of art at Athens. He assumed that Memmius' shrine was also at Athens. Avianius is known to have had business interests in Sicyon, cared for in his absence by another freedman, Hammonius, and to have had reason to visit Cibyra. Hatzfeld further conjectured that the Sicyonian business was a factory for the mass-production of bronze statues (for which the city was noted) and that it was iron which drew Avianius to Cibyra in 46 B.C.[4] But these details of the business interests of Cicero's Campanian *familiaris* go beyond the one known fact. Avianius Evander is the only sure connecting-link between Aemilius Avianius and trade in statues, for the Avianius who supplied Cicero might be the freedman and not the patron. But it is possible that Aemilius' business included the trade in, or even the manufacture of, works of art. On the other hand, the great factory at Athens is mere hypothesis, especially as there is no need to assume that Memmius' shrine was located there: it is more likely to have been at Rome,[5] as it was the shrine where the *sacra gentilicia* were performed. Moreover, if the factory had been so important, it would surely have had a more convenient and permanent location. Nothing suggests, in the letter of Cicero, that Evander was not a freelance artist, who might well encounter difficulties in obtaining a studio. We know something of the type of works dealt in by Evander or his patron from Cicero's letter to Fadius Gallus,[6] and we know also from Pliny of a specific work carried out by Evander, the restoration of the head of a statue of Diana by Timotheus.[7] The work of such men as Evander was doubtless commercialized to meet the demands of men like Cicero, who bought statues rather

---

[1] *NH* xxxvi. 32.
[2] *Fam.* vii. 23. 2.
[3] *Trafiquants*, p. 74.
[4] Cic. *Fam.* xiii. 21.
[5] Cf. Tyrrell and Purser, *The Correspondence of Cicero*, iii. 219. Contra, A. J. N. Wilson, *Emigration from Italy in the Republican Age of Rome* (Manchester, 1966), p. 197.
[6] *Fam.* vii. 23. 2 f.
[7] *NH* xxxvi. 32.

as a discerning modern householder might purchase wallpaper or carpets, but Evander was certainly eminent of his type. He was patronized by Cicero, and later M. Antonius took him to Alexandria and Octavian moved him back to Rome.[1] His fame was great enough for early Horatian commentators to identify him with the Evander mentioned by Horace.[2]

Hatzfeld's hypothesis that the manufacture of works of art in Greece for the Italian market was highly organized, is borne out more convincingly by the example of the Cossutii.[3] The interest of this *gens* in the east went back to the architect who was employed in Athens in 174 B.C.[4] and inscriptions of the family and its freedmen are found in Athens, Paros, Delos, and Erythraea. In Italy a statue of Pan at Lanuvium bears the inscription 'M. Cossutius Marci Cerdo',[5] and a fragment of drapery found in Rome has the name 'M. Cossutius Menelaus'.[6] Both artists were probably freedmen. It appears, then, that the family specialized in producing sculptures: its agents in the eastern Mediterranean were conveniently situated for the marble quarries of Paros and Teos, and the artists employed were freedmen, most likely Greeks. They may sometimes have been independent of the firm.

Both as craftsmen in commercial ventures, privately employed house-decorators, and, though perhaps rarely, as independent and original painters and sculptors, freedmen played their part in the expanding Roman market for works of art.

(*e*) *On the Stage and in the Circus and Arena*

In what we should now call the world of entertainment, freedmen probably outnumbered *ingenui*. Native forms of drama, however, such as the Atellane farces, the legitimate stage—comedy and tragedy, the arena and the circus, all claimed native recruits,

---

[1] Porph. *ad* Hor. *Sat*. i. 3. 90.
[2] Hor. *Sat*. i. 3. 90 f.: 'mensave catillum Evandri manibus tritum deiecit'. The identification would at least fit in with Horace's mention of many other figures from Cicero's letters. (See Carcopino, *Cicero: The Secrets of his Correspondence* (tr. E. O. Lorimer, London, 1951), pp. 525 ff.) Wickham, ad loc., would understand a reference to the Arcadian Evander, because of the difficulty of translating 'tritum' as 'turned'. But his other argument that Evander only came to Rome in 30 B.C. is unsafe.
[3] *Trafiquants*, p. 228.   [4] p. 133.
[5] *IG* xiv. 1249.   [6] *IG* xiv. 1250.

though not normally of high social standing. Singers, *cithara*-players, *mimi*, *tibicines*, and many actors and gladiators were of slave or freed status.

Histriones were officially subject to certain disabilities,[1] which reflected social prejudice.[2] But the prejudice could be overcome in the case of an actor of real talent, and that it was not inextricably linked with foreign or servile origin is indicated by the fact that Augustus was able to use even *equites Romani* on the stage, until the Senate stopped the practice.[3] Thus, several of the actors known to us only by *nomen gentile*[4] were probably ingenuous. The great Q. Roscius Gallus himself, a native of Lanuvium, the friend of Sulla,[5] Catulus,[6] and Cicero, who earned half a million sesterces a year,[7] was presumably free throughout his life.[8]

Yet the usual status of *histriones* was slave or freed.[9] We hear of two pupils of Roscius, Eros[10] and the slave Panurgus,[11] and we may deduce that slave actors usually had to prove their worth on the stage before they were manumitted: a certain Antipho who was manumitted before his début was a miserable flop.[12] The actor of *fabulae togatae*, Stephanio, scourged and banished in the time of Augustus,[13] was probably a freedman, as, to guess rashly from the name, Aesopus the grave tragic actor and friend of Cicero[14] may also have been.

The Greek mime and the later Roman pantomime were an entirely different matter. To act in a mime rendered a citizen *infamis* and both the show and its male and female performers were of patent immorality. Only slaves and *libertini* could afford to take part. A young *mima* called Eucharis, in an ancient inscription,[15] had

---

[1] Suet. *DA* 45. 3.   [2] Cic. *Rep.* iv. 13.   [3] Suet. *DA* 43. 3.
[4] e.g. Fufius the *tragoedus* (Hor. *Sat.* ii. 3. 60); Burbuleius (Pliny, *NH* vii. 55).
[5] Plut. *Sulla*, 36.   [6] Cic. *Nat. Deor.* i. 79.   [7] Pliny, *NH* vii. 128.
[8] The only hint of servile origin is that given by the context of Pliny but this is outweighed by Cicero's testimony that he was born at Lanuvium (*Nat. Deor.* i. 79) and brought up there as an *ingenuus*. Nor could he have been a slave of the Social War, for he was famous by 91 B.C. (Cic. *de Or.* i. 130) and in 80–79 B.C. was Sulla's friend.
[9] Sometimes peregrine (Plut. *Brut.* 21).   [10] Cic. *Rosc. Com.* 30.
[11] Cic. *Rosc. Com.* 27 ff.
[12] Cic. *Att.* iv. 15. 6. He seems to have been young, for 'in Andromacha tamen maior fuit quam Astyanax, in ceteris parem habuit neminem'.
[13] Suet. *DA* 45. 4.   [14] Cic. *Div.* i. 80.
[15] *CIL* i. 1214 = Degr. 803.

already undergone a thorough training and won her freedom at the age of fourteen. She received an extravagant epitaph from her *patrona* or parents. The *mimae*[1] Arbuscula,[2] Galeria Copiola, who had first appeared in 82 B.C. and reached the age of 103 in A.D. 8,[3] and Bacchis, who performed at the *ludi* of Brutus in 44 B.C.,[4] and the *mimi* Sorex and Metrobius, Sulla's cronies,[5] were all probably freed, if not slaves. The mime was a career which could produce acquaintance with the great, and high financial rewards. Sulla's predilection for the society of mimes has been mentioned. In 76 B.C. Cicero remarked on the earning capacities of the *mima* Dionysia —two hundred thousand sesterces a year,[6] which, if she was independent and free and not paying her wages to a master, or (in part) to a patron, meant that she was very comfortably off.[7] The lady's fame was still great in 62 B.C.[8] M. Antonius followed Sulla's example in choosing mimes as his companions, Sergius and the notorious Cytheris. Of the former[9] it can only be said that, as he had a *nomen gentile* and so was not a slave, he was presumably a freedman. Volumnia[10] Cytheris was the freedwoman of Volumnius Eutrapelus.[11] Of her professional career we know nothing but the bare fact that she had been a mime,[12] so she probably retired early from the stage when she took up the more profitable career of *meretrix, maîtresse en titre* to Antony.[13] In the time of Augustus, the mime developed under the guidance of Pylades and Bathyllus, who introduced Italian choreography, of a tragic and comic type respectively.[14] Pylades also, instead of both singing and dancing, introduced a chorus and piper and limited himself to mime proper.[15] He was a Cilician[15] freedman of Augustus,[16] while Bathyllus of

[1] On whom see now C. Garton, *CQ* 14 (1964), 238 f.
[2] Cic. *Att.* iv. 15. 6; Hor *Sat.* i. 10. 77.
[3] Pliny, *NH* vii. 158. [4] Cic. *Att.* xv. 27. 3.
[5] Plut. *Sulla*, 36. [6] Cic. *Rosc. Com.* 23.
[7] Cf. the earnings of Roscius Gallus (HS 500,000); Verrius Flaccus (HS 100,000, p. 124); Remmius Palaemon (HS 400,000, Suet. *Gram.* 23).
[8] Gell. i. 5. [9] Cic. *Phil.* ii. 62; Plut. *Ant.* 9. 4.
[10] Cic. *Phil.* ii. 58. [11] Serv. *ad* Verg. *Ecl.* x. 1.
[12] Cic. *Phil.* ii. 69. But we may note that Eutrapelus may have been patron also of an actor named Volumnius, captured by Brutus at Philippi (Plut. *Brut.* 45. 4 ff.).
[13] Cic. *Att.* x. 10. 5, 16 . 5; xv. 22; *Phil.* ii. 20, 58 ff., 69. Plut. *Ant.* 9. 4. Auct. *Vir. Ill.* 82. 2. [14] Athen. i. 20 d.
[15] Suet. *frr.* (ed. Renan), p. 301. 25. [16] Jerome on 22 B.C.

LEARNED PROFESSIONS AND FINE ARTS 141

Alexandria had Maecenas as patron.[1] Hylas, the pupil and rival of Pylades,[2] was no doubt also a freedman, conceivably of Pylades himself. The rivalry and quarrels of this formidable trio caused a public excitement which Augustus at first ignored,[3] but later checked by banishing Pylades.[4] Hylas also on one occasion was flogged.[5] Pylades was recalled in 18 B.C. and there is a story that he told Augustus that it was better for him that the people should interest themselves in the quarrels of dancers than in politics.[6] Mimes in fact became part of the imperial bread-and-circuses programme, and it is significant that *liberti* of the emperor and of Maecenas were prominent.

Musicians and singers were also usually freedmen or slaves. They often formed part of a luxurious *familia*, for instance that of Chrysogonus, Piso, or Antony.[7] A college of *tibicines*[8] and the guild of *Cantores Graeci*[9] had mainly freedmen *magistri*. The most famous singer of the age, Tigellius, may, to judge from hints in Cicero and the epigram of Calvus, have been a freedman.[10]

Gladiators, because of the dangers of their occupation, were generally slaves, but some free men were reduced to this career[11] and others apparently found that the profits or thrills outweighed the risks, for even men of the highest social standing sometimes fought in the arena, usually as amateurs.[12] For slave gladiators, we need only cite Spartacus and his followers,[13] or the Caesarian band at Capua to whom Lentulus offered liberty in 49 B.C.[14] Freedmen are not directly attested for the republican period, though one known

[1] Sen. *Controv.* x, pr. 8; Schol. Pers. v. 123.
[2] Macrob. ii. 7. 12 ff.
[3] Tac. *Ann.* i. 54.   [4] Suet. *DA* 45. 4.
[5] Suet. *DA* 45. 4; cf. the punishment of Stephanio (p. 139). Tac. *Ann.* i. 77 and Suet. *DA* 45. 4 agree that Augustus abrogated the magistrates' ancient powers of *coercitio* against actors, Suetonius adding that exception was made for the time when games were being held. Stephanio, Hylas, and Pylades were punished on the orders of the *princeps*.
[6] Dio, liv. 17. 4.
[7] Cic. *Rosc. Am.* 134; *Pis.* 89; Plut. *Ant.* 24. 2.
[8] *CIL* i. 989 = Degr. 775.   [9] *CIL* i. 2519 = Degr. 771.
[10] Cic. *Fam.* vii. 24; Porph. *ad* Hor. *Sat.* i. 3. 4; Appendix 6.
[11] Cic. *Fam.* x. 32. 3.
[12] Dio, xlviii. 43. 2 f.; li. 22. 4 (senators); at Caesar's games, it is alleged, two men, one an ex-senator and barrister, one of praetorian family, fought to the death (Suet. *DJ* 39).
[13] Oros. v. 24.   [14] Caes. *BC* i. 14.

gladiator, Aeserninus,[1] could have been a public freedman of Aesernia. It is also logical to suppose that some at least of the gladiators employed as bullies by Clodius,[2] Milo,[3] Ap. Claudius,[4] D. Brutus,[5] and Considius[6] won their freedom, which would surely be held out as bait by their bosses as it was to Caesar's men if they would join the Pompeians. Libertine gladiators are attested for the Empire,[7] and as they could not be forced to remain in the arena after manumission[8] it is to be supposed that the profession might be attractive. The same applies to charioteers, on whom the evidence is yet scantier for our period.

Prostitutes, whom we may append here, were naturally often freedwomen. Horace indeed makes the *libertina* the mistress and harlot *par excellence*.[9] Of the more noted *hetaerae*, Cytheris has been mentioned; Chelido, the mistress of Verres and a famous courtesan of the 70s,[10] may, on the shaky evidence of her name, have been a freedwoman. Fecenia Hispala continued to ply her trade after manumission.[11] Among common *meretrices*, most of the girls were foreign,[12] which means most often freedwomen or slaves. In classical law,[13] it was forbidden to compel a woman to continue to prostitute herself after manumission, but the law would be hard to enforce, even if the freedwoman wished to avail herself of it. Many will have worked for their *patronus*, a pimp or bath-owner perhaps, and others as casual prostitutes, women such as the mime-actresses and servants at inns.

(iv) *Private Service*

Many freedmen did not work on their own after manumission. In any case, many were in the position of having to perform *operae* for their old masters; many worked full time for them. Of the

[1] The famous 'Samnite' mentioned by Lucilius (136) and Cicero (*Tusc.* iv. 48).
[2] Cic. *Sest.* 78; Dio, xxxix. 7. 2.   [3] Cic. *Vat.* 40; Dio, xxxix. 8. 1.
[4] Cic. *Sest.* 85.   [5] App. *BC* ii. 53, etc.
[6] Auct. *Bell. Afr.* 76; 93.   [7] Duff, *Freedmen*, p. 105.
[8] *Dig.* xxxviii. 1. 38.
[9] *Epod.* xiv. 15 f.; *Sat.* i. 2. 48; *Od.* i. 27. 16; i. 33. 14 f., etc. Cf. Plaut, *Cist.* 38 f.; *Pseud.* 176.
[10] Cic. ii *Verr.* i. 104, 106, 120, 136 f., etc.
[11] Livy, xxxix. 9. 5.
[12] Propert. ii. 23. 21; Juv. i. 3. 62 ff.   [13] *Dig.* xxxviii. i. 38.

freedmen we have dealt with in various jobs, in industries such as the potteries, in trades and professions, a large number were in the employ of their patrons. In many cases, it was impossible to do more than guess if a freedman was independent of his patron or not. Some of this section, therefore, will be recapitulatory.

Some *libertini* were not well qualified for work outside the household where they had worked as slaves. Among the vast numbers freed, many will have been the humble domestics of the type neglected by the literary sources, maids, litter-bearers, footmen, cooks, and the *tuttofare* of the poorer slave owner. Like the despised 'operarius homo' whom Cicero thought so unimportant among his freed staff,[1] there will have been many workers whose jobs were undefined or not worth defining by their owners, and who, though they achieved their freedom, were hardly equipped to earn their living alone. The *familia* of a Roman of position was large: even the bachelor Horace, with his simple tastes, had, during the lean years in Rome, three *pueri* to serve his frugal supper.[2] Tigellius went from one extreme to the other: 'habebat saepe ducentos, Saepe decem servos'.[3] The household of the wealthy had a large variety of workers: 'Familiam vero quantam et quam variis cum artificiis habeat quid ego dicam?' says Cicero of Chrysogonus, 'Mitto hasce artes volgares, coquos, pistores, lecticarios; animi et aurium causa tot homines habet ut cotidiano cantu vocum et nervorum et tibiarum nocturnisque conviviis tota vicinitas personet.'[4] Cooks, bakers, and litter-bearers were part of the essential staff; musicians and singers were not. Like the slave attendants of comedy,[5] the general domestic workers, and still more the specialized slaves, won freedom in large numbers.

The management of the household of a rich man was entrusted to one servant[6] and he was likely to be a freedman. In the country, we hear of *dispensatores* or stewards, who may have been freed.[7]

---

[1] Cic. *Att.* vii. 2. 8. [2] Hor. *Sat.* i. 6. 116.
[3] Hor. *Sat.* i. 3. 11 f. [4] *Rosc. Am.* 134.
[5] e.g. Plaut. *Capt.* 948; *Epid.* 726 ff.; *Men.* 1023 ff.; *Miles* 1194; *Rud.* 927 ff., 1217 ff.; Ter. *Ad.* 960 ff. [6] Cic. *Rep.* i. 61.
[7] Cicero's steward at Tusculum, Ummius, cannot have been his own freedman. but may possibly have been *libertinus*, not *ingenuus* (Cic. *Fam.* xvi. 14. 2); Q. Cicero's dispensator at the Arcanum, Herus, may have been freed, not slave (Cic. *QF* iii. 1. 1).

A known *libertus* who was employed as a steward is Philotimus, freedman of Terentia, who was employed by Cicero on such matters as the repair of a boundary-wall at his town-house.[1] But he was not attached to any one residence, nor does Cicero actually call him his *dispensator*.[2] When Cicero lent his *Cumanum* to Pilia, he lent her his *vilici* and *procuratores* too.[3] Bailiffs (*vilici*) were often slaves, though occasionally the job seems to have gone to a trusted freedman who had retired from another post, and we should expect that slaves experienced in agriculture might sometimes be promoted to *vilici* and freed.[4] Besides being in charge of farm work at Italian villas such as those of Q. Cicero at Arpinum or Clodius' *Albanum*,[5] *vilici* were employed on the great estates possessed by Romans in the Empire.[6] Especially in distant places, one would expect freedmen rather than slaves.

Working under these bailiffs and stewards were the farm and domestic servants of whom we know little. In the households of the emperors or of a Trimalchio, they were highly organized with subordinate departmental heads and intense specialization,[7] but there is no evidence of this for the more modest families of the late Republic. A full staff of domestic servants was not maintained in all a rich Roman's many houses and *deversoria*: a skeleton staff was kept in each, but most of the necessary domestics moved round when the master did.[8] Even the humble sweeper could hope for freedom if he caught his master's eye.[9] Voltacilius Plotus, the rhetorician, had allegedly been a chained door-keeper;[10] the notorious Geganius Clesippus was a fuller.[11] Personal servants had a good chance of manumission, either for good service or because they accumulated *peculium* more easily,[12] and probably many of the *libertinae* attested by inscriptions from the *columbaria* were ladies'

---

[1] Cic. *Att.* ii. 4. 7; cf. *QF* iii. 9. 7; *Fam.* xiv. 18. 2.
[2] Only 'qui (domesticas res) dispensavit', which clearly refers to Philotimus, though he is not named (*Att.* xi. 1. 1).
[3] Cic. *Att.* xiv. 16. 1.   [4] p. 107.
[5] Cic. *QF* iii. 1. 5; Asc. *Mil.* 35 A.
[6] e.g. Cic. ii. *Verr.* v. 15 (Sicily); *Flacc.* 11 (Asia).
[7] Duff, *Freedmen*, pp. 143 ff.   [8] Park, *Plebs*, p. 60.
[9] Phaedr. ii. 4.   [10] Suet. *Rhet.* 3.
[11] Though he did not gain his freedom for services in the laundry: Pliny, *NH* xxxiv. 11. Cf. *CIL* i. 1004 = Degr. 696.
[12] Cf. Ter. *Heaut.* 300 f. on the chances a maid enjoyed of receiving tips.

PRIVATE SERVICE 145

maids. They might remain in service after their manumission, as apparently did Julia Phoebe, maid to the daughter of Augustus.[1] But we hear little of the more ordinary servants, the cooks, barbers, valets, and footmen, after their manumission.

For arbitrary reasons we know a lot about letter-carriers, since Cicero in his correspondence often mentions who was delivering the letter. Some slaves and freedmen seem to have been primarily used as letter-carriers, others were only incidentally so employed. Cicero used either his own *domestici tabellarii*,[2] or the *tabellarii publicanorum*,[3] friends,[4] friends' agents,[5] or his own and his correspondents' freedmen. Cicero himself had probably seven or eight *tabellarii* over the period covered by his extant correspondence, and of these two were certainly freedmen. Probably some of the five whose status is not known were also freed,[6] since letter-carrying was a responsible job.[7] *Liberti* who were not primarily *tabellarii* were often entrusted with important letters, when they were travelling on other business, or because it was convenient for other reasons. Philotimus carried mail for Cicero on several occasions,[8] and so did Cilix and Phania, freedmen of Appius Claudius;[9] Diochares, *libertus* of Caesar,[10] and others. These freedmen were given letters to deliver much as ingenuous friends were. In some cases *liberti* were picked to carry particularly vital letters, such as those sent to the consuls in 44 B.C. by Pompeius and Libo.[11]

Freedmen naturally formed the backbone of a Roman's suite of attendants, for instance of Q. Cicero on the occasion when he made a speech from the *rostra* and had to be rescued by his slaves and freedmen;[12] of M. Marcellus on the day of his murder,[13] and of

---

[1] She committed suicide when her mistress was disgraced (Suet. *DA* 65. 2). Another *ancilla*, *liberta* of Aemilia Tertia, was married off to a *conlibertus*, so presumably gave up her work (Val. Max. vi. 7. 1). See Maxey, *Occupation of the Lower Classes*, pp. 40 ff.
[2] Cic. *Fam.* ii. 7l. 3. [3] Ibid viii. 7. 1.; *Att.* v. 15. 3.
[4] e.g. Cic. *Att.* ii. 24. 1; *Fam.* vii. 15; *QF* iii. 1. 21.
[5] e.g. Cic. *QF* ii. 12. 3—letters to Quintus went by Caesar's regular *tabellarii* to Gaul.   [6] See Appendix 3, p. 253.
[7] Letter-carriers had to be trustworthy (Cic. *Att.* v. 17. 1; cf. ibid. 15. 3). Letters were often lost (e.g. Cic. *QF* iii. 9. 6); damaged (e.g. ibid. ii. 10. 4); intercepted or stolen (id. *Fam.* ii. 9. 1; *Att.* vii. 9. 1; *Fam.* x. 31. 1).
[8] Cic. *Att.* vi. 3. 1; ix. 5. 1; x. 7. 2, etc.
[9] Cic. *Fam.* iii. 1. 1; iii. 1. 2.   [10] Cic. *Att.* xi. 6. 7.
[11] Cic. *Att.* xvi. 4. 1.   [12] Cic. *Sest.* 76.   [13] Cic. *Fam.* iv. 12. 3.

Caesar when he visited Cicero at Puteoli in 45 B.C.[1] The word 'pedisequi' (footmen) would probably describe many of these, and we know that Atticus at least took care to educate his footmen so that they could carry out a variety of commissions.[2] Even military attendants, the general's bodyguard, were often *libertini*, for instance Cassius' shield-bearer Pindarus,[3] and all Antony's spearmen on the retreat from Armenia.[4]

Slaves with a specialist training clearly had the best possible chance of being manumitted, since freedom, if anything, increased their usefulness. Chrysippus, the freedman of the architect Cyrus;[5] Julius Modestus, the freedman and pupil of Hyginus;[6] Tiro;[7] Gnipho;[8] Terence;[9] Voltacilius Plotus;[10] Publilius the mime-writer,[11] these and many others were chosen for a specialist education by their patrons. Many, though not all, of such slaves were retained as their master's employees on manumission; others who set up in a profession on their own were often liable to work occasionally for their patron in the performance of *operae*. Or the *operae* might be performed for a third party while the patron received cash—a situation that was likely to arise in the case of specialists such as doctors and teachers.[12] Our sources are never explicit about the position of *liberti* found working for their patrons, whether they were full-time employees, given maintenance and pay; or performing occasional *operae*, with a food allowance for each day's work, but supporting themselves by outside work; or set up in business by the patron and paying him rent but keeping the profits, or paying a percentage of the profits. In the case of employees such as the Arretine foremen, who were generally freedmen who had been trained in the same firm as slaves, one would expect that wages were paid. Professional men like Tiro, living with their patron and working when there was work to be done may have had a more

---

[1] Cic. *Att.* xiii. 52; cf. App. *BC* ii. 119 for Caesar's escort on the Ides of March.
[2] Nep. *Att.* 13. 3.
[3] Pindarus had been with Cassius at least since 53 B.C. (Plut. *Brut.* 43. 7), but at the time of Philippi was only 'nuper manumissus' (Val. Max. vi. 8. 4).
[4] Plut. *Ant.* 48. 3 (δορυφόροι). [5] p. 134.
[6] Suet. *Gram.* 20.
[7] pp. 260 f.   [8] p. 115.   [9] p. 112.   [10] p. 118.
[11] Macrob. *Sat.* ii. 7. 6: 'maiore cura eruditus'.   [12] p. 76.

casual type of remuneration and of course their keep.[1] Nothing as sordid as a salary is ever mentioned in Cicero's letters, but Tiro had money, for he was able to buy a country estate and we know that Cicero authorized him to draw on his agents for funds.[2] Other freedmen had a good chance to line their own pockets as their patron's agents, for instance, Sulla's Chrysogonus, but these too depended also on the generosity of the *patronus* as did L. Aurelius Cottae Maximi l. Zosimus, whose patron was in the habit of making presents equal to the equestrian census.[3]

We may recapitulate briefly here those freedmen in the professions who appear to have been still in the employ of their patrons. Teachers and scholars naturally often found work in their patron's household, educating his children or assisting his own literary efforts. Some *paedagogi* were or became freedmen, for instance Augustus' old tutor Sphaerus,[4] and when that emperor limited the right to manumit, he allowed a master between the ages of eighteen and twenty to free his *paedagogus*.[5] But we do not know if a *paedagogus* was normally freed after a boy had outgrown his services, as is suggested by this regulation. Among *grammatici*, Lutatius Daphnis[6] was probably a literary collaborator with Catulus; Cornelius Epicadus[7] Sulla's literary assistant; Pompeius Lenaeus[8] was a scholar who made himself useful to Pompey, especially in the east; Dionysius[9] and Apollonius[10] were literary assistants to Atticus and the Younger P. Crassus respectively. The *rhetor* Voltacilius Plotus[11] worked for his patron.

Doctors, slave or freed and sometimes peregrine, formed a normal part of a rich Roman's staff. Young Julius Caesar, for instance, was attended by his doctor when a prisoner of the pirates.[12]

---

[1] Tiro had holidays and long sick-leave and, though he was hard-worked as Cicero's chief secretary, had time to attend to his own affairs. See pp. 261 f.
[2] Cic. *Fam.* xvi. 4. 2.   [3] *ILS* 1949 = *EJ* 358.
[4] Dio, xlviii. 33. 1. He had a public funeral in 40 B.C.
[5] Ulp. xl. 2. 13. For *paedagogi* who were still slaves see Plut. *Cato Min.* 1. 5; *Ant.* 81.
[6] p. 114.   [7] p. 114.   [8] p. 119.
[9] pp. 119 f.   [10] p. 121.   [11] pp. 118 f.
[12] Suet. *DJ* 4. If the friend mentioned by Plutarch (*Caes.* 2. 1) as having stayed with Caesar is to be identified with the doctor, then he will have been a freedman or *peregrinus*. See also Cic. *Har. Resp.* 35; *Pis.* 83 for Piso's confidential doctor, who is unlikely to have been a slave; Plut. *Caes.* 34. 3 f.—a slave.

Cato's doctor, Cleanthes, who was with him at Utica and tried to save him, was one of his most trusted freedmen.[1] Architects probably also continued as employees of their patrons: this may have been the case with Vettius Chrysippus,[2] whose patron was a professional architect, and with Trebatius Rufio,[3] whose patron was not. Artists, in the same way as craftsmen and artisans, often continued to work for the 'firms' in which they had trained.[4]

Clerical staff, since they were necessarily in private service, have not so far been discussed, except in so far as they also carried out functions such as teaching and research. The staff of a Roman might be large and complex, as was, for example, that of Atticus, whose publishing business meant that he needed an efficient organization, and, later, the imperial secretariat, which Augustus began to develop. Roman politicians, too, needed a number of clerks and secretaries. Nepos describes Atticus' staff, designed for use, of highly educated slaves, excellent readers, and a large number of copyists—and even his lackeys were capable of carrying out all these functions.[5] *Anagnostae* (readers) were a luxury which most Romans of culture seem to have permitted themselves—naturally, when one considers the inconvenience of reading a roll for oneself, perhaps in a poor light, and aloud. Cicero was much attached to a boy reader of his, a slave who died before the manumission that would doubtless have been his reward.[6] Other readers are mentioned, but their status is not given.[7] *Librarii* did a variety of jobs, of which the most important was copying. Individual copyists of Atticus are mentioned several times in Cicero's letters to his

---

[1] Plut. *Cato Min.* 70. 2 ff.

[2] It is not quite certain that Chrysippus worked as a junior partner or employee of Cyrus after manumission, but as Cicero in 59 B.C. mentions the former as working for him (*Att.* ii. 4. 7), while in 60 and 56 B.C. it was the patron (*Att.* ii. 3. 2; *QF* ii. 2. 2 ff.), this is likely. Perhaps, when Cyrus died in 52 B.C., Chrysippus took over the firm.

[3] Cic. *Fam.* vii. 20. 1; *CIL* vi. 16120.

[4] e.g. the Veturii, Trebonii, and Cossutii (pp. 97 f., 138 f.).

[5] Nep. *Att.* 13. 3: 'usus est familia, si utilitate iudicandum est, optima—namque in ea erant pueri litteratissimi, anagnostae optimi, et plurimi librarii, ut ne pedisequus quidem quisquam esset, qui non utrumque horum pulchre facere posset.'   [6] Sositheus, p. 253.

[7] Nor are they designated as *anagnostae*, so they may primarily have had other jobs: M. Marius' Protogenes (Cic. *Fam.* vii. 1. 3); Atticus' Salvius (Cic. *Att.* xvi. 2. 6).

PRIVATE SERVICE

publisher, as engaged in copying the text of his works.[1] Various men alluded to as being likely to be asked by Atticus to check references for Cicero are also probably his *librarii*.[2] Other 'librarioli' were especially skilled in book-production, and Cicero borrowed a couple to help Tyrannio as *glutinatores* (that is, to stick the sheets together to form the roll) in his new library at Antium.[3] None of these employees of Atticus is distinguished as being *libertus*, but some at least probably had been freed.[4] We hear of a copyist of Virgil's who was a freedman.[5] Perhaps an agent in Atticus' publishing business, and certainly useful in other ways, was the scholar M. Pomponius Dionysius, who gave Cicero some help in writing the *Republic*.[6]

Secretaries, especially the more confidential ones, were often freedmen. Tiro is an obvious example.[7] Atticus' Alexis, Tiro's opposite number,[8] is naturally assumed to be a freedman. Many of the highly educated freedmen of whom we hear as attached to the service of public men were probably their secretaries. Apollonius, the literary freedman of P. Crassus, may have served him in this capacity; Q. Cicero's trusted freedman Statius, who was deep in all his affairs, acted as secretary at least while his patron was governing Asia,[9] but as he was not highly educated,[10] perhaps he did not always carry out this function.[11] Augustus used several freedmen as secretaries, Marathus,[12] his *a memoria*, and Hilarion and Polybius,[13]

---

[1] Salvius (Cic. *Att.* xiii. 44. 3); Antaeus (ibid.); Pharnaces (*Att.* xiii. 29. 3.)
[2] Antiochus (Cic. *Att.* xiii. 23. 3); Syrus (*Att.* xii. 22. 2); Satyrus (ibid.).
[3] Cic. *Att.* iv. 4 a; 5. 3; 8. 2 (56 B.C.).
[4] There is a possible *librarius* and *libertus* of Cicero himself at *Att.* xiii. 33. 1, but it is dubious.
[5] Suet. *Vita Verg.* 34: Eros.
[6] Cic. *Att.* vi. 2. 3; vii. 3. 10.
[7] On whom pp. 259 ff.
[8] Cic. *Att.* xii. 10: 'imaginem Tironis'. He is referred to in Cic. *Att.* v. 20. 9; vii. 2. 1; vii. 7. 7; xvi. 15. 1.
[9] Cic. *QF* i. 2. 8.
[10] Cic. *Fam.* xvi. 16. 2—at least he was not to be compared with Tiro.
[11] Statius was not in Asia during the whole of Q. Cicero's term of office (p. 158, n. 4). His correspondence seems to have been dealt with by Theopompus (Cic. *QF* i. 2. 9; ii. 10. 4), whom Münzer (*RE* v. A. 2. 2174) suggests is to be identified with Theopompus of Cnidos, Caesar's favourite (Strabo, xiv. 656; Plut. *Caes.* 48 and perhaps Cic. *Att.* xiii. 7. 1).
[12] Suet. *DA* 79.
[13] Suet. *DA* 101.

who helped him to copy his will. Maecenas had a freedman secretary[1] too. But public men might also use freeborn Romans or foreigners as their confidential secretaries.[2]

Accountants (*ratiocinatores*) were essential to a businessman or a senator with financial interests. Cicero had a freedman who had worked as an accountant, but who, when we hear of him in 61 B.C. was (according to his patron, who admittedly had reason to disown him) no longer in his employ.[3] In 45-44 B.C. Atticus' freedman or possibly slave, Eros, was keeping Cicero's accounts, with help from Tiro.[4] In the interval between Hilarus' departure[5] and the advent of Eros, Cicero's steward Terentius Philotimus and a subordinate staff were responsible for the accounts, but this arrangement fell through with the divorce from Terentia in 46 B.C., if not before.

Dispensatores, apart from controlling country estates, were also employed to co-ordinate all financial business. Philotimus was given a free hand with many of Cicero's domestic arrangements, saw to such things as the maintenance of the town-house or the purchase of a new *deversorium*, and dealt with Cicero's ever-complex debts and payments.[6]

Freedmen were also employed as financial agents of other kinds. A procurator was a legally responsible representative in business affairs, and it is quite common to find *liberti* acting as procurators for their patrons. Strictly, a procurator was the representative of someone who was absent. The word might also be applied more loosely, to anyone acting as the agent of another.[7] It is with

[1] Dio, lv. 7. 6.
[2] Q. Cicero may have done so (p. 149, n. 11); Caesar had the Vocontian Pompeius Trogus (Justin, xliii. 5. 11 f.; Syme, *PBSR* N.S. 1 (1938), 15); Augustus offered a job as *ab epistulis* to Horace (Suet. *Vita Hor.*).
[3] Hilarus. See pp. 256 f.
[4] Cic. *Att.* xii. 18. 3; xii. 21. 4; xiii. 2. 1; xiii. 12. 4; xiii. 30. 2; xiii. 50. 5; xv. 15. 1.
[5] For which the *terminus ante quem* is 61 B.C.
[6] pp. 263 ff.
[7] Cic. *Caec.* 57: 'Non enim alia causa est aequitatis in uno servo et in pluribus, non alia ratio iuris in hoc genere dumtaxat, utrum me tuus procurator deiecerit, is qui legitime procurator dicitur, omnium rerum eius qui in Italia non sit absitve rei publicae causa quasi quidam paene dominus, hoc est alieni iuris vicarius, an tuus colonus aut vicinus aut cliens aut libertus aut quivis qui illam vim deiectionemque tuo rogatu aut tuo nomine fecerit.' See H. G. Pflaum, *Les Procurateurs équestres sous le haut empire romain* (Paris, 1950), p. 10; Kaser, *Röm. Privatrecht*, pp. 230 ff.; Nicolet, *L'Ordre équestre*, pp. 424 ff.

freedmen who came under the juristic definition of procurators that we are here concerned. Procurators were much used in the late Republic, both in the provinces as agents for people in Rome, and in Rome itself, especially by politicians.[1] As they were often employed only for a specific and quick commission, they were not socially on a par with regular employees. Often, they were friends of the person for whom they stood proxy, as Fufius Calenus was procurator for Antony in Rome in 43 B.C.[2] or P. Sulla for P. Sittius when the latter was abroad.[3] The procurator might be socially superior to the man whom he represented: T. Pinarius, a friend, though not a very important one, of the Cicerones and Atticus,[4] was apparently agent for Dionysius, Atticus' freedman, in Africa in 43 B.C.[5] The good standing and wealth of the procurator was, in fact, an indication that he might be honest and influential enough to protect one's interests.[6] The practice formed part of the reciprocal performance of services between Romans, even services that had to be repeated frequently, or which took up a large part of a man's time. But for permanent procuratorships, the control, for instance, of a money-lending business or estates in the provinces, an agent who could devote himself almost entirely to the work would be needed, and for this *liberti* were especially useful. Thus, C. Avianius Hammonius, freedman of M. Aemilius Avianius, was procurator in a banking business at Sicyon;[7] Cn. Otacilius Naso had three freedmen in charge of *negotia* in Sicily.[8] Many of the agents of Atticus found in Corcyra and Asia were presumably procurators,

---

[1] e.g. procurators of A. Trebonius in Cilicia (Cic. *Fam.* i. 3. 2); of Caerellia on estates in Asia (ibid. xiii. 72. 1); of Dolabella in Rome (id. *Att.* vi. 18. 5); of Cicero at the *Cumanum* (ibid. xiv. 16. 1).

[2] Cic. *Phil.* xii. 18.

[3] Cic. *Sulla*, 56.

[4] Cic. *Att.* vi. 1. 23; viii. 15. 1; *QF* iii. 1. 22; He had been on the Gallic campaign.

[5] Cic. *Fam.* xii. 24.

[6] e.g. the procurator of P. Quinctius, Alfenus, to whom the former always entrusted his affairs when he went to Gaul: 'eques Romanus locuples, sui negoti bene gerens' (Cic. *Quinct.* 62). See Nicolet, *L'Ordre équestre*, pp. 426 ff., who counts four named procurators of libertine status to eight *equites*, and suggests that the latter were more commonly employed and that this was due to their sounder position.

[7] Cic. *Fam.* xiii. 21.

[8] Ibid. 33.

and several, if not all, of them were freedmen.[1] Those in Greece were probably working on the Epirot estates, while the procurators in Asia seem to have had a pair of specific commissions. Cicero himself used a freedman, Philotimus, as procurator, for he often acted in his patron's name during his absence[2] and had perhaps been Cicero's accredited agent during his provincial governorship, when Cicero began to suspect dishonesty and asked Atticus to check up.[3] Other *liberti* are found with powers over the fortunes of their patrons that suggest a similar position to that of Philotimus.[4] *Liberti* were also used as procurators to deal with specific missions, especially the collection of debt in the provinces[5] or mediation in confidential or disputed matters.[6]

When speaking of the employees of a businessman in the provinces, Cicero commonly distinguished *procuratores*, *liberti*, and *familia*.[7] The procurators had freedmen and slaves working under them. If the *negotiator* himself was in charge of his affairs, for instance resident in Delos or Athens, his staff was again composed of his freedmen and slaves.[8] Slaves of the public companies also continued to work in the same business after manumission. The jobs given to freedmen by their patrons were multifarious, as we see from the examples of Tiro or Philotimus: either as procurator or merely as servant they might rent a house,[9] arrange free seats at the games for a politican's fellow tribesmen,[10] or entertain guests on their patron's behalf.[11]

Romans in public life exploited the services of freedmen as

---

[1] In Corcyra: Areus and Eutychides in 51 B.C. (Cic. *Att.* v. 9. 1). The latter was a freedman (ibid. iv. 15. 1). Alexio was there in 50 B.C. (ibid. vii. 2. 3. Cf. xii. 53; xiii. 25. 3). In Asia: Philogenes, a freedman (ibid. v. 13. 2; vi. 2. 1; vii. 5. 3; vii. 7. 2), and ? Democritus (ibid. vi. 1. 13). On Atticus' business activities see R. Leslie, *The Epicureanism of Titus Pomponius Atticus* (diss. Philadelphia, 1950), pp. 21 ff.

[2] e.g. Cic. *Att.* viii. 7. 3.   [3] p. 264.

[4] Turius Eros, freedman of the *negotiator* Q. Turius, in Africa, who on the death of the patron tried to embezzle the property (Cic. *Fam.* xii. 26); Rupa (whose name suggests libertinity), who on the death of the elder Curio planned to give games to secure popularity for the son (ibid. ii. 3. 1).

[5] e.g. Cic. *Fam.* xiii. 14; *Flacc.* 47. (For collection of debt for the freedman by the patron see Suet. *DJ* 2.)

[6] e.g. Cic. *Flacc.* 89.   [7] *Fam.* i. 3; xii. 29. 2.
[8] p. 104.   [9] Cic. *Pis.* 61 (a freedman of Piso).
[10] Cic. *QF* iii. 1. 1. (Philotimus.)   [11] Cic. *Fam.* xvi. 22. 2 (Tiro).

confidential agents just as businessmen did. *Liberti* could be trusted and controlled because of their position of dependence.[1] They could be used for a variety of services in electioneering and in cementing *amicitiae*; their advice and knowledge of certain sections of society might even be useful. *Liberti* who were used as political agents seem generally to have been those who were trusted also with most responsibility in their patron's private service: thus Statius, who was in Q. Cicero's confidence, for example over the divorce from Pomponia,[2] also took part in the administration of Asia. Involvement in a patron's political affairs was a natural development from employment in private matters, and from the necessity of studying a patron's political loyalties a freedman often developed political opinions of his own.[3] *Liberti* as political agents for their patrons are discussed in the next chapter.[4]

(v) *The Public Service*

Although the magistracies were closed to freedmen, the civil service was wide open.[5] The fact that the ruling classes were accustomed to employ *liberti* for confidential work as procurators made it natural that they should use them also as *apparitores* to the magistrates and that even freedmen without an official position on a governor's staff should often have more influence than the regular civil servants. A further reason for employing freedmen may well have been that a reasonable standard of education, and, in the eastern provinces, a knowledge of Greek were desirable, and freedmen had these qualifications more often than the humble *ingenuus*. Moreover, with the exception of the *scribae*, who were sometimes recognized as an order in the state coming immediately below the *tribuni aerarii* in importance,[6] civil servants did not stand high: even slaves were sometimes employed as *viatores* (messengers) and *praecones* (criers),

---

[1] 'quibus illi (sc. maiores nostri) quidem non multo secus ac servis imperabant' (Cic. *QF* i. 1. 13). [2] Cic. *Att.* vi. 2. 1.
[3] e.g. Statius' prophecy that young Q. Cicero would join Brutus (Cic. *Att.* xv. 19. 2). Philotimus was a die-hard Optimate (ibid. ix. 7. 6. Cf. vii. 23). Tiro held views on Hirtius and Pansa (Cic. *Fam.* xvi. 27. 1). [4] pp. 177 ff.
[5] See, with reservations, Tac. *Ann.* xiii. 27.
[6] Cic. *Dom.* 27; *Cat.* iv. 15.

an expedient prohibited by the *Lex Cornelia de xx quaestoribus* of 81 B.C.[1] and again in 38 B.C.[2]

The *apparitores* formed five bodies, the *scribae*, *accensi* (personal attendants on magistrates with *imperium*), *lictores*, *viatores*, and *praecones*, all of which were subdivided into *decuriae*.[3] To these officials we may add the *haruspices* and *interpretes*; functionaries attached to magistrates for extraordinary commissions, such as the surveyors assigned to the land commission proposed by Rullus,[4] and the *calatores* normally attendant on the priests.

The scribes, who formed an *ordo*[5] and often received the gold ring,[6] were drawn mostly from ingenuous Romans.[7] Horace became a *scriba quaestorius* when deprived of his patrimony[8] and another freedman's son, Cn. Flavius, had served as aedilician scribe.[9] When freedmen are found as *scribae*, they are often men of a certain standing, either through the eminence of their patron or their own merits. Thus one Cornelius, a scribe and profiteer of Sullan days, was possibly one of the dictator's own freedmen.[10] The scribe to Cicero's quaestor in Cilicia, Mescinius, was the governor's freedman, in whom he reposed great confidence, M. Tullius.[11] An unnamed *libertus* of Seius served as scribe to Varro, his patron's friend.[12] Sarmentus, the wit and probably freedman of Maecenas,[13] held the post of *scriba quaestorius*[14] and pretended to equestrian dignity.[15] A freedman of Octavia is found as a *scriba librarius*.[16]

The *accensi*, who, unlike the other *apparitores*, were appointed for a year only and by the magistrate concerned, were generally his own *liberti* or at least *libertini*. Cicero, advising his brother, urged:

> Accensus sit eo numero quo eum maiores nostri esse voluerunt, qui hoc non in beneficii loco sed in laboris ac muneris non temere nisi libertis suis deferebant: quibus illi quidem non multo secus ac servis imperabant.[17]

---

[1] Bruns, *Fontes*, 12. 8, 12.
[2] Dio, xlviii. 43.
[3] Jones, *Studies*, pp. 154 ff.
[4] Cic. *Leg. ag.* ii. 32.
[5] Cic. *Cat.* iv. 15; *Mur.* 42.
[6] Cic. ii. *Verr.* iii. 185.
[7] e.g. *CIL* i. 1313 = Degr. 812; *CIL* i. 1490 = Degr. 813.
[8] Suet. *Vita Hor*. See also E. Fraenkel, *Horace* (Oxford, 1957), pp. 14 f.
[9] Livy, ix. 46.
[10] Sall. *Hist. Or. Lepidi*, 17; Münzer, *RE* iv. 1. 1250, p. 61, n. 5.
[11] Cic. *Fam.* v. 20 and pp. 258 f.
[12] Varro, *RR* iii. 2. 14.
[13] Hor. *Sat.* i. 5. App. 7.
[14] Hor. *Sat.* 1. 5. 66.
[15] Schol. Juv. v. 3.
[16] *ILS* 1877 = *EJ* 149.
[17] *QF* i. 1. 13.

Only very rarely do we hear of *accensi* who need not have been freedmen, for instance P. Tettius and L. Volteius,[1] but in such cases it is likely that the speaker refers to them *honoris causa* in a way which does not mark their freed status, just as Cicero never refers to the scribe Tullius with his *cognomen*. Among libertine *accensi*, we may cite Verres' catspaw, Timarchides[2] and Gabinius' Antiochus,[3] both *accensi* to their patrons; P. Cornelius Lentuli l. Pausanias, *accensus* to Cicero in Cilicia and perhaps previously to his patron in the same province;[4] C. Julius Caesaris l. Salvius, a freedman of Julius who held other appointments too;[5] Q. Considius Q. l. Eros, *accensus consularis*;[6] M. Caelius M. l. Phileros, *accensus* of T. Sextius, the Caesarian opponent of Cornificius in Africa in 43 B.C.[7] The *accensi*, then, were almost always freedmen of the consuls, praetors and censors[8] whom they served, or freedmen of other patrons who were connected with the magistrates, and so to be trusted. But there are traces of *accensi* who made a career in the civil service: Pausanias, if he served two governors of Cilicia, and possibly Eros, who does not mention under which individual consul he served, so may have been with several, and later a *libertus* of Augustus, who was *accensus* to Germanicus in A.D. 12 or 18 and to Calvisius Sabinus in 26.[9] Such men were not, obviously, full-time *accensi*: their appointments were sporadic and

[1] Cic. ii. *Verr*. i. 71; i. 155 ff.
[2] Cic. ii. *Verr*. ii. 69. 133 ff., etc.
[3] Cic. *Att*. iv. 18. 4.
[4] Cic. *Fam*. iii. 7. 4 f. See Tyrrell and Purser iii. 170 for the suggestion about service under Lentulus (in 56–3 B.C.). It is attractive as it accounts for Cicero's choice of Pausanias. There seems to be no exact parallel, but cf. the later practice of maintaining officials in the same province and not changing them with the governor (Jones, *Studies*, pp. 163 f.).
[5] *CIL* xiv. 2105 = *ILS* 9039. As he was *Lupercus* he will have been freed by Julius, not Augustus. He was also *viator tribunicius*.
[6] *CIL* vi. 1933 = *ILS* 1923. His patron was perhaps Q. Considius Gallus (Cic. *Fam*. xii. 26. 1), probably son of the senator Q. Considius (Cic. *Cluent*. 107).
[7] *CIL* x. 6104 = *ILS* 1945 = *EJ* 330. Sextius had been appointed to Africa Nova by Caesar in 44 B.C. and was supported by the triumvirs in 43 (*MRR* ii. 330, 349). The only likely patrons for Phileros are the Caesarian M. Caelius Rufus or his father, who had estates in Africa (Cic. *Cael*. 73).
[8] For an *accensus censorius* see *AE* 1959, 147. Jones (*Studies* x, n. 10) mentions only praetors and consuls as having *accensi*. They also attended *privati* who gave funeral games (Cic. *Legg*. ii. 61).
[9] *ILS* 1948 = *EJ* 147.

they often held other posts too, as did Eros, but they were no longer the mere amateur agents of their patrons envisaged by the ancestral practice which Cicero had described.

In 38 B.C., a *senatus consultum* was necessary to forbid slaves to serve as lictors.[1] By implication, freedmen both could and did perform this work, and in fact libertine lictors are attested.[2] Lower still in the hierarchy of civil servants came the messengers, among whom *ingenui* seem to have been a rarity.[3] Geganius Clesippus, freedman of a certain Gegania, served as *viator tribunicius*,[4] as did C. Julius Salvius,[5] and one L. Eprius Chilo who was probably a freedman.[6] Q. Considius Eros had been a messenger to the plebeian aediles.[7] *Praecones* no doubt followed the same pattern, though sure instances are lacking.[8] Valerius, the crier of Verres, could have been a freedman,[9] and Aemilius, a *praeco* who supported Aemilianus in 142 B.C., probably was an ex-slave, as is suggested by the context in which he is named.[10]

Of the other officials, *haruspices*, practitioners of a native Italian art, naturally tended to be *ingenui*,[11] although one freedman at least is known.[12] Interpreters were probably often freedmen like the celebrated Greek Cn. Publicius Menander,[13] although *ingenui* were not behindhand.[14]

It is interesting to note how *libertini* made their way in the public service. Clearly an influential patron and the good education which he no doubt obtained advantaged a scribe such as M. Tullius. We have seen how a patron's connections might put a freedman in the way of further employment, as in the case of Cornelius Pausanias and of course the various freedmen of Caesar and later the imperial

[1] Dio, xlviii. 43. 3.
[2] *CIL* i. 1289 = Degr. 796; cf. *CIL* i. 1320.
[3] Val. Max. ix. 1. 8.
[4] *CIL* i. 1004 = Degr. 696.
[5] *CIL* xiv. 2105.
[6] *CIL* i. 1570 = Degr. 977.
[7] *CIL* vi. 1933.
[8] Except perhaps *AE* 1959, 147.
[9] Cic. ii. *Verr*. iii. 54.
[10] Plut. *Paull*. 39. He was a κῆρυξ. From the *nomen* he could have been a freedman of Scipio's family; Plutarch stresses Scipio's dependence on ἀγεννεῖς and δεδουλευκότες.
[11] e.g. *CIL* i. 2127 = Degr. 791.
[12] *CIL* i. 1835 = Degr. 788.
[13] Cic. *Balb*. 28.
[14] e.g. Verres' C. Claudius C. f. Palatina (Cic. ii. *Verr*. ii. 107 f.), and perhaps Cicero's 'amicus atque interpres', Marcilius (*Fam*. xiii. 54), who may, however, have been a go-between, not an interpreter, though the latter seems more likely.

house. A freedman in the *ordo scribarum* might hope to see his son an *eques* or even a senator.[1] Lower down the scale, the *apparitor* might rise to be a scribe or *accensus*. Q. Considius Eros rose from messenger to the plebeian aedile to be attendant on the consuls. His success was marked by a further appointment as *Lupercus*. Julius Salvius had been *viator* before becoming *accensus*. M. Caelius Phileros, who served in Africa, collected municipal posts in the Caesarian colonies there: he was aedile at Carthage, where he built a temple, and twice duumvir at Clupea. Then retiring to Italy he became Augustalis at Formiae (one of the first) and spent some more of what must have been a considerable fortune on the restoration of the temple of Neptune.[2]

With the early principate, the system became more organized and better able to exploit and favour the capacity of *libertini*. M. Aurelius Cottae Maximi l. Zosimus attracts attention thanks to the eulogy of his patron's kindnesses which the patron had inscribed on his tomb. Zosimus was *accensus* to Cotta[3] and his son became military tribune through his patron's influence. Also from the reign of Tiberius we have a monument to Q. Fabius Africani l. Cytisus.[4] His patron was the consul of 10 B.C. and his wife was a freedwoman of Livia. Cytisus was a treasury messenger and then scribe copyist to the tribunes and to the quaestors. His wife's former husband had been a mere *viator*, but his own brother was also a *scriba quaestorius*, and his stepson became *primus pilus* and married a freeborn woman. Such were the advantages of imperial or noble patrons and the rewards of a successful career. The ex-civil servant may reach the *libertina nobilitas*, represented in the Republic by the religious guilds and by local organizations, in the principate by the *Augustalitas*.

Of what effect was the work done by freedmen in the civil service? The influence of the *apparitores* for good and ill receives adequate testimony in the letters and speeches of Cicero. The *scribae*, as a permanent body, had a great advantage over the annual magistrates whose staff they were. Cicero goes so far as to say that

[1] Cic. *Off.* ii. 29.
[2] *EJ* 330.
[3] ? cos. A.D. 20, but see *PIRA* I.[2] A1488; *CIL* xiv. 2298 = *ILS* 1949 = *EJ* 358.
[4] *CIL* vi. 1815 = *ILS* 1926 = *EJ* 151.

they both controlled the laws, since they were responsible for making and keeping copies,[1] and that they kept many magistrates in ignorance, doling out only that information which suited themselves.[2] The quaestor's office staff in fact was completely unaccustomed to interference from the quaestor.[3] *Apparitores*, especially in the provinces, had opportunity both for exercising influence over the magistrate and for private transactions with the public. Cicero commended the employment of freedmen or *accensi* because their loyalty to the magistrate was thus assured, but Statius should have been a warning to him. This freedman of Q. Cicero, in spite of the fact that he held no official position in the province,[4] was, according to report, the power behind the throne in Asia during his patron's term of office in 59 B.C. As Cicero so wisely advised his brother, a slave should not be allowd to handle public business:

Ac si quis est ex servis egregie fidelis, sit in domesticis rebus et privatis: quae res ad officium imperii tui atque ad aliquam partem rei publicae pertinebunt, de iis rebus ne quid attingat. (*QF* i. 1. 17.)

The rule applied, with modification, to a governor's freedmen. But it was more honoured in the breach than in the observance, even by Cicero himself. The danger was proportionately increased when a magistrate's freedman was also endowed with public office as his *accensus* or other civil servant. His authority with the magistrate

[1] Cic. *Legg.* iii. 46: 'Eae leges sunt quas apparitores nostri volunt.'
[2] Ibid. 48: 'Animadverto plerosque in magistratibus ignoratione iuris sui tantum sapere quantum apparitores velint.'
[3] Plut. *Cato Min.* 16 ff.
[4] Statius was not, in my opinion, *accensus* to his patron. He was freed during Q. Cicero's governorship (Cic. *Att.* ii. 18. 4) against Cicero's advice (ibid. 19. 1). He had gone out to Asia after his master (Cic. *QF* i. 2. 8) and found Q. Cicero's official correspondence dangerously disorganized. By reforming the system and advising Quintus in other matters, he quickly became important (ibid. i. 2. 3, 8), but he was not so indispensable that he could not be sent home in advance of his patron, in October (ibid. 1). Statius, then, was a private secretary and confidential freedman, who after his brief notoriety returned to his work as a household administrator (Cic. *Att.* v. 1. 3; vi. 2. 1, etc.). It is natural that even if he had been *accensus* he would not have been sharply criticized in the formal letter on good government which Cicero wrote for his brother (*QF* i. 1) in which he does not appear, but the fact that he was not in the province for long and is not elsewhere called an *apparitor* or *accensus* allows the belief that he was not a public servant. Tiro, who was certainly not *accensus*, also performed 'officia . . . provincialia' for his patron (Cic. *Fam.* xvi. 4. 3).

was often too great.[1] Even if it was not, provincials and citizens would probably still expect to be able to influence the governor or judge through his servant. If the magistrate were himself a villain, the employment of his *liberti* on the staff could not but aggravate the effects of his rule on the governed: Rome lacked to a great extent the check on corruption which is provided by a professional civil service. The careers of freedmen were bound up with the success or failure of their patrons: like Verres' *scriba* who served him when he was legate, praetor, and propraetor,[2] the freedman was the perfect companion in crime. Verres' *accensus* and freedman, Timarchides, was his right-hand man in all his extortions. He exploited his position to the utmost, taking bribes from wretched defendants, selling decrees and letters, and feathering his own nest as well as supporting his patron.[3] The lower offices also gave opportunity for peculation or oppression, as witness the conduct of Verres' lictor.[4] But corruption was not *caused* by the employment of *libertini*. Verres' scribe and perhaps his lictor were *ingenui*, who enjoyed peculiar advantages because they were working with Verres—or perhaps it is truer to say that they were just unlucky enough to be found out. The system itself, based on purchase of posts, opened the door to corruption. The taking of perquisites was accepted custom; other, illegal methods of recouping and self-enrichment went on unchecked as it did in the higher strata of the public administration.[5] Freedmen, more involved with the magistrates who were often their own patrons[6] and for whom they often at times worked as political agents, had divided loyalties to an even greater extent than had the ingenuous members of the *decuriae*, and the risk the state ran in employing them was consequently higher.

[1] Cf. Cicero's praise for the praetor C. Octavius 'apud quem primus lictor quievit, tacuit accensus, quotiens quisque voluit dixit et quam voluit diu' (*QF* i. 1. 21).
[2] Cic. ii. *Verr*. iii. 187, not a freedman.
[3] 'Timarchidem fugitivum omnibus oppidis per triennius scitote regnasse' (Cic. ii. *Verr*. ii. 136). For his operations see, for instance, ibid. 69, 75, 80, 108, 133 f.
[4] Cic. ii. *Verr*. v. 114 ff.
[5] Jones, *Studies*, p. 156.
[6] Cf. the attack on Antiochus because he was freedman of Gabinius (Cic. *Att*. iv. 18. 4).

Conclusions

The part played by *libertini* in almost all types of work was important. As agents of their patrons, they were employed in all sorts of industry and trade (with the almost complete exception of agriculture), often as foremen with slave subordinates. Usually, they had served an apprenticeship as slaves in the same business. They might be entrusted with a whole factory, or with a firm's business in a foreign port, or with a merchant ship. They are often found running shops, especially in luxury trades, for which Greek and eastern freedmen were probably particularly adapted. Such men may be managers or may have been set up in business by their patron, to whom they would pay a percentage of the profits or a fixed return. Either explanation fits the inscriptions which show several *ingenui* and *liberti* of the same *gens* engaged in the same trade in different places or at different dates. Some of these men may also have been completely independent of the patron, especially as, even in luxury trades, the craftsman did not have to have a large capital, since he did not always own the material on which he worked. In businesses which required considerable capital, freedmen were exceptional, though some controlled vast interests, often, it appears, when they had inherited from their patrons.[1] Others had a more modest success story, for example the Arretine potters or Eurysaces the baker.

Freedmen were widely used in all sorts of administrative duties by patrons, in charge of houses, land, financial affairs. Both education and trustworthiness fitted them for confidential posts. Similarly, the high standard of culture to which many freedmen attained, thanks to careful training by upper-class Roman masters or to having been enslaved after an education in the cultured eastern world, made them much more suitable than Italian *ingenui* for employment in the learned professions and the arts. The contempt in which learning and most of the arts as a profession were held in Rome gave slaves and freedmen a virtual monopoly in such work, and ability normally gained recognition in manumission. In the service of the state officials too, the double qualification

[1] As may have happened in the case of Caecilius Isidorus (p. 109) and as Petronius relates of Trimalchio (*Cena*, 76. 2).

CONCLUSIONS

of education and attachment to a patron made freedmen desirable employees in work which was still hardly distinguished from private service to a magistrate.

Obviously, not all freedmen were the highly trained clients of Roman aristocrats or businessmen. The vast majority were no better educated than common *ingenui*, and they either continued working for their patrons in humble capacities or took unskilled or semi-skilled work. Many were old when they gained their freedom, poor, and with little prospect of self-sufficiency. They merged in the mass of the *plebs frumentaria*, in the poor urns of the *columbaria*, and the anonymous graves of the Esquiline. Their contribution to Roman life cannot be estimated. It is their more fortunate or energetic brothers who give the impression of a basically valuable activity in nearly all fields of economic life. It was freedmen who were able to give an impetus to development in scholarship and the arts and crafts and to assist in the expansion of trade and industry. They did not stand alone in this, but without their contribution the achievement of the first century B.C. would have been smaller, and of a different character.

IV

POLITICS

(i) The 'Ordo Libertinus'

THE last century of the Republic was a time when large sections of the population had reason to be discontented with their economic, social, and political lot, when politicians fully realized the need to exploit this discontent and to seek support from as many quarters as possible, and when civil war and revolution provided more opportunity than ever before for ability, or unscrupulousness, to assert itself against mere right of birth. It is against such a background that we see a new prominence of the *ordo libertinus* in political life and the rise of individual freedmen, phenomena which are not explained by the frequency of manumission and the consequently large number of ex-slaves in the citizen body, but which seem to indicate a high degree of political awareness in the freedman, and a high level of competence, drive, and even patriotism.

Operae pretium est . . . libertinorum hominum studia cognoscere qui, sua virtute fortunam huius civitatis consecuti, vere hanc suam patriam esse iudicant, quam quidam hic nati, et summo nati loco, non patriam suam sed urbem hostium esse iudicaverunt.[1]

Libertini as a class became a distinguishable force in politics, to be spoken of in the same breath as other *ordines* in the state.[2] The effect of this position for good or ill was already a matter for appraisal in the Augustan age. Dionysius held[3] that the Roman state was polluted by the admixture of freedmen citizens, many of whom

---

[1] Cic. *Cat.* iv. 16.
[2] There was some justification for calling them an order, since, as the equestrian order was marked off by certain privileges, so the freedmen were distinguished by certain handicaps. The term is not very common: cf. Livy, xliii. 12. 9; xlii. 27. 3; Auct. *Vir. Ill.* 73. See now Nicolet, *L'Ordre équestre*, p. 168.
[3] iv. 24: εἰς τοσαύτην σύγχυσιν ἥκει τὰ πράγματα καὶ τὰ καλὰ τῆς Ῥωμαίων πόλεως οὕτως ἄτιμα καὶ ῥυπαρὰ γέγονεν ὥσθ' οἱ μὲν ἀπὸ λῃστείας καὶ τοιχωρυχίας καὶ πορνείας καὶ παντὸς ἄλλου πονηροῦ πόρου χρηματισάμενοι, τούτων ὠνοῦνται τῶν χρημάτων τὴν ἐλευθερίαν καὶ εὐθὺς εἰσι Ῥωμαῖοι.

had gained their freedom by purchasing it with the ill-gotten gains of highway robbery, breaking and entering, and pimping. He put the blame on the low moral standards of the manumitted; to others the salient point was their foreign blood and the equality which they at once obtained on manumission.[1] Already in the late second century Scipio Aemilianus had been able to comment on the prevalence of freedmen in popular gatherings, alleging even that they were his own ex-prisoners.[2] Describing canvassing methods for the *Comitia Centuriata*, the author of the *Commentariolum Petitionis* told the candidate to remember always the peculiar composition of the electorate:

'Roma est', civitas ex nationum conventu constituta, in qua multae insidiae, multa fallacia, multa in omni genere vitia versantur, multorum adrogantia, multorum contumacia, multorum malevolentia, multorum superbia, multorum odium ac molestia perferenda est. Video esse magni consili atque artis in tot hominum cuiusque modi vitiis tantisque versantem vitare offensionem, vitare fabulam, vitare insidias, esse unum hominem accomodatum ad tantam morum ac sermonum ac voluntatum varietatem.[3]

He was referring to *cives Romani*, who would mostly be *libertini* rather than enfranchised *peregrini*. Freedmen would also have constituted the majority of the aliens whom Cicero mentions as troublesome or influential in the *contiones*, the Greeks, Asians and Jews.[4] The numbers of these alien freedmen, as we have seen, cannot be determined, though it appears that they were large and concentrated in Rome itself. They would therefore probably outnumber *ingenui* in some *contiones*, and indeed at the *comitia*, but there weight of numbers did not count, since the freedmen were at this period confined to the urban tribes and disposed of only four votes.[5] Their position in the *Comitia Centuriata* may have been

---

[1] App. *BC* ii. 120: ... διαφθαρμένης ἐκ πολλοῦ τῆς πολιτείας. παμμεγεθές τε γὰρ ἐστιν ἤδη τὸ πλῆθος ὑπὸ ξενίας καὶ ὁ ἐξελεύθερος αὐτοῖς ἰσοπολίτης ἐστίν.

[2] Vell. ii. 4. 4; Val. Max. vi. 2. 3; Plut. *Mor.* 201E; Brunt, *JRS* 52 (1962), 70, n. 19; Astin, *CQ* 10 (1960), 135 ff.

[3] 54.

[4] *Flacc.* 17; 66; cf. Philo, *Leg.* 155. Of course, non-citizens also took part in such meetings: cf. App. *BC* ii. 120 (with special reference to slaves).

[5] pp. 49 ff. Some wealthy and influential individuals may have secured membership of a rustic tribe.

that they were placed in the appropriate urban classes of their census rating.[1] They are certainly found exercising a strong influence on the voting of both assemblies. What factors may have produced such influence? Concentration in the *Urbs* is relevant. So is the fact that they could be easily approached, through patron or *collegium*,[2] and in some cases at least, through national groupings, such as the strong Jewish network. Another factor which might maximize the influence of freedmen was that, to a certain extent, they represented an élite: the fact that they had won their freedom 'sua virtute', or less reputably, indicates a certain measure of ability, loyalty, or ambition which might be higher than that of the mass of the *ingenui*. The freedman had had to develop before manumission qualities which might serve him well in politics, not the least of which were diplomacy, discretion, ability to please, possibly deceit and unscrupulousness. The other side of this picture is that the freedman might have a chip on his shoulder which impelled him to assert himself. Lastly, since it was the wealthy and powerful who owned and manumitted most slaves,[3] the proportion of freedmen from such families was high, and the freedmen of the great would normally possess more ambition, education, backing, and cash.

Many of the motives which actuated *libertini* were shared by other sections of the population and were not peculiar to them. For instance the concern for the sanctity of *provocatio* which was shown by the crowd rebuked by Aemilianus was common to the whole *plebs*. One question concerned *libertini* alone: the inequality of their position in the tribes. The legislation on this subject has already been described.[4] Here we have only to develop the significance of the question in party politics. It was suggested by Taylor that until the *Lex Tabellaria* of 139 B.C., reformers were mainly interested in freedmen living in the country but registered in the city tribes, and that after this date the interest shifted to those living in Rome.[5] She also held that in the earlier period it was the 'patricians' who wished to increase their own power by having their

---

[1] pp. 51 f.   [2] *Comm. Pet.* 29 f.
[3] Cf. Brunt, *JRS* 48 (1958), 165.   [4] pp. 39 ff.
[5] *Voting Districts*, pp. 141, 146.

freedmen in the rustic tribes, while later it was the *Populares* who courted this group.[1] The latter theory is too schematic. As Last pointed out,[2] both Appius Claudius and Sulpicius Rufus sought the support of the freedmen for a minority group in the ruling class, but in the intervening years the nobility itself sometimes acquiesced in the dispersion of freedmen through all the tribes. Some reformers were concerned to distribute *libertini* who resided in the country,[3] but it has been argued[4] that Appius Claudius himself anticipated the first century radicals by distributing freedmen who actually lived in Rome. It is clear that the *humiles* who benefited formed a *factio* loyal to him, not to their patrons. The *Lex Tabellaria* may not have removed the burden of adherence to the patron's politics as has been supposed. It was of course natural that the *Populares* in their search for support should have attempted to win the freedmen and put them in a better position to vote. But it was not tried till 88 B.C., when Sulpicius, perhaps on the pretext of rewarding the good service done by twelve cohorts of *libertini* during the Social War,[5] brought in a distribution bill. We do not hear of any agitation by freedmen comparable to the allied agitation for the franchise, probably because they were not organized as were the Italians. We have seen that the bill would have permitted freedmen to vote in the same tribe as their patrons, and that this would have swamped their patrons' votes.[6] It was a dangerous expedient and though Cornelius and Manilius had some claim to be considered responsible politicians, it was not a measure which commended itself to Pompey or Crassus,[7] or to Caesar.[8] It is easy to see why: if we are right in thinking that the population of the *Urbs*

---

[1] *Party Politics in the Age of Caesar* (California, 1949), p. 54.
[2] *Gnomon*, 22 (1950), 364 f.
[3] The censors who preceded Gracchus and Pulcher.
[4] pp. 39 ff.
[5] App. *BC* i. 212; Macrob. i. 11. 32; Livy, *Ep*. lxxiv (wrongly saying that this was the first time that freedmen had served); cf. Botsford, *Roman Assemblies*, p. 404, n. 1, for a suggestion that Sulpicius tried to reward only the twelve cohorts, not all freedmen. But this conflicts with the evidence that Sulpicius' bill was taken over by later politicians, so it does not seem that its scope could have been so limited.
[6] Cic. *Mil*. 87; Asc. *Mil*. 52C.
[7] Dio, xxxvi. 42. 2.
[8] Taylor, *Party Politics*, p. 55.

was mainly libertine, it would have given the freedmen the whip hand over all other sections of the community, except when a majority of voters from the country could come to Rome for a *comitia* of unusual importance. Therefore the redistribution of freedmen through all the tribes would have had a cataclysmic effect on the rights of native Romans, and the scheme did not appeal to the more responsible politicians.

Attempts to put freedmen in the rustic tribes failed. Yet there is evidence that they exercised considerable influence over the voting. The *Commentariolum* recommended wooing the *libertini* because of their influence in the *Centuriata*:

> Quam ob rem omnis centurias multis et variis amicitiis cura ut confirmatas habeas. Et primum, id quod ante oculos est, senatores equitesque Romanos, ceterorum ordinum navos homines et gratiosos complectere. Multi homines urbani industrii, multi libertini in foro gratiosi navique versantur. Quos per te, quos per communis amicos poteris, summa cura ut cupidi tui sint elaborato, appetito, adlegato, summo beneficio te adfici ostendito.'[1]

The suggestion must be that *libertini* were members of the elective assembly and that some of them had considerable influence on the vote, so that their opinion was as worth taking into account as that of certain other 'urbani'. Presumably the latter were freeborn city-dwellers and both they and the freedmen were registered in the *classes* of the urban tribes, in contrast to the senators and *equites* who were normally registered in the country districts. To be influential the freedmen and the 'urbani' must have been those in the wealthier classes, who carried most weight. They thus represented a city influence, in which Cicero was poor, for most of his support came from the *municipia*. Some of these energetic and politically-minded freedmen will have had wealthy and powerful patrons, or they will have belonged to the solid *bourgeoisie*, men such as those whom Cicero praised in the *Pro Sestio* in the notorious phrase, 'Sunt etiam libertini optimates'.[2] Besides voting themselves, they influenced the vote of others. The *Commentariolum*[3] advised Cicero to see that his own freedmen and slaves spoke well of him,

[1] 29 [2] 97. [3] 17.

and Julius Caesar was noted for the attention which he gave to conciliating the slaves and freedmen of those whom he wished to win.[1] In 142 B.C., according to his rival Claudius, Scipio Aemilianus in his candidature for the censorship had been supported by a crowd of ignoble men and ex-slaves, who were familiar with the ways of the forum and able to call up a crowd and control a political situation.[2] The language[3] recalls the *forensis factio* of Appius Claudius. Aemilianus' clients were urban freedmen of much the same type. But possibly they were led by men closely connected with Scipio himself. Dionysius of Halicarnassus[4] made Servius Tullius say that freedmen would serve their patrons in legislative and electoral assemblies, and this was one of the ways they did it.

The richer *libertini* will have been those who exerted influence on and in the *Centuriata*. The view taken by Cicero (in public) was that they were energetic and Optimate in sympathy: the speech of Claudius shows them as a noisy clique rallying the mob. But the real *forensis factio* acted in the *Comitia Tributa* and *Concilium Plebis* and it will not have been made up of wealthy *liberti* of the nobles as much as the *opifices* and *tabernarii*. It was this group which supported Appius Claudius and elected Flavius to the curule aedileship of 304 B.C. The urban tribes in the late Republic could normally be relied on to support the radicals, and in these tribes freedmen and their sons must have formed the majority. The *Palatina*, according to Cicero, was a plague-spot, 'per quam omnes illae pestes vexare rem publicam dicebantur'.[5] It was Clodius' own tribe, and among its known members are a freedman and three others of probable freed descent.[6]

But pressure was not exerted only by and through the vote.

---

[1] Suet. *DJ* 27. 1; Dio, xl. 60. 4.

[2] Plut. *Paull.* 38. 3. The names of two supporters, Licinius Philonicus and the *praeco* (civil servant) Aemilius (ibid. 38. 4), suggest that these included *liberti* of the upper classes. Aemilius could have been a freedman of Scipio himself. Licinius could have been a freedman of the Crassi, but two possible patrons, P. Crassus Dives and C. Crassus, were probably not friends of Scipio (A. E. Astin, *Scipio Aemilianus* (Oxford, 1967), pp. 91 f.).

[3] ἀνθρώπους ἀγεννεῖς καὶ δεδουλευκότας, ἀγοραίους δὲ καὶ δυναμένους ὄχλον συναγαγεῖν καὶ σπουδαρχίᾳ καὶ κραυγῇ πάντα πράγματα βιάσασθαι.

[4] iv. 22. [5] *Sest.* 114.

[6] Taylor, *Voting Districts*, p. 148.

Even non-citizens had begun to make themselves felt in *contiones*, and vocal *libertini* in the city could show what they wanted in a way which could worry politicians. We recall the importance attached to demonstrations in the theatre against the triumvirs; the shouting against Flaccus in the lawcourts; the behaviour of *contiones* from that of Carbo after the death of Tiberius Gracchus (consisting in large part of *libertini* according to Aemilianus) to those of Clodius; the *operae* who shouted down Pompey at the trial of Milo in 56 B.C.; the funeral of Caesar when Antony roused the slaves and the poor.[1] Such popular demonstrations were the sounding-board of the Republic, although like all such protests they exaggerated the importance of a minority group. The *plebs Romana* was normally the group involved and Cicero affected to believe that their power meant control by freedmen or even slaves.[2]

But although the freedmen were strong and sometimes active in the political life of the capital, it cannot be said that any consistent purpose can be attributed to them as a pressure group. They were largely the tools of politicians: they did not, like the *socii*, band together to obtain their rights. Nor was the *ordo libertinus* more than a tenuous concept, except in cases when magisterial action, such as conscription, defined the class. Unlike the *ordo equester*, the freedmen had no common goal towards which they could work: the class was too disparate to share common ambitions. Attribution to the country tribes was probably earnestly desired mainly by the wealthiest freedmen, but such men might well think they could more easily obtain it through their patrons than through the radicals. Hence they would be Optimate and pin their faith on the sanctity of property. The poorer freedmen shared their grievances with the ingenuous poor and their actions cannot be identified with those of the *ordo libertinus* either.

(ii) *The Collegia*

We now turn to methods of putting illegal pressure on voters and politicians, the methods exploited by revolutionaries like Catiline

[1] 'servique et egentes' (Cic. *Att.* xiv. 10. 1).
[2] *Att.* ii. 16. 1: 'agro Campano diviso, quod vectigal superest domesticum praeter vicesimam? quae mihi videtur una contiuncula clamore pedisequorum nostrorum esse peritura.' Cf. ibid. 1. 8.

and Clodius, who did not merely use their own *liberti* or those of their friends, but sought *clientela* from the urban mob.[1] One way of uniting the *opifices* and *tabernarii* was through the professional *collegia*. We have seen that there is reason to suppose that the majority of such tradesmen and craftsmen were freedmen, though native Romans were no doubt much employed in such trades as building. The question of the *collegia* is therefore relevant to the subject of *libertini*. Here, I shall outline briefly what I consider to have been the history of the *collegia* in the fifties and sixties B.C., and then argue that these colleges contained a large admixture of freedmen.

The legislation on the *collegia* in these years is a complex and difficult problem, and cannot be investigated fully here. I accept in the main the conclusions of F. M. De Robertis.[2] From early times, *collegia* had been allowed by law without any statutory legislation having been deemed necessary. The state interfered only when an association appeared dangerous, as in the case of the *senatusconsultum de Bacchanalibus*.[3] But in the sixties began a spate of legislation and *senatusconsulta* inspired by a new political threat from various kinds of association. *Collegia* were being used for electoral corruption and intimidation. These were trade and religious guilds, especially the organizations in the *vici* in the fifties, and political clubs, *sodalicia* or *sodalitates*, catering for the rich. The influence of freedmen will have been confined almost entirely to the *collegia*, the lower-class bodies.[4] In 64 B.C.[5] a *senatusconsultum* was passed against certain colleges which seemed to be in conflict with the public interest.[6] Only colleges which had a bona-fide purpose and which were of service to the community were allowed to continue.[7]

[1] See now P. A. Brunt, *Past and Present* 35 (1966), 3 ff.
[2] *Il Diritto Associativo Romano dai collegi della reppublica alle corporazioni del basso impero* (Bari, 1938), pp. 131 ff.
[3] De Robertis, *Diritto Associativo*, pp. 53 ff.
[4] I shall use '*collegium*' generically for the trade associations and religious and local guilds, though these might have a variety of titles. Cf. De Robertis, *Diritto Associativo*, pp. 14 f.; J. P. Waltzing, *Étude historique sur les corporations professionelles chez les romains jusqu'à la chute de l'empire d'Occident* (Louvain, 1895–6), iv, pp. 236 ff.   [5] De Robertis, *Diritto Associativo*, pp. 77 f.
[6] Asc. *Pis.* 7A: '... collegia sublata sunt quae adversus rem publicam videbantur esse *constituta*.'
[7] Asc. *Corn.* 75D: 'Frequenter tum etiam coetus factiosorum hominum sine

Those dissolved had been used for political purposes, they had the name 'collegia',[1] and some of them were of ancient foundation, so not all had been founded for political reasons.[2] The decree was apparently comprehensive and dissolved all colleges with very few exceptions. There is debate on the subject of the colleges at which it was primarily aimed. Mommsen[3] claimed that these were the 'collegia compitalicia', as he named the organizations which he held to have existed in the *vici* to carry on the cult of the *Lares*. Waltzing,[4] denying the existence of such colleges, thought that the professional guilds were those mainly affected. It seems reasonable to suppose, however, in spite of the lack of explicit evidence, that professional guilds might also have been regional in organization. Two passages attest the colleges affected: Asconius,[5] commenting on the holding of *ludi compitalicii* by Sex. Cloelius[6] before the restoration of the colleges by Clodius,[7] says 'Solebant autem magistri collegiorum ludos facere, sicut magistri vicorum faciebant Compitalicios praetextati, qui ludi sublatis collegiis discussi sunt.'[8] Sex. Cloelius, though not a *magister*, held compitalician games with the approval of Clodius. There were no colleges in being at this time, and thus no properly appointed officials. This is, I think, the simplest interpretation of Cicero and Asconius. Whatever name it had, some sort of organization seems to have existed, and this had been dissolved by the *senatusconsultum* of 64 B.C. The other passage concerns a college of Cornelii. Asconius' comment (in his notes on

publica auctoritate malo publico fiebant: propter quod postea collegia et S.C. et pluribus legibus sunt sublata praeter pauca atque certa quae utilitas civitatis desiderasset, sicut fabrorum fictorumque (fictorumque Manutius; lictorumque Σ).

[1] De Robertis, *Diritto Associativo*, p. 88.
[2] Dio, xxxviii. 12; cf. perhaps Cic. *Sest.* 55.
[3] *De Collegiis et Sodaliciis Romanorum* (Kiel, 1843), pp. 57, 74. Cf. pp. 198 f.
[4] *Corporations*, i. pp. 98 ff.
[5] *Pis.* 7A.
[6] Not Clodius. See D. R. Shackleton-Bailey, *CQ* 10 (1960), 41 f.
[7] Cic. *Pis.* 8.
[8] The punctuation of this passage is disputed. Most texts, including Clark's, insert commas after 'facere' and 'faciebant', but this is awkward Latin. It seems preferable to adopt the punctuation suggested by Max Cohn, *Zum römischen Vereinsrecht* (Berlin, 1873), p. 40, n. 62 (cf. De Robertis, *Diritto Associativo*, p. 84, n. 45) of one comma after 'facere'. The *magistri vici* held *ludi compitalicii*, those of other colleges also held games but did not participate in the compital celebrations, according to Festus, s.v. *piscatorii ludi*.

the *Pro Cornelio* of 65 B.C.) on the *senatusconsultum* was apropos of an argument introduced by Cicero to show that a certain Philerotis who was involved in the case was not a slave of his client. The orator said that there were so many Cornelii that there must exist several owning slaves of this name. There were indeed so many that they formed a college.[1] This college then existed in 65 B.C. and Asconius believed it to have been one of those dissolved the following year. It appears to have consisted of freedmen of Sulla. We have an inscription set up in honour of Sulla as dictator by certain *libertini*, who are thought to have formed a permanent *collegium* and not to have joined together merely for this occasion, though the inscription does not vouch for it.[2] They are further credibly identified with the ten thousand Cornelii (or some of them), who were freed by Sulla and used to safeguard himself when he retired. These men were picked for their youth and strength from the slaves of the proscribed,[3] and were based on Rome itself.[4] Possibly ex-slaves of Marius were of their number, since the inscription was found at Minturnae.[5] Such a band, though no doubt it had some pretext for existing other than Sulla's security,[6] was a perfect weapon for sedition, especially if its members were still in Rome in 65 B.C.[7] De Robertis also holds that we know of a college of gladiators which was dissolved with that of the Cornelii, but this rests on a patent mistranslation.[8] Lastly, the exclusion of certain professional colleges, such as that of the *fabri*, from the ban makes it clear that other professional guilds *were* affected.

[1] . . . Cornelios vero ita multos ut collegium . . . constitutum sit? (Cic. *apud* Asc. *Corn.* 75c.
[2] *CIL* i. 722 = Degr. 353. Cf. Waltzing, *Corporations*, i. p. 107; De Robertis, *Diritto Associativo*, p. 75; Münzer in *RE* iv. 1. 1250.
[3] App. *BC* i. 100.
[4] Ibid., 104.
[5] Gabba *ad* App. *BC* i. 100. Cf. *CIL* x. 6028.
[6] There were other *collegia* formed by the freedmen of one *familia*. See Waltzing, *Corporations*, i. p. 264.
[7] De Robertis (*Diritto Associativo*, p. 103, n. 21) further connects with these Cornelii the *sodalitas* mentioned in *Comm. Pet.* 19: 'Sodalitates hominum ad ambitionem gratiosissimorum tibi obligasti, C. Fundani, Q. Galli, C. Cornelii, C. Orchivi . . .' But to do so, he had to take all these names to be nominative plural, where grammar would demand accusative. In fact they are genitive singular and the aristocratic club of which Cicero's client was a member is meant.
[8] *Diritto Associativo*, p. 87, n. 52.

The *senatusconsultum* was clearly aimed against potential revolutionary groups. Now we know that Catiline in the following year had keen support from the artisans of Rome, though they failed him at the last.[1] These are named in our sources 'urbana plebes'[2] and, in the case of those stirred up by the slaves and freedmen of Lentulus and Cethegus to rescue their masters, 'opifices atque tabernarii'[3] or χειροτέχναι.[4] Cicero, regaining the loyalty of the disaffected, said that there were no craftsmen so wretched or rash that they did not prefer peace and quiet to revolution.[5] I have argued[6] that the shopkeepers and craftsmen of Rome were predominantly freedmen, and the use of the word 'servitia' to describe a section of the discontented here suggests that many of them were of freed status.[7]

The *senatusconsultum* of 64 B.C. seems to have been effective: the Catilinarians were not organized for sufficiently rapid action, and the freedmen and clients of Lentulus failed to get in touch fast enough with the mob-leaders.[8] The discontent of the poor remained exactly as before, and the lesson had been learnt by the next exploiter of their misery. Clodius took over some of Catiline's remaining men, for instance L. Sergius, who may have been his freedman. He was noted as an agitator among the shopkeeping class.[9] In 61 B.C. Clodius was using *operae* made up, according to Cicero, of slaves.[10] Runaway slaves and even slaves with a lesser measure of independence may have been among the malcontents, but Cicero probably meant that freedmen were involved, as the

---

[1] Sall. *BC* 37; 48. 1; Cic. *Cat.* iv. 17.
[2] Sall. *BC* 37. 5.
[3] Sall. *BC* 50. 1.
[4] App. *BC* ii. 5.
[5] *Cat.* iv. 17: 'nulli sunt inventi tam aut fortuna miseri aut voluntate perditi qui non illum ipsum sellae atque operis et quaestus cotidiani locum, qui non cubile ac lectulum suum, qui denique non cursum hunc otiosum vitae suae salvum esse velint.'
[6] pp. 95 ff.
[7] See Appendix 4 on the use of such expressions to mean freedmen.
[8] Sall. *BC* 50. 1: 'duces multitudinum qui pretio rem publicam vexare soliti erant.'
[9] Cic. *Dom.* 13: 'Quis est Sergius? armiger Catilinae, stipator tui corporis, signifer seditionis, concitator tabernariorum, damnatus iniuriarum, percussor, lapidator, fori depopulator, obsessor curiae.'
[10] *Att.* i. 13. 3; 14. 5; 16. 5.

COLLEGIA

word was often used pejoratively of freedmen.[1] In 60 B.C., in fact, Cicero envisaged kow-towing to slaves and *libertini* as the alternative to conciliating the *equites*.[2] Such were the forces marshalled by Clodius and Crassus.

In 58 B.C. Clodius took his opportunity to reconstitute the colleges. He restored those abolished in 64, revived the *Compitalia* and founded innumerable new colleges 'ex omni faece urbis ac servitio concitata'.[3] These new associations were apparently based on the organizations for the cult of the *Lares* and thus adopted the convenient *vicus* divisions.[4] The most exact information that we have from the slanted remarks of Cicero on the subject is that given in the following passages:

Post Red. ad Quir. 13. Cum homines in tribunali Aurelio palam conscribi centuriarique vidissem . . .

Post Red. in Sen. 33. Cum viderem . . . servos simulatione collegiorum nominatim esse conscriptos . . .

Sest. 34. Isdem consulibus inspectantibus servorum dilectus habebatur pro tribunali Aurelio nomine collegiorum cum vicatim homines conscriberentur, decuriarentur, ad vim, ad manus, ad caedem, ad direptionem incitarentur.

Dom. 13. Cum desperatis ducibus decuriatos ac descriptos haberes exercitus perditorum . . .

Dom. 54. Cum in tribunali Aurelio conscribebas palam non modo liberos sed etiam servos ex omnibus vicis concitatos . . .[5]

All these passages are in the same strain and concentrate not on the law itself but the paramilitary character of the organizations which Clodius was able to set up after passing the law. The main points about the new colleges are that they were organized *vicatim*; that their members were divided into *decuriae*;[6] that they were

[1] Appendix 4.
[2] *Att.* ii. 18. 8.
[3] Cic. *Pis.* 9; cf. Asc. *Pis.* 7B; De Robertis, *Diritto Associativo*, pp. 94 f.; Waltzing, *Corporations*, i. pp. 111 f.
[4] De Robertis, *Diritto Associativo*, p. 96.
[5] Cf. also *Pis.* 11: 'dilectus servorum'. Cicero mentioned the law also at *Att.* iii. 15. 1.
[6] It is not clear whether these formed an integral part of the new *collegia* or a parallel organization. (De Robertis, *Diritto Associativo*, p. 107, n. 38, inclined to the latter view.) Cicero concentrates on the *decuriae* to such an extent that one cannot tell if there were members of colleges outside them, or even whole colleges not so arranged.

commanded by *duces*, and that they were enrolled by Clodius personally. These colleges were based probably on the old structure of *collegia* in the *vici*, and the celebration of the *Compitalia* by Clodius helped recruitment, exploiting religious feelings.[1] Thus technically they will have been local trade and religious colleges, though Cicero naturally regarded them as paramilitary organizations for purposes of intimidation, which is what Clodius too intended. Again, the members of the new colleges on whom Cicero concentrates were slaves, who would naturally be prominent in the cult side of the associations, and whom, as non-citizens, he could most safely attack. But freedmen were no doubt members too and could be included in his remarks on slaves.

In reference to the *operae Clodianae*[2] in general the same personnel appears. They were 'hired bands of slaves as well as paupers',[3] 'servi' or 'servitium',[4] and 'sicarii'[5] or 'latrones'.[6] Although slaves[7] might be used to force free voters to support Clodius, or to fight against Optimate bodyguards,[8] they will not have accounted for all Clodius' power in the *Concilium Plebis* and *Comitia Tributa*. Though Cicero accused Piso of having obtained his command without a single vote cast by a free man,[9] and such abuses were possible, there must have been many free voters present, and probably Cicero is counting *libertini* as slaves. Cicero elsewhere[10] claimed that it was the shopkeepers and artisans who had voted against him. These would probably not be slaves. Such calmer statements suggest that the intemperate use of 'servi' among so many other pejorative expressions covers ex-slaves as well. The taunt was commonly

[1] De Robertis, *Diritto Associativo*, p. 96.
[2] Who might include men not in the *collegia*, but who seem generally equivalent to the *decuriati*.
[3] Cic. *Dom.* 79: 'conductis operis non solum egentium sed etiam servorum'. Cf. ibid. 45.
[4] Cic. *Dom.* 89; *Sest.* 47, 53.
[5] Cic. *Sest.* 53.
[6] Cic. *Sest.* 76; *Legg.* iii. 45.
[7] Few masters would have encouraged their slaves to follow Clodius, except artisans who were themselves Clodians. Perhaps many were χωρὶς οἰκοῦντες or even *fugitivi*.
[8] Cf. Cicero's brush with the *operae* (Cic. *Att.* iv. 3. 2 f.). On the use of slaves to intimidate see Cic. *Dom.* 79; *Sest.* 53; *Legg.* iii. 45.
[9] Cic. *Pis.* 57: 'nullo ferente suffragium libero'.
[10] *Dom.* 90; *Acad. Pr.* ii. 144.

used against freedmen, especially those who had allegedly shown themselves unworthy of their freedom and citizenship. This view is also supported by the optimistic passage in which Cicero said that Clodius had been deserted by his free lieutenants Gellius and Decimus,[1] and reduced to canvassing support from slaves by offering them freedom.[2] He could not have been reduced to this unless he previously had had free support.

The Clodian *operae*, I conclude, were recruited from the poor city population, including slaves, but with a large admixture of freedmen *opifices* and *tabernarii*. They were used to intimidate voters, to attack opponents, and to cast their own votes. They were organized on military lines, and Cicero claimed that they were hired.[3] Possibly there were funds from Crassus.[4] But the genuine discontents of the poor in Rome might have sufficed by themselves to keep these bands together. Their leaders were Clodius' own henchmen, some of them also of freed origin, others impoverished *ingenui*.[5]

The *operae* finally went too far when they shouted down Pompey on 6 February, 56 B.C.[6] Pompey believed that Crassus was subsidizing Clodius, and, of course, through him the *operae*.[7] Pompey summoned his own supporters from Picenum. On 10 February, the Senate passed a resolution, 'ut sodalitates decuriatique discederent: lexque de eis ferretur, ut qui non discessissent, ea poena quae est de vi tenerentur.'[8] It has been held[9] that the 'decuriae' in question were those of the tribes and the 'sodalitates' were the aristocratic political clubs which controlled them. But the logic of events suggests that trouble caused by Clodians and offensive to

---

[1] Gellius was an *eques Romanus* (Cic. *Sest.* 110), Decimus a freeborn *designator*.
[2] *Att.* iv. 3. 2.
[3] *Dom.* 79, 89; cf. *Sest.* 112.
[4] Cf. Cic. *QF* ii. 3. 4.
[5] Sergius (Cic. *Dom.* 13, cf. 89) was possibly a freedman; Damio was *libertus* of Clodius (Asc. *Mil.* 46D f.); others were *ingenui*: Fidulius, a leader in the *Concilium Plebis* (Cic. *Dom.* 79); M. Lollius (ibid. 13, cf. 89); Plaguleius (ibid.); Titius of Reate (Cic. *Sest.* 80, 112); Lentidius (ibid. 80); Scato the Marsian (Cic. *Dom.* 116; *Att.* iv. 5. 2, vi. 1. 15). The form of *nomen* or specific mention of origin show that most of them came from outside Rome.
[6] Cic. *QF* ii. 3. 2.   [7] Ibid. ii. 3. 4.
[8] Ibid. ii. 3. 5
[9] Waltzing, *Corporations*, i. pp. 111 f.

the Optimates would be followed by senatorial action against the Clodians, not against Optimate clubs. Pompey was briefly at this point in alliance with the Senate, and awaiting armed supporters capable of disposing of Clodius' toughs, so at last the Senate had a chance to take action, and attack the freedom of association conceded by Clodius' law in 58 B.C.[1] The *decuriae* in question were surely those of Clodius, to which Cicero paid so much attention, the organizations for the use of force in the *comitia* which were part of, or connected with, the colleges. These latter, being religious bodies, would technically have been *sodalitates*. Thus the resolution was aimed only at the Clodian *collegia* in the *vici* and at the *decuriae*, which were not bona-fide associations but created as a cover for terrorism and intimidation. Various other *collegia* are known to have continued to function.[2]

The following year, with the patching-up of the triumvirate, saw the counter-action of Crassus, the *Lex Licinia de sodaliciis*. On this, I accept fully the thesis of De Robertis, that it was not the law proposed by the *senatusconsultum* of the previous year, but one of much larger scope, condemning not only the Clodian colleges which aimed at *vis*, but also at the aristocratic clubs still in existence, which worked through bribery. Thus men who committed *ambitus* and those who organized groups for purposes of intimidation in the tribes might be accused under this law, for having been involved in illegal political associations.[3] The arguments for this wider view of the *Lex de sodaliciis* cannot be explored here, as its relevance to the Clodian colleges, already quashed by administrative action in the previous year, is only secondary.[4] But it is unlikely that the law was fully effective. Bribery and violence were rife in the next two years and order was only restored by Pompey in 52 B.C. when he called in the troops. Clodius, apart from his alleged plans to distribute the freedmen through all the tribes, which would have

---

[1] De Robertis, *Diritto Associativo*, pp. 100 f.
[2] De Robertis, *Diritto Associativo*, p. 109. But as the law envisaged by the *senatusconsultum* was not passed, it relied on the will of the magistrates to carry it out, till 55 B.C.
[3] Cic. *Planc.* 45: 'decuriasse . . . conscripsisse, sequestrem fuisse, pronuntiasse, divisisse.'
[4] See De Robertis, *Diritto Associativo*, pp. 110 f.

shattered the voting power of the aristocrats, was also probably back at his old tricks, recruiting *decuriae*.[1]

So when Caesar put down all except bona-fide colleges during his dictatorship, political clubs were surely involved. He is said to have banned all but the colleges of ancient constitution.[2] One of the reprieved guilds was the religious organization of the Jews.[3] The law[4] fell into neglect in the civil wars after Caesar's death and Augustus revived it.[5]

In these political *collegia*, freedmen played an important part in those organized on a religious, professional, or local basis, which worked through intimidation (*vis*). The composition of the Clodian *decuriae* and *operae* proved to be strongly libertine, although slaves and displaced Italians[6] and ingenuous shopkeepers and artisans were also recruited and the leaders were not normally freedmen. The *collegia* thus provided an outlet for the artisan freedman of the city and showed that he was not always satisfied with his political or—more important—his economic lot. But the *operae* could not hold the field against the professional fighters, often gladiators,[7] who were called in, still less against the troops of Pompey.

(iii) Liberti *as Political Agents*

The freedmen who had influence in the *Comitia Centuriata* and whom Cicero called Optimates were obviously a different type from the discontented workmen who joined the seditious colleges. These were the rich freedmen, often those of noble patrons, men

---

[1] Cic. *Mil.* 25: 'Convocabat tribus, se interponebat, Collinam novam dilectu perditissimorum civium conscribebat.' This may not have been a muster on the old pattern of *vicus* divisions, perhaps no *collegium* was involved, but it was surely 'decuriari' as forbidden by the *Lex Licinia*. For the language, cf. Cic. *Dom.* 54; *Sest.* 34; *Post Red. in Sen.* 33; *Post Red. ad Quir.* 13.

[2] Suet. *DJ* 42. 3: 'Cuncta collegia praeter antiquitus constituta distraxit.' For trouble caused by colleges at this time, cf. the agitation over the false Marius (Val. Max. ix. 15. 1).

[3] Joseph. *Ant.* xiv. 10. 8.

[4] For the neat proof that it was a law see De Robertis, *Diritto Associativo*, p. 176. Cf. also Waltzing, *Corporations*, i. pp. 113 ff.

[5] Suet. *DA.* 32. 1: 'plurimae factiones titulo collegii novi ad nullius non facinoris societatem coibant. Igitur . . . collegia praeter antiqua et legitima dissolvit.' Cf. *CIL* vi. 4416.

[6] p. 175, n. 5, and Sall. *BC* 37. 5.

[7] e.g. Cic. *Sest.* 78, 85.

who had a vested interest in the *status quo*.[1] Usually freedmen of whom we hear as active in politics were attached to a politician. There is one example of a man with personal political influence who is likely to have been a freedman, the Sardinian Phamea, who promised his help to Cicero in his campaign for the consulship, although Cicero in the end did not avail himself of it.[2] But most freedmen of importance in politics were agents or subordinates of Roman nobles.

Liberti were traditionally used in political contexts. As agents of *vis* against opponents they were exploited, for instance, by Tiberius Gracchus against Octavius,[3] and the friends of Cicero were prepared to use them in 59 B.C.[4] The *liberti* of Lentulus and Cethegus raised the shopkeepers in 63 B.C.;[5] Damio, freedman of Clodius, besieged Pompey in his own house.[6] Such examples are put in the shade by the *Bardyaei*, Marius' freedmen terrorists, who on one estimate numbered over four thousand and who murdered their ex-masters and Marius' opponents,[7] or the ten thousand Cornelii freed by Sulla from among the fittest slaves of the proscribed and intended to help safeguard himself.[8]

But these examples of the use of freedmen in strong-arm tactics are less interesting than their employment as confidential go-betweens and administrators. They are found doing a variety of jobs and the freedom, or at least the openness, with which they were used reached a high point in the Second Triumvirate. For this reason, after a quick survey, I shall consider the habits of individual politicians in respect to the delegation of work to their freedmen, or those of others.

A reference in Plutarch to Cato Uticensis' freedman Butas, whom he used particularly for political work,[9] suggests that it would have been natural for a Roman politician to have a *libertus* or *liberti* specialized in political matters. But in the case of Cicero, of

[1] pp. 166 f. [2] Below, p. 186 and Appendix 6.
[3] Plut. *Ti. Gracch.* 12. 4. [4] Cic. *QF* i. 2. 16.
[5] App. *BC* ii. 5. [6] Asc. *Mil.* 46D f.
[7] Plut. *Mar.* 41. 2, 43, 44. 6; *Sert.* 5. 5; App. *BC* i. 74.
[8] p. 171.
[9] Plut. *Cato Min.* 70. 3: ᾧ μάλιστα πρὸς τὰς πολιτικὰς πραξεῖς ἐχρῆτο. Knaack in *RE* ii. 1. 1080 suggested that Butas was to be identified with a *grammaticus* of the same name (Plut. *Quaest. Rom.* 21; Arnob. v. 18).

whom we know so much more, there is no hint that the freedmen with whom he discussed politics, Tiro or Philotimus,[1] were anything of this kind. Philotimus was primarily a steward and Tiro a secretary, but as employees with their patron's interests supposedly at heart, they were expected to take an interest in politics as they concerned him. Philotimus, in fact, took strong Pompeian views of his own, which Cicero failed to appreciate.[2] But if we do not find *liberti* who definitely concerned themselves only with their patron's political affairs, we find many confidential freedmen who were often engaged in them. An educated and able man, bound securely to his patron by ties of duty and self-interest,[3] was an invaluable confidant and go-between. He could come and go more easily than his patron: it was for a freedman to keep his ear to the ground in Rome, or to deal with the *tribules*,[4] and if his patron[5] or a friend of his patron[6] were disgraced or in exile, negotiate discreetly with friends and enemies for his restoration. Freedmen were commonly used as political agents when the patron was absent from Rome, just as freedmen procurators sometimes dealt with business interests. Appius Claudius' pair of freedmen Phania and Cilix operated a shuttle-service when he was in Cilicia, carrying letters back and forth and gathering information. Cicero said of Phania that he knew as much about politics as did the Republic itself.[7] Phania, at least in part, carried out the job which Caelius was to do the following year for Cicero, with the limitation that he was a freedman, not a senator, and that he was not permanently in Rome. Cilix took over when Phania went back to Cilicia with letters. Such freedmen maintained friendly contact with their patron's political *amici* in the capital. Cilix and Phania had the job of keeping their patron

[1] pp. 262 and pp. 263 f.
[2] Cic. *Att.* vii. 23. 1 f.; viii. 16. 1; ix. 7. 6; xii. 44. 3.
[3] See Cicero's remarks on *accensi*, *QF* i. 1. 13.
[4] Cf. Philotimus in 54, p. 263. On the *tribules*, Cic. *QF* iii. 1. 1.
[5] Cf. Theudas, *libertus* of Trebianus (Cic. *Fam.* vi. 10. 1), and the probable freedman Philargyrus, agent of A. Torquatus (Cic. *Fam.* vi. 1. 6 and perhaps *Att.* ix. 15. 5).
[6] Cf. Trypho, freedman of Livineius Regulus who worked on Cicero's behalf (Cic. *Fam.* xiii. 60).
[7] *Fam.* iii. 1. 1: 'Si ipsa respublica tibi narrare posset, quomodo sese haberet, non facilius ex ea cognoscere posses quam ex liberto tuo Phania, ita est homo non modo prudens verum etiam, quod iuvet, curiosus.'

informed of Cicero's attitude and convincing Cicero of Appius Claudius' goodwill towards him. Here is Cicero's testimony to the eloquence and tact with which Cilix carried out his duty:

> Cilix, libertus tuus, antea mihi minus fuit notus [that is, than Phania] sed, ut mihi reddidit a te litteras plenas et amoris et offici, mirifice ipse suo sermone subsecutus est humanitatem litterarum tuarum. Iucunda mihi eius oratio fuit, cum de animo tuo, de sermonibus, quos de me haberes cotidie, mihi narraret; quid quaeris? biduo factus est mihi familiaris, ita tamen, ut Phaniam valde sim desideratus. Quem cum Romam remittes, quod, ut putabamus, celeriter eras facturus, omnibus ei de rebus, quas agi, quas curari a me voles, mandata des velim.[1]

The social graces served freedmen as well as *ingenui* in oiling the wheels of political co-operation. In this particular case, if the two freedmen succeeded in assuring Cicero of Appius Claudius' goodwill, it would be likely to ensure that the handing-over of command in Cilicia would be smooth and that Cicero would not promote a prosecution of his predecessor. Cicero in fact took notice of the opinion of Phania on the question of where he should enter his province.[2] More crucial negotiations carried out by freedmen will be mentioned later in discussion of the freedmen of the triumvirs.[3]

It has been mentioned that the paucity of civil servants encouraged the use of a governor's own assistants on the staff. *Ingenui* who were often relations or personal friends of course formed the *cohors*.[4] A promagistrate might try to obtain the services of his own or his friends' freedmen who were in the pool of civil servants, as Cicero had his *scriba* Tullius and Lentulus Spinther's freedman Pausanias as his *accensus*. But there would be scope for private freedmen staff to work on provincial business too. Cicero was accompanied by a number of his own *liberti*, including Tiro and Chrysippus,[5] companion to young Marcus, as well as Dionysius,[6] Atticus' freedman and tutor to the two boys. Although the two latter were cultivated men to whom secretarial business might well have been entrusted, it is naturally Tiro of whose work we are told. Unfortunately, it is defined only as 'officia provincialia'.[7] But we

---

[1] Cic. *Fam.* iii. 1. 2. [2] Cic. *Fam.* iii. 5. 3; 6 1 f. [3] p. 187.
[4] e.g. Q. Cicero and a Lucius Tullius were *legati* to Cicero.
[5] pp. 257, 261. [6] p. 120.
[7] Cic. *Fam.* xvi. 4. 3.

get a clearer idea of how a private secretary might deal with public affairs from the notorious example of Statius. He held no official position on Q. Cicero's staff,[1] but nevertheless as his patron's regular secretary (for Quintus seems to have had no other) stepped into the breach when he arrived in the province and found the official correspondence in disorder. Letters demanding settlement of debts and written by the creditors themselves had been sent out ratified by the governor although not checked.[2] This is in itself an index of a staff-shortage, or at least a shortage of responsible staff. Statius took on the work of reading and checking such requests and recommending what decision should be taken. Although a sensible delegation of authority, this occasioned the disapproval of those who did not trust Statius as his patron did. Quintus' gravest error was to allow the influence which his freedman had on decisions to be seen. His enemies, who had exploited the confusions produced by his earlier secretarial methods now attacked his secretary's undue influence. He was said to have persuaded Quintus to take various severe decisions:[3] he may have been involved in some of the angry letters which Cicero himself saw.[4] He was certainly thought of as a power behind the throne, and to avoid talk he had to be sent home early, to show that he was not indispensable.[5] Most of the scandal probably had little basis, for it was rife before Statius' arrival and manumission,[6] but the trouble was that Statius' position of authority was too blatant. Cicero admits how in conversation with himself Statius tended to use language which suggested that he controlled his patron, 'Id mihi non placuit: monui, suasi, deterrui'.[7] A freedman, in fine, could be allowed to guide his patron's judgement, but must not be seen to do so: 'quibus in rebus etiam si fidelitas summa est ... tamen species ipsa tam gratiosi liberti aut servi dignitatem habere nullam potest'.[7]

If Q. Cicero relied on a freedman for help in public business scandal might be provoked, but other politicians could do the same with impunity. Sulla had also trusted his freedmen too far, as is clear from the example of Chrysogonus. Not only in the *Pro Roscio*

[1] p. 158, n. 4. [2] Cic. *QF* i. 2. 8.
[3] Ibid. i. 2. 3. [4] Ibid. i. 2. 6 f.
[5] Ibid. i. 2. 1 f. [6] Cic. *Att.* ii. 18. 4; 19. 1.
[7] Ibid. i. 2. 3.

Amerino but later in tranquillity, Cicero describes the licence of Sullan times and how freedmen were sent out to ruin and rob provinces and allowed to plot and oppress and kill:

> Qui ... dimissiones libertorum ad defaenerandas diripiendasque provincias, qui expulsiones vicinorum, qui latrocinia in agris, qui cum servis, cum libertis, cum clientibus societates, ... qui caedes municipiorum, qui illam Sullani temporis messem recordetur ...[1]

Sulla, it appears, not only gave freedmen too free a rein but deliberately connived at their doings. This seems to have been the case with Chrysogonus. He is listed by Pliny with other freedmen of great men who rose high:

> *NH* xxxv. 200. Talem in catasta videre Chrysogonum Sullae, Amphionem Q. Catuli, *H*ectorem L. Luculli, Demetrium Pompei, Augenque Demetri quamquam et ipsa Pompei credita est, Hipparchum M. Antoni, Menam et Menecratem Sex. Pompei, aliosque deinceps, quos enumerare iam non est, sanguine Quiritium et proscriptionum licentia ditatos. Hoc est insigne venaliciis gregibus opprobriumque insolentis fortunae.

These, I take it, were all freedmen who became rich and powerful in some way, not necessarily the same way for each of them. Nothing further is known of Amphio[2] and the name of the freedman of Lucullus is not known for certain.[3] Demetrius[4] and Chrysogonus both enriched themselves and acquired a position through their patrons' favour; Hipparchus was remarkable for his desertion of a position of trust under Antony and subsequent success in Corinthian life,[5] and the freedmen of Sextus Pompey were of course his admirals.[6] No more is known of Auge. Only a general 'Cinderella story' will fit all these people. It is not true that they all obtained influence in state affairs or even that they won their patron's favour for sexual reasons (in spite of the presence of Auge in the list). Only

---

[1] *Parad.* vi. 2. 46; cf. Plut. *Sulla*, 33. 2.
[2] Except that his patron had an interest in Pacuvius' treatment of the legendary Amphio (Cic. *de Or.* ii. 155).
[3] The manuscripts have 'interfectorem' and 'rectorem'. A name is surely needed. 'Interfectorem' would recall the tale that Lucullus was accidentally killed by a freedman lover, Callisthenes (Plut. *Lucull.* 43). 'Interfectorem' might then be a gloss on his name. But the story does not rest on strong authority, nor do we know that Callisthenes had influence on Lucullus nor of any other freedman who was powerful.
[4] pp. 184 f.
[5] Plut. *Ant.* 67. 7; Stein in *RE* viii. 2. 1664 f.
[6] pp. 188 ff.

Chrysogonus, Demetrius, Hipparchus, and the Pompeian admirals have any known significance for Roman politics. It is not suggested that all of them, like the others whom Pliny omits, won wealth through proscriptions, though this was true at least of Chrysogonus, or civil war, as in the case of the last three.

We are nowhere directly told Chrysogonus' function as freedman and slave[1] of Sulla. He had a separate establishment on the Palatine, an escort of *togati* when he visited the *forum*, just like a Roman noble, clients in the *municipia*.[2] Cicero, keen to disassociate him as much as possible from Sulla, stressed his *gratia, potentia*, and *dominatio*;[3] he was 'adulescens vel potentissimus hoc tempore nostrae civitatis'.[4] His influence is confirmed by the course of events as Cicero narrates them: the Elder Roscius entered on the closed proscription-lists; the commission sent by the town council of Ameria bamboozled the Younger Roscius accused.[5] Cicero denies that Sulla had any knowledge of the plot.[6] He protests that it is self-evident that the dictator himself had nothing to do with it, and if Chrysogonus tried, as bad freedmen always did, to throw the blame on his patron, he was wasting his time, for everyone knew that the pressure of business prevented Sulla from supervising everything and checking every abuse.[7] But Plutarch claims[8] that Sulla was involved and that he had Roscius brought to trial and entrusted the handling of the evidence to his freedman. While Plutarch seems to have had no evidence to clinch this version, it is likely enough to be true and that Cicero by his deft disassociation of Chrysogonus from Sulla gave the latter the opportunity to disown his tool. It

---

[1] It has been suggested that Chrysogonus was not an ex-slave of Sulla's own, but one of the ten thousand Cornelii who had been slaves of the proscribed (see Gabba on App. *BC* i. 100). But in view of the position of trust and wealth which Sulla gave him, it seems more likely that he was from Sulla's own *familia*. Cf. also Cic. *Rosc. Am.* 22, 25. We may argue too that it would be odd for Cicero to have omitted a point which would have whitewashed Sulla and blackened Chrysogonus still more.

[2] Cic. *Rosc. Am.* 133 ff.; 105 f.
[3] *Rosc. Am.* 28, 122; 35; 140.
[4] Ibid. 6.
[5] Ibid. 21; 25; 28 f. respectively.
[6] Ibid. 22.
[7] Ibid. 130: 'Quae omnia si, quem ad modum solent liberti nequam et improbi facere, in patronum suum voluerit conferre, nihil egerit; nemo est enim, qui nesciat propter magnitudinem rerum multa multos *partim invito*, partim imprudente L. Sulla commisisse.'
[8] *Cic.* 3. 5.

further suggests what I should in any case argue, that Chrysogonus was an agent for Sulla, if not in this matter, when he may have been marauding on his own account, then in other and probably political affairs. He was present at the siege of Volterrae,[1] and his power and especially the respect in which he was held by the *nobiles*[2] are unlikely to have been independent of his being accepted as an agent of Sulla. In view of the ease with which he falsified the proscription-list, according at least to Cicero, he perhaps held some secretarial and very probably some political position. The *liberti* whom Sulla is said to have allowed to plunder provinces would have been the same sort of agent. Some of the odium of the proscriptions and confiscations could be shifted on to the shoulders of freedmen, and it would have been beneath the dignity of most *ingenui* to undertake such work. A freedman could be trusted to be a better tool and could be discarded or transferred if necessary. This did not of course prevent such a tool making huge personal profits on the side: the perquisites for a man like Chrysogonus, who prevented the Amerian delegation from approaching his patron, would have been those usually open to a servant who could guarantee an audience or present a petition to his master when it was likely to be granted. So freedmen were among the worst profiteers of the period.[3]

The influence of back-stage politicians reached a new level when the real decisions came to be made by the *principes viri* instead of the Senate and magistrates. Men like Theophanes of Mytilene, Demetrius of Gadara, Tigellius the Sardinian, Cornelius Balbus of Gades, became important in the circle of Caesar and Pompey, men, that is, of slave or provincial[4] origin. On Pompey's freedman Demetrius—Theophanes was a *peregrinus* enfranchised by Pompey—the evidence is tantalizingly fragmentary. This is inevitable, for the political services of a freedman, as we have seen in the case of Statius, were not to be paraded, and scandal was wilder than the

---

[1] Cic. *Rosc. Am.* 18, etc.   [2] Cic. *Rosc. Am.* 140.
[3] Cic. *Parad.* vi. 2. 46; Sall. *Hist., Or. Lep.* 17: mentioning the profiteers Vettius Picens and 'scriba Cornelius'. The former will be a freeborn Picentine; on the latter see p. 61, n. 5.
[4] For a full account of Greeks in the political life of the eastern part of the empire, see Bowersock, *Augustus and the Greek World*, pp. 1 ff.

reality. Demetrius accompanied Pompey in the East and was already his freedman in 64 B.C. when Cato bumped into him at Antioch.[1] Possibly he had been acquired and freed during the campaign, but Pompey may have taken him with him from Rome. According to Plutarch, he was the most influential of Pompey's companions and, like the rest, was allowed to get out of hand, although in other respects he was quite a clever young man. He was obviously assumed to have Pompey's ear, hence the adulation of the Antiochenes which so infuriated Cato. In fact his personal ascendancy over his patron, examples of which are given by Plutarch, would also allow him to dispense political patronage. His own town of Gadara received re-foundation at Pompey's hands for his sake.[2] In fact a native freedman would have been a sensible choice of agent for the conqueror of the East: he could interpret local conditions just as he could exploit the inhabitants of Antioch to his own honour and glory. Demetrius was proverbial for his wealth,[3] doubtless obtained mainly in the East. In Rome, his employment by Pompey continued on the same lines: in 59 B.C. we find Cicero asking Atticus to pump him for information on the plans of Pompey and Crassus.[4] Apart from this, the information we have is wild. Seneca relates that he was wealthier than Pompey, and Dio claims that there was a tale that he and not his patron paid for the Theatre of Pompey, with spoils from the East.[5]

Caesar seems to have preferred provincial or ingenuous Roman agents to freedmen. He was notable for the loyalty of his supporters, some of them, like Balbus, ex-Pompeian. He put the son of one of his freedmen in charge of three legions at Alexandria, but if the man was ingenuous, as is to be presumed, Rufio—or Rufinus,

---

[1] Plut. *Pomp.* 40. 1.
[2] Jos. *B.J.* i. 155.
[3] Sen. *Tranq.* 8. 6; Dio, xxxix. 38. 6.
[4] *Att.* iv. 11. 1.
[5] Sen. *Tranq.* 8. 6; Dio, xxxix. 38. 6. A Demetrius who appears in 45 B.C. as a person whom Cicero wished to conciliate (*Fam.* xvi. 22. 2; 17. 2; 19) has been identified with Pompeius Demetrius. But the name was very common. A further identification has been made with a certain 'Pompei servus, libertus Caesaris' who embezzled Pompeian property (Cic. *Phil.* xiii. 12). There is no evidence to support this. If Cicero were speaking technically, a man named C. Julius (*cognomen*) Pompeianus would be meant (see Münzer in *RE* iv. 2. 2803). Just possibly, it could refer to a freedman of Pompey who had deserted to Caesar and so become a client and as it were freedman of the latter (cf. Cic. *Mil.* 89 for the idea).

for the name is uncertain—was entitled to serve as *tribunus militum*.[1] Suetonius also claims that Caesar put his own slaves in charge of the mint and of *vectigalia*, but does not substantiate the charge. It could be a generalization from a hostile source,[2] but Caesar could have anticipated the use of slaves and *liberti* by Augustus in a secretariat dealing with public moneys.[3] Tigellius the Sardinian, who was probably, like his uncle Phamea, of libertine origin,[4] was on the fringes of the Caesarian ruling group. In 52 or 51 B.C. he had been offended because Cicero was unable to defend Phamea, as he had promised, because the trial was unfortunately fixed for a day when Cicero was otherwise engaged. Phamea was put out and Tigellius, whether or not he started a feud at once, was blaming Cicero for having broken his promise in 45 B.C. Cicero claimed that he was unperturbed by the attack of a man who had been knocked down by Calvus' epigram of 'Sardi Tigelli putidum caput venit', for he would not kow-tow to everyone: 'ego non omnibus servio'. But he was troubled enough to write urgent letters to Atticus and Fadius Gallus, asking them to find out what was going on.[5] Clearly the danger was that, in spite of his good relations with other Caesarians such as Balbus the Younger,[6] Tigellius might prejudice Caesar against him. The anxiety of Cicero seems excessive unless the quarrel might have had such repercussions as disgrace with Caesar. But the motives remain outside the political field, except in so far as personal *amicitiae* might influence political *amicitiae*.[7] Tigellius moved in the ruling class: he was a friend of Caesar, Cleopatra,[8] and Augustus,[9] so that he was in a position to show off his acquaintance with kings and tetrarchs.[10] His adherence to the Caesarians, as far as can be seen, was based on personal friendship, and he charmed people by his abilities as a singer and a wit.

[1] Suet. *DJ* 76. The *De Bello Alexandrino* is silent.
[2] The remark that Rufio/Rufinus had had homosexual relations with Caesar ('exoleto suo') suggests that Suetonius may have been affected by slanderous accounts here.
[3] Suet. *DA* 101. 4.   [4] Appendix 6.
[5] Cic. *Att.* xiii. 49; 51; *Fam.* vii. 24.
[6] e.g. Cic. *Att.* xiii. 49. 2.
[7] For a reminder that the friends of the great may be detached from politics see Hor. *Sat.* ii. 6. 51 ff.
[8] Porph. *ad* Hor. *Sat.* i. 2. 1.   [9] Hor. *Sat.* i. 3. 4 f.
[10] Hor. *Sat.* i. 3. 12 f.: 'modo reges atque tetrarchas, Omnia magna loquens'.

In the wars and disturbances of the triumviral period the mediation and adhesion of freedmen seem to have been more important than ever before. Octavian was started off on the road to power by the support of loyal Caesarians, among whom freedmen were most prominent.[1] By his adoption he acquired the rights of patron over a useful number of rich *liberti*.[2] It was a *clientela* worth putting second to that of the legions. In the breakdown of republican rule, negotiations between military leaders became more and more weighty and secret, and the destinies of the world were controlled by the discussions which took place between generals. As intermediaries, they tended to use freedmen, as had always been customary, but now more than ever because it was hard to trust anyone else. Sextus Pompeius and Scribonius Libo thus sent two freedmen to carry confidential letters to the Senate and Antony in 44 B.C.[3] Antony used his freedman Callias as an emissary to negotiate a marriage between his daughter and Lepidus' son in 37 B.C., something which would have been possible earlier too, but the difference was that as soon as he heard that Callias had been sent, Octavian suspected a plot.[4] *Liberti* were used as pledges of good faith, either offered by their patrons as hostages (as appears to have been the case when Lepidus sent a certain Apella to Plancus)[5] or restored when captured by opponents.[6] Octavian's staff of freedmen is better known than that of any of the others. In these years we hear of Helenus, Philadelphus, Epaphroditus, and Thyrsus.[7] The latter two were employed on delicate missions to Cleopatra, Thyrsus because of his tact and persuasiveness. Epaphroditus was accompanied in his mission to keep Cleopatra alive by a Roman *eques*, so the responsibility was not given entirely to a freedman.

But these were minor intermediaries and the fact that each is

[1] App. *BC* iii. 11. [2] App. *BC* iii. 94.
[3] They were Philo, freedman of Pompey, and Hilarus, freedman of Libo (Cic. *Att.* xvi. 4. 1). Philo may have been the violent Pompeian mentioned as active in Lusitania (Auct. *Bell. Hisp.* 35. 2).
[4] App. *BC* v. 93.
[5] Cic. *Fam.* x. 17. 3. The name suggests that he was a freedman, presumably a Jew.
[6] Helenus, a freedman in the service of Octavian, was restored by Menas (Dio, xlviii. 30).
[7] Dio, xlviii. 30; App. *BC* v. 331; Plut. *Ant.* 79. 6, Dio, li. 114, 13. 4; Plut. *Ant.* 732, Dio, li. 86 f. respectively.

known only from one mission shows that they were not of great individual importance. The freedmen of Sextus Pompeius were a different matter. He was held to be the freedman of his freedman and the slave of his slaves.[1] There were various reasons for their prominent position in the fleet. The aristocratic followers of Pompey were hardly material for admirals. Obedience, as Pompeius Magnus had found in the campaign of Pharsalia, was hard to extract from nobles. Freedmen made better lieutenants,[2] if loyal. But the clinching argument was that Sextus Pompeius had in the freedmen inherited from his father the best naval commanders available. The general efficiency of his fleet and tactics is evident, but we are also able to deduce various things about the *praefecti*. Their names were Menas (alias Menodorus), Menecrates, Apollophanes, and Demochares.[3] We know from Velleius that Menas and Menecrates were *liberti* of Cn. Pompeius.[4] Other sources call them *liberti* of Sextus, but the confusion is easy[5] and the Roman and nearly contemporary Velleius is to be preferred. Appian held that Demochares and Apollophanes were also *liberti* of Sextus,[6] but these two may well have been technically freedmen of Magnus, clients owing *operae* and duty to his son. The names of Menas-Menodorus and of Menecrates suggest Anatolian origin, and as Plutarch refers to Menas as a pirate,[7] it is suggested that he was one of the pirates captured by Pompey in his campaign of 67 B.C.[8] Menecrates is not called a pirate, but he might well have come from the same net.[9] The period they spent as slaves may have been brief, like that of Tyrannio of Amisus and perhaps Pompeius Demetrius, but they were nevertheless Pompey's freedmen. Perhaps they had been pirate captains and were swiftly released in recognition of their potential usefulness. Certainly they served the son well,

[1] Vell. ii. 73. 1.
[2] See M. Hadas, *Sextus Pompey* (New York, 1930), p. 83.
[3] Who also had aliases: Demochas and Papias.
[4] ii. 73. 3: 'paternos libertos'. Cf. Porph. *ad* Hor. *Epod.* iv.
[5] Cf. App. *BC* iii. 390; Suet. *Gram.* 12.
[6] *BC* v. 356, cf. 351.
[7] *Ant.* 32. 1.
[8] Münzer in *RE* xv. 1. 774 f.
[9] Such origin would also have helped Augustus' claim that this was a pirate war: *RG* 25; Strabo, v. 243; Vell. ii. 73. 3; Lucan vi. 421; Flor. ii. 18. 1; cf. Hadas, *Sextus Pompey*, p. 70.

except for Menas who was a congenital traitor. They were given considerable responsibility to plan their own commands. Thus Menas was sent with part of the fleet to Sardinia in 40 B.C. to damage enemy territory. He ravaged Etruria and seized Sardinia.[1] Pompey also paid attention to his lieutenants' advice on strategy. Menas, for instance, advised him to have nothing to do with Octavian's overtures but to play a waiting game and starve Italy out, a policy which was opposed by Staius Murcus.[2] Pompey got rid of the latter, again, according to our source, on the freedman's advice.[3] But he does not seem to have followed his lieutenant blindly, as Velleius thought. He did not restore Menas to the position of trust which he had previously enjoyed after he had deserted to Octavian and, after receiving great rewards for his treachery, returned to his patron again.[4] He decided the strategy which should be employed, allowing the necessary room for adaptation and opportunism by his subordinates. Apart from the dangerous rivalry between Menas and Menecrates,[5] it was the obstinacy of noble supporters which was the main threat to unity. The anti-Pompeian tradition naturally asserted that Pompey's supporters were riff-raff and he himself was inefficient and weak. The traitor Menas was nevertheless a valued prize for Octavian: he was given the *anulus aureus* and a high command, under Calvisius.[6] Clearly, Menas' abilities were appreciated by others than Pompey, although Octavian did not trust him with an independent command, which is said to have rankled.[7] Nor can Pompey's dependence on freedmen commanders have been as dangerous as Augustan and later writers affected to believe, for the war was a serious civil conflict, although Augustus played it down as a mere suppression of pirates.

Menas controlled Sardinia for Pompeius. Freedmen are found doing similar work for the triumvirs. The influx of freedmen's sons

[1] App. *BC* v. 238; Dio, xlviii. 30.
[2] App. *BC* v. 293.　　　　　　　　　　　　　　　　[3] Ibid. v. 297.
[4] Ibid. v. 400; Dio, xlviii. 54. 7.　　　　　　　　[5] App. *BC* v. 343, etc.
[6] Probably as *praefectus classis*, pp. 65 f. But on his second desertion of Pompey, Octavian received him less warmly. He was sent to Pannonia, where he died in a skirmish (Dio, xlix. 37. 6). See *MRR* ii, p. 410 for the suggestion that he may still have ranked as prefect or legate.
[7] Dio, xlviii. 54. 7.

into the Senate, and even the rise of some more dubious characters under their patronage have already been mentioned.[1] In or just after 39 B.C. Cyprus was controlled on Antony's behalf by a freedman of Caesar, Demetrius.[2] Probably Antony's steward at Corinth was concerned with public affairs and not just a private procurator.[3] A freedman's son, Vedius Pollio, settled Asia in perhaps 31 or 30 B.C. for Octavian.[4] Another freedman of Julius Caesar's,[5] Licinus, was procurator with the important job of organization in Gaul[6] up to the visit of Augustus himself in 16 or 15 B.C. We do not know when he was sent out but according to Seneca he had been there a long time: 'Licinus multos annos regnavit',[7] conceivably since before 27 B.C., for with the beginnings of his constitutional power Augustus became more careful in choosing subordinates for their respectability. He was himself a Gaul and it seems likely that Caesar may have had his eye on him for work in his native province and that he would have had some experience in administration before Augustus gave him this important post. For assessing the resources of the new and untapped province Licinus must have been well adapted: he may have belonged to the ruling class and have spent only a short period as war-prisoner and slave. The reports on his activities are uniformly unfavourable: he showed barbaric arrogance, cheated the natives with clever tricks and yet was not disowned by Augustus.[8] As the *princeps* kept him in the province for a considerable time and did not repudiate his actions

---

[1] pp. 61 f.
[2] Dio, xlviii. 40. 6. He has been conjecturally identified with Demetrius of Gadara (Münzer in *RE* iv. 2. 2803, no. 50) which is not convincing as the name was common. Cf. p. 185, n. 5.
[3] Plut. *Ant.* 67. 9: διοικητής. He was a private employee, but probably not confined to private business in the Achaean capital.   [4] pp. 233 f.
[5] Dio, liv. 21. Suet. *DA* 67 takes him to have been a freedman of Augustus, but as he was not concerned with Licinus' precise origins and Dio was, we may accept the latter. J. E. B. Mayor, on Juv. *Sat.* i. 109, suggested that Licinus had been freed by Caesar's will, which would explain the confusion, but it was frequently difficult to determine whether a freedman Julius was *libertus* of Caesar or Augustus (especially as the latter bore both *cognomina*). See too the obscurity as to who had freed Menas, p. 188.
[6] As his headquarters were at Lugdunum, he may have been concerned not with the whole of Gaul, but with Lugdunensis and perhaps Aquitania which were later the charge of the procurator at Lugdunum. See O. Brogan, *Roman Gaul* (London, 1953), p. 25.
[7] *Ludus*, 6.   [8] Dio, liv. 21.

afterwards, many of the details, picturesque though they are, are to be discarded. Unlike Vedius Pollio, Licinus did not fall out of favour, but returned to Italy, where he enjoyed large estates,[1] a fortune comparable to that of Crassus,[2] a notoriety equal to that of Pallas and Narcissus,[3] and finally a tomb startling enough to find mention in the works of more than one satirist.[4]

Licinus is compared by Suetonius as a *libertus* held in special honour by Augustus with a certain Celadus.[5] Of him nothing further is known, but there may be traces of other parallels. Allegedly, Areius the Alexandrian philosopher took over as procurator in Sicily from a certain Theodorus.[6] It has been argued[7] that this is a mistake for Athenodorus, who would be the philosopher from Tarsus, but the correction is unnecessary. Bowersock has recently suggested that the procurator could have been the freedman Theodorus of Gadara.[8] This seems likely, though the name was too common to make it at all certain. There was a certain Eros, who was διοικῶν[9] in Egypt and whom Augustus punished for perverse extravagance. As the magistrate διοικητής was a creation of the second century A.D., Bowersock conjectures that Eros' office was that of Idiologus. He considers him to have been a freedman, presumably on the grounds that the name was often servile. This again is possible, but not proved.

Freedmen are found in the period of the Triumvirate as military commanders—Helenus, Menas, Demetrius. The common denominator of the later cases, the freedmen important under Octavian's monarchy, was finance. In the work of reconstruction and organization, the *constitutio* of Asia, the assessment of taxation, Augustus needed expert subordinates, in spite of the energy with which he toured the western provinces to organize for himself. For the first

---

[1] Pers. ii. 36; Sen. *Epp.* 119. 9.   [2] Juv. i. 109.
[3] Sidon. Apoll. v. 7. 3.
[4] Mart. viii. 3. 5 f.; *Anthol.* 77 (*Poetae Latini minores*, ed. Baehrens, p. 64):
    Marmoreo Licinus tumulo iacet, at Cato nullo,
    Pompeius parvo; credimus esse deos?
[5] *DA* 67.   [6] Plut. *Apopth.* 207.
[7] C. Cichorius, *Römischen Studien* (Leipzig, 1922), pp. 280 ff.
[8] *Augustus and the Greek World*, p. 40. On this Theodorus, C. Cichorius, *Rom und Mytilene* (Leipzig, 1888), pp. 62 ff.
[9] Plut. *Apopth.* 207B; Bowersock, *Augustus and the Greek World*, p. 40.

time, the empire was being put on a sound financial footing, and plans were being made for the provinces as a whole.[1] In his search for men to administer the work, Augustus notoriously used *novi*—men like Cornelius Gallus—for his own supporters were new men and the old ruling order had been nearly wiped out. But senators and *equites* could not do everything. In the first confusion after the civil wars, Augustus used the freedmen whom he could lay hands on more easily for financial jobs. We can discern a care in the selection of a Celt for Gaul and probably Greeks for Sicily and Egypt. Later the *princeps* avoided giving freedmen such official posts, but in the early days of his rule they were probably the most reliable and expert men to be had—though Licinus and perhaps Eros took advantage of their power. But freedmen continued to do most of the accounting and census work for the empire and the official ruling class was kept in the dark about the work done by the emperor's own personal secretariat, consisting of slaves and freedmen.[2] Like the *liberti* of republican governors who had helped them with their provincial business, these imperial freedmen wielded a power which caused no scandal until flaunted by Claudius. But the senators who at the death of Augustus were bidden to consult slaves and freedmen about the state of the empire[3] might well have stopped to think.

The end of the Republic and the early part of Augustus' reign marked a high point in the opportunities for freedmen in public life. Great commands and principate necessitated large, loyal, and skilled staff, and the freedmen were qualified, often by birth and education, to make themselves useful in dealing with provincials, by business experience to administer public finances, and because of obligation to their patron to be trusted. When strife between dynasts finally ended and freeborn Romans became willing to settle down and accept the rule of one man and co-operate in the work of empire, the necessity for extraordinary appointments to freedmen was removed. But their usefulness behind the scenes continued, just as it had been in the days of republican politicians and governors, although modified in scope because power was in the hands of the *princeps*.

---

[1] G. H. Stevenson, *CAH* x, pp. 189 ff.
[2] R. Syme, *The Roman Revolution*, p. 410.   [3] Suet. *DA* 101. 4.

Conclusions

The first century B.C. marks the highest point so far in the political importance of the freedman. But except for the distribution question, we know of no policy on which all *libertini* were united, and this was a problem which had caused sporadic interest in the preceding two centuries also. Indeed, the *ordo libertinus* was not homogeneous, for richer freedmen may have suffered less under restrictions as to tribe, and Cicero could regard a section of the order as Optimate. Moreover, even if freedmen had been united in their aims, there was no organization to hold them together. They were normally approachable through their patrons or their trade, and in some cases through national groups. Clodius alone found a practicable method of organizing freedmen for political purposes, but again they were not recruited *qua* freedmen and the interests they served were not specifically those of freedmen, though Clodius was said to be reviving the bill of Sulpicius in 62 B.C.

Individual *libertini* attained positions of more importance than had hitherto been usual, but they were normally agents of ingenuous politicians. The confidential and traditionally hidden nature of their work makes it impossible to assess the extent to which they influenced politics through their patrons and the extent to which they were merely tools. But there are indications that men like Statius were not just agents. A Pompeius Demetrius or a Julius Licinus might well make constructive suggestions for future policy. As long as the patron retained his position as magistrate, such subordinates carried out many of the functions which were later entrusted to a permanent civil service.

We have evidence for the discontent of poor *libertini* and for the ambitions of the better-off. The social and economic problems of the *plebs frumentaria* were not confined to ex-slaves, and were not solved. Nor, except for commanding some influence at elections, did the rich freedman find much outlet for political ambition. Those who were lucky enough to have patrons in the governing class could alone play an effective, though unadvertised, part in the political life of the nation.

V

RELIGION

GENERALIZATIONS on the religious beliefs of freedmen as a class would be inaccurate and possibly meaningless; conclusions can, however, be drawn about the religious practices of individuals and groups of freedmen. The share taken by *libertini* in various cults illustrates both the predicament of a world presented with the options of a ritualistic dogma-less religion and individualistic mystery cults, and the particular need of an ex-slave to assert himself in order to find a place in this as in other fields.

(i) *The State Religion*

In the offering of worship on behalf of the Roman state, the freedman like the humble *ingenuus*, had little share. The priests were recruited from the governing class, and to neither the *summa collegia* (those of the *pontifices, septemviri epulones, quindecimviri sacris faciundis* and *augures*), nor to the *Salii, sodales Titii, fratres Arvales* or the *fetiales* could a freedman belong. Normally too, servile descent barred a girl from serving as a Vestal.[1]

In a humble way *libertini* had their role in the great public sacrifices, since many of the attendants on priests came from their ranks. *Lictores, calatores* (criers and attendants), and *viatores* were needed.[2] Sulla in his capacity as augur had his favourite freedman Epicadus as *calator*.[3] Under the Principate, we hear of freedmen as lictors and messengers and the same will have been true of the Republic, though none of the known lictors and messengers[4] is known to have been in attendance on the priests. *Pullarii* and

---

[1] Anyone 'cuius parentes alter ambove servierunt servierunt aut in negotiis sordidis versantur' was ineligible (Gell. i. 12. 5). In A.D. 5 lack of recruits forced Augustus to permit the candidature of the daughters of *libertini* but the lot did not fall on any of them (Dio, lv. 22. 5).
[2] Cf. Duff, *Freedmen*, p. 130; Marquardt, *Römische Staatsverwaltung*, iii, pp. 224 f.
[3] Suet. *Gram.* 12.   [4] p. 156.

STATE RELIGION

victimarii, the keepers of the sacred chickens and the assistants at sacrifices, will also have often been freedmen, as later.[1] Also essential to the performance of a sacrifice were the musicians, the 'collegium tibicinum et fidicinum Romanorum qui sacris praesto sunt',[2] and among pipers of republican times freedmen were common.[3] They are found too as *aeditui* (temple curators).[4]

Another essential function, that of taking the auspices, does not seem to have often been entrusted to freedmen. One *haruspex* in an inscription gives filiation and tribe,[5] and others mentioned in the literary sources seem to have been freeborn too,[6] but we do hear of one freedman in this profession.[7, 8]

In the minor religious boards[9] the freedman had a part to play. Among these that of the *Luperci* was in the time of Cicero in decline and looked on as not quite respectable, at least in some quarters.[10] As a witness in the trial of Clodius, L. Herennius had adduced membership of this *sodalitas* as evidence of Caelius' bad character, in spite of the fact that he too was a member, and Cicero comments scathingly on the rough and primitive nature of a priesthood which allowed its members not only to accuse each other but also to make membership a ground of accusation.[11] Similarly in 46 B.C. he failed to sympathize with his brother's elation that young Quintus was a *Lupercus*.[12] Caesar was trying to restore the Lupercalia, allotting funds to the college and creating new members, such as young Q. Cicero and M. Antonius, but the policy failed.[13] Considering the nature of the race which was one of the main functions of the priests

---

[1] Marquardt, *Römische Staatsverwaltung*, iii, p. 225.
[2] *CIL* vi. 2191 of A.D. 102. See Marquardt, *Römische Staatsverwaltung*, p. 226.
[3] *CIL* i. 988, 989 = Degr. 185 add. 175.
[4] *CIL* i. 1443: six libertine *magistri* from a college of temple employees. See Marquardt, *Römische Staatsverwaltung*, p. 214.
[5] *CIL* i. 2127 = Degr. 791.
[6] e.g. Suet. *DJ* 81; Plut. *Sulla* 9. 3; cf. Cic. *Div.* i. 72; ii. *Verr.* iii. 28.
[7] *CIL* i. 1835 = Degr. 788.
[8] Temple slaves and occasionally *liberti* (like Agonis, *liberta* of Venus Erycina, Cic. *Div. in Caec.* 55 f. etc.) are held not to have been *servi publici* but serfs. So these were not true *libertini*. Latin had no proper word for a freed serf. See R. M. Haywood, *AJP* 54 (1933), 145 ff.
[9] See Waltzing, *Corporations*, i, pp. 34 ff.
[10] Suet. *DA* 31. 4; G. Wissowa, *Religion und Cultus der Römer* (Munich, 1902), p. 560.
[11] *Cael.* 26.   [12] *Att.* xii. 5. 1.
[13] Cic. *Phil.* xiii. 31; Suet. *DA* 31. 4.

it is not surprising that it came to be abandoned to raffish aristocrats and freedmen. Cicero's remarks to Atticus at the time of his nephew's elevation to the college[1] are probably not to be taken to imply that his brother's freedman Statius was also a *Lupercus*, but many freedmen are known to have held this priesthood: the notorious Geganius Clesippus, the lover of his patroness;[2] Q. Considius Q. l. Eros;[3] C. Curtius Postumi l. Helenus,[4] and C. Julius Caesaris l. Salvius.[5] Except for Clesippus, these were all *liberti* of powerful patrons, Salvius of the dictator himself, and probably his nominee, as Eros and Helenus would also perhaps have been, as they were doubtless freedmen of prominent Caesarians. They were all, with the exception of Helenus, civil servants, *accensi* or *viatores*. All therefore had the backing of patron, wealth (as in the case of Clesippus), and position, for the public service conferred that on its officials.

Geganius is also interesting because, like one other known to us from this period,[6] he was a 'pluralist'. He was a *magister Capitolinus* as well as a *Lupercus*. Of this college, founded after the Gallic invasion to celebrate the *Ludi Capitolini*, nothing is heard after Augustus' re-organization of the *regiones*.[7] Originally, the qualification for membership had been domicile.[8] Probably this rule had lapsed. The *Capitolini*, like the *Luperci*, seem to have been rather a mixed bunch: Cicero in 56 B.C. had a spicy bit of gossip about one

[1] *Att.* xii. 5. 1:'Quintus pater ... nihil sapit qui laetetur Luperco filio et Statio, ut cernat duplici dedecore cumulatam domum. Addo etiam Philotimum tertium.' Tyrrell and Purser, *The Correspondence of Cicero*, iv. 471, took it that Statius, like Philotimus, was referred to as an unqualified disgrace. Münzer (*RE* iii. A. 2. 2215) held that Statius had been elected with young Quintus.
[2] *CIL* i. 1004 = Degr. 696: 'Clesippus Geganius Mag. Capit. Mag. Luperc. Viat. Tr.' Cf. Pliny, *NH* xxxiv. 11.
[3] *CIL* vi. 1933: 'Viator aed. pl. Lege Papiria Lupercus Quinctial. vetus. Accensus cos. magister trium decuriar.' 'vetus' is thought to mean 'of last year' to distinguish it from 'designatus'. See also p. 155 and n. 6.
[4] *CIL* vi. 32437. This is the only office he claims. He would have been a freedman of the Caesarian Curtius Postumus (Cic. *Fam.* vi. 12. 2 etc.).
[5] *CIL* xiv. 2105: 'Accensus, magister Lupercorum, viator tribunicius.'
[6] *CIL* xiv. 2105: 'A. Castricius Myrio Talenti f., tr. mil., praef. eq. et classis, mag. colleg. Luperc. et Capitolinor. et Mercurial. et paganor. Aventin., xxvivir.' Mommsen in his note supposed that the father Myrio was *peregrinus*, but he could have been a freedman.
[7] Mommsen on *CIL* xiv. 2105.
[8] Livy, v. 50. 4: 'collegiumque ad eam rem M. Furius dictator constitueret ex iis qui in Capitolio atque arce habitarent.'

of them and his expulsion from the college.¹ The members were clearly not aristocratic or well known, for Cicero had to explain the identity of the blackballed *eques*, but again, like the *Luperci*, they were men of a certain position. The three known *magistri* were an *eques*, the ingenuous son of a peregrine or freedman with a distinguished military and civil career,² and a freedman of wealth. Freedmen were probably members of the sister college of *Mercuriales* from the Aventine, especially as this was a college of merchants, but the only known members are the two freeborn *Capitolini* just mentioned.

The other hills and outlying districts of Rome had similar organizations for holding festivals and making dedications, but the two of which we have inscriptional evidence, the Janiculum, and the *Mons Oppius*,³ do not mention freedmen *magistri*. We have a possible parallel, however, in the *pagi* of Capua. This 'urbs trunca sine senatu, sine plebe, sine magistratibus',⁴ was of course a very special case. Here religious boards of *magistri* not only made dedications to various deities, but also carried out works which would normally have been done by the municipal authorities, of which Rome had deprived the rebellious town. The *Magistri Pagi* exercised an authority superior to that of the religious boards.⁵ Both classes of *magistri* included freedmen: the two surviving lists of *Magistri Pagi*, each with the normal complement of twelve men, have twelve and three freedmen members.⁶ Thus what local government there was in Capua was shared by *ingenui* and *libertini*. The prerequisite for such service was wealth, and Capua produced an amazing number of freedmen ready to expend their own money in the service of the city. As Frederiksen has pointed out, they formed the 'libertina nobilitas' of their day, as the freedmen who held the Augustan sevirate did later.⁷ If Capua drew on the freedman class

---

[1] *QF* ii. 5. 2: 'M. Furium Flaccum equitem Romanum, hominem nequam, Capitolini et Mercuriales de collegio eiecerunt, praesentem ad pedes unius cuiusque iacentem.'   [2] p. 196, n. 6.
[3] *CIL* i. 1000, 1001, 1002, 1003 = Degr. 699, 700, 702, 698.
[4] Livy, xxxi. 29. 11.
[5] M. Frederiksen, *PBSR* 14 (1959), 88 f., 92 f.
[6] They are the *Pagus Herculaneus* in 94 B.C. and an unspecified board in 71 B.C. (*CIL* i. 682 = Degr .719. Frederiksen, *PBSR* 14 80 ff. (1959), no. 17; *CIL* i. 686 Degr. 722. Frederiksen, no. 20.
[7] *PBSR* 14 (1959), 93 f.

for such services, it seems likely that Rome herself, also with a prosperous freed population, did the same.

In the *vici*, men of servile origin played the main part in the cult of the *Lares* at the cross-roads (*compita*), and in the dedications to other deities such as *Stata Mater*, who protected the city against fire.[1] The organization of the *vici* is a matter for controversy. It has already been argued that trade guilds probably had a local basis and the dissolution in 64 B.C. of colleges which had held compital games has been mentioned. Waltzing held[2] that the inhabitants of the *vici* did not form proper *collegia*, but merely elected *magistri*. Mommsen had previously postulated 'collegia compitalicia' which elected the *magistri vici*.[3] Now as Rome was divided into *montes* and *pagi*, a further subdivision into *vici* with *collegia* might seem unnecessary. But, while the whole population was concerned with the state worship of the larger districts, the cult of the *Lares* interested slaves in particular. So a society (a subdivision of the *vicus*) would have been needed to elect slave or freed officers. (Would *ingenui* have even known whom to vote for?) Various considerations back Mommsen's hypothesis, but do not of course prove that the colleges bore the name which he conjectured. The analogy of Delos cannot be exact, but there probably colleges existed.[4] It is likely that later they existed also at Rome.[5] Thirdly, a passage of Asconius can be read to show that there were *collegia* actually responsible for this cult: 'Solebant autem magistri collegiorum ludos facere, sicut magistri vicorum faciebant ludos praetextati, qui ludi sublatis collegiis discussi sunt.'[6] In my opinion, Asconius is here saying that officers of certain (presumably trade) guilds had held games, and that the *magistri vicorum*, officers appointed in the *vici*, had also been in the habit of holding compitalician games, but that both sorts of celebration were suspended by the *senatusconsultum* which banned the *collegia* in 64 B.C. The obvious deduction is that the

---

[1] Dedications (god unknown): *CIL* i. 1002, 2514 = Degr. 702, 704; *Stata Mater*: *ILS* 3306–9; Degr. 259; cf. Duff, *Freedmen*, p. 131; F. Bömer, *Untersuchungen über die Religion der Sklaven in Griechenland und Rom*, i (Mainz, 1958), pp. 32 f.
[2] *Corporations*, i. pp. 40 f., 98 f.
[3] *De Collegiis*, pp. 74 ff. [4] pp. 199 f.
[5] De Robertis, *Diritto Associativo*, p. 81.
[6] *Pis.* 7A. For the punctuation adopted see p. 170, n. 9.

magistri vicorum represented *collegia*, for how otherwise could their office have lapsed? Finally, as De Robertis has pointed out,[1] the organization of guilds in the *vici* by Clodius in 58 B.C. suggests that there had been similar *collegia* there previously. None of these arguments clinches the problem by itself, but together they increase the probability that Mommsen's guess was right.[2]

What is not in doubt is that the office of *magister vici* was entrusted to freedmen just as it was later when Augustus linked it with the worship of the *princeps* and made the sevirate the highest object of a freedman's ambition.[3] Livy made a second century character speak scornfully of the low station of the *magistri vicorum* and this may well be evidence of pre-Augustan views.[4] No doubt they were held in disesteem because many were ex-slaves. The worship of the *Lares* was also carried out by slaves, at the *compita* as in the household.[5] It seems that the inferior functionaries, the *ministri*, were slaves, but the *magistri* were freedmen. From Rome itself, only freedmen officers are attested;[6] from Capua an inscription gives as *ministri Laribus* thirteen slaves with a freedman at their head.[7]

The Competeliasts of Delos are not strictly analogous, since in the districts of a foreign city the whole population was not concerned with the worship of the *Lares*: in such a case, one would suppose that a college would naturally have existed to elect the *magistri*, though it will still be the names of officers or their subordinates which appear on inscriptions. As the names are all in Greek,

[1] *Diritto Associativo*, p. 82.
[2] Cf. also Minturnae, where the *magistri* probably represented *collegia* which were compital. See Johnson, *Excavations at Minturnae*, ii, pp. 120 f. Frederiksen, *PBSR* 14 (1959), 86 f., concluded that the Capuan colleges were not compital.
[3] Duff, *Freedmen*, pp. 133 ff.
[4] xxxiv. 7. 2. L. Valerius in 195 B.C.: 'hic Romae infimo generi, magistris vicorum, togae praetextae habendae ius permittemus...' Bömer, *Untersuchungen*, i. p. 35, has suggested that, as Livy personally would have avoided offending Augustus, he had reason to believe this was a second century attitude.
[5] Dion. iv. 14, mentions only slaves. He dates the practice to the reign of Servius Tullius and adds the more reliable information that these slave officials wore no badge of slavery, which softened the hardship of their condition. The *magistri* wore the striped official robe (Livy, xxxiv. 7. 2; Asc. *Pis.* 7A).
[6] *CIL* i. 1002 = Degr. 702 (a freedman *magister vici Sulpicei*); *CIL* i. 2514 = Degr. 704 (four freedmen *magistri vici*).
[7] *CIL* i. 681 = Degr. 718.

the distinction between members of a cult society and its officials is not made.[1] But the important point is that on Delos, as at Rome, public worship of the *Lares* was entrusted to freedmen and slaves.

(ii) *Other religious* Collegia

Other religious colleges are found in many parts of the empire, dedicated to the worship of various deities, and distinct from the state cults which were served by the *summa collegia*.[2] They were not needed in Rome itself because there the state cult was an official responsibility. But in Delos the Roman and Italian merchants, in Minturnae the devotees of certain deities not catered for by temples, in Capua where normal town authorities were lacking— and in many other towns about which we are less adequately informed—*magistri* made dedications and carried out public works sometimes only remotely connected with cults. It seems natural to assume that such *magistri* had the backing of a society, *collegium*. However, Frederiksen[3] interpreted *collegium* in this context as meaning a board of colleagues, in the same way as the *summa collegia*, the Roman priestly colleges, were committees. But, though the *magistri* of *pagi* were probably not elected by a society, it does not follow that there was no guild behind the committees of other religious organizations. The existence of colleges is borne out to some extent by the Greek versions of the Delian inscriptions, where the names Apolloniastae, Posidoniastae, Hermaistae, suggest a body of worshippers.[4] It would put the religious colleges of this type on a par with the professional bodies with which they were often identical, rather than with the boards of priests of the City. The parallel to the Apolloniasts and the votaries of *Spes*, Ceres, Mercury, and probably Venus at Minturnae[5] is surely the Bacchanals of Rome rather than the college of augurs.[6] I would accept in the main Johnson's outline of the organization of the

[1] J. Hatzfeld, *BCH* 1912, 182 f.; *Trafiquants*, pp. 343 f., 272.
[2] Johnson, *Minturnae*, pp. 119 f.
[3] *PBSR* 14 (1959), 85. He backs this hypothesis by reference to the *Pagus Herculaneus* inscription (*CIL* i. 682 = Degr. 179 = Frederiksen no. 17) which refers to 'conlegium sive magistri', who are ordered to see to certain works by the *Pagus*.
[4] Hatzfeld, *Trafiquants*, pp. 272 f.   [5] Johnson, *Minturnae*, p. 116.
[6] On the confusion produced by the lack of a generic term for associations, see De Robertis, *Diritto Associativo*, pp. 12 ff.

Minturnensian cults: that there were colleges of worshippers who chose *magistri* (probably annually), who might be women or slaves.[1] At Delos and Capua the boards were composed of *ingenui* and freedmen in more or less equal numbers, taken as a whole, though some boards may exclude one class completely. At Minturnae, only *libertini* and slaves appear (in contrast to the other cities where slaves were involved only in the worship of the *Lares*). The importance of freedmen in all these cases is an index of their importance in a trading society. At Delos, in spite of the fact that they were probably usually subordinates in business, they were given parity with their employers on the religious boards.[2] In Capua, they performed expensive liturgies which indicate their wealth and their willingness to use it in public works. In Minturnae, where the boards were less important since freeborn citizens were otherwise occupied, the expenditure expected of *magistri* was less, but nevertheless no doubt considerable for the slaves who held office, and it has been taken to have constituted a proof that a slave deserved manumission, or, retrospectively, that a freedman was worthy of the citizenship which he had acquired.[3]

The professional colleges also performed religious functions. It is not certain whether the cult colleges at Delos had a professional basis, if the Hermaistae were bankers and the Posidoniastae merchants.[4] At Capua we have a 'collegium mercatorum' performing the same type of function as the religious bodies.[5] The cult objects of these colleges will have reflected the interests of their members just as the dedications at Minturnae to *Spes* and Mercury and Ceres expressed the trading or agricultural occupations of their donors. The activities of the colleges (if that is what they were) already described, those of Delos and the Campanian cities, no doubt included others not specifically religious, for instance social gatherings. Apart from them, we hear of few professional organizations for the wealthy business man.

[1] *Minturnae*, p. 120.
[2] Hatzfeld, *BCH* 1912, 536, n. 8.
[3] Johnson, *Minturnae*, p. 122. There appears to have been no distinction between Italians and Romans in their attitude to *libertini* in this context (ibid., pp. 117 f.).
[4] As suggested by Hatzfeld, *Trafiquants*, p. 275; cf. *BCH* 1912, 180.
[5] *CIL* i. 672 = Degr. 705 = Frederiksen, *PBSR* 14 (1959), no. 1.

The humbler trade guilds also had religious functions. The college of scribes and actors[1] worshipped Minerva and the fullers of Spoleto are also found invoking her aid.[2] The colleges of small tradesmen of whom we hear from dedicatory inscriptions had predominantly freed *magistri* and slave *ministri*, on the same pattern as the *vici*.[3] Those known are mostly of humble traders, butchers, cooks, sellers of violets, cattle-dealers, and the like. As we have seen, freedmen probably outnumbered free-born in this type of employment, but it seems likely too that even when *ingenui* took part in a trade, they were often represented on the committee of their guild by freedmen, for ingenuous *magistri* are more rarely found than ingenuous craftsmen.[4] This is the impression that is given by the patchy *corpus* of republican inscriptions. Possibly the freedman, excluded from certain other activities, found he had time and ambition for committee work which an *ingenuus* might lack.[5]

The objects of cult of the freedman-dominated colleges were appropriate to the status of the worshippers. Fortune, 'praesens vel imo tollere de gradu | mortale corpus',[6] was a favourite, and it is probably not just because of distortion caused by the accident of the survival of the Praenestine inscriptions that this appears to have been the case. Fortune was indeed a fitting object of worship to the humble and the freedman. Several guilds are known to have paid her honour.[7] *Mens Bona* was also worshipped, another forwarder of careers.[8]

An important work carried out by the colleges was to provide for the dead. There is little evidence from our period, but we may deduce from later evidence[9] that they were much used by freedmen who were not given a place in the tombs of their patrons, that is, by the end of the Republic, the great majority of ex-slaves, and who

---

[1] Festus, 492. 22.   [2] *CIL* i. 1406 = Degr. 930.
[3] *CIL* i. 1446 = Degr. 103 add. But slave *magistri* were also possible (cf. *CIL* vi. 287—but it is likely that all the members of this college were slaves).
[4] *CIL* i. 1618 = Degr. 231 is a rare example of ingenuous officers, equal in number to freedmen.
[5] e.g. *CIL* i. 977, 980 = Degr. 96, 99.
[6] Hor. *Od.* i. 35. 2 f.
[7] *CIL* i. 1446, 1447 = Degr. 103, 104. Also 105a. Bömer, *Untersuchungen*, i, pp. 140 f.
[8] *CIL* i. 1510, 1616 = Degr. 225, 226; Bömer, *Untersuchungen*, i, pp. 154 f.
[9] See Barrow, *Slavery*, p. 146 f.

lacked the wealth to provide for their own family tomb. We know of a college at Cos which seems to have been funerary,[1] and the same work was done by ordinary professional guilds, of which the *Societas Cantorum Graecorum*, which was probably made up of freedmen and perhaps slaves, has left an inscription showing that one of the committee gave a gift or money for the preparation of a common tomb.[2]

Dedications by freedmen to various Roman deities indicate individual as well as corporate allegiance to the native cults, but the evidence is too scanty to allow any conclusions about the origin or particular beliefs of the freedmen who honoured the Bona Dea,[3] Hercules,[4] Juno *Sospes*,[5] Diana of Nemi,[6] or abstract figures such as *Honos*[7] or *Concordia*,[8] although the latter had a social significance, standing for absence of class-hatred. The formula, 'servus vovit, liber solvit', indicating that the *ex voto* was in gratitude for manumission, is naturally fairly common.[9] Oddly, no dedication to *Libertas* herself survives, though the manumission of the slave volunteers in the Second Punic War had been represented by paintings in her temple.[10]

In all these activities of freedmen in priestly colleges, *pagi* and *vici*, and private trade or funerary colleges, one can surely see an urge to assert themselves in a society in which many of them were strangers. Few in the first century B.C. can have been *vernae* or Italians: many, then, came from alien backgrounds, and their predominance in many colleges wholly or partly concerned with specifically native cults (especially the *Lares*)[11] and their dedications

---

[1] *CIG* 2520: a funerary inscription of seven freedmen from four different *gentes*, so it is almost certainly a college.

[2] *CIL* i. 2519 = Degr. 771.   [3] *CIL* i. 972 = Degr. 56.

[4] *CIL* i. 982, 1617, 1697 = Degr. 127, 140, 141.

[5] *CIL* i. 1430 = Degr. 170.   [6] *CIL* i. 1480 = Degr. 85.

[7] *CIL* i. 31 = Degr. 157.

[8] *CIL* i. 1508 = Degr. 71. Cf. Flavius' dedication of the temple to Concord in 304 B.C., p. 57.

[9] e.g. *CIL* i. 972, 1617 = Degr. 56, 140.   [10] Livy, xxiv. 16. 19.

[11] There is, I think, no direct evidence in this period for the participation of freedmen in the household cult of the *Lares*, but it is probable that if resident in the patron's house they continued the cult practised as slaves. As *patresfamilias* too many must have honoured their own household gods. Horace's affection for the *Lares* probably derives from childhood experience in a freedman's home (e.g. *Od.* iii. 23).

to local gods, while they were not extraordinary in a polytheistic society which could often identify one local deity with another and believed always in propitiating the gods of the country in which one happened to be, seem to show a strong social need to identify with the Roman culture.

(iii) *Foreign Cults*

The opposite side of the coin is the involvement of freedmen with foreign cults, and, it seems, their great influence in introducing new religions to Rome. 'Nationes in familiis habemus, quibus diversi ritus, externa sacra aut nulla sunt', as Tacitus made C. Cassius say in Nero's reign.[1] It is in fact difficult to see how the mystery cults could have spread without the influence of Rome's imported slaves and freedmen. The first appearance of *Chaldaei* in Italy in the second century can definitely be linked with the influx of Syrian slaves after the war with Antiochus.[2] We also know that the worship of Atargatis was strong among slaves in Sicily at the time of the revolt of 134 B.C.[3] The evidence is slight but enough to indicate a strong element of slave and consequently of freed worshippers in such cults. This is borne out by the share of the slave and later freedwoman Fecenia Hispala in the Bacchanalian worship. Her story reflects the popular nature of such orgiastic cults.[4] With these hints to go on, we may conjecture that Phrygian and other freedmen took advantage of the official sanction given to the worship of the *Magna Mater*,[5] that freedmen in the trading centres of Puteoli and Pompeii participated in the cult of Isis[6] and helped its

[1] *Ann.* xiv. 44.
[2] Reis in *RE* ii. 2, 1816; Bömer, *Untersuchungen*, i, p. 188; cf. Val. Max. i. 3. 2; Livy, *Per. Ox.* liv.
[3] Florus ii. 7. See F. Cumont, *Les Religions orientales dans la paganisme romaine* (Paris, 1929), p. 97.
[4] Livy, xxxix. 9 ff.
[5] The *sodalitates Magnae Matris*, dating back to 204 B.C., were recruited from noble families, 'principes civitatis' (Gell. ii. 24. 2; Waltzing, *Corporations*, i. p. 36), for instance the elder Cato (Cic. *Sen.* 45). Presumably no freedman was ever admitted. The priesthood was limited to Phrygians and non-citizens, so *libertini* were excluded from this office too (Cumont, *Religions orientales*, p. 49).
[6] The *Serapeum* at Puteoli was established before 105 B.C., the *Iseum* at Pompeii was roughly contemporaneous. The worshippers were of Greek extraction, including slaves and freedmen with few native *ingenui* according to Hatzfeld, *Trafiquants*, pp. 360 f.

spread to Rome, where it soon obtained a strong hold on the *opifices*, a large proportion of whom were of course of servile origin.[1] We hear of a priestess of Isis called Usia Prima, daughter of Rabirius Postumus Hermodorus, who was presumably a freedman, probably Egyptian, of Rabirius Postumus.[2] Mithraism seems to have started in Rome as early as 67 B.C. but its appeal at this date was more limited than that of the Syrian, Egyptian, and Phrygian religions.[3]

The importance of these oriental religions for us is twofold. First, they provided for freedmen and slaves a valuable outlet, either the release of crude orgies, or the idealistic faith in future life and redemption, both of which would be precious to men whom the world had perhaps treated badly, enslaving them to other men who were not necessarily their moral or intellectual superiors. It was such men that Christianity was later able to recruit, with the hope of the world to come and the faith that made slavery and suffering in this life tolerable. Secondly, the influence which a slave or freedman might have on a Roman master in this matter was great. As educated Greeks turned their masters' eyes to philosophy, so no doubt many Syrians caught their interest in Atargatis or Cybele. Our literary sources deal with the class of Romans most resistant to superstition, so this point is hard to substantiate for the Republic, but we can compare the influence which Christians who were of Caesar's household had later on highly placed Romans.[4]

Finally, we have definite evidence on the maintenance of a foreign religion by groups of *libertini* in the case of the Jews, whose staunch monotheism and obedience to the Temple of course made them a special case, but who were probably paralleled by devotees of other cults. Philo tells us that Augustus co-operated with the Jews, who were settled in Trastevere in large numbers and were mostly freedmen who had been brought to Rome as prisoners of war.[5]

---

[1] The college of the *pastophoroi* dated its foundation to the time of Sulla (Lucian, *Met.* xi. 30). The Senate banned the cult in 59, 58, 53, and 48 B.C.

[2] *CIL* vi. 2246.

[3] Clearly the followers of Isis were organized into societies which were regarded as a political threat (Cumont, *Religions orientales*, pp. 76 f). The triumvirs' plan to build a temple to Isis in 43 B.C. may have been a bid for popular favour (ibid.). Cumont, *Religions orientales*, pp. 129 ff.

[4] Paul, Philippians 4. 22, cf. Romans 16. 3 ff., where the Christians of Rome have predominantly Greek names.   [5] *Leg. ad Gaium.* 155.

There had been Jews in Rome even in the second century, for they were expelled with the Chaldaeans in 139 B.C.,[1] but the first great influx will have been that of Pompey's prisoners. Already in 59 B.C. there was a strong Jewish element in Rome: 'scis quanta sit manus, quanta concordia, quantum valeat in contionibus', says Cicero.[2] Rome did not attract many *peregrini*: the Jews of the Aurelian steps were therefore probably of libertine status or extraction. The fact that they were strong at *contiones* does not necessarily in itself imply citizenship, but it is probable that the Jews of the *Diaspora* had been coming into Rome for a long period as slaves,[3] and that, rapidly winning freedom themselves, they had continued, with their usual *concordia*, to buy and manumit their fellow countrymen, as bidden by the Law.[4] The attitude a true Roman would have to even such a sedate religion as Judaeism is typified by Cicero's appeals to regard it as a 'barbara superstitio',[5] but the unpopularity of the cult in Rome was mainly due to the fact that it refused (despite attempts to identify Jehovah with Jupiter Capitolinus) to be assimilated into the hotch-potch of pantheism: even before the conquest of Jerusalem, the Jews held themselves apart.[6] Like the votaries of Isis, but to a greater extent, they constituted a political threat. Julius Caesar, however, treated them well and did not touch the synagogues when he dissolved other *collegia*.[7] The Jews repaid him by mourning him, along with other foreigners, after his murder.[8] Augustus also allowed the Jews to practise their religion in peace, have synagogues, send tribute to Jerusalem, and even made arrangements for them to receive the dole when the normal distribution fell on the Sabbath.[9] This last point of course shows that the Jews in Rome included many citizens, and makes it probable that they were mainly freedmen. This is confirmed by an

---

[1] Cumont, *Religions orientales*, p. 152.　　　　　　　　　[2] *Flacc.* 66.
[3] Cf. Cic. *Prov. Cons.* 10: the Jews and Syrians were born to slavery.
[4] Leviticus 25. 47 ff.　　　　　　　　　　　　　　　　　[5] *Flacc.* 67.
[6] Cic. *Flacc.* 69: 'Stantibus Hierosolymis pacatisque Iudaeis tamen istorum religio sacrorum a splendore huius imperi, gravitate nominis nostri, maiorum institutis abhorrebat; nunc vero hoc magis, quod illa gens quid de nostro imperio sentiret ostendit armis; quam cara dis immortalibus esset docuit, quod est victa, quod elocata, quod serva facta.'
[7] Jos. *Ant.* xiv. 10. 8; cf. Suet. *DJ* 42. 2.
[8] Suet. *DJ* 84. 5.
[9] Philo, *Leg. ad Gaium*, 155.

interesting mention of a synagogue called that of the *Libertini*, members of which were present in Jerusalem, with communities from Cyrene, Alexandria, Cilicia, and Asia, at the time of Stephen's martyrdom, and which as it had a Latin name, was surely located in the West and probably in Rome itself.[1]

Conclusions

The case of the Jews shows how a slave might keep his religious beliefs intact, and this was surely true to a lesser extent of the less strict sects. Oriental slaves and freedmen will normally have practised and spread their native religions in Rome. The state in republican times was already beginning the custom of entrusting specific functions to freedmen, which later bore fruit in the sevirate and which was a force to foster local patriotism and group-feeling, to give the freedman an outlet in public service. But the *magistri vicorum* were despised, at least by upper-class Romans, and the more important priesthoods such as those of the *Luperci* and *Capitolini* were open only to the favoured freedmen. So for many the mystery cults, with their promises of spiritual equality, and Judaeism, and later Christianity, which drew many converts from the poor and enslaved, provided what they most needed.

[1] Acts 6. 9: .... ἐκ τῆς συναγωγῆς τῆς λεγομένης Λιβερτίνων.

VI
FAMILY AND SOCIAL LIFE

(i) *The Family*

To a man who had passed through slavery, which could at the worst stamp him as morally inferior and destined to be a chattel,[1] the normal contacts of society and the pleasures of family life must have been especially precious. It may not be over imaginative to discern in many of the inscriptions set up by *libertini* to their dead[2] and in the relationship of Horace to his freedman father, an intensity of family loyalty and affection which was hardly to be met with so often among the ingenuous population and which was perhaps produced by the peculiar circumstances in which a freedman came to have a family at all. For a man who legally had no parents—'Ius tibi natorum vel septem, Zoile, detur, Dum matrem nemo det tibi, nemo patrem', as Martial brutally put it[3]—the possession of wife, children, and friends was of great significance.

Even as a slave, more especially in the wealthier households where there was more leisure, and also for those who were in business and did not live in their masters' households, the freedman had enjoyed some liberty to make friends. The religious and trade guilds provided social contact with equals and sometimes with *ingenui*, giving slaves a sense of security and self-importance. In public gatherings slaves were indistinguishable from free Romans[4] and could share in the amusements of the ingenuous poor. Especially favoured slaves, Tiro for instance, might in their own right enjoy the friendship of their master's equals. In a society which depended for its existence and efficiency on slaves, the personalities and affections of the more useful slave agents could not be overlooked.

---

[1] Ar. *Pol.* 1253B ff.; Cic. *Prov. Cons.* 10; *Phil.* vi. 18, etc.
[2] e.g. *CIL* i. 1221 = Degr. 793. Though epitaphs were often composed in the lifetime of those whom they eulogized, and therefore idealized relationships, they reflected current values.
[3] xi. 12. 1 f.   [4] App. *BC* ii. 120.

Inside the household or even, on occasion, outside it, the slave was often allowed to contract a quasi-marriage or *contubernium*,[1] at least in the *familia urbana*. This arrangement was admitted to make him more contented and reliable.[2] Such relationships had no legal force, but were often respected by the master (and, one might add, the slave, though Galatea does not seem to have had any difficulty in leaving Tityrus)[3]—as long, no doubt, as financial interests did not oblige him to separate the pair by selling one or both, or the female slave did not attract one of the *domini*. Freedom offered the only security for a slave to lead an almost independent life, even though it might lack material comforts which he had enjoyed before. Together with his *contubernalis*, he might try to save as much as possible of his *peculium* in order eventually to purchase manumission.[4] Often one of the pair must have achieved freedom first, either on the master's initiative or through his own thrift. Many *contubernia* will have been split by this event. But inscriptional evidence quite often attests the permanence of *contubernia* or attachments formed during slavery when both *contubernales* were freed together,[5] or the one freed first then bought and manumitted his partner, or the patron later decided to manumit the second.

Collaboration between *libertus* and patron to secure the freedom of a *contubernalis* is not unexampled. We have a monument to C. Caninius C. f.,[6] whose son manumitted a slave who in his turn freed a slave-girl and married her. Presumably, she had been a fellow slave of her future husband, who, on achieving his own liberty, either bought her from, or was given her by, young Caninius. For the *libertini* manumission of the wife by the husband rather than by the common owner presented the great advantage that she was free of legal obligations to a third party, since her husband became her patron. The same applied when a freed parent redeemed his children from slavery.[7] Thus at least some of the

---

[1] See Tenney Frank, *AHR* 21 (1916), p. 697.
[2] Varro, *RR* ii. 17.
[3] Verg. *Ecl.* i. 30. [4] Verg. *Ecl.* i. 32.
[5] Ter. *Ad.* 973 ff. has two *contubernales* freed together.
[6] *CIL* i. 1216.
[7] Cf. Gaius, i. 19 (*Lex Aelia Sentia*).

monuments to pairs of *libertini*[1] with the same name probably belonged not to *conliberti* but to ex-*conservi*, and the husband was patron of the wife.[2] We may note also, though the point is obvious, that *coniuges* were often freed by different members of the same family, the wife especially often being 'Gaiae liberta', freedwoman of the lady of the house or one of the daughters.[3] One detailed monument is left by a couple of *conliberti* who had been slaves together since the wife was seven.[4]

Freedmen who did not marry *conlibertae* generally, because perhaps of prejudice against marriage with *ingenuae*, married other freedwomen.[5] In the case of the freedmen of the great Roman families, the marriages are of interest as indicating the social hierarchy among freedmen and the opportunities for social life which they enjoyed. For instance, the doctor of Pansa, Glyco, who was probably a freedman, was married to a sister of M. Brutus' Achilles, whose status was probably freed too.[6] A freedman of L. Aurelius Cotta, presumably the consul of 65 B.C., was husband of a *liberta* of Livia Drusilla, Octavian's future wife.[7] Not all freedmen of upper-class Romans married similarly highly placed *libertinae*[8], however, which probably shows, not that class distinctions were non-existent among freedmen, but that the lower servants of aristocrats were not unlikely to marry into the class of freedmen of humbler families. In the lower strata, we may note a tendency for freedmen to find wives in the same trade or firm.[9]

Apart from the special case of a freedwoman marrying her patron who had been a slave with her, marriages between ex-slave and

---

[1] Space on the poorer monuments rarely permitted explicit references to marriage, but it may be assumed in nearly all cases where a couple appears alone. For instance, *CIL* i. 1221, 1413, 2527 = Degr. 793, 809, 795, attest marriage; the great majority do not: e.g. *CIL* i. 1364 = Degr. 428.

[2] e.g. probably, *CIL* i. 1638 = Degr. 956. *CIL* i. 1332 = Degr. 928: the wife may have freed the husband.

[3] e.g. *CIL* i. 1331, 1333.   [4] *CIL* i. 1221 = Degr. 793.

[5] e.g. *CIL* i. 1332, 1928 = Degr. 928, 49.   [6] Cic. *Ad Brut.* i. 6. 2.

[7] *CIL* i. 1258 = Degr. 413. As Livia practically dropped the *cognomen* Drusilla after her marriage in 38 B.C., she presumably freed Galatea before that date and the monument itself is not likely to be much later.

[8] e.g. *CIL* i. 1220 = Degr. 365 (a *libertus* of Q. Pompeius Bithynicus) and *CIL* i. 1274 = Degr. 767 (moving down the social scale, a freedman of Clodius' friend, C. Causinius Schola of Interamna).

[9] *CIL* xiv. 4233.

THE FAMILY

ex-master occurred. The *Lex Aelia Sentia* allowed marriage as one of the motives for manumission by a master under the age of twenty.[1] We know of one family where one of the sons married a freedwoman of his father, who was, however, a freedman himself.[2] Snobbishness about free birth would have been out of place in such a family. But 'mixed marriages' seem to have been acceptable enough among the lower classes in general.[3] Naturally enough, it was usually an *ingenuus* who married a freedwoman, not a freedman who married above his station. Even aristocrats sometimes stooped to *mésalliances* of this kind: L. Gellius Publicola, an *eques*, brother of the consul of 72 B.C. and stepson of L. Philippus, is now, but possibly was not then, notorious, for he was grilled by Cicero on the grounds that he had married a freedwoman 'ut credo, non libidinis causa, sed ut plebicola videretur'.[4] If a gentleman took a freedwoman for his wife, he was clearly the victim of an irresponsible passion: family advantage and the qualities of a *materfamilias* should have been the criteria in choosing a wife.[5] The prejudice seems to have been shared by Augustus, who discountenanced marriages between nobles and freedwomen (or freedmen).[6] The proper relationship with a freedwoman 'libidinis causa' was to make her a concubine, 'quippe cum honestius sit patrono libertam concubinam quam matremfamilias habere'.[7] The arrangement was not in any way disreputable,[8] and gratitude at least might be shown to the concubine. Q. Brutius Q. f., for instance, shared his monument with his *liberta* who seems to have been his mistress.[9] Concubinage seems sometimes to have been preferred even when marriage would have been socially permissible: a widower might,

[1] Gaius, i. 19; *Dig.* xl. 2. 13.
[2] *CIL* i. 1570 = Degr. 977.
[3] e.g. *CIL* i. 1289, 1528 = Degr. 796, 949.
[4] *Sest.* 110; p. 84. If Ellis, on Catullus lxxiv ff., is right in thinking that the Gellius attacked in those poems was the nephew of Cicero's Gellius, then the aunt whom he allegedly seduced could be the 'libertina uxor'.
[5] Cf. the shamefulness of Antony's having sons whose grandfather was a freedman, Cic. *Phil.* ii. 3; *Att.* xvi. 11. 1, etc.
[6] pp. 82 ff.
[7] *Dig.* xxv. 7. 1 *pr.* Note that the *ingenuus*' own freedwoman is thought of here.
[8] Kaser, *Röm. Privatrecht*, i, pp. 125 ff.; Duff, *Freedmen*, pp. 62 f.; J. P. V. D. Balsdon, *Roman Women* (London, 1962), pp. 231 ff.
[9] *CIL* i. 1259 = Degr. 802: 'Brutia Q. l. Rufa, pia patrono, dum vixsit, placuit.'

for instance, take a concubine[1] rather than remarry and give his children a stepmother. An acknowledged concubine had some security and permanence, but more transient liaisons must have been common in a slave society.[2] Horace recommends affairs with freedwomen as being discreet.[3]

What we should like to know about the freedman's family is at what age he was able to marry, and whether the number of ingenuous children born to him was high. Obviously circumstances might differ widely from one case to another, and our sources do not allow statistical considerations. A freedman might of course have produced children in slavery. Still more common than *vernae* born in *contubernium* would be children of slave-women, often by the free men of the household. The production of slave children was sometimes at least considered desirable,[4] even though in the Republic, with its seemingly inexhaustible supplies of imported grown slaves, it was a luxury.[5] If a freedman had children born in slavery whom he could or did recognize as his own, he might attempt to buy or manumit them. The freed six-year-old Optatus may have been one of these children.[6] But such child *liberti* may also have been the offspring of an *ancilla* and the master of the house or another free member of the family, who were freed instead of being recognized as sons. One would expect perhaps that if a slave-woman who had a young child were freed, it might be simpler for the patron to let her keep the child, rather than go to the expense of bringing it up, but perhaps such women were not particularly likely to be freed.

Most of the children of freedmen known to us were *ingenui*. This is partly no doubt due to the nature of the sources: we hear of sons of *libertini* who were able to play a part in public life precisely because they were ingenuous.[7] But the inscriptions too rarely attest families of which both father and child were freed. It is

---

[1] As is probably the case in *CIL* i. 2527 = Degr. 795, where both wife and concubine are mentioned. Cf. Hor. *Sat.* i. 2. 117.
[2] e.g. Hor. *Od.* ii. 4. 1.
[3] *Sat.* i. 2. 48. But freedwomen might be demanding or promiscuous: *Epod.* xiv. 15 f., *Od.* i. 33. 14 ff.
[4] Varro, *RR* ii. 1. 26.
[5] Cf. Hor. *Epod.* ii. 65; Nep. *Att.* 13. 4.   [6] *CIL* i. 1223.
[7] e.g. Cn. Flavius, P. Furius, P. Popilius, C. Thoranius, Julius 'Rufio'.

likely that any children born in slavery rarely formed part of a freedman's effective family.[1] Occasionally, family unity could survive the most adverse circumstances—we know, for example, of a daughter, who, though freed by a different patron, could yet set up a monument to her freedman father.[2] In the *familiae* of great nobles, slave breeding might perhaps be encouraged and the father be expected to train a son to succeed him after his own manumission, as later happened in the imperial civil service.[3] So Antony had two freedmen, father and son, the father being his agent at Corinth and the son his favourite Hipparchus.[4]

Effective children of a freedman, then, tended to be those born in freedom. How many children would *libertini* have? The controlling factor being usually the age of the wife rather than that of the husband, much depends on the age at which slave-women were freed. *Libertini*, as we have seen, did not often match with *ingenuae*, though freedwomen married freeborn men more often. Some *libertinae* were certainly of an age to produce ingenuous children.[5] One freedman's daughter and probably freedwoman herself, died at the age of twenty, after giving birth to twins 'leiberum semen duplex . . . patrono auxsilium ac decus'.[6] The suggestion may be that the children's father was her patron. Freeing a slave mistress might be a sensible move to ensure the free birth of the children. If this is so, the age of twenty may be lower than was normal for slave women. Horaea, who also gives an indication of age—she had been freed and ruled the household 'a pupula', was also freed for special reasons, to marry the son of the house.[7] Q. Pompeius Sosus and his wife were married for sixty years, but we do not know if a period of *contubernium* is included in this reckoning nor if they had children.[8] A freedwoman whose age at death we know was certainly freed young, but had barely reached child-bearing age at the time of her death at fourteen.[9] Another freedwoman's monument

---

[1] Ingenuous children: *CIL* i. 1570, 1227, 1365, 1837 = Degr. 977, 919, 927, 971, and perhaps *CIL* i. 1209, 1349 = Degr. 821, 943.
[2] *CIL* i. 2210. [3] Jones, *Studies*, x, pp. 159 f.
[4] pp. 182, 190. [5] e.g. *CIL* i. 1837, 1227 = Degr. 971, 919.
[6] *CIL* i. 1215. 'patrono' could mean that she was client of her father's patron, but it seems less likely.
[7] *CIL* i. 1570 = Degr. 977. [8] *CIL* i. 1220 = Degr. 365.
[9] *CIL* i. 1214 = Degr. 803.

mentions that she died at forty, but does not say when she was freed. She had known her husband since childhood, but the *contubernium* is not dated and despite the length of the inscription no children are mentioned.[1] The smallness of freedmen's families gives the impression that the childbearing years after manumission tended to be short. More than two children are rarely found on inscriptions.[2] The large family of Aurelius Zosimus[3] is accounted for by the generosity of his patron. He may have been freed young (nothing is known of his wife); his patron encouraged him to bring up his children (a suggestion that many, because of poverty, got rid of their new-born children) and helped with jobs for the sons and dowries for the daughters. Among all the *liberti* of Cicero known to us, we hear of none who were married and had children. Tiro was obviously a bachelor; the others mainly lived with their patron and do not seem to have had their own establishments, but may of course have had families. Marriage may have been rare for such men, or more likely postponed till late in life, as was the case with freeborn men. Late manumission is likely except when the master was rich and generous. Again we have few data. Tiro was perhaps freed young.[4] Terence died young, but left a daughter, clearly ingenuous.[5] Pompeius Demetrius was married to the courtesan Flora (probably a freedwoman), but though she was attractive and presumably therefore young, we hear of no children.[6] Infant mortality will have accounted for the shortage of children to some extent; freedwomen may have been subfertile. Like the freeborn, the freedmen may have intentionally limited their families,[7] but the extent of the practice cannot be ascertained.

It seems likely, then, that the size of libertine families was small. But the proportion of libertine blood in the veins of the Roman

---

[1] *CIL* i. 1221 = Degr. 793. The end is lost but children would naturally have been mentioned in the verses assigned to the husband.
[2] e.g. *CIL* i. 1570 = Degr. 977.   [3] *CIL* xiv. 2298. 5 ff. = *EJ* 358.
[4] p. 260.   [5] Suet. *Vita Ter.* 5.   [6] Plut. *Pomp.* 2. 3 f.
[7] By abortion (Juv. vi. 595 ff., cf. 366 ff..) or exposure of the newly-born (Suet. *DA* 65. 4; *Claud.* 27.), rather than by the mainly ineffectual methods of contraception current in the late Republic, according to M. K. Hopkins, *Comparative Studies in Society and History*, 8 (1965) 124 ff., especially 149 ff. I am not convinced that the treatment of a pair of alleged bastards in the imperial house justifies Hopkins in thinking exposure was common, and the prevalence of abortion may be similarly disputed.

people increased steadily. This fact has been exaggerated. Tenney Frank, it will be remembered, put the proportion of the population with freed or alien ancestry at ninety per cent. But when Tacitus says that nearly every senator had a freed ancestor—'non aliunde originem trahi'[1]—it is in a partisan speech, and in any case does not mean that all his ascendants were freedmen. The same will have been true of the libertine admixture in the *plebs*. The *libertini* did not have to have a higher birth-rate than the *ingenui* in order to make an effect on the racial purity of Rome. It was enough that there was intermarriage, and that the ingenuous birth-rate was also low, especially in the last years of the Republic, when war disposed of, or checked the philoprogenitiveness of, so many freeborn Romans of military age.[2]

(ii) *Social Relationships*

In considering a freedman's social contacts outside his family, there are two questions we may ask. What sort of relationship did a freedman have with his patron? How far did he become integrated in society, that of other freedmen, or of *ingenui*? As we are not considering an ideal or average freedman, the answers, as far as there are any, will vary in different cases.

The inscriptional evidence on the relations between patron and freedman is slanted in favour of good relations, since hostility is only exceptionally recorded on tombs, while the *officium* owed to the patron is often exemplified. The old idea of the unity of the *familia*—family, slaves, and freedmen together—and of the paternal status of the patron had made it customary to bury all in the same tomb. But by the later Republic, the large size of households made the custom impractical, while fashion made it distasteful to the upper classes. Lower down in the social scale, it was still possible. Where we find only the formula 'libertis libertabusque'[3] nothing is proved for affection felt by the patron, but where freedmen are named,[4] we may argue that the old idea of the family still had

---
[1] Tac. *Ann.* xiii. 27; cf. Syme, *Tacitus*, ii, pp. 612 f.
[2] Cf. on the families of slaves and freedmen in a later age, B. Rawson, *CP* 61 (1966), 70 ff.
[3] e.g. *CIL* i. 1236, 1638 = Degr. 940, 956.
[4] e.g. *CIL* i. 1401, 939 and previous note.

reality. Patrons who opened their tombs to their *liberti* were often *libertini* themselves. Freeborn Romans who mentioned freedmen by name on their tombs seem to have been childless[1] or tradesmen who had worked in close contact with their freed subordinates.[2] Separate tombs were occasionally set up by patron to freedmen[3] and often by freedmen to patron. This might be in order to comply with the terms of the patron's will, when manumission was made by will, or freedmen were left bequests, on this condition.[4] But the phrase 'de sua pecunia faciundum coeravit'[5] recurs, so the duty was sometimes undertaken voluntarily. Eulogies of the patron and the sharing of a tomb primarily intended for the freedman himself indicate a closer relationship. Again such patrons were often of freed status[6] too or bourgeois who had worked closely with their freedmen.[7] *Conliberti* too were often on such terms of interdependence that they chose to be buried together.[8]

Bequests to freedmen will also sometimes have indicated affection and gratitude, though not always, for we know from Petronius that a crafty patron might leave money and freedom to his slaves and make sure that they knew it, in order to obtain good service.[9] But Horace suggests that freedmen were often named heirs in the absence of sons.[10] In the Principate it was common to leave *alimenta* to freedmen.[11] An inscription from Venusia shows a perfumer who freed his slaves in his will and (if it is rightly interpreted) left a bequest to the entire *familia*.[12] Literature furnishes more detailed examples. Cicero commended L. Nostius Zoilus, co-heir with himself under his patron's will, as 'patroni iudicio ornatus'.[13] A victim of Verres, P. Trebonius P. l., was among the heirs of his patron on condition that he, and the others, helped his patron's proscribed brother, who was debarred from inheriting. Only the freedman was faithful to his obligation.[14] Possibly a warmer loyalty was involved than the strong sense of duty praised by Cicero:

---

[1] *CIL* i. 1919.   [2] e.g. *CIL* i. 1334b = Degr. 823.
[3] e.g. *CIL* i. 1259 = Degr. 802 (probably a freed mistress).
[4] Cf. *CIL* i. 1519   [5] e.g. *CIL* i. 1236 = Degr. 940.
[6] *CIL* i. 1236, 1928 = Degr. 940, 49.   [7] *CIL* i. 1596 = Degr. 938.
[8] *CIL* i. 1398, 1585 = Degr. 816, 922. *CIL* x. 6028.
[9] *Cena*, 71.   [10] *Sat.* ii. 3. 122; 5. 71.
[11] *Dig.* xxxiv. 1.   [12] *CIL* i.1703 = Degr. 825.
[13] *Fam.* xiii. 46.   [14] Cic. ii. *Verr.* i. 123 f.

Utrum reprehendis, quod patronum iuvabat eum qui tum in miseriis erat, an, quod alterius patroni mortui voluntatem conservabat, a quo summum beneficium acceperat ?[1]

Verres, however, considered it scandalous that a freedman should be heir to a rich *eques*. An even more striking example of devotion is provided by an undated tale told by Pliny of a freedman who, though left sole heir to his patron's property, preferred to throw himself on the pyre.[2] Such bequests to freedmen took place of course in the absence of *sui heredes*. The *heredes* might indeed get little out of the legacy once they had paid debts and settled other bequests,[3] but to be named heir was nevertheless an honour, and as the testator was at liberty to choose as *heredes* reputable men whose presence in the will would have also a certain snob appeal, the choice of a freedman shows both that the patron trusted him to be a responsible executor and that he had a particular kindness for him, as Cicero pointed out in the case of Zoilus.

Apart from these conventional ways of showing affection, gratitude, or dutifulness, we hear of others. Freedmen were, naturally, praised for their attitude towards their patrons: *officium*, *fides*, *fidelitas*, or *benevolentia*.[4] Such good qualities might be dramatically demonstrated: the freedmen of Asuvius of Larinum helped to bring his murderers to book;[5] a freedman of Pompey buried his murdered patron;[6] Cicero mentions the witty freedman L. Aelius who to avenge the wrongs of his patron brought the latter's enemy to trial;[7] during the triumvirs' proscription several owed their lives to freedmen,[8] notable among these being the celebrated T. Vinius Philopoemen.[9]

The patron's approval was the conventional guarantee of virtue in a freedman.[10] It could be of varying degrees of warmth. Our

[1] Cicero seems to be using 'patronum' of the proscribed brother without meaning that Trebonius was his *libertus* (joint freedman of the two brothers), for he goes on to imply that only P. Trebonius had manumitted. In this case the relationship with the proscribed brother will have been that of a client.
[2] *NH* vii. 122. Contrast Cic. *Fam.* xii. 26 for lack of respect for a patron's will.
[3] See J. A. Crook, *Law and Life of Rome* (London, 1967), pp. 118 ff.
[4] e.g. Cic. *Fam.* xiii. 21. 2; iv. 9. 1; iii. 6. 1; iv. 9. 1, respectively.
[5] Cic. *Cluent.* 38.   [6] Plut. *Pomp.* 80, cf. 78.   [7] *Scaur.* 23.
[8] App. *BC* iv. 187 f., 198. But others betrayed their patrons, ibid. 101, 107 ff., 120.   [9] Suet. *DA* 27. 2; Dio, xlvii. 7. 4; App. *BC* iv. 187.
[10] Cic. *Cluent.* 52.

sources regularly speak of the esteem in which a patron held a freedman in terms of 'honor et usus',[1] 'gratia' or 'gratus'[2] and their Greek equivalents,[3] 'acceptus' or 'acceptissimus'.[4] A cold, patronizing appreciation was often all a patron's feeling for his freedman amounted to, as one would expect. Cicero, writing to Atticus about the defection of his freedman Chrysippus, was particularly annoyed because he was an educated man, while the disappearance of his companion, a mere *operarius*, was trivial: 'Chrysippum vero, quem ego propter litterularum nescioquid libenter vidi, in honore habui, discedere a puero insciente me!'[5] But appreciation of a freedman's culture or talents was often part of a warmer feeling. Q. Cicero, congratulating his brother on the manumission of Tiro (and the fact that it was a matter of congratulation is significant) remarks on his literary talents, as outweighing even the virtue of faithfulness: 'Si enim mihi Stati fidelitas est tantae voluptati, quanti esse in isto haec eadem bona debent, additis litteris, sermonibus, humanitate, quae sunt his ipsis commodis potiora!'[6]

Relationship between patron and freedman could include *voluptas*, as Quintus Cicero points out. Pleasure in social contacts depends mainly on similarity of ideas and interests. *A priori*, then, the freedmen closest to their patrons would be those of the same culture and tastes. It is thus unsurprising that the freedmen of whom we hear in the closest social contact with their patrons were those who would have made the same sort of contribution as any other friends. This would apply to the lower classes, but we have no direct evidence to show the *opifices* and *tabernarii* dicing, lounging in the *Campus* or visiting the games together with their freedmen. In the upper classes, where we hear of such friendships, we can often see what the bond might be. The clearest case is that of Cicero and Tiro, where shared intellectual interests provided a firm basis for understanding. In spite of the smears attempted by some of the ancients and recent writers such as Carcopino,[7] the correspondence between the two shows that the worst Cicero could

[1] Suet. *DA* 67: many of Augustus' *liberti*, especially Celadus and Licinus.
[2] Val. Max. vi. 1. 4; Suet. *Gram.* 12: Epicadus with Sulla and Faustus.
[3] Plut. *Pomp.* 40. 1: Demetrius; Dio, xlviii. 30: Helenus with Augustus.
[4] Suet. *DA* 67: Polus. [5] *Att.* vii. 2. 8.
[6] Cic. *Fam.* xvi. 16. 2. [7] Appendix 3, p. 262, n. 17.

be accused of was feather-bedding his freedman, and the worst fault of Tiro an excessive devotion to his patron's family. The letters of all the Cicerones to Tiro are affectionate and familiar, though Quintus repels by his effusiveness[1] and young Marcus by his patent toadying and insincerity.[2] But they live up to Quintus' remark on Tiro's manumission, that he was their friend henceforth and not their slave, since he was too good for that position in life.[3] Cicero himself loaded Tiro with work, but was properly grateful for it. He treated him with the utmost solicitude during his frequent illnesses, and did not stint him for funds, doctors, or attendants.[4] He took an interest in Tiro's own work[5] and confided to him his political secrets and personal feelings.[6] Finally, the terms on which they stood were such that Cicero could afford to laugh at his exslave, and even on such a thorny subject as his status.[7] As we have no example of a letter from Tiro to his patron, a similar familiarity from the freedman cannot be cited, but Q. Cicero accused Tiro of having hauled him over the coals on one occasion,[8] and young Marcus had some fear of Tiro's opinion.[9] Young Marcus, like his father, indulged in good-tempered teasing of the freedman. Tiro, in fact, was treated consistently as one of the family, so deep in its secrets and affections, so identified with it that even his purchase of a farm at Puteoli could be interpreted not as a gesture of independence, but as indicating his willingness to share it with the Cicerones.[10] If Tiro ever resented this attitude, we do not hear of it, and his devotion to his patron's memory, shown by the publication of various Ciceroniana, surely disproves any such idea.[11]

Although a freedman could never be an equal (except perhaps, in practice, though not in theory, when the patron was also *libertinus*) the formal code of the *patronus–libertus* relationship, once

---

[1] Cic. *Fam.* xvi. 27. 2: 'Ego vos a. d. III Kal. videbo tuosque, etiamsi te veniens in medio foro videro, dissuaviabor'. But this is partly humorous and probably entirely sincere.
[2] Ibid. xvi. 21.
[3] Ibid. xvi. 16. 1.
[4] e.g. ibid. xvi. 4, 5, 15.
[5] Ibid. xvi. 18. 3.
[6] Ibid. xvi. 23. 2.
[7] Ibid. xvi. 18. 1; cf. *Dom.* 22, *Fam.* ix. 32.
[8] *Fam.* xvi. 27. 1.
[9] Ibid. xvi. 21.
[10] Ibid. xvi. 21. 7.
[11] For other cultured *liberti* on close terms with their patrons, cf. Pompeius Lenaeus (Suet. *Gram.* 15) and probably Tullius Laurea (Appendix 3, p. 259) both of whom defended their patron's memory.

accepted, made intimacy easier between them than it was for *ingenui* with a large social gulf between them. Patron and freedman, each aware of his position, could, if there was intellectual or other parity, create a satisfactory and generous relationship.

The degree to which freedmen mixed with freeborn Romans is hard to tell as regards the poorer classes. In the trade and religious *collegia* they were in frequent contact, and on such boards as those of the Capuan *magistri*,[1] to take a well-documented example, freedmen appear to have had parity with *ingenui*. In the city *plebs*, especially as represented in the Clodian gangs,[2] there appears to have been little class distinction between freedmen and freeborn, though perhaps there were few of the latter. This would be natural if, as has been argued,[3] most of the shopkeepers and craftsmen were freedmen, leaving labouring jobs to the poor ingenuous *conducticii*, so that from the point of employment, *ingenui* might well be lower on the social scale. The occurrence of mixed marriages[4] is also evidence for a lack of class prejudice among the common people in Rome and the country districts.

In the upper classes, on whose social life we have detailed information, a more exclusive attitude was inevitable. The importance of birth and origin need not be laboured here.[5] There was a great divide between the gentleman, *liber* and *ingenuus*, and the ex-slave,[6] which was why a distinguished man like Tyrannio of Amisus should never have been admitted to be a slave.[7] When a freedman became his patron's friend or confidential agent, however, he was likely to form similar relationships with other *ingenui*. In many cases such *amicitia*[8] was a politic alliance rather than real friendship, just as it was in the greater world of Roman politics. So Cicero claimed a warm appreciation of Appius Claudius' confidential freedman, Phania, whom he clearly did not really like,[9] and an even stronger friendship for his other freedman Cilix, who, he says, became his intimate within a couple of days.[10] A political

---

[1] p. 197.　　[2] pp. 173 ff.　　[3] pp. 95 ff.　　[4] p. 211.
[5] Cf. e.g. Cic. *Cael.* 4; *Phil.* iii. 15.
[6] Cic. *Pis.* 67.　　[7] p. 116.
[8] For *amicitia* with social inferiors see Brunt, *Proc. Camb. Phil. Soc.* N.S. 2 (1965), 8.
[9] *Fam.* ii. 1. 2; 13. 2.　　[10] *Fam.* ii. 1. 2.

SOCIAL RELATIONSHIPS

transaction is clothed in the polite fiction of a personal liking. The type of *amicitia* involved between freedman and *ingenuus* is to be observed in such contexts as Cicero's letter of introduction for L. Cossinius Anchialus to Sulpicius, where the word is specifically used of the attitude which he hopes the governor will adopt. He explains that Anchialus is 'probatissimus' both to his patron and to his patron's *necessarii*, of whom Cicero himself is one.[1] The pattern is repeated in three other letters commending freedmen: L. Livineius Trypho, the freedman of Regulus, was loved by Cicero for his own sake (*diligere* is the word) and he had performed notable *officia* at the time of Cicero's exile, even braving the wintry sea;[2] C. Avianius Hammonius, the freedman of Aemilius Avianius, had shown as much *fides* and *benevolentia* to Cicero in the same painful period as if he had been his own freedman;[3] Curtius Mithres, freedman of Cicero's intimate friend Postumus, had also treated Cicero as if he had been his own patron:

me colit et observat aeque atque illum ipsum patronum suum. Apud eum ego sic Ephesi fui, quotienscumque fui, tamquam domi meae, multaque acciderunt in quibus et benevolentiam eius erga me experirer et fidem. Itaque si quid aut mihi aut meorum cuipiam in Asia opus est, ad hunc scribere consuevi, huius cum opera et fide tum domo et re uti tamquam mea.[4]

This last man stands out from the others in that his services to Cicero seem to have been independent of the orders of his patron: he entertained Cicero in his own house and in the style to which he was accustomed. His social standing probably depended on wealth.

Entertaining[5] *ingenui* of importance seems to be a sign of high social standing in a freedman: it has been mentioned for Tiro.[6] Another example is likely in Pompeius Vindullus, probably a freedman rather than a client of Pompeius Magnus.[7] It was this man who was host to Pompey's close friend Vedius, who deposited incriminating baggage which was found on Vindullus' death.[8] M. Aemilius Philemon, freedman of Lepidus, also belongs to this select few. He entertained Cicero as a guest at his Pomptine villa

---

[1] *Fam.* xiii. 23.   [2] *Fam.* xiii. 60; *Att.* iii. 17. 1.
[3] *Fam.* xiii. 21.   [4] *Fam.* xiii. 69.
[5] On *hospitium* see E. Badian, *Foreign Clientelae*, pp. 11 f., 155.
[6] p. 219.   [7] See Syme, *JRS* 51 (1961), 23, n. 5. Above, p. 104.
[8] Cic. *Att.* vi. 1. 25.

in 53 B.C., while Cicero was taking a holiday.[1] We know from Asconius that he was a 'notus homo', a man of some influence and position: he was an important and weighty, though perhaps unreliable witness against Milo in 52 B.C.[2]

The writing of personal letters may also be taken as proof of friendship between some freedmen and the friends of their patrons. Thus Tiro wrote to Atticus and Cicero wished Alexis, Atticus' secretary (and presumably freedman) to do the same with him, instead of merely sending greetings.[3] The avidity with which Cicero desired to receive the salutations of certain freedmen, and the care with which he sent them to others, are amusingly exemplified in his correspondence with Atticus concerning Dionysius.[4]

Living with an *ingenuus* other than the patron is often a proof, or at least a concomitant, of familiarity. Certain freedmen, either through an arrangement with their patron—often, probably, because he himself could not find a use for their *operae* and lent them to friends[5]—or because they were free agents after the *operae* were ended or the patron dead, worked for other *ingenui*. Thus Dionysius worked more often for Cicero than for his patron Atticus in the period in which we have knowledge of him. Cicero to begin with had nothing but praise for him, 'Dionysium semper equidem, ut scis, dilexi, sed cotidie pluris facio et me hercule in primis quod te amat nec tui mentionem intermitti sinit.'[6] He is praised for his love of Atticus and of Cicero and for his devotion to learning. But Cicero later reacted equally violently against the freedman, after he was reluctant to join him in 49 B.C.,[7] but finally forgave him in 45.[8] Another inmate of Cicero's household was the doctor Alexio, probably a freedman but not Cicero's own,[9] whose death in 44 B.C. caused Cicero to lament the loss of his affection, culture, and amiability.[10] The freedman architect Vettius Chrysippus, who often

---

[1] Cic. *Fam.* vii. 18. 3.
[2] Asc. *Mil.* 37A.   [3] *Att.* v. 20. 9; cf. p. 149.
[4] Greetings from Cicero to Dionysius: *Att.* iv. 14. 2; 15. 10; 19. 2; greetings from Dionysius to Atticus: *Att.* iv. 11. 2; a message of thanks expected by Cicero from Dionysius, and not sent: *Att.* viii. 4.   [5] p. 76.
[6] *Att.* v. 9. 3 (51 B.C.). Cf. *Att.* vi. 1. 12 (50 B.C.): 'Dionysius mihi quidem in amoribus est.'
[7] *Att.* vii. 18. 3, etc.   [8] *Att.* xiii. 2. 6.   [9] Appendix 3, p. 254.
[10] *Att.* xv. 1. 1: 'amorem erga me, humanitatem, suavitatem'.

worked for Cicero, probably also lived in the house, at least while on the job, since Cicero calls him 'homo prope domesticus',[1] which seems to admit only of a literal meaning. Apollonius, freedman of the young P. Crassus, after his patron's death at Carrhae, turned to cultivating such friends of Crassus as Caesar and Cicero, both of whom he visited in the provinces.[2] The scholar Caecilius Epirota, freedman of Atticus, sacked by his patron in 30 or 29 B.C., went to live with Cornelius Gallus.[3] An instance from the triumviral period is Timagenes of Alexandria. This man had, according to *Suda*, been a war-captive of Gabinius and was brought to Rome in 55 B.C., but later freed. Seneca repeats splendid, but unhappily improbable, tales that he had been first a prisoner, then a cook, then a litter-bearer, and then a friend of Caesar (that is, Octavian).[4] He had Antonian connections and bitterly attacked Octavian, his wife, and whole household, in which, it seems, he was a resident or at least an *habitué*.[5] Previously he had written a monograph on the deeds of Octavian, which he burnt when he was finally forbidden the house. Was his change of front due to Antonian partisanship? At any rate, his exclusion from Octavian's home is said to have had no effect on his intimacy with others. He betook himself to the '*contubernium*' of Asinius Pollio, another historian and Antonian, and with him passed an old age as obstinate as ever, though Pollio, less recalcitrant, asked Octavian if he should throw his lodger out.[6]

These freedmen who worked closely or lived with *ingenui* other than their patrons would naturally be said to have two patrons. As an ingenuous client could multiply patrons,[7] so could a freedman. Such *libertini* with extra patrons are Mallius Glaucia, the client and intimate of T. Roscius,[8] or Cicero's Hilarus, who is called client of Atticus.[9] The *liberti* of others whom Clodius is said to have threatened to make his own by the distribution law would really

[1] *Fam.* vii. 14. 1.
[2] Cic. *Fam.* xiii. 16.
[3] Suet. *Gram.* 16.
[4] *Controv.* x. 5. 22: 'ex captivo cocus, ex coco lecticarius, ex lecticario usque in intimam amicitiam Caesaris felix'.
[5] Sen. *de Ira* iii. 23. 4 ff. [6] Sen. *de Ira* iii. 23. 5.
[7] Cf. von Premerstein, *RE* iv. 1. 23 ff. [8] Cic. *Rosc. Am.* 19.
[9] Cic. *Att.* i. 12. 2. Cf. pp. 73, 150; Appendix 3, p. 256

have been his clients.[1] Dionysius, named Marcus in honour of Cicero,[2] might also consider Cicero his patron.

The appellation 'familiaris' indicated a close degree of intimacy. Terence lived on familiar terms with many of the nobility, especially Scipio and Laelius,[3] Epirota on very familiar terms with Gallus, to the latter's discredit,[4] while Augustus' freedman Hyginus, the Palatine librarian, was intimate with Ovid and the consular historian Clodius Licinus, who claimed also to have supplied him with money in his impoverished old age.[5] The notorious Phamea, who was probably a freedman,[6] besides having useful political friends,[7] is called by Cicero 'mihi sane familiaris'[8] and entertained people like Paetus to elegant dinners.[9] Freedmen were also given the title of 'amicus' by *ingenui*.[10]

The participation of the more influential freedmen at dinners and similar social events was accepted in the late Republic. When Cicero entertained Caesar at Puteoli, he provided three *triclinia* for his followers, one for the 'liberti lautiores', one for the 'liberti minus lauti', one for slaves.[11] On this occasion segregation was convenient.[12] But Suetonius found it worth remark that Augustus never entertained freedmen at his own table with the exception of Pompeius Menas,[13] on whom he had conferred the gold ring. The practice of Suetonius' day and of earlier times was less rigid: Pompeius Magnus for instance had had conspicuously different ideas, and it was not the fact that his freedman Demetrius took part in his parties that caused comment, but that he was allowed to behave with such bad manners.[14] As for the practice of inviting freedwomen to bachelor dinners[15], that and the familiarity which

[1] Cic. *Mil.* 89. [2] Cic. *Att.* iv. 14. 1.
[3] Suet. *Vita Ter.* 1: 'cum multis nobilibus familiariter vixit, sed maxime cum Scipione Africano et C. Laelio.' Living in the household cannot be implied: Terence visited many houses.
[4] Suet. *Gram.* 16: 'vixitque una familiarissime.'
[5] Suet. *Gram.* 20: 'fuitque familiarissimus Ovidio poetae et Clodio Licino consulari historico.'
[6] Appendix 6. [7] Cic. *Att.* xiii. 49.
[8] *Fam.* vii. 24. 2. [9] Cic. *Fam.* ix. 16. 8.
[10] e.g. Cic. *Att.* vii. 18. 3. [11] Cic. *Att.* xiii. 52.
[12] Contrast Pliny, *Epp.* ii. 6. 2 where differentiation of service to freedmen guests for less adequate reasons is attacked as being in bad taste.
[13] *DA* 74 (on the authority of Valerius Messalla).
[14] Plut. *Pomp.* 40. 1. [15] Cic. *Fam.* ix. 26. 2.

SOCIAL RELATIONSHIPS

Volumnia Cytheris enjoyed with the upper classes at Rome, especially with Antonius,[1] are little to the point in a consideration of the opportunities for social climbing open to freedmen and freedwomen as a class. Birth or origin have only minor influence on the careers of courtesans, if they are sufficiently talented. The same applies to professional actors, and in Rome to the *mimi* in particular, though serious actors might have the entrée to society because of their value as models for oratory.[2] But we may note in passing that Volumnia and others adopted a most effective method of social climbing.

That society of the triumviral period was as capable as the Republic of remembering a man's servile origins against him if it wished to exclude him is sufficiently shown by Horace, when he remarks that Maecenas was above that snobbery which led many others to despise him as the son of a freedman.[3] But Tigellius the Sardinian, who was probably freed, moved in the circles of Caesar and Octavian as well as on the fringes of society.[4] Maecenas' friends included, as well as Horace, the freedman's son, Sarmentus, who was probably a full-blown freedman,[5] and whose likeable qualities are shown by the fact that he was taken on the journey to Brundisium. Interesting details of his career are noted. Dellius is said to have offended Cleopatra by saying that while the Antonians were drinking vinegar Sarmentus was enjoying Falernian in Rome. Plutarch comments that he was a favourite of Octavian.[6] Juvenal also knows him as a buffoon who entertained Caesar.[7] From probably slave origins he had reached a position of some intimacy with the ruling class, but one bought at the cost of being a butt and a jester (if not worse, as propaganda suggested) and accompanied by unpopularity—his appearance in the Fourteen Rows provoked an outcry. The fact that the Antonians and the urban *plebs* picked on him shows that he could be considered a discredit to the party of Octavian, even if a minor one. He was one of the mushrooms of

---
[1] p. 140.
[2] Sulla and Antony were noted for their taste for low company: Plut. *Sulla* 36. 2; Cic. *Phil.* ii. 15, 67, 101. These were often freedmen or slaves, pp. 139 ff. Aesopus, perhaps a freedman, was a friend of Cicero (Cic. *Div.* i. 80).
[3] *Sat.* i. 6. 1 ff.
[4] Ibid. 2. 1 f. See Appendix 6. [5] Appendix 7.
[6] Plut. *Ant.* 59. 8. [7] *Sat.* v. 3 f.

the age of the civil wars; like Tigellius and the dandy pilloried in Horace's fifth epode his origins are said to have been servile[1] and, like them, he excited 'liberrima indignatio'. To these products of the rise of Octavian we can add Licinus, Menas, and the rest, whose importance in state affairs will have allowed them to make a show in Roman society, even though the aristocracy tried to ignore them.

The parallel question to that of the treatment *libertini* were given in ingenuous society is what relationship they were likely to have with other freedmen. But as social history was not written by freedmen, evidence is largely lacking. Freedmen clearly mixed with their *conliberti*, the other ex-slaves of the same family.[2] But the hierarchy in the households of the rich caused deep class distinctions even among *conliberti*. Caesar had his 'liberti lautiores' and his 'liberti minus lauti'. The distinction between educated freedmen and mere labourers was marked.[3] As the more important freedmen of nobles sometimes married freedwomen of other nobles,[4] mixing with other *libertini* who were on the same level and had patrons in the same class in society seems to have been normal. Other connections were provided by work or nationality. Scholars and poets; colleagues like the librarians Hyginus and Melissus; craftsmen and tradesmen who met in the guilds; national groups like the Jews; Egyptians who maintained their allegiance to Isis; freedmen in such groupings will have been bound together or separated by personal feelings too.

Despite a general class prejudice against freedmen, they were able to make their way in society on certain terms. They were normally expected to know their place, but after that *ingenui* might find pleasure in their company because of their learning, wit, or other qualities, not least their wealth. As long as a freedman did not forget that he was not an equal, all was well. It was when Demetrius flaunted his influence with Pompey, or Tigellius and Sarmentus their wealth and the fact that great men found them amusing, that protests were heard. Civil war and proscription produced freedmen who had grown rich and climbed high, thanks to the importance of

---

[1] Not even libertine, which is why I take them to have been freedmen.
[2] p. 216.   [3] Cic. *Att.* vii. 2. 8.   [4] p. 210.

comparative parvenus like Sulla and Octavian, with consequent disruption of old social classes, and the uncomfortable situation in which old aristocrats found themselves less well-off, influential, and eye-catching on the *Via Appia* than an ex-slave who had until recently been at the beck and call of a master.

Conclusions

In his family and social life the freedman was naturally limited by the circumstances that part of his life had been spent as a slave (which normally gave him less time to enjoy family relationships than an ingenuous Roman had) and by a certain amount of class discrimination. The 'class' of a freedman, however, depended not so much on his freed status as on the social position of his patron. The freedman of a shopkeeper would belong inevitably to the lower orders, while the freedman of an aristocrat, though never an equal, had often the opportunity to mix in high society and cultured circles, a chance which was denied to the poor *ingenuus* unless in exceptional circumstances. The freedman's position was often similar to that of the free alien who gained the citizenship without passing through the cataclysm of slavery which could both lower a man and eventually raise him from his original status. Only a narrow barrier separated the two categories and it is sometimes hard to distinguish free-lance provincials like the *rhetor* Nicias of Cos,[1] who moved in the circle of Roman politicians between his home and the capital, and freedmen like Demetrius of Gadara. The freedman might be more closely attached to an individual patron and based on Rome rather than on the provinces. Demetrius retained his links with Gadara and had influence of his own in the East; the same was true for Licinus in Gaul, presumably. Others had lost their original ties, and the freedman might thus be a better Roman than an enfranchised provincial could be, and therefore a more useful agent, with a greater part to play in the society of Rome itself. Culture and accomplishments, which won favour for provincials, were the chief qualifications for freedmen also, and no distinction can be made between Licinius Apollonius or Licinius

[1] Syme, *JRS* 51 (1961), 25 ff.; Bowersock, *Augustus and the Greek World*, pp. 45 f.

Tyrannio, the freedmen scholars, and the Greeks Theophanes of Mytilene[1] and Antiochus of Ascalon,[2] just as in political life the activities of Theophanes[3] and Pompey's other henchman Demetrius were on the same plane. If a general distinction may be drawn, it is that the freedman may have had more influence with his patron, while a foreign noble clearly had immeasurably more personal power on his own territory. The prestige and influence each enjoyed in Roman society at large would vary accordingly, a local dynast outranking a great freedman (but not necessarily having more power behind the scenes) and a great freedman being far more important than an ordinary provincial client.

[1] *FGH* ii. B. 188.
[2] Plut. *Lucull.* 28. 7
[3] Cic. *Att.* v. 11. 3; Caes. *BC* iii. 18. 3, etc.

VII

THE SONS OF FREEDMEN

THE sons of freedmen were, in my opinion,[1] free from the legal handicaps from which their fathers suffered.[2] I see no reason to believe that they were forbidden by law to be *equites equo publico*, jurors under the Gracchan Law, senators, or magistrates. In private law, they were free from obligations to their father's patron, except that they owed the *fides* due from clients, and they excluded him from the right to inherit, even if they were emancipated or adopted by others, but not if they were disinherited. If there were any legal drawback to marriages between freedmen and freeborn, this did not apply to their sons. If Suetonius were right on the antique use of the word 'libertinus' to mean sons of freedmen this might suggest that there were some legal drawbacks attached to the position, but there is no evidence that he was right and no corroborative instances support him.

But there were consequences of the status of parents which affected the sons. When freedmen were confined to the urban tribes their sons would inherit the registration, though probably they could attempt to arrange a transfer if they had country property. Many of the members of the urban tribes attested appear to have been sons or descendants of freedmen.[3] This would of course limit the power of their vote in the same way as that of their fathers.

We have seen that a good many of the sons of freedmen became magistrates, for instance Flavius, Furius, and Thoranius,[4] and senators like Popillius and perhaps Gellius and the protégés of Caesar and the triumvirs.[5] Attacks were often made on such men, but not on legal grounds. The prejudice appears to have been social, like that against men from the country towns. The criticisms of

---

[1] pp. 52 ff.
[2] They were citizens *optimo iure Quiritium* by the Lex Terentia of 189 B.C. See A. Berger, *Encyclopedic Dictionary of Roman Law*, p. 560.
[3] Taylor, *Voting Districts*, p. 148.
[4] And possibly Claudius Glycias and L. Equitius.   [5] pp. 56 ff.

their opponents often referred to a servile background in the crudest terms, ignoring the fact that the fathers of such men had been manumitted. In spite of the deeply held belief that *libertas* and *civitas* went together,[1] we often find that freedmen were regarded as second-class citizens[2] and this reflected also on their sons. Thus Cicero accused Equitius, in effect, of being a runaway slave,[3] and mocked the senator Gellius, probably a freedman's son, when he read letters to the Senate, with the remark that he was one of those who had cried aloud for his freedom.[4]

This prejudice was based on moral theories, that slavery signified or produced low moral standards, trickery, lack of dignity, unscrupulousness. The idea can clearly be seen in Cicero's attacks on Sextus Naevius, who seems to have been a freedman's son.[5] According to the advocate, his client C. Quinctius had formed a partnership with Naevius, who was a man of good credit, but not educated in such a way

ut iura societatis et officia certi patris familias nosse posset; non quo ei deesset ingenium; nam neque parum facetus scurra Sex. Naevius neque inhumanus praeco umquam est existimatus. Quid ergo est? Cum ei natura nihil melius quam vocem dedisset, pater nihil praeter libertatem reliquisset, vocem in quaestum contulit, libertate usus est quo impunius dicax esset.[6]

Every phrase tells. Whether Naevius was actually a freedman's son, or illegitimate, or in some other way deprived of the stable background provided by a *paterfamilias*, the passage powerfully illustrates the upper-class idea that the poor or those without a proper home and family were bound to be out of touch with the *mos maiorum*.

Such moral prejudice against the sons of freedmen would be almost confined to the upper classes. For the lower and middle class we have at this date little evidence about how the sons of

[1] e.g. Cic. *Caec*. 96 f.; *Red. in Sen*. 2; *Dom*. 77; *Sest*. 1; *Balb*. 24.
[2] e.g. Cic. ii *Verr*. i. 127: Verres thought that *libertini* were not *liberi*.
[3] *Rab. Perd*. 20: 'ille ex compedibus atque ergastulo Gracchus'.
[4] Plut. *Cic*. 27. 2. Gellius was not a *praeco* or *apparitor* but a senator and was probably among the signatories to the *senatusconsultum* about the Jews in 44 B.C. (Joseph. *Ant*. xiv. 220).
[5] See especially Cic. *Quinct*. 11 and 55, 95.
[6] *Quinct*. 11.

freedmen lived and worked, since inscriptions rarely mention the name of the father or give *cognomen*. As *cognomina* began to be generally used by the poorer classes in imperial times, they have been used to draw conclusions about the libertine element in the population and Frank[1] concluded from inscriptional evidence that the population of Rome was ninety per cent of freed stock. He took it that a Greek *cognomen* was evidence of recent foreign extraction and secondly that a Greek *cognomen* for a child or one parent was evidence that both parents were foreign. But if *ingenui* married freed persons quite frequently—and this was probably increasingly true from Augustus onwards—Frank's second premiss is unconvincing. Since, too, there was a shortage of Latin names, freeborn parents might use Greek names for their children too. But Frank showed that there was a prejudice in favour of Latin names, for parents with Greek *cognomina* gave Latin names nearly as often as Greek, while parents with Latin names rarely gave Greek ones to their children. This seems, as Frank argued, to mean that there was a prejudice against Greek names, as they might suggest servile origin. Latin slave names[2] also tended to be avoided in the second generation. But the prejudice was probably less radical than Frank admitted. After all, many Greek-named parents gave their sons Greek names, and the foreign *cognomina* did not die out, as his argument suggests that they should have done in the course of a few generations from a slave ancestor. Statistics in this case exaggerate. We know from Aquileia that Greek names might be fashionable rather than not.[3] I should therefore, especially as Frank's calculations include freedmen who may have only been free a short part of their lives and thus distort the statistics, consider that his figures for the proportion of people with slave ancestors are too high, even when we remember that those who, he suggests, had slave ascendants may have had one freedman great-grandfather and seven freeborn great-grandparents. Frank's study is, however, good evidence for the infiltration of the Roman

[1] *AHR* 21 (1916), 689 ff.
[2] But see P. R. C. Weaver, *CQ* 14 (1964), 311 ff., for a caution against making a rigid distinction between servile and ingenuous names.
[3] A. Calderini, *Aquileia Romana* (Milan, 1930), pp. 417 ff. Taylor, *AJP* 82 (1961), 126 f., refuses to allow that this was of general application.

population by foreigners, mainly freedmen and their children. I take it, therefore, as evidence for lack of prejudice against the descendants of freedmen among the lower classes. In fact we have evidence for the way in which freedmen's descendants were absorbed even among the upper classes, for Tacitus is a witness for this in his own day, if not at an earlier date.[1]

We find in our period too that the sons of freedmen, like freedmen themselves, tried sometimes to conceal their origins.[2] Fathers might give their sons Latin names, as Larcius Nicia[3] selected 'Rufus' for one of his sons, a name which could be borne by aristocrats, though red hair had servile connections. The procurator and freedman Julius Licinus rejoiced in a name which did nothing to show his origins. Horace's name was unexceptionable; Vedius Pollio's was an asset. Like freedmen[4] the sons of freedmen often dropped or, like some other *ingenui*, never had a *cognomen*. All the sons of *libertini* who entered politics, with the possible exception of Claudius Glycias, were in this category—Flavius, Furius, Thoranius, Popillius. Only when they had to give full filiation would the lack of a grandfather betray them.

The instinct for a 'libertino patre natus' to try to forget his father's status is shown best by Horace, who took the courageous decision not to prevaricate.[5] But a freedman's son had to expect a good deal of contempt, especially if he was successful. Horace met it often, because he had been Brutus' officer and was Maecenas' friend, 'quem rodunt omnes libertino patre natum'.[6] The poet's indignation and hurt show through the words: he was criticized in spite of his qualities for his birth which those qualities could never cancel out.

Other freedmen's sons had tougher hides, for instance Helvius Mancia who fought verbal battles with Antonius and Caesar in the nineties and eighties[7] and survived to accuse Libo before the censors of 70 B.C. and to call Pompey an 'adulescentulus carnifex'.[8] The

[1] That is, Nero's reign: *Ann.* xiii. 27.
[2] e.g. Pasicles who had the more respectable *cognomen* Pansa too (Suet. *Gram.* 18).
[3] *CIL* i. 1570 = Degr. 977.
[4] e.g. M. Tullius, M. Cicero's freedman and scribe, p. 258.
[5] *Sat.* i. 6. 58 ff.   [6] Ibid. 46.   [7] Cic. *de Or.* ii. 274, 266.
[8] Val. Max. vi. 2. 8. Cf. Münzer, *RE* viii. i. 229, for the dating.

THE SONS OF FREEDMEN

son of Aesopus who so irritated Cicero[1] may have been another, for his father was probably a freedman.[2] He was a friend of Dolabella, rival of Antony, and a notorious wastrel.[3]

The sons of freedmen might have useful backing, chiefly money, if their fathers were of the select band of wealthy freedmen, and the patronage of the father's ex-owner. The son of Aesopus was able to make his way in society because of wealth bequeathed by his father,[4] and Horace's father, though not rich, was able to spend lavishly on his son's education.[5] Julius Rufio reached an equestrian post, thanks to the patronage of Caesar,[6] as did the son of Aurelius Zosimus later with the help of Cotta.[7] Other sons of freedmen, in spite of their birth, might make their own way, without support from their father's patron, often winning patronage from others. Those we know of as magistrates seem to have come far by their own abilities, though it is hard to guess if patronage was won by success or produced it. Probably both are true. Flavius was a man of ability and had the support of Appius Claudius. The most interesting example is not of a magistrate but of an *eques* who held power equal to that of a proconsul. This is Vedius Pollio,[8] of libertine parentage,[9] who became one of the extraordinarily powerful *equites* for whom the Principate was notable[10] and settled the province of Asia as agent for Octavian, probably in 31 to 30 B.C.[11] Syme, who has discussed him thoroughly in a recent article, shows that he may have been the same as the 'magnus nebulo' P. Vedius who was a friend of Pompey and stayed with Pompeius Vindullus at Laodicea in 50 B.C.[12] Vedius Pollio was noted for his extravagance, which finally gave Augustus a pretext for breaking with him. It was probably also the motive: the young Octavian had desperately needed subordinates who had organizing ability and could have no political ambitions apart from

---

[1] *Att.* xi. 15. 3.   [2] p. 139.
[3] Pliny, *NH* ix. 122; Hor. *Sat.* ii. 3. 239.
[4] Pliny, *NH* ix. 122: 'relictus ab eo in amplis opibus heres.'
[5] Hor. *Sat.* i. 6. 71 ff.
[6] p. 64.   [7] p. 64.
[8] See Syme, *JRS* 51 (1961), 23 ff.
[9] Dio, liv. 23.   [10] Tac. *Ann.* xii. 60.
[11] *CIL* iii. 7124. See Syme, *JRS* 51 (1961), 28, for full citation of sources.
[12] Cic. *Att.* vi. 1. 25; cf. Syme, *JRS* 52 (1961), 21 f. He is possibly to be identified too with 'Vidius' (Cic. *Fam.* ix. 10. 1) and Pollio, friend of Herod (Joseph. *Ant.* xv. 343).

him, but Augustus, the *princeps* of a united empire, had trouble in keeping up the appearance of a restored Republic and a revival of morality when a freedman's son was building palaces and Pausilypon and rearing his lampreys on a diet of slaves.[1] Like Gallus, Vedius Pollio seems to have been dropped. Vedius had ambitions of making his mark on the state: he asked for some fine public work to be erected at Pausilypon, but Augustus razed the house to the ground and then did not mention Vedius' name on the colonnade which he put up in its place. The emperors' agents were not to aspire to personal glory, as Gallus also learnt. The sons of freedmen in public life could never wholly shake off the disadvantages of their origin. Those who were members of the Senate were perpetually at the mercy of a hostile censor, as were those who had the *equus publicus*. Even the protégé of Augustus was only powerful on sufferance, while his master approved, though this fate was shared by *ingenui* under the Principate.

The grandsons of freedmen finally threw off the *damnosa hereditas* of slavery. They rejoiced in the full filiation. Unfortunately for our purposes this makes them hard to identify and we have to rely often on suspect *cognomina* to betray descendants of freedmen.[2] This method is dangerously unreliable. One example of a success story of a libertine family may be cited, since it does not rely on such conjectures. A. Gabinius, the tribune of 139 B.C., was descended from slaves.[3] The Pompeian tribune of 67 B.C. was almost certainly a direct descendant,[4] who was firmly established, for he did not stop at the tribunate but went on to hold the consulship.

The ambitions of freedmen, forbidden free scope for themselves, were naturally concentrated on their sons. This has been documented for the Principate in an investigation[5] of the part played by freedmen's sons and descendants in municipal government. A freedman might buy for his son positions from which he himself was excluded. So too Horace's father refused to send him to the

[1] Dio, liv. 23.
[2] As does, for example, P. Willems, *Le Sénat*, i, p. 188, suspecting 'Cimber' and 'Damasippus' of indicating libertine origins.
[3] p. 58.
[4] Other A. Gabinii held office in the interval, *MRR* ii, p. 570; E. Badian, *Philol.* 103 (1959), 87.
[5] M. L. Gordon, *JRS* 21 (1931), 65 ff.

local school attended by the sons of centurions, but insisted on giving him the education of an *eques* or senator.[1] The direct result of this was that Horace mixed in high society at Athens and took an equestrian post under Brutus. In spite of his modest social ambitions for his son,[2] the elder Horatius had a good idea of the value of education. He won the noblest epitaph that a freedman's son could ever have given his father for his start in life:

> at hoc nunc
> laus illi debetur et a me gratia maior.
> nil me paeniteat sanum patris huius, eoque
> non, ut magna dolo factum negat esse suo pars,
> quod non ingenuos habeat clarosque parentis,
> sic me defendam. longe mea discrepat istis
> et vox et ratio: nam si natura iuberet
> a certis annis aevum remeare peractum
> atque alios legere ad fastum quoscumque parentis,
> optaret sibi quisque, meis contentus honestos
> fascibus et sellis nollem mihi sumere, demens
> iudicio vulgi, sanus fortasse tuo, quod
> nollem onus haud umquam solitus portare molestum.[3]

What of the daughters of freedmen? Their history is scantier still. The quickest way for them to rise in society was to marry a freeborn Roman, as did the daughter of Terence,[4] and what, from the point of view of the aristocracy was a shocking *mésalliance* was no doubt from the point of view of the freedman a brilliant match, as when, if we may trust Cicero so far, M. Antonius married the daughter of a freedman Q. Fadius.[5]

Conclusions

The sons of freedmen were almost, but not quite, exempt from the consequences of their parents' original servile status. As clients of the manumitter or his descendants, they had to maintain *fides*, but the advantage might well be with themselves if a powerful patron chose to further their careers. Libertine origin did not bar

---

[1] Hor. *Sat.* i. 6. 71 ff. [2] Ibid. 85 ff.
[3] Ibid. 87 ff. [4] Suet. *Vita Ter.* 5.
[5] *Phil.* ii. 3, iii. 17, xiii. 23; *Att.* xvi. 11. 1 (where the *praenomen* is C.).

them from public life, so long as they had the backing of wealth or patronage, though for high office it was a handicap. But in society they still ran the risks of sneers and enmities, which indeed in slanderous Rome were common to men of all backgrounds. In short, the son of a freed slave was almost wholly integrated into society.

VIII
CONCLUSIONS

THE close link, almost identification, between *libertas* and *civitas* in the Roman mind[1] meant that freedmen were never to be deprived of the basic rights of citizenship, although these were in subtle ways limited. The constant recruitment of freedmen into the citizen body which was thus allowed might be considered advantageous because it gave soldiers to the state.[2] But it was also recognized as having a radical effect on the composition of the *populus Romanus* which might be regarded as the constant passing over from slavery of those who least deserved freedom and citizenship. Augustus tried to put a brake on rash manumission, for instance by limiting the number of slaves who could be freed by will, and reducing the right of young masters to manumit.[3] His regulation of informal manumission by the *Lex Junia* should also have acted as a check on the rash freeing of slaves, since though informally freed *liberti* had previously had some protection from the praetor, their status was now better defined.[4] A more direct measure against the freeing of criminal slaves was that which made them *dediticii*, without the rights of citizenship.[5] This was on the lines of action recommended by Dionysius,[6] that the state should inspect candidates for manumission (censors or consuls being the magistrates responsible) and that only the worthy should receive the citizenship, the rest being shipped off to some colony. But the law must have been hard to enforce, since it affected slaves punished by their masters, and

---

[1] Cic. *Caec.* 96: 'si semel civitas adimi potest, retineri libertas non potest. Qui enim potest iure Quiritium liber esse is qui in numero Quiritium non est?'; *Dom.* 77: 'sed cum hoc iuris a maioribus proditum sit, ut nemo civis Romanus aut libertatem aut civitatem possit amittere, nisi ipse auctor factus sit...' Cf. *Caec.* 99–100; *Red. in Sen.* 2; *Sest.* 1; *Balb.* 24; Livy, xlv. 15. 3 f.; A. Momigliano, *JRS* 31 (1941), 160 f.

[2] Dion. Hal. iv. 22; Dio, lvi. 7. 6. Also citizens in general: Plaut. *Pers.* 474 f. (a woman).

[3] Duff, *Freedmen*, pp. 30 ff. [4] Ibid., pp. 75 ff.
[5] Ibid., pp. 73 ff. [6] iv. 24.

such slaves were unlikely to be freed, or, if they were, would be freed by masters, who, like those complained of by Dionysius, would not be in the least likely to advertise their freedmen's immoral character. The law probably became a dead letter, but we do not know how soon.

The state was thus concerned about the effects on society of the indiscriminate admission of ex-slaves to citizenship, but did not do anything about it, except to encourage masters to pause for thought before manumitting. It is hardly true that it was the most unscrupulous and clever slaves who were freed, as Dionysius suggests, but success in getting freedom depended in part on such talents. A slave was by his position prevented from having much freedom of choice 'nec turpe est quod dominus iubet'.[1] The moral effects of slavery could be catastrophic.

Two points have been made about the effect of freedmen on the native population, that they diluted the ingenuous stock with racial characteristics which corrupted,[2] and that the moral training of slavery handicapped even the best of freedmen with a vulgarity of outlook which was one of the worst evils of the empire.[3] The first hypothesis is sweeping and inaccurate; the second valid up to a point. Since Tenney Frank wrote his article on race mixture in 1916,[4] the whole theory of racial purity has been discredited and it would hardly be suggested any longer that if freedmen originated in the eastern half of the empire they necessarily possessed determinable racial characteristics which would, by a sort of chemical formula, spoil the special virtues of the Roman people. The racial mixture would certainly dilute the Roman character; a sudden influx of immigrants may alter the society of a nation, but in the case of Rome, where the new citizens had served a period of probation in Roman households and where most of the slaves who won their freedom were of a Hellenistic culture very like that of their masters, there was no convulsion such as the Southern States were

---

[1] Petr. *Cena*, 75. Cf. Publilius, *Sent.* 525; Warde Fowler, *Social Life at Rome in the Age of Cicero* (London, 1908), pp. 227 f. *Liberti* might be similarly intimidated: *Dig.* xliv. 5. 1. 5.
[2] e.g. Duff, *Freedmen*, pp. 205 f.
[3] M. L. Gordon, *JRS* 21 (1931), 77.
[4] *AHR* 21 (1916), 689 ff.

to suffer, and little race hatred. Divisions were of classes rather than culture, race, or colour. On the whole, freedmen adopted a Roman way of life.

Miss Gordon's point that freedmen were morally handicapped by the experience of slavery and through no fault of their own is based on the evidence for materialistic values clearly shown in municipal life in the imperial period. We may here take the opportunity to examine some republican examples of the ambitions and values of freedmen. 'Libertinae opes', famous in imperial times, were a familiar phenomenon in the late Republic. The triumvirs in 31 B.C. imposed a special tax on freedmen, after a capital tax on those with more than 200,000 sesterces had led to riots by the freedmen.[1] They had also been affected in 43 B.C. by a tax on those with over 400,000 sesterces.[2] These are not large fortunes, though the latter figure puts its holders in the same class as the *equites*.[3] The freedmen of great families often had much greater capital, for instance, Pompeius Demetrius, who is said to have been worth 4,000 talents.[4] The freedmen of Caesar were many and wealthy.[5] A freedman might make a respectable fortune in trade, like Vergilius Eurysaces, or even a great one, like Trimalchio, but most of the outstandingly rich freedmen won their money either by exploiting the position won for them by their patron's status, as did Demetrius, Chrysogonus, or Julius Licinus,[6] or by inheriting from a childless patron, as perhaps did Caecilius Isidorus from the Caecilii Metelli,[7] M. Caelius Phileros from M. Caelius Rufus[8] and certainly Geganius Clesippus from his patroness.[9] It was in fact a recognized custom that in the event of childlessness a freedman inherited.[10]

---

[1] Dio, l. 10. 4; 20. 3; li. 3. 3.
[2] App. *BC* iv. 34. 146.
[3] See Brunt, 2me *Conférence internationale d'histoire économique* (1962), 117, n. 1.
[4] Plut. *Pomp.* 2. 4; 40.   [5] App. *BC* iii. 94.
[6] For his wealth and ostentation see Dio, liv. 21. 2 ff.; Juv. *Sat.* i. 109; Pers. ii. 36; Mart. viii. 3. 5 f.; *Anthol.* 77; Sen. *Epp.* cxix. 9, cxx. 19; Sidon. Ap. v. 7. 3.
[7] Pliny, *NH* xxxiii. 134 f.
[8] *CIL* x. 6104 = *ILS* 1945 = *EJ* 330.
[9] Pliny, *NH* xxxiv. 11 f.
[10] Hor. *Sat.* ii. 3. 122; 5. 71; Phaedr. 54. 11 f.

CONCLUSIONS

Freedmen's wealth, then, might put them on a par with rich *ingenui*—Isidorus' real estate was compared with land held by Crassus, which was worth 200 million sesterces. Wealth might open the door to social success: Phamea, probably, and Chrysogonus are cases in point. The charge usually made against wealthy freedmen was, however, their ostentation. Chrysogonus lived on the Palatine;[1] a certain Marcius Sotericus 'libertinus homo' had a villa at Tusculum which he sold to Crassus.[2] This may have been the same as the villa owned by a freedman next door to that of L. Lucullus, which is mentioned in another context by Cicero.[3] Licinus and Geganius had offensively extravagant tombs. Isidorus on his tomb gave vulgar details of his wealth. But the ostentation of others took the form of public works—Caelius Phileros, for example, built temples at Carthage and Formiae. Freedmen did not necessarily fritter away their wealth in banquets, like Eros,[4] or on the latest food-warmers, like Chrysogonus.[5] But such ostentation in any case, though more objectionable when shown by a parvenu freedman, was common to the aristocracy—the Optimate *piscinarii* showed the way to Vedius Pollio, the freedman's son. It cannot therefore be said that slavery was responsible for such vulgarity of outlook. Freedmen emulated the upper classes, and it was precisely this that the latter resented.[6]

Apart from such notorious freedmen as Chrysogonus or Licinus, *libertini* do not stand out from their contemporaries for false values. On the contrary, many brought the idealism of Greece to the ancient Roman pragmatism. If we read Horace's account of his father the freedman we feel that it is full of what we should be inclined to regard as typically Roman virtues: common sense, a strict moral code, dislike of sham and ostentation.[7] Freedmen were not necessarily out of tune with their Roman environment. Often they both absorbed much that was good in native life and contributed to Rome their own culture and values. The fertilizing

[1] p. 183.
[2] Cic. *Balb.* 56. Marcius' patron cannot be conjectured as a number of Marcii are known.
[3] *Legg.* ii. 30.   [4] Plut. *Apopth.* 207B.   [5] Cic. *Rosc. Am.* 133.
[6] Moreover, in the economic circumstances of the time, high-living and expensive public works were the chief outlets for wealth.
[7] We know nothing of Horatius' race or origin.

CONCLUSIONS 241

influence of Greek literature was mainly brought to Rome by freedmen. Other graftings on the Roman character are harder to pin-point, but it is probable that freedmen had considerable influence in the spread of foreign religious cults, and this, though it could be pernicious, brought a much-needed spiritual outlet to Rome. Jews, Greeks, and Asiatics might well contribute good influences to their patrons, contemporary society, and their own descendants.

The freedmen in fact counted men of all types among their number. Tiro, Horatius, Licinus, Menas, Eurysaces give a strangely mixed cross-section in character, life, and the effect they had on Romans. I doubt if it could be said that slavery had a corrupting influence on all of them. In the first two, there is no evidence that their characters had been harmed or vulgarized in the least, and it is arguable that Licinus and Menas (who were probably slaves only a short time) would have been no better if they had never passed through slavery. Any sort of social handicap may be reckoned likely to damage a man's morals, likeability, or chances of success, but it may also be surmounted or ignored. The ancients might hold, indeed, that slavery opened the door to great opportunities. It was not, for an educated Greek, 'a compulsory initiation into a higher culture', as it has been called, but for all freedmen of Romans it was the gateway to the coveted citizenship.[1] Slaves might well feel themselves to be 'viscera magnarum domuum dominique futuri'.[2]

What views did freedmen themselves have on slavery? It was not for the ancient world a subject which encouraged much discussion of the validity of the institution. So the freedmen authors whose works have come down to us do not attack slavery itself. They may attack abuses, but they do not counsel the slaves to rebel. Terence admits mention of brutal slave-punishments into his comedies apparently without a tremor.[3] His humanity shows itself only occasionally in pity for the hard life of slaves[4] and manumission is a less frequent motif in his plays[5] than in those of Plautus.

[1] Cf. Livy, xli. 9. 11; Petron. *Cena* 57.   [2] Juv. *Sat.* iii. 72.
[3] e.g. *Andr.* 200, 214, 600, 621, 786, 860 ff. The subject is rather less prominent in the other plays.
[4] *Phorm.* 43 f.   [5] *Ad.* 960 ff., 973 ff.

He accepts the commonly held views about the good slave and the dutiful freedman.[1] Publilius Syrus, though the gnomic *Sententiae* which are all we have left of his mimes present us only with a limited sample of his writings, had basically accepted the current view that a slave had to resign himself and that the system was necessary.[2] He appears to have put some stress, however, on the Stoic views about the real slave (the man who is a slave to his passions)[3] and he had a lofty view about the proper conduct of an *ingenuus*.[4] His one direct statement on freedmen echoes the best Roman sentiment, 'Probus libertus sine natura est filius'.[5] Phaedrus shows much of the same philosophic resignation and pessimism, in his case too a reflection of the literary genre as much as of his own views, though certainly his own experience of slavery and of exile must have helped to form his work, as he himself states.[6] Criticism of the 'potentes' is common,[7] but so is the preaching of resignation and patience to the 'humiles' in the hope of eventual reward or revenge.[8] The slave is told to bear cruel treatment, for if he offends, worse will follow: Aesop tells a runaway slave, after listening to the tale of his wrongs:

> 'audi; cum male nil feceris,
> haec experiris, ut refers, incommodo;
> quid si peccaris? quae te passurum putas?'
> Tali consilio est a fuga deterritus.[9]

Phaedrus calls on the slave to behave properly;[10] he laughs at those who show mock-keenness about their work in order to catch the master's eye and win freedom,[11] yet he attacks also the cruelty of masters[12] and talks of the sweetness of freedom.[13] Most notable is the freedman's claim that slavery does not devalue a man's character or worth and that he and Aesop may occupy a high place in literature, in words which recall Horace's proud modesty on the subject of his own birth:

[1] Ter. *Ad.* 479 ff., 886, 891 ff.; *Andr.* 37 ff. Cf. Plaut. *Pers.* 838 ff.
[2] *Sent.* 607: 'Qui invitus servit, fit miser, servit tamen.' 468: 'Ni gradus servetur nulli tutus est summus locus.'   [3] Ibid. 219, 256, 356.
[4] Ibid. 11. 111, 264, 271, 314.   [5] Ibid. 489.   [6] Phaedr. 43. 15 ff.
[7] Ibid. e.g. 3. 6 ff.; 6. 1; 16. 1 f.; 31; 39. 1.   [8] Ibid. 29.   [9] Ibid. 123.
[10] Ibid. 130.   [11] Ibid. 38.   [12] Ibid. 115, 120, 123.
[13] 51 etc., not necessarily freedom from slavery but political and personal freedom in general.

CONCLUSIONS

Aesopi ingenio statuam posuere Attici
servomque collocarunt aeterna in basi,
patere honoris scirent ut cuncti viam
nec generi tribui sed virtuti gloriam.
Quoniam occuparat, alter ne primus foret,
ne solus ille studui, quod superfuit;
nec haec invidia, verum est aemulatio.
Quodsi labori faverit Latium meo,
plures habebit quos opponat Graeciae;
si livor obtrectare curam voluerit,
non tamen eripiet laudis conscientiam.[1]

It is hardly surprising that freedmen seem to have accepted without question the inevitability of the institution of slavery. They cared, however, about the behaviour of individual masters and slaves and as philosophers they tended to hold that a man could triumph over slavery. Freedmen of rich patrons and well educated, such men as our authors may not have represented the feelings of the humbler slaves and freedmen, although the monuments of some of the artisans reflect a similar pride in achievement and the triumph over the handicap of slavery. In spite of the bitterness of Phaedrus against the oppressor and the consciousness, at times, that he was one of the 'humiles', no freedman author comes near championing either slaves or freedmen as a class.[2]

As freedmen did not react violently against slavery, so society did not react violently against freedmen. Contemporary Romans, though they inveighed against individual freedmen whose wealth or influence was too ostentatious, and though they attached great importance to the duty owed to a patron, do not seem to have followed a consistent policy of keeping freedmen in their place. The major legal handicap from which freedmen suffered in public law, that of being confined to the urban tribes, was of ancient origin, and sense in fact sanctioned limitation of political rights for such new citizens. Attempts to change the arrangement occurred at widely separated dates, for diverse motives. Distribution was attempted by the democrats of the first century in order to unchain the valuable city vote, but this, like Appius Claudius' parallel move,

[1] Phaedr. 42.
[2] See, for a different view, E. M. Schtajerman, *Die Krise der Sklavenhalterordnung im Westen des römischen Reiches* (Berlin, 1964), pp. 67 ff., 112 ff.

was designed to obtain *clientela* and was not an altruistic liberal measure. In the field of private law, there seems to have been no progressive tightening-up, if the Rutilian innovation has been rightly taken as liberal, for other praetorian rulings at the same period—on wills—diminished the privileges of freedmen.

The explosive rise to power of the moneyed classes outside the Senate in the late Republic was accompanied by the sporadic appearance of influential freedmen. They either had highly placed patrons or supporters, or wealth—or both. At the same time humbler freedmen acquired a better position than before because of the new importance of trade and industry, in which they played a far more important role than did freeborn Romans as subordinates and managers, and which again depended on the growth of the empire and the consequent influx of slaves. In this context, freedmen became commoner and more important to all classes of society, as artisans, as agents in business ventures, in private life, in the civil service. There was therefore, it seems, some breaking-down of the social barriers, though it is difficult to judge how much this depended on the numerical increase in gifted freedmen, for to a Terence there had been few barriers in the second century. In the first century more freedmen got to the top, that is, as near to the top as was permitted to those of their station. Finally, in the triumviral period the few 'top freedmen' were more important in public life than ever before, because of the overpowering position of a few dynasts who were their employers. This situation was continued in fact, but with more discretion, under Augustus.

We can discern an improvement in the position of freedmen as individuals (though not in the legal position of the *ordo libertinus*) consequent on the breakdown of the exclusive oligarchy, the vast influx of freedmen, and the political situation which intensified the need for *clientela* and for reliable agents. Finally alarm was caused, it seems, by two things. The power of the mob had been demonstrated by the Clodian gangs in the fifties. Julius Caesar put down the *collegia*, left in obscurity Clodius' bill to distribute freedmen among all the tribes, and shipped off many freedmen among his colonists. Secondly, during the triumviral period public opinion was shocked by the spectacle of freedmen in high command, albeit

CONCLUSIONS

as personal agents of the dynasts. The experiment was not overtly continued by Augustus once he had settled the empire. He also brought in measures to check the rate of manumission and to give an outlet to the ambitions and energies of freedmen in the civil service and the Augustan sevirate. The action of Caesar and Augustus comes as the culmination to the *laissez-faire* policy of the Republic, during which at various times *ad hoc* measures had been applied to check freedmen or to improve their position, and which had finally resulted in their numbers, ability, and potential dangerousness being demonstrated all too clearly. Augustus and Caesar took steps to provide freedmen with a solution to their discontents —Caesar providing work and the chance of a magistracy in his colonies, Augustus allowing freedmen the prestige of a priesthood and a niche in the administration. This was constructive policy. In the Republic too the potential of freedmen had been realized by the individual patron or employer as it affected his own success in trade or his own political aims. Cicero took the political ideas of the Optimate *libertini* into account and Clodius took up the cause of the poor city freedmen and in his organization of the *collegia* produced an idea which prefigured that of Augustus. But no consistent policy on freedmen could be followed under the republican system. Praetorian edicts might run counter to each other; tribunes and censors tried to distribute freedmen among all the tribes or confine them to the city tribes.

It was as individuals that freedmen won success and made their mark on society. As a class, they lacked cohesion of purpose, identity of origin or conditions of slavery and manumission. As individuals, suffering perhaps from resentment against slavery or their political disabilities as freedmen, spurred by ambition or helped by a patron, they were throughout the late Republic in the forefront of development in the arts and in industry, innovators in religious ideas and essential subordinates in the change from republicanism to Principate. Their talents and energy were among the forces which shaped the political and social revolution.

APPENDIX 1

Freedmen whose Origin is Attested

EGYPT

Bathyllus of Alexandria,[1] freedman of Maecenas.[2]
Timagenes of Alexandria, a prisoner of Gabinius in 55 B.C.[3] Patron not mentioned.

SYRIA

Pompeius Demetrius of Gadara.[4] Possibly a war-prisoner, he was freed by Pompey before 64 B.C.[5]
Publilius the mime-writer, 'natione Syrus'.[6]
Manilius, as Publilius' cousin,[7] presumably came from Syria too.
Staberius Eros, who was brought to Rome on the same ship as Publilius and Manilius,[7] will almost certainly have been Syrian too. Probably all three were Sullan captives, in 84 or 83 B.C.[8]
Terentius Tyranno, Phoenician, son of Artemidorus, freedman of Terentia,[9] allegedly the divorced wife of Cicero, but perhaps the wife of Maecenas.
Theodorus of Gadara, son of prisoners of the Mithridatic Wars.[10] He may have been *verna*.

ASIA

Cornelius Alexander Polyhistor, of Miletus, captured by Cornelius Lentulus in 82 B.C., and freed by him.[11]
Licinius Tyrannio of Amisus, captured by Lucullus, freed by Murena, 71 B.C.[12]

---

[1] Athen. 1. 20D.   [2] Schol. Pers. 5. 123.   [3] *Suda* s.v. Timagenes.
[4] Jos. *BJ* 155.   [5] Plut. *Pomp.* 40.
[6] Jerome *Chron.* on 43 B.C. Pliny, *NH* xxxv. 199 has the dubious reading 'Antiochius'.   [7] Pliny, *NH* xxxv. 199.
[8] The Syrian M. Pompilius Andronicus (Suet. *Gram.* 8) is not attested as a freedman, though he could have been one.
[9] *Suda* s.v. Tyrannio the Younger.
[10] *Suda* s.v. Theodorus; cf. Bowersock, *Augustus and the Greek World*, p. 35.
[11] *Suda* s.v. Alexander of Miletus. L. Cornelius Lentulus was proconsul, probably in Asia, in 82 B.C. See *MRR* ii, p. 68.
[12] *Suda* s.v. Tyrannio the Elder; Plut. *Lucull.* 19. 8. See *MRR* ii, p. 123 for the date.

FREEDMEN WHOSE ORIGIN IS ATTESTED 247

? L. Manneius Q. Menecrates, son of Demetrius, of Tralles, in the time of Pompey.[1] He was probably another war-prisoner.
? L. Lutatius Paccius, 'thurarius de familia rege Mitredatis'.[2]

CILICIA

Julius Pylades, freedman of Augustus.[3]

THRACE

Phaedrus, who states his origin in his poems, and also his slavery.[4] The manuscripts of his work call him freedman of Augustus.

GREECE

Publicius Menander, the interpreter and public freedman probably in the mid second century.[5]

Ateius Philologus or Praetextatus, born at Athens.[6] He was in Rome till at least 29 B.C.[7] and may have been a Sullan prisoner.

(Pompeius Lenaeus, freedman of Pompey, if a conjecture of editors is right, may have been kidnapped as a child from Athens.[8])

M. Vaccius M. l. Theophilus, Q. Vibius Q. l. Simius, and L. Aurelius L. l. Philo, of the collegium of *Cantores Graeci* in Rome,[9] were presumably Greek.

SARDINIA

Phamea and Tigellius were probably freedmen and Sardinian.[10]

AFRICA

P. Terentius Afer, born at Carthage and freed by Terentius Lucanus, after being presumably sold to Rome.[11]

SPAIN

Julius Hyginus, freedman of Augustus, a war-prisoner of Caesar's, probably from Spain.[12]

GAUL

Our sources often fail to distinguish between Cisalpina, Narbonensis, and Comata.

---

[1] *CIL* i. 1684 = Degr. 799, with the comment 'Omissum more Graeco f. potius quam l.' I think that a *peregrinus* is less likely than a freed doctor and would understand 'Q. l.'
[2] *CIL* i. 1334 = Degr. 817, 823.
[3] Suet. *frr.* (ed. Renan), p. 301. 25; Jerome on 22 B.C.
[4] 43. 30 ff.; 44. 17 ff.   [5] Cic. *Balb.* 28; *Dig.* xlix. 15. 5. 3.
[6] Suet. *Gram.* 10.   [7] Goetz in *RE* ii. 2. 1910.
[8] Suet. *Gram.* 15: 'Traditur autem puer adhuc *Athenis* subreptus . . .' See under SPAIN.
[9] *CIL* i. 2519 = Degr. 771.   [10] Appendix 5.
[11] Suet. *Vita Ter.* 1.
[12] Alternatively from Alexandria, Suet. *Gram.* 20.

APPENDIX 1

Caecilius Statius, either an Insubrian or from Mediolanum.[1]

Antonius Gnipho, an *ingenuus* exposed and freed by his *nutritor*.[2] (His slavery was thus illegal.[3])

? Valerius Cato, according to one tradition the freedman of a certain Bursenus from Gaul, according to himself a freeborn orphan illegally enslaved.[4]

Julius Licinus, a Caesarian captive from Comata, freedman of Caesar and client of Augustus.[5]

ITALY

Livius Andronicus of Tarentum, probably captured in 272 B.C., freed by Salinator.[6]

C. Cilnius Melissus, a freeborn child who was exposed, and freed by Maecenas. He came from Spoletium.[7]

L. Crassicius Pasicles or Pansa of Tarentum. Patron unknown. He may have been enslaved during the civil wars.[8]

? Pompeius Lenaeus. A scholiast states that 'Lenius' was from Suessa Aurunca,[9] but it is likely that he was confusing Lenaeus with the more celebrated satirist Lucilius.

VERNAE

Caecilius Epirota, freedman of Atticus, born at Tusculum.[10]

Theodorus of Gadara, if he was born after his mother was a slave.

Antonius Hipparchus, freedman of M. Antonius, was presumably home-bred since his father was also a freedman of Antony.[11]

Antonius Musa and his brother Euphorbus,[12] both probably in Antony's service until Musa went to Octavian and Euphorbus to Juba, are likely to have been *vernae* for the same reason as the above.

? Billienus the freedman, 'verna Demetri'.[13]

'Herennia T. l. Vern.'
? 'Plotia T. l. Ve-' } of Minturnae.[14]

---

[1] Jerome, *Chron.* on 179 B.C.   [2] Suet. *Gram.* 7.
[3] Watson, *Law of Persons*, p. 171.   [4] Suet. *Gram.* 11.
[5] Dio, liv. 21. 2 f.
[6] Jerome, *Chron.* on 188 B.C. Cic. *Brut.* 71.   [7] Suet. *Gram.* 21.
[8] Suet. *Gram.* 18. Cf. M. Aurius (Cic. *Cluent.* 21); the wife of Ceius (ibid. 162), a woman of Arretium (Cic. *Caec.* 97). Italian freedmen after the conquest of Italy and before the troubles of the first century were probably mainly *vernae*. Cf. App. *Mithr.* 85 f.
[9] On Juv. *Sat.* i. 20.
[10] Suet. *Gram.* 16. Atticus specialized in home-bred slaves (Nep. *Att.* 13. 4), but it will not follow that all his freedmen had been *vernae* since some must have been inherited from his father and uncle, who are not known to have shared his fad.
[11] Plut. *Ant.* 67. 7.   [12] Pliny, *NH* xxv. 77.   [13] Cic. *Fam.* viii. 15. 2
[14] Johnson, *Minturnae*, inscrr. 11. 6; 3. 1.

FREEDMEN WHOSE ORIGIN IS ATTESTED

This list of named freedmen may be supplemented by testimony to groups of freedmen and to unnamed individuals.

SYRIANS
A freedman of, perhaps, Ap. Claudius Pulcher.[1]

JEWS
A colony of Jewish freedmen in Trastevere.[2]

ITALIANS
Italian freedmen in Asia.[3]

---

[1] Plut. *Lucull.* 21.
[2] Philo, *Leg. ad Gaium*, 155; cf. Acts 6. 8.
[3] App. *Mithr.* 85 f.

APPENDIX 2

Nomenclature of Freedmen

THE following notes are not meant to be an exhaustive treatment,[1] but merely to clarify references in the text.

The classic formal manner of naming a freedman, corresponding to 'M. Tullius M. f. Cicero' for an *ingenuus*, was of the pattern 'M. Tullius M. l. Tiro'—'Marcus Tullius Marci libertus Tiro'.[2] If the manumitter was a woman, 'Ↄ.' or 'Gaiae' was used in place of the patron's *praenomen*.[3] The freedman took a gentile name which was the same as that of his patron or of one of his patrons, or, in the case of a public authority, was derived from 'publicum' or from a proper name, as for instance Publicius or Veronius.[4] It was in early times usual for him to take a *praenomen* different from that of his patron,[5] later he normally assumed the same one. When *libertini* regularly used a *cognomen*, it mattered less if all those in one household were Marci Tullii.[6] Choice of a *praenomen* other than that of the patron might not be arbitrary, as we know from the example of M. Pomponius T. l. Dionysius, the freedman of Atticus named in compliment to Cicero.[7] If the manumitter was a woman, the freedman would probably take the *praenomen* of her father or *tutor* who authorized the manumission. Where there were more than one patron the freedman might take his name from one or neither.[8]

The *cognomen* adopted was normally the freedman's old slave name.[9] It is not always given either in inscriptions or in literary texts. (Ingenuous Romans of the lower classes often had no *cognomen* at this date, but as slaves had to have some name, freedmen possessed a *cognomen*, and the omission of it is rare.[10]) When the *cognomen* was omitted, some

---

[1] For which see Duff, *Freedmen*, pp. 52 ff.
[2] e.g. Degr. 943: D. Octavius D. l. Modiarius.   [3] e.g. Degr. 724, 809.
[4] See L. Halkin, *Ant. Class* 4 (1935), pp. 125 f.   [5] e.g. Degr. 90, 97, 98.
[6] For variations of Degr. 816: the freedmen of C., P., and P. Trebonii were P. Trebonius —l. Nicostratus, M. Trebonius C. P. l. Malchio, D. Trebonius C. l. Olophantus, M. Trebonius C. P. l. Macedo, A. Trebonius C. P. l. Alexander.
[7] Cic. *Att.* iv. 15. 1.
[8] Degr. 922: 'L. Annius L., L., C. l. Niceporus'; Degr. 70: 'T. Terentius L., C. l.
[9] Degr. 913: 'M. Pinarius P. l. Marpor'; 946: 'Truttedia . . . P. Truttedi Amphionis lib., nomine servile Appia . . .'
[10] According to Degrassi, probably not later than 71 B.C. (vol. ii, p. 500, citing nos. 96, 154, 157, 170, 289, 714).

NOMENCLATURE OF FREEDMEN

other identifying word was often used, referring to profession or tribe.[1] A freedman sometimes changed his slave name to something more respectable, for instance L. Ateius Praetextatus 'Philologus ab semet nominatus' and L. Crassicius Pasicles, who changed his name to Pansa.[2] Sometimes, like *ingenui*,[3] a freedman used two surnames, as did Saevius Nicanor Postumius.[4]

Libertine nomenclature, like that of *ingenui* and slaves, was subject to constant changes and variations. Inversion of *nomen* and *cognomen* is common in the inscriptions,[5] sometimes, no doubt, for stylistic reasons, as 'Tiro Tullius' in Gellius.[6] The patron's name might be omitted[7] or emphasized by using his *gentilicium* instead of his *praenomen*.[8] Precision was sometimes sought in the case of *patronae* by giving the family name instead of 'Gaiae'.[9] Aristocratic patrons tended to be identified with most care,[10] doubtless for reasons of prestige: in the same way a freedman of the *princeps* later was 'Aug. l.' and his freedman in turn stressed that he was 'Augusti liberti l.'[11] Tribe was very rarely mentioned in inscriptions to freedmen. It has been thought that they were not allowed to claim tribe on their monuments; Taylor[12] supposes rather that they were not proud of belonging to the urban tribes and this seems more probable. The one sure republican example is of a freedman in the Palatine tribe,[13] which was one of the more respectable city tribes. A freedman's town of origin is rarely given, and the same applies to the naming of his father.[14]

---

[1] e.g. Degr. 714: 'M. Ocratius M. l. pist(or)'; 210: 'M. Livius M. l. Pal(atina)'; Cic. *Fam.* v. 20. 1: 'M. Tullius scriba meus'.
[2] Suet. *Gram.* 10; 18.
[3] Cf. Degr. vol. ii, p. 498.
[4] Suet. *Gram.* 5.
[5] e.g. Degr. 696: 'Clesippus Geganius'; also 878, 971, etc.
[6] vi. 3. 8.
[7] e.g. Degr. 259.
[8] e.g. Degr. 365, 767, 797.
[9] e.g. Degr. 97: 'T. Corneli Ɔor l.'
[10] e.g. Degr. 427: 'Cn. Pompeius Cn. Magni l.': probably, that is, of Sex. Pompeius.
[11] *CIL* vi. 7462.
[12] *Voting Districts*, p. 147.
[13] Degr. 210.
[14] Degr. 799.

APPENDIX 3

The Freedmen of M. Cicero

CONSIDERING that Cicero was a humane master who took a personal interest in his slaves,[1] and probably a generous manumitter,[2] we may be surprised to find that his correspondence and other sources yield a mere half-dozen certain *liberti*, Tiro, Laurea, the *scriba* M. Tullius (these two being traditionally identified), Chrysippus, Aegypta, Hilarus, Eros, and probably Phaetho. A much more impressive list is given by Drumann and Groebe, who discover twenty-five slaves and freedmen,[3] a list which Carcopino,[4] in the interests of proving Cicero's extravagance and love of luxury, has adroitly expanded to twenty-six, by the simple expedient of counting Clodius Philhetaerus twice over. However, on examination the list proves to suffer either from omissions or from unjustifiable additions: if Terentia's slave Orpheus[5] is to be included, why not her freedman Philotimus? There are also inaccuracies. We have no evidence on the status of Philargyrus,[6] who is mentioned once in passing; Pelops of Byzantium,[7] who failed to get an honorary decree passed for Cicero, was surely an ingenuous provincial; Pescennius and Sallustius[8] were presumably freeborn friends. Sallustius may in fact have been pro-quaestor in Syria in 50 B.C.[9] The list reduces itself rapidly and Cicero's household is found to have included at various times (for we need not assume that the personnel was static, as Carcopino appears to do) the following slaves and freedmen:

[1] Cf. e.g. his grief at the death of the young reader Sositheus ('me . . . plus quam servi mors debere videbatur commoverat'. *Att.* i. 12. 4) and the devotion shown by his slaves in the last crisis (Plut. *Cic.* 47. 9); also Cic. *Off.* i. 41.

[2] The runaway slave Dionysius in 46 B.C. had no difficulty in convincing various friends of Cicero in Illyricum that he had recently been manumitted.

[3] W. Drumann and P. Groebe, *Geschichte Roms* vi: *M. Tullius Cicero* (Leipzig, 1929), pp. 353 ff. They list Acastus, Aegypta, Alexio, Anteros, Aristocritus, Chrysippus, Clodius Philhetaerus, Demea, Dexippus, Dionysius, another Dionysius, Hermia, Hilarus, Laurea (or M. Tullius the scribe), Mario, Menander, Metrodorus, Orpheus, Pelops, Pescennius, Philargyrus, Pollex, Sallustius, Sosithes, Spintharus.

[4] *Secrets*, i, p. 128, Eng. tr., p. 77. He was misled probably by Drumann and Groebe vi, p. 356.

[5] Cic. *Fam.* xiv. 4. 4.   [6] *Att.* i. 15. 5.

[7] *Att.* xiv. 8. 1.

[8] *Fam.* xiv. 4. 6. They are taken by Park, *Plebs*, p. 62, n. 1, to have been freedmen of some other patron, but temporarily in Cicero's service.

[9] See Münzer, *RE* i. A. 2. 1912 f.

THE FREEDMEN OF M. CICERO

SLAVES

[1]Sositheus, *anagnostes*; died in 61 B.C.
[2]Dionysius, *anagnostes*; ran away in 46 B.C., still missing in 44.
[3]Pollex, *a pedibus*.
[4]Acastus, who carried a letter in 50 B.C.

SLAVES OR FREEDMEN

[5]Spintharus, secretary.

Tabellarii

[6]Aristocritus, who took letters between Cicero and Terentia in 58 B.C.
[7]Dexippus, who also went between Cicero and Terentia in 58 B.C.
[8]Hermia, who went to Q. Cicero in Asia in 59 B.C. and from Tiro to Cicero in 54 or 53 B.C.
[9]Mario, who went between Tiro and Cicero in 50 B.C.
[10]Menander, who went between Tiro and Cicero in 54 or 53 B.C.

FREEDMEN

Tiro, secretary.
M. Tullius, *scriba*.
Laurea, later a poet, possibly a secretary.
Chrysippus, literary assistant, etc.
Eros, probably a literary assistant.
Hilarus, *ratiocinator*
Aegypta, *tabellarius*.
? Phaetho, mainly *tabellarius*.

Unnamed

An *operarius*, who absconded with Chrysippus.[11]
A freedman employed in buying statues in about 62 B.C.[12]

OTHER FREEDMEN, NOT HIS OWN, WHO WERE IN CICERO'S OCCASIONAL OR PERMANENT EMPLOY

[13]Terentius Philotimus, freedman of Terentia, the steward employed by Cicero at least from 59 to 47 B.C.
[14]Eros, slave or freedman of Atticus, *ratiocinator* for Cicero 45–44 B.C.

---

[1] *Att.* i. 12. 4.
[2] *Fam.* xiii. 77. 3; v. 9. 2, 10 A. 1, 11. 3.
[3] *Att.* viii. 5. 1.
[4] *Att.* vi. 9. 1.
[5] *Att.* xiii. 25. 3.
[6] *Fam.* xiv. 3. 1, 4.
[7] Ibid. 3.
[8] *QF* i. 2. 12; *Fam.* xvi. 15. 2.
[9] *Fam.* xvi. 1. 1, 3, 2, 5. 1.
[10] *Fam.* xvi. 13. 'Andricus' in *Fam.* xvi. 14. 1 is surely Menander. Others on Drumann and Groebe's list as letter-carriers, Demea (*Att.* xiii. 30. 1) and Anteros (*Att.* ix. 14. 2), seem more likely to have belonged to Atticus.
[11] *Att.* vii. 2. 8.
[12] *Fam.* vii. 23. 3.
[13] pp. 143, 145, 153, 173.
[14] p. 150.

APPENDIX 3

[1] M. Pomponius Dionysius, *libertus* of Atticus and *protégé* of Cicero, tutor to young Marcus and Quintus in 51–50 and supposed to teach them at other times.

[2] Licinius Tyrannio, *libertus* of Murena, helped with the libraries of Cicero in 56 B.C. and Q. Cicero in 54, and in 56 taught young Q. Cicero.

[3] Cyrus, a freeborn alien or freedman, employed by Cicero from 60 to 55 B.C.

[4] Vettius Chrysippus, *libertus* of Cyrus, regularly employed by Cicero both during and after the lifetime of his patron.

[5] Metrodorus, a doctor who attended Tiro at Tusculum, probably in 45 B.C. If he was the same as the doctor who looked after Tiro there in the year of his manumission (?54 or 53 B.C.)[6] he was paid a fee and so cannot have been Cicero's own freedman. A Metrodorus is heard of travelling in 44 B.C. from Sinuessa to Rome and was made use of to carry a letter from Cicero to Atticus.[7] If this was the same man (the name is common) it suggests a position of some dependence on Cicero. He could have been *libertinus* or *peregrinus*.

[8] Alexio, another doctor, who died in May 44 B.C. He was Cicero's personal doctor and friend. Cicero knew that he was heir in the first degree, which would be consistent with his having been Alexio's patron, but as he did not know who the *secundi heredes* were it is probably more likely that Alexio was not his own *libertus*. He again could have been a *libertinus* or a free immigrant.

[9] Ummius, who received orders from Cicero to pay Tiro's doctor in 54 or 53 B.C. and so may have been the steward at the *Formianum*, cannot in any case have been Cicero's own freedman. As stewards were normally slaves or freedmen, he could have been the freedman of another patron. But it is probably better to reckon that he was not Cicero's *dispensator*.

[10] Clodius Philhetaerus was to some extent under Cicero's orders in 58 B.C. His name might suggest the freedman, but as we have no evidence for the kind of job he might have been doing for Cicero, it

---

[1] pp. 119 ff., 222.
[2] *Att.* iv. 4A. 1; *QF* iii. 4. 5, 5. 6, 6; *QF* ii. 4. 2.
[3] *Att.* ii. 3. 2; *QF* ii. 2. 2; *Att.* iv. 10. 2. If a freedman, he had no patron alive in 52 B.C., for he was able to name Cicero and Clodius as his heirs (Cic. *Mil.* 46 ff.).
[4] In 59 (*Att.* ii. 4. 7) and in 54 and 44 B.C. (*Att.* xiii. 29. 2; xiv. 9. 1).
[5] *Fam.* xvi. 20.   [6] *Fam.* xvi. 14. 1.
[7] *Att.* xv. 1A. 2.
[8] *Att.* xv. 1. 1; xv. 2. 4. He is on Drumann and Groebe's list.
[9] *Fam.* xvi. 14. 1.
[10] *Fam.* xiv. 4. 6: 'Clodium Philhetaerum, quod valetudine oculorum impediebatur, hominem fidelem remisi.'

is unjustifiable to call him a freedman in Cicero's employ,[1] still less a freedman of Cicero's own.[2]

The above list of employees, some or any of whom may have been *libertini*, is important as indicating the services for which Cicero had to go outside his own staff.[3] He used freelance architects and, probably, doctors. In his various literary activities and in the education of his son and nephew he could not, obviously, draw all his helpers from his own *familia*, so he seized eagerly on the services of Dionysius, Tyrannio, and others. The staff as we know it was not large. The above lists give us probably seven of his own freedmen (plus two whose names are not mentioned), four slaves, and six of uncertain status. All, except Pollex and the freed *operarius*, belong to the administrative staff or to the letter-carriers (though no doubt those whom we meet only as letter-carriers could have had other jobs too). Clearly we are only seeing the top of the iceberg, those servants who were doing important work or those naturally mentioned in correspondence. It is apparent from Cicero's one passing reference to the *operarius* that this class of slaves—even though he freed them—interested him little. Relatively large numbers of domestic staff in the *familia urbana* and the skeleton staff of the villas, and outside workers, both slave and freed, are unknown. But from the known list some guess may be made about the rate of manumission in Cicero's household. Of the slaves, young Sositheus would have been an early candidate for manumission; Dionysius too was easily believed when he claimed to have been freed. The *tabellarii* perhaps show a suspiciously rapid turn-over: Aegypta was probably a slave in 54 or 53 B.C., but he is named as a freedman in 45; Aristocritus and Dexippus are mentioned only in 58 B.C., Menander only in 54 or 53, Mario only in 50. This perhaps indicates that they had left Cicero's employ, more probably for freedom than for another master. (It could mean that they were being used in other ways, but this seems unlikely to be true in so many cases.) We should not in any case expect Cicero to have had as many as seven *tabellarii* employed simultaneously. One would, without this evidence, have been inclined to think that few of Cicero's deserving, and none of his really valued, slaves remained for long without their liberty, unless his public utterances[4] were not honoured by private practice. His readiness to free his entire household in 58, rather than let it fall into the hands of his enemies, was rather a surrender to *force*

---

[1] Park, *Plebs*, p. 62, n. 1.
[2] Drumann and Groebe, vi, p. 354, with inexplicable inattention to the *nomen*.
[3] Cicero naturally employed many other professional men and craftsmen, but not permanently or repeatedly. Other architects who worked for him were Diphilus in 54 B.C. (*QF* iii. 1. 1 f., 9. 7) and Cluatius in 45 B.C. (*Att.* xii. 18. 1, 36. 2). The slave engineer Cillo was called in once in 54 B.C. (*QF* iii. 1. 3).
[4] *Rab. Perd.* 15; *Phil.* viii. 32.

majeure than a philanthropic decision, for most of the slaves were to remain so if he succeeded in keeping his property.[1] On the whole, it seems likely, however, that the proportion of freedmen to slaves in all the more confidential or important posts was high. Unfortunately the most obvious test-case for this view, that of Tiro, cannot be applied with certainty, since the age at which he was freed is disputable.

We may now examine briefly the histories of individual freedmen of Cicero, in order to see what light they cast on Cicero's attitude to manumission, his treatment of his freedmen, and their careers. Leaving Tiro, for the present, on one side, I treat the others in order of their appearance.

1. HILARUS

He is known of definitely only in 61 B.C., when he was a freedman and out of Cicero's employ. Cicero wrote to Atticus, then on the point of departure for Epirus:

> Libertum ego habeo, sane nequam hominem, Hilarum dico, ratiocinatorem et clientem tuum. De eo mihi Valerius interpres nuntiat Thyillusque se audisse scribit haec: esse hominem cum Antonio: Antonio porro in cogendis pecuniis dictitare partem mihi quaeri et a me custodem communis quaestus libertum esse missum. Non sum mediocriter commotus, neque tamen credidi sed certe aliquid sermonis fuit. Totum investiga, cognosce, perspice, et nebulonem illum, si quo pacto potes, ex istis locis amove.[2]

Cicero at this time was embarrassed politically by the claim of his ex-colleague Antonius that he should oppose his recall from Macedonia. Antonius had apparently been going to lend Cicero money in consideration of Cicero's allowing the province to go to him, but Antonius did not carry out his part of the bargain.[3] The authority for Valerius' statement was Cn. Plancius, military tribune to Antonius, so the report about Hilarus was no idle rumour. Cicero repudiates the truth of Antonius' suggestion that the two ex-consuls had agreed to exploit the province for their mutual advantage. He bore Antonius a grudge after,[4] mainly, as far as we can tell, because of the Hilarus affair. It is to be assumed that Cicero was genuinely not responsible for Hilarus' actions, *pace* Carcopino, who holds that Cicero was implicated and that he would not admit it even to Atticus.[5] Possibly the freedman had some private affairs in Macedonia—this or his financial ability might account for his being a client of Atticus—and Antony had picked him as a useful liaison with his ex-colleague, or with more sinister intentions of incriminating Cicero.

---

[1] *Fam.* xiv. 4. 4: 'praeterquam oppido pauci. Sed haec minora sunt.'
[2] *Att.* i. 12. 2.   [3] *Att.* i. 12. 1.   [4] *Fam.* v. 3. 2 f.
[5] *Secrets*, pp. 214 ff., Eng. tr. pp. 131 f.

Münzer conjectured that the same man reappears as a *librarius* who is twice found carrying letters in the early summer of 45 B.C.,[1] but the name is a common one,[2] our Hilarus was strictly an accountant, we do not even know if this man was in the employ of Cicero or Atticus and surely Cicero should not have been reconciled so easily with his wicked freedman.[3]

2. PHAETHO

He is thought by Drumann and Groebe[4] to have been a freedman of Q. Cicero, but more likely belonged to Marcus. Cicero sent him in the spring of 58 B.C. to intercept his brother on his way home from Asia, but Phaetho was unsuccessful.[5] He was later sent to Quintus in Rome with a letter.[6]

3. CHRYSIPPUS

In 54 B.C., when he first appears, Chrysippus had had the difficult job of improving Q. Cicero's library.[7] He was in fact a literary freedman of M. Cicero, as we learn from references to him in 50, from which it appears that he had been the companion of young Marcus in the East.[8] As the boy was with his father for most of the homeward voyage, Chrysippus' desertion of his post here mentioned is probably to be put during young Marcus' and Quintus' visit to Deiotarus.[9] The reaction of Cicero is, however, more interesting than the circumstances:

> Illud tamen de Chrysippo—nam de altero illo minus sum admiratus, operario homine; sed tamen ne illo quidem quicquam improbius. Chrysippum vero quem ego propter litterularum nescio quid libenter vidi, in honore habui discedere a puero insciente me! Mitto alia quae audio multa, mitto furta; fugam non fero qua mihi nihil visum est sceleratius. Itaque usurpavi vetus illud Drusi, ut ferunt, praetoris in eo qui eadem liber non iuraret, me istos liberos non addixisse, praesertim cum adesset nemo a quo recte vindicarentur. Id tu, ut videbitur, ita accipies; ego tibi adsentiar.[10]

The legal crux concerns us elsewhere; the interesting points here are that Chrysippus and the *operarius* had apparently been manumitted before Cicero as presiding magistrate, *vindicta*, since he should have said 'Addico', which means that the manumission is to be dated to 66,

---

[1] *Att.* xii. 37. 1; xiii. 19. 1; *RE* viii. 2. 1604 f.
[2] Cf. *ILS* iii, pp. 202 f.
[3] A subjective argument and one which Carcopino would reject: he uses the reappearance of a Hilarus in the correspondence to show that when the scandal had died down Cicero no longer needed to repudiate his agent.
[4] vi, p. 662.   [5] *Att.* iii. 8. 2.
[6] *QF* i. 4. 4. The letter was probably *QF* i. 3.
[7] *QF* iii. 4. 5, 5/6. 6.   [8] *Att.* vii. 2. 8, 5. 2.
[9] The letters to Atticus do not necessarily imply that he had only just defected.
[10] *Att.* vii. 2. 8.

63, or, most likely, to Cicero's proconsulate in 51–50 B.C., and secondly that looking after young Marcus was apparently part of Chrysippus' *operae*. Cicero attacks his freedman in two ways: (*a*) Chrysippus had not repeated the oath taken before manumission to perform *operae*. This suggests that the manumission is to be dated to 51–50, but even so Cicero should have done something about it at the time of manumission and not waited till Chrysippus, after apparently performing for a time what his patron intended to be *operae*, went away and abandoned his charge. Possibly, however, the similarity with the case judged by Drusus was not exact, and Cicero may mean failure to perform *operae* which had been promised, rather than failure to repeat the promise. Watson[1] holds that the similarity is slighter still, nothing more than the denial of the manumission on technical grounds and that the flaw in the case of Chrysippus was (*b*) because the master was not represented (because Cicero was taking the magistrate's part). We do not know what success Cicero had—if he could not lay hands on Chrysippus, he could not even use his legal arguments, neither of which seems to have been strong.[2]

4. AEGYPTA

A kindly man and a friend of Tiro, Aegypta was sent to bear him company during his illness at Tusculum in, probably, 54 or 53 B.C.[3] He is elsewhere mentioned as a bearer of letters and a bringer of news.[4]

5. M. TULLIUS

Referred to only by *nomen* and *praenomen*, and as 'scriba meus' or 'servus meus'[5] (that is, freedman), Tullius first appears in 51 B.C., when he delivered a letter from Atticus.[6] As he was *scriba* to Cicero in Cilicia in 51–50, he had presumably been manumitted some considerable time before in order to be by this date a member of the *ordo scribarum*—something of a distinction for a freedman.[7] Cicero, who in his previous provincial office, twenty years earlier, had had *scribae quaestorii* who were probably *ingenui* and anyway not his own *liberti*,[8] took care to secure his own freedman for his own province. Such things could be managed.[9] Cicero relied completely on Tullius, his quaestor Mescinius Rufus, and the latter's cousin Mindius for an accurate presentation of accounts, or so he assured the unhappy Rufus in 49.[10] After Cicero's return to Italy, he was technically still proconsul, and could not even get rid of his

---

[1] *Law of Persons*, p. 191 f.
[2] The Chrysippus of *Att.* xi. 2. 3 is almost certainly Vettius Chrysippus.
[3] *Fam.* xvi. 15.
[4] *Att.* viii. 15. 1 (49 B.C.); xii. 37. 1; xiii. 3. 2 (45 B.C.).
[5] *Fam.* v. 20. 1, 2. [6] *Att.* v. 4. 1.
[7] Cf. *ILS* iii, pp. 433 f. and p. 154.
[8] ii. *Verr.* iii. 182: they were called L. Mamilius and L. Sergius.
[9] ii. *Verr.* iii. 187. [10] *Fam.* v. 20. 2.

lictors.[1] Therefore Tullius as one of his *comites* naturally remained attached to him. At the time of the letter to Rufus, Tullius was absent in the country,[2] but during the following month, February, he was used as a confidential letter-carrier between Cicero and Pompey; Cicero stresses his reliability by calling him his 'necessarius'.[3] Tullius, though he probably returned to the pool of scribes and to his career, continued to make himself useful to Cicero. In 45 we hear that he had certain funds belonging to Cicero in his care, which Cicero told Atticus were not earmarked 'nomine voti', but which he thought of using for the shrine to Tullia.[4] Tullius' position of trust and the way in which Cicero speaks of him are interesting. 'Servus meus' expresses the moral, though not the legal position of duty in which the *libertus* found himself; 'necessarius' is a rather vague word, covering relations, friends, clients, and dependants. Tullius definitely came into the last two categories and this fits the letter to Pompey: probably the main notion was dependence, not friendship, in this context.

6. LAUREA

This freedman of Cicero is mentioned only by Pliny.[5] He is often identified, without proof, with M. Tullius the scribe. After his patron's death, Laurea celebrated in verse the appearance of medicinal springs at the villa once owned by Cicero near Puteoli, the *Academia*, 'ut protinus noscatur', says Pliny enthusiastically, 'etiam ministeriorum haustus ex illa maiestate ingeni'. The tribute is, for a date soon after the proscriptions, a sufficiently bold one to Cicero's literary glory:

> ... Nimirum locus ipse sui Ciceronis honori
> Hoc dedit, hac fontes cum patefecit ope,
> Ut, quoniam totum legitur sine fine per orbem,
> Sint plures oculis quae medeantur aquae.

7. EROS

He is mentioned only by Plutarch,[6] as having been manumitted because of his good advice to put off a forensic speech till the following day, to avoid spoiling its eloquence since time was running short.

8. TIRO

We have very detailed information on the activities of Cicero's most trusted and versatile freedman. His career was a long one, since he lived till the age of a hundred, or so we are assured. Jerome[7] under 4 B.C. has the entry 'M. Tullius Tiro... in Puteolano praedio usque ad

---

[1] *Fam.* v. 20. 4.   [2] *Fam.* v. 20. 9.
[3] *Att.* viii. 11B. 4. Cf. *Att.* viii. 1. 2: 'hominem certum misi ex comitibus meis.'
[4] *Att.* xiii. 22. 4.   [5] *NH* xxxi. 6–8.   [6] *Apopth. Cic.* 21.
[7] *Apud* Euseb. *Chron.* Olympiad 194.

centesimum annum consenescit.' Groebe[1] has therefore put Tiro's birth in 103 B.C., assuming that Jerome implies that Tiro died in 4 B.C. From other evidence, items which, though in themselves inconclusive, seem to add up to Tiro's having been born considerably later, I think that Jerome will either have to be disbelieved or interpreted as meaning something other than that Tiro died in 4 B.C. 'Consenescit' could mean retirement rather than death in that year.[2] For, if he had been born in 103, he would have been a mere three years junior to Cicero,[3] and the whole tone of their relationship seems to have been against this. Tiro is described by Aulus Gellius as *alumnus*[4] of Cicero; Cicero himself in 50 B.C. called him *adulescens*,[5] which would be very odd, even despite Roman inexactness about age,[6] if Tiro had been at that time fifty-three. Moreover, if the manumission is rightly dated to 54 or 53 B.C., this peerless slave would, if the date of his birth is put in 103, have reached the ripe age of fifty before winning his freedom, which is most implausible.[7]

If we reject, therefore, the dating of his birth to 103, we can assume that Tiro won his freedom early in life. He does not appear in Cicero's correspondence till 54 B.C., when he had the responsible job of sending political reports to Q. Cicero.[8] *Ex silentio*, we might reasonably think that Tiro had only recently reached an age when he was equipped for such a duty; on the other hand, the affection in which he was held by the Tullii and by Atticus in the late fifties B.C. suggest that he was a long-standing member of the *familia*. Groebe in fact conjectured that he was a *verna* and Gellius' description of a thorough education and the application of the word *alumnus* to him in relation to Cicero suggest that his

---

[1] *RE* viii A. 2. 1319.
[2] 'He (retires to and) grows old in his farm at Puteoli.' I am reluctant to discard the entry entirely, as at least the mention of the *praedium* is circumstantial and plausible.
[3] Born 106 (Cic. *Brut.* 161; Gell. xv. 28. 3).
[4] xiii. 9, cf. vi. 3. 8.   [5] *Att.* vi. 7. 2; vii. 2. 3.
[6] According to Varro, 'adulescens' could be used for a man up to the age of thirty (*L.L.* ii. 14. 2). Cicero in fact used it of men up to quaestorian age (*Rep.* i. 18; *Fam.* ii. 15. 4) though this is not to be pressed, while Valerius Maximus (vii. 5. 2) has it of a candidate for the aedileship. Apart from giving a rough indication of age, the word can be evaluative, expressing admiration of a youthful prodigy, as often of Octavian, or disapproval of one already far gone in sin. Perhaps its use to describe freedmen might be connected with the patronizing manner in which slaves of any age were called 'pueri' (it is applied to Chrysogonus, Cic. *Rosc. Am.* 6) but it seems more likely, in default of a large number of examples, that this pejorative use and Cicero's affectionate use of it for Tiro do not depend on libertine status and that the word set a certain age limit. Groebe in fact thought that 'adulescens' here could be explained entirely as an affectionate usage, and suggested that Atticus checked Cicero for exaggeration in *Att.* vi. 7. 2, but the text 'adulescentem, ut nosti (et adde, si quid vis), probum' (*Att.* vii. 2. 3) conveys to me, at least, the opposite impression.
[7] Contrast Cic. *Phil.* viii. 32.   [8] *QF* iii. 1. 10.

master had trained him specially.[1] Tiro's manumission is convincingly dated to 54, though 53 would also be possible.[2] The dating depends on finding a year between the manumission of Statius in 59[3] and the death of Pompey, in which Pompey could have been at Cumae and Q. Cicero separated from Marcus in mid April. Only 54 or 53 qualifies. The manumission was a great event in the family, preceded by Cicero's anxiety over Tiro's health (he was lying ill at Tusculum while Cicero waited at Cumae)[4] and followed by a congratulatory letter from Quintus.[5] The actual manumission presumably took place at the villa at Formiae, where Tiro was told to meet Cicero.[6] It may have been informal. If Pompey accompanied Cicero from Cumae to Formiae, there is, however, a strong likelihood that the ceremony was the full *vindicta* manumission, with Pompey, in his capacity as proconsul, presiding. But the reference to Pompey does not suggest that he was staying long.[7] If the manumission was informal, we must assume that it was repeated formally (perhaps in Rome soon after) for Tiro bore the *tria nomina*, M. Tullius Tiro.

Tiro continued to render what sound like almost full-time services to Cicero: 'Innumerabilia tua sunt in me officia domestica, forensia, urbana, provincialia, in re privata, in publica, in studiis, in litteris nostris'.[8] His work for Cicero was broken only by his periods of illhealth, just before his manumission; on the way home from Cilicia, from June 50 to May 49; again in 45. Primarily a secretary, he took dictation of letters,[9] except the most confidential,[10] and normally of literary works, using a shorthand system of his own;[11] he superintended copyists (who might be unable to read Cicero's writing).[12] He kept copies of letters, at least the more important and in 44 B.C. had about seventy designed for publication.[13] He also kept up his own correspondence, partly on Cicero's behalf, but also as a personal matter, with Q. Cicero,

---

[1] *RE* vii A. 2. 1319; Gell. vi. 3. 8: 'ab ineunte aetate liberaliter instituto'; xiii. 9.
[2] Tyrrell and Purser, *Correspondence of Cicero*, vi. 923, on *Fam.* xvi. 13.
[3] Mentioned in *Fam.* xvi. 16.
[4] *Fam.* xvi. 15: 'Incredibili sum sollicitudine de tua valetudine, qua si me liberaris, ego te omni cura liberabo.'
[5] Ibid. 16: 'Mihi gratissimum fecisti cum eum indignum illa fortuna ac nobis amicum quam servum esse maluisti', etc.
[6] Ibid. 10.
[7] Ibid. 10. 2: 'Pompeius erat apud me, cum haec scribebam, hilare et libenter. Ei cupienti audire nostra dixi sine te omnia mea muta esse.' The reading 'Pomponius' has been suggested, but Atticus became Caecilius in September 58, and wherever Cicero was in April 58 he certainly was not relaxing at Cumae and Formiae. Earlier years are improbable.
[8] Ibid. 4. 3.   [9] *QF* iii. 1. 19.   [10] *Att.* xiii. 9. 1.
[11] *Att.* xiii. 25. 3; cf. Plut. *Cato Min.* 23. 3.
[12] *Fam.* xvi. 22. 1.
[13] *Att.* xiii. 6. 3 (45 B.C.); xvi. 5. 5; *Fam.* xvi. 17. 1.

with Atticus, and with young Marcus, whose undergraduate letter in 44 was a model of conciliation.[1] But he was far more than a mere secretary. He helped Cicero in his literary works, not only in practical ways by proof-reading,[2] but also inspiring his Muse,[3] and no doubt checking details of fact, as did Dionysius.[4] Cicero confided in him on political topics and his own intentions.[5]

Tiro was also employed by Cicero in his financial affairs, after the loss of Philotimus, in collaboration with Atticus and Eros.[6] Any commission from cataloguing a library[7] to arranging the lease of market-gardens at Tusculum,[8] from entertaining friends of his patron[9] or preparing for a dinner-party[10] to finding a Greek *librarius* to send to young Marcus in Athens,[11] all was grist to Tiro's mill. But he still found time to invent a system of shorthand[12] or to write verse in the Sophoclean style;[13] he had his own business interests;[14] he was not above going to Rome from Tusculum to see the games,[15] and in 44 B.C. he bought himself a farm, probably that near Puteoli mentioned by Jerome, which would have been near the *Academia*.[16]

Tiro's long-term services to posterity, with which he must have been busy in the long period of his life which fell after the loss of his patron, were a collection of the letters of Cicero, begun perhaps in 45 B.C.;[17] the edition of at least some of his public works, including the *Verrines* and the *De Gloria*;[18] a collection, according to a dubious tradition, of Cicero's *Ioci* in three volumes,[19] and a 'Life' of Cicero, a work of some length and

[1] Q. Cicero: *QF* iii. 7. 10 (on political events in 54 B.C.); *Fam.* xvi. 27 (44 B.C.). *Fam.* xvi. 3–6 are joint letters to Tiro from all the Tullii Cicerones, *Fam.* xvi. 8 from Q. Cicero alone. Atticus: *Att.* v. 20. 9 (51 B.C.); vi. 7. 2 (50 B.C.). Young M. Cicero: *Fam.* xvi. 21.

[2] Cf. *Fam.* xvi. 22. Gell. i. 7, xv. 6. 2, may refer to texts published after Cicero's death.

[3] *Att.* xii. 34. 1; *Fam.* xvi. 10. 2.

[4] *Att.* vi. 2. 3; vii. 3. 10.

[5] *Fam.* xvi. 11. The tone is familiar, even if references to Caesar as 'amicus noster' and to Antony and Pompey in similar words do not mean that Tiro could regard them in the same light in relation to himself. *Fam.* xvi. 23 is in a similar vein ('Atticus noster') and includes the interesting statement, 'Ego tamen Antoni inveteratam sine ulla offensione amicitiam retinere sane volo scribamque ad eum, sed non ante quam te videro' (2).

[6] *Att.* xii. 19. 4, 51. 3; xv. 15. 3, 17. 2, 18. 1, 20. 4; *Fam.* xvi. 24. 1 f.
[7] *Fam.* xvi. 20.   [8] Ibid. 18. 2.   [9] Ibid. 22. 2.
[10] Ibid. 22. 1.   [11] Ibid. 21. 8.   [12] *Att.* xiii. 25. 3.
[13] *Fam.* xvi. 18. 3.
[14] Ibid. 23. 2—unless the contract was Cicero's own.
[15] Ibid. 20.   [16] Ibid. 21. 7.
[17] *Att.* xvi. 5. 5; *Fam.* xvi. 17. 1; Nep. *Att.* 16. 3. I do not accept the principal thesis of Carcopino, *Secrets*, that the publication of Cicero's correspondence was meant to discredit Cicero and that Tiro was an accessory to the scheme.
[18] Quint. x. 7. 31; Gell. i. 7; xv. 16. 2.
[19] Macrob. *Sat.* ii. 1. 12; Quint. vi. 3. 5.

Important Notice to All Customers

Bellwether Books has made every effort to inspect each book prior to shipment to ensure there are no markings and/or inscriptions of an offensive nature in the book you have purchased. However, the majorities of our titles are publisher returns, and while appearing in 'like new' condition, they may have some markings that we did not catch.

If you do find offensive markings in this book, please return the book and upon receipt back to us, we will ship another copy, if available, to you at no additional charge, or credit your account back the full amount (purchase price plus shipping & handling) should this copy be unavailable.

Thanks for purchasing from Bellwether Books, and we hope you enjoy your book!

For any questions or concerns, kindly email us at info@bellwetherbookstore.com

81369414

Order Number:
Title: Roman Freedmen During the Late Republic (Malone Society

SKU: oxHC15JULw-063a-0198142803
Special: Amazon/108-9776027-4792245
Recipient: Robert McHugh
10125 S. Eleanor Av

Palos HillsIL, US 60465

Shipping Method: Expedited
Buyer: Robert J. Mchugh, ydn55wdm0t5115d@marketplace.
Quantity: 1

Location: [ox-063a]

complexity, since Book iv referred to Pompey's defence of Milo in 56 B.C.[1] This last was a source used and respected by Tacitus and Plutarch.[2] In his own right Tiro was a noted grammarian and literary critic, whose *Pandects*, other works on Latin style and syntax and miscellaneous questions, and letters on literary subjects are frequently quoted in the *Noctes Atticae*.[3]

The career of Tiro perhaps provides one of the better excuses for the institution of slavery and manumission. He was trained and encouraged to use his talents to the full; he was treated with affection and trust by his patron and his family, with friendliness by his patron's friends.[4] His libertine status was accepted easily enough to be joked about.[5] There is a world of difference between the easy exchange of teasing between Tiro and Cicero of his brother, and the patronizing criticism of Aulus Gellius,[6] who evidently felt that even Tiro's superior education did not justify a freedman in pulling to pieces a speech by the Elder Cato.

9. TERENTIUS PHILOTIMUS

Since, as the freedman of Terentia,[7] Philotimus was part of Cicero's household and even at times regarded by Cicero as a freedman of his own,[8] he is relevant to this discussion of Cicero's freedmen. Between 59 and 49 B.C. and occasionally in 48/7, he served Cicero in a variety of ways, primarily as *dispensator* and manager of the town-house. Thus he kept Cicero's accounts and paid out money;[9] saw to the maintenance[10] and in 49 B.C. the defence[11] of Cicero's houses or the purchase of new property.[12] During the absence of Cicero from Rome he would treat the *tribules* to free circus-seats on Cicero's behalf[13] and arrange for the forwarding of letters.[14] He also frequently carried letters to and from Cicero, presumably when consultation between the two was needed or when the letters were important.[15] He also took upon himself the duty of sending Cicero reports on politics when his patron was absent from the city,[16] but Cicero consistently criticized his judgement, reliability, and

[1] Asc. *Mil.*, B. 48.
[2] Tac. *Dial.* 172; Plut. *Cic.* 41. 3, 49. 2. Gellius' account (iv. 10. 6) of Caesar's procedure in the Senate in 59 B.C. is probably drawn from this work.
[3] xiii. 9; vi. 3. 8 (a letter to Cicero's friend Q. Axius); x. 1. 7.
[4] Lepta (*Fam.* xvi. 4. 4), Mescinius (*Fam.* xvi. 4. 3), Varro (*Fam.* xvi. 12. 6), Curius (*Fam.* vii. 29; xvi. 4. 2).
[5] *Fam.* xvi. 18. 1.   [6] vi. 3. 8 ff.   [7] *Att.* vi. 4. 3.
[8] *Att.* x. 7. 2. It is hardly credible that an otherwise unknown freedman of Cicero called Philotimus is meant.
[9] *Att.* v. 4. 3; v. 19. 2 (51 B.C.); vi. 1. 19 (50 B.C.); viii. 7. 3 (49 B.C.).
[10] *Att.* ii. 4. 7; *QF* iii. 7. 7.   [11] *Fam.* xiv. 18. 2.
[12] A *deversorium*, *Att.* x. 5. 3.
[13] *QF* iii. 1. 1. (54 B.C.).   [14] *Fam.* iii. 9. 1; iv. 2. 1.
[15] e.g. *Att.* ix. 5. 1; v. 3. 1. Cicero said that a letter from Sulpicius should have been carried by Philotimus in person (*Fam.* iv. 2. 1).
[16] *Att.* vii. 23. 1, 24; viii. 16. 1; ix. 7. 6; x. 9. 1 (49 B.C.); xii. 44. 4 (45 B.C.).

partisanship: 'cuius hominis, quam insulsi et quam saepe pro Pompeio mentientis!'[1]

But Philotimus had his own business affairs, probably in the Chersonese in 50 B.C., and *negotia* in Asia in 47 which were expected to involve him in an important lawsuit at Ephesus.[2] These affairs were thought by Cicero to interfere with the proper performance of his duty to his patron. When the friends of Milo banded together to buy his property in 52 B.C., Philotimus was one of the purchasers, presumably with Cicero's encouragement at the least, but mishandled the affair badly enough to endanger Cicero's relationship with his exiled client.[3] In fact Cicero soon came to suspect Philotimus of sharp practice,[4] and Atticus found that some of Cicero's money had been misappropriated.[5] The precise nature of the trouble is by no means clear, but Cicero accused Philotimus of theft and apparently suspected that Terentia was involved.[6] He decided to put his financial affairs in the hands of Atticus,[7] but in fact in 50 and 49 B.C. Philotimus seems to have continued in his old duties,[8] although perhaps under Atticus' supervision. Meanwhile the rift between Cicero and Terentia grew wider and the position of Philotimus more awkward.[9] In early 48 Philotimus played truant[10] and probably ceased to be Cicero's steward then or soon after, but in 47 he carried out the important commission of bringing Caesar's letter from the East.[11] He remained as antipathetic as ever to Cicero, but in spite of the divorce in 46 continued to write to him, at least on public affairs.[12]

We may say that Cicero had a 'servant problem': one of his slaves ran away; two of his freedmen absconded; a freedman might prove untrustworthy as did Philotimus perhaps (though possibly through loyalty to his real *patrona*), or his independence might damage his patron's interests, as happened with Hilarus. No doubt in some of these cases the freedman was not as black as he was painted by Cicero: one feels that Cicero was too apt to take offence where none was intended or to suspect an injury. On the other hand, he was lucky in such freedmen, in or out of his own service, as M. Tullius the scribe and Tiro, and his constant appreciation of the latter is the best illustration of the *humanitas*[13] which could exist between patron and freedman.

---

[1] *Att.* x. 9. 1.   [2] *Att.* vi. 1. 19; xi. 24. 4.
[3] *Att.* v. 8. 2 f.; *Fam.* viii. 3. 2.   [4] *Att.* vi. 4. 3; 5. 1.
[5] *Att.* vii. 3. 1.   [6] *Att.* vi. 4. 3.   [7] *Att.* vii. 1. 9.   [8] *Att.* x. 7. 2, 15. 1.
[9] In 47 Cicero writes 'Auditum ex Philotimo est eam scelerate quaedam facere' (*Att.* xi. 16. 5), probably alluding to the ungenerous provision for the children in his wife's will.
[10] *Att.* xi. 1. 1: 'De quibus (sc. domesticis rebus) acerbissime adflictor quod qui eas dispensavit neque adest istic neque ubi terrarum sit scio.'
[11] *Att.* xi. 23. 2, 19. 2, 24. 4; *Fam.* xiv. 24. 23.   [12] *Att.* xii. 44. 4.
[13] On the meaning of the term see Gell. xiii. 17 and Schulz, *Principles*, pp. 189 ff., especially pp. 215 f.

APPENDIX 4

The Application of the word servus to a Freedman

IN early times 'servus' was used to describe any freedman, as is stated in the comment on the *Lex Cincia*, 'servis liberti continentur': the word 'slaves' covers freedmen too.[1] A freedwoman on an inscription also terms herself 'ancilla'.[2]

In the late Republic this usage survived probably only when the patron wished to stress the dependence of his freedman upon himself and the usual use of 'servi' for freedmen was pejorative. An example of the former is Cicero's description of M. Tullius as his slave when he particularly wanted to assure a correspondent of his trustworthiness.[3]

As a pejorative, the contemptuous 'servus' was common. Cicero says that when radical politicians called a *contio* and ordered all the shops to be closed so that their supporters would attend, the opposition spokesmen would attack all those at the meeting as exiles, slaves, and madmen.[4] Not all these shopkeepers and their customers would have been freedmen, but the passage shows that Cicero's own mud-slinging should be recognized as such. Examples are 'servi nequissimi' of Chrysogonus[5] (where Cicero compares the freedman's *dominatio* with that of the *equites*) and the bitter reference to Clodius' distribution bill as an attempt to turn the slaves of Cicero and his friends into Clodius' own freedmen,[6] where 'slave' stands for freedman and 'freedman' for client. Many references to the Clodians as slaves,[7] although freeborn Romans may be included, probably allude especially to the freedmen. The factual basis

[1] *Fr. Vat.* 307. See Mommsen, *StR.* iii, p. 428; *Gesammelte Schriften* (Berlin, 1907), iii, pp. 21 f.
[2] *CIL* i. 2273 = Degr. 981: 'Plotia L. et Fufiae l. Prune haec vocitatast ancilla . . .'
[3] *Fam.* v. 20. 2.
[4] *Acad. Pr.* ii. 144: 'Quid me igitur, Luculle, in invidiam et tamquam in contionem vocas, et quidem, ut seditiosi tribuni solent, occludi tabernas iubes? Quo enim spectat illud cum artificia tolli quereris a nobis nisi ut opifices concitentur? Qui si undique omnes convenerint facile contra vos incitabuntur! Expromam primum illa invidiosa, quod eos omnes qui in contione stabunt exsules servos insanos esse dicatis . . .' Cf. Scaurus *apud* Cic. *de Or* ii. 257; Diod. xxxvii. 13.
[5] *Rosc. Am.* 140. Cf. Pliny, *Epp.* viii. 6, on Pallas, where he is throughout called a slave.
[6] *Mil.* 89: 'servos nostros libertos suos effecisset.' Cf. ibid. 87 and Asc. *Mil.* 52C.
[7] Cic. *Dom.* 89, 92; *Sest.* 47; *Pis.* 11.

APPENDIX 4

of the taunt was no doubt that many shopkeepers were freedmen. Similarly, a henchman of Verres called slave and 'vix liberum' may have been a freedman.[1] Verres himself is said to have thought that freedmen were not in fact free.[2] Outside Cicero, the rhetorical taunt probably recurs in Velleius' remark that Sextus Pompey was 'libertorum suorum libertus servorumque servus',[3] for the second part of the phrase probably does not expand the information given by the first half: freedmen are meant again.

[1] Apronius (Cic. ii. *Verr.* iii. 91, 134), Turpio is also mentioned.
[2] ii. *Verr.* i. 127. But the phrase is used of *ingenui*. Cf. D. R. Shackleton Bailey, *Cicero's Letters to Atticus* i (Cambridge, 1965), pp. 331 f.
[3] Vell. ii. 73. 1.

APPENDIX 5

Lutatius Paccius

LUTATIUS PACCIUS is attested by three inscriptions. Of these the first[1] runs: 'Ego sum L. Lutatius Paccius thurarius de familia rege [sic] Mitredatis [sic].' The Mithridates in question is almost certainly Mithridates VI of Pontus.[2] Mommsen argued that Paccius was a prisoner of the Mithridatic Wars and an ex-member of the king's household. We may thus assume that he was a freedman. He mentions his antecedents in Mithridates' service because a training on the staff of a monarch so notoriously interested in drugs and poisons would have been of professional value to him as a perfumer. He may have been a slave before his capture by the Romans, as the word 'familia' suggests.[3]

The *nomen* would naturally suggest that Paccius' patron was Q. Lutatius Catulus (which would mean that Paccius had been captured in the Sullan campaigns). But Paccius had the *praenomen* L., although this does not prove that his patron had the same. However, another inscription[4] attests (L. L)utatius L. l. Pamphilus, L. Lutatius L. l. Seleucus, L. Lutatius L. l. Paccius. The *cognomen* is unusual[5] and it was not the normal practice to give a slave one's own *cognomen*, so it is more likely that this is our Paccius than that it is one of his own freedmen. Thus, his patron seems to have been Lucius like himself, probably a poor relation of Catulus.[6]

Paccius commemorated himself and several freedmen on a third inscription,[7] like the first found on the *Via Appia* and from his own tomb. On the left it reads 'C. Quinctilius C. l. Pamphilus unguentari(us) sibi et patrono et libertis suis posterisque eorum et Faustae l. nostrae', and

[1] *CIL* i. 1334a = Degr. 817.
[2] Not the Bosporan king who came to Rome in the reign of Claudius (Tac. *Ann.* xii. 21). See Mommsen and Degrassi ad locc.
[3] Hatzfeld (*Trafiquants*, pp. 135 f.), held that 'ex familia' meant 'by appointment', presumably to Mithridates after the Peace of Dardanus or, later, to his son Philopator. He thinks that the *cognomen* Paccius is more consonant with Italian origin. The theory is unconvincing. Hatzfeld further conjectured that Paccius worked in Campania, where the rose-essence was famous, but there is no evidence to show that he did.
[4] *CIL* vi. 21728.
[5] It is common as a *nomen*. Cf. Degr. ii, p. 418.
[6] *RE* lists no L. Lutatius at this date.
[7] *CIL* i. 1334b = Degr. 823.

on the right, 'L. Lutatius[1] Paccius thurar(ius) sibi et Seleuco, Pamphilo, Tryphoni, Philotae liberteis posterisque eorum.' As the two patrons seem to have had Fausta as a common freedwoman, they were probably business-partners and not just friends. Seleucus and Pamphilus reappear on the second inscription and it is a fair assumption that the links with their patron were close and that they were also perfumers.

[1] The omission of patron after 'Lutatius' may be accounted for by (a) the fact that he was not buried in the tomb like the patron of Quinctilius Pamphilus, (b) the mention of Paccius' trade, which is to identify him. The patron may well have been dead and Paccius was able to avoid making his libertinity explicit.

APPENDIX 6

Tigellius and Phamea

THE known facts about Tigellius relevant to his origin and status are these:

Cicero's in 45 B.C. wrote to M. Fadius Gallus, who was worried about Cicero's being on bad terms with Tigellius, that, although he was friendly with most Caesarians, he would not be servile to this one: 'ego non omnibus, mi Galle, servio'. He goes on: 'Id ego in lucris pono, non ferre hominem pestilentiorem patria sua; eumque addictum iam tum puto esse Calvi Licini Hipponacteo praeconio.[1] The auctioneer's advertisement which had knocked Tigellius down, the epigram of Calvus, has been partly preserved and runs 'Sardi Tigelli putidum caput venit'.[2] Referring to this, after explaining the cause of Tigellius' dislike, which was that Cicero had been unable to defend his uncle or grandfather Phamea in 52 or 51 B.C., Cicero says 'Habes "Sardos venales alium alio nequiorem."'

All these jokes, both of Calvus and Cicero, become much more pointed if Tigellius had been a slave. That he was Sardinian is certain, or two jokes are meaningless.

I agree with Ullman's arguments[3] that the Sardinian Tigellius of Cicero and Calvus is to be identified with Horace's singer Tigellius, also a friend of Caesar's.[4] I would also agree that Horace's Tigellius Hermogenes[5] was the same man,[6] though this makes little difference to the present argument. If both these identifications are accepted, we have the further information that Tigellius was a singer and had a Greek *cognomen*. Both profession and name suggest freed status, for a *peregrinus* from Sardinia is unlikely.

Ullman argues that Phamea (whose 'nepos'[7] Tigellius was, probably nephew rather than grandson) was a freedman. 'Judging from his foreign name and the probability that he was a rich parvenu,[8] it is altogether likely that Phamea was a freedman.'[9] He then argues from the status of Phamea to that of Tigellius. But the nephew of a freedman might well

---

[1] *Fam.* vii. 24. 1 f.   [2] Porph. on Hor. *Sat.* i. 3. 4.
[3] *CP* 10 (1915), 270 ff.
[4] *Sat.* i. 2. 1 ff.; 3. 1 ff. Cicero also calls him a *tibicen* (*Fam.* vii. 24. 2).
[5] *Sat.* i. 3. 129 f.; 9. 25; 10. 16 ff., 80 ff.
[6] Contra, Fraenkel, *Horace*, p. 86, n. 2.
[7] Cic. *Fam.* vii. 24. 2.
[8] Cic *Att.* ix. 9. 4; *Fam.* ix. 16. 8.   [9] *CP* 10 (1915), 271.

have been ingenuous. If, however, the arguments for Tigellius' having been a slave are accepted, then we can more cogently argue from the probable status of the nephew to the probable status of the uncle. The very vagueness of Cicero's taunts[1] may be another index to the social standing which the freedman had acquired.

[1] No *cognomen* is mentioned. In spite of his protests, Cicero was genuinely worried about the feud (*Att.* xiii. 49. 1; 51. 2) and the omission of a *cognomen* which smacks of low origin might be *honoris causa*.

APPENDIX 7

Sarmentus

A *scurra* Sarmentus appears prominently in Horace's satire on the journey to Brundisium and is mentioned by later authorities. Horace begins his description of the battle between Sarmentus and Messius Cicirrus in the Homeric manner by giving their ancestry:

> Messi clarum genus Osci,
> Sarmenti domina exstat; ab his maioribus orti...[1]

During the discussion, Cicirrus again mocks Sarmentus with his ambiguous social position:

> multa Cicirrus ad haec: donasset iamne catenam
> ex voto Laribus, quaerebat; scriba quod esset,
> nilo deterius dominae ius esse. rogabat
> denique cur umquam fugisset, cui satis una
> farris libra foret, gracili sic tamque pusillo.[2]

Porphyrio comments on line 51 that Sarmentus and Cicirrus were 'ambo et urbanitate et audacia noti, equites tamen Romani.' He explains the taunts of Cicirrus by Sarmentus' having been a slave and being a freedman. The Scholiast on Juvenal v. 3 had more information, that Sarmentus was 'natione Tuscus e domo M. Favoni, incertum libertus an servus'. He then grew so bold because of the high favour in which he stood because of his wit and looks, that he usurped equestrian privileges and caused public indignation by sitting in the Fourteen Rows. Called to account, he based his defence entirely on the argument that he had been freed by Maecenas: 'concessam sibi libertatem a Maecenate, ad quem sectio bonorum Favoni pertinuerat.' He was acquitted.

On the authority of Horace, it can be taken that Sarmentus had certainly been a slave: he had no 'maiores'. But, as Sarmentus was a favourite with Maecenas and Octavian,[3] the joke is not to be too bitter. Cicirrus' allusion to Sarmentus' having run away should not be taken seriously: other freedmen were called *fugitivi*,[4] which was a vivid variant on the common pejorative *servi*.[5] The point of Cicirrus' rough

---

[1] *Sat.* i. 5. 54 f.   [2] Ibid. 65 ff.
[3] Schol. Juv. v. 3 f.; Plut. *Ant.* 59. 8. Scandal had it that he had a homosexual relationship with Octavian, but this may well have been Antonian propaganda.
[4] Timarchides (Cic. ii. *Verr.* ii. 136).   [5] Appendix 4.

joking is merely that, in spite of Sarmentus' position as *scriba quaestorius*, the most honourable class of civil servant, the stigma of slavery cannot be wiped out. Horace does not decide one way or the other, who it was who had freed Sarmentus. Most likely the circumstantial report of the trial given by the scholiast is right in saying that Maecenas was responsible. Doubt existed as to whether Favonius had freed him, for the scholiast admits it, and a mistake could easily occur, since Maecenas was certainly *patronus* in the sense that Sarmentus was his client,[1] but if the statement of Sarmentus at the trial has been rightly reported, then he had been slave successively to Favonius and Maecenas, and freed by the latter. This patronage no doubt helped him to his post as *scriba*. It is possible that he was also granted the *anulus aureus* by Octavian, if he usurped equestrian privileges—and Porphyrio's statement that he was an *eques Romanus* is thus most simply explained.

If we press the remark of the scholiast that he was a Tuscan, it is possible that Sarmentus was freeborn and had been wrongfully enslaved. Maecenas may have established his client's right. The joking of Horace would then be even less wounding to the subject. Such a history would be quite possible in the period of the civil wars, but it is difficult to believe that it will fit the necessary time-scheme.[2] If the story of Sarmentus' reply in court is reliable, this explanation will not do. The easiest theory is therefore that if Tuscan he was a *verna*.

[1] A common difficulty. Cf. the confusion about the freedmen clients of Sex. Pompeius, *liberti* of Magnus, whom many authorities call freedmen of the son (p. 188).

[2] A Tuscan would most naturally be enslaved during the Sullan wars, but Sarmentus was obviously too young for this to have happened to him. He could have been abandoned in infancy, as allegedly was Maecenas' Spoletine freedman, Melissus (Suet. *Gram.* 21).

APPENDIX 8

The Position of Freedmen in the Italian Communities which had not obtained the Roman Franchise

IT seems likely that Roman custom was the same as that of other Italic races in regard to manumission. Freedmen in other Italian communities had the citizenship and bore the *tria nomina*. Thus in our inscriptional evidence it is only rarely possible to distinguish, on the basis of an Etruscan or Oscan *cognomen*, the freedman of an ally from one of an Etruscan or Oscan Roman citizen.

The freedman of an unenfranchised Italian followed his patron's name and citizenship. This may be clearly seen from the Capuan inscriptions before the enfranchisement of Italy, since there were few resident Roman citizens. Similarly, in the Roman colony of Minturnae, there is no distinction in regard to citizenship of Minturnae between the freedmen of Roman residents and Oscans, for both appear together on the *magistri* lists.[1] The likelihood that there was no distinction between Rome and other Italian cities (from early times) is indicated also by the tradition of manumission of foreign slaves ordered by Rome as a reward for services. Thus in the second Punic War Capuan slaves were given freedom and presumably Capuan citizenship.[2]

Libertini were probably *de facto* if not *de iure* excluded from office in Italian as in Roman law. They had, however, important functions on religious boards, and as a social class they had a considerable influence because of their wealth. These points are treated in the text.

[1] Cf. *CIL* i. 1804 = Degr. 605 (Vestini).
[2] Livy, xxvii. 3. 5.

BIBLIOGRAPHY

This list includes only books and articles which have been cited in the notes. Certain standard works, including collections of inscriptions, are to be found in the List of Abbreviations.

ALBERTARIO, E. *Studi di diritto romano*, i (Milan, 1933), *Persone e famiglia*.

ALLBUTT, T. C., *Greek medicine in Rome* (London, 1921).

ARANGIO-RUIZ, A. V., *Istituzioni di diritto romano* (9th edition, Naples, 1947).

ARNOLD, W. T., *The Roman system of provincial administration to the accession of Constantine the Great* (Oxford, 1914, 3rd edition, revised by E. S. Bouchier).

ASTIN, A. E., '*Dicta Scipionis* of 131 B.C.', *CQ* N.S. 10 (1960), 135 ff.

BADIAN, E., 'Caepio and Norbanus', *Hist.* 6 (1957), 318 ff.

—— *Foreign Clientelae 264–70 B.C.* (Oxford, 1958).

—— 'The early career of A. Gabinius (*cos.* 58 B.C.)', *Philol.* 103 (1959), 87 ff.

—— Review of Taylor, L. R., *The voting districts of the Roman Republic*, *JRS* 52 (1962), 200 ff.

BALSDON, J. P. V. D., *Roman women. Their history and habits* (Oxford, 1962).

—— 'The *Commentariolum Petitionis*', *CQ* N.S. 13 (1963), 242 ff.

BANG, M., 'Die Herkunft der römischen Sklaven', *Röm. Mitt.* 25 (1910), 223 ff.; 27 (1912), 189 ff.

BARROW, R. H., *Slavery in the Roman Empire* (London, 1928).

BEARE, W. *The Roman stage. A short history of Latin drama in the time of the Republic* (London, 1950).

BELOCH, J., *Historische Beiträge zur Bevölkerungslehre*, i (Leipzig, 1886), *Die Bevölkerung der griechisch-römischen Welt*.

BELOW, K. H., *Der Arzt im römischen recht* (Münchener Beiträge zur Papyrusforschung und antiken Rechtsgeschichte 37) (Munich, 1953).

BERCHEM, D. VAN, *Les Distributions de blé et d'argent à la plèbe romaine sous l'empire* (Geneva, 1939).

BERGER, A., *Encyclopedic dictionary of Roman law* (Transactions of the American Philosophical Society N.S. 43, part 2) (Philadelphia, 1953).

BISCARDI, A., *Manumissio per mensam e affrancazioni pretorie* (Florence, 1939).

BÖMER, F., *Untersuchungen über die Religion der Sklaven in Griechenland und Rom*. i (Akademie der Wissenschaften und der Literatur im Mainz, Abhandlungen der geistes- und sozial-wissenschaftlichen Klasse, Jahrgang 1957, nr. 7), 1958.

BIBLIOGRAPHY

BOTSFORD, G. W., *The Roman assemblies* (New York, 1909).
BOWERSOCK, G. W., *Augustus and the Greek world* (Oxford, 1965).
BROGAN, O., *Roman Gaul* (London, 1953).
BRUNT, P. A., Review of Westermann, W. L. *The slave systems of Greek and Roman antiquity*, *JRS* 48 (1958), 164 ff.
—— 'The army and the land in the Roman revolution', *JRS* 52 (1962), 69 ff.
—— 'Italian aims at the time of the Social war', *JRS* 55 (1965), 90 ff.
—— '*Amicitia* in the Late Roman Republic', *Proc. Camb. Phil. Soc.* N.S. 2 (1965), 1 ff.
—— 'The Roman mob', *Past and Present*, 35 (1966), 3 ff.
BUCKLAND, W. W., *The Roman law of slavery: the condition of the slave in private law from Augustus to Justinian* (Cambridge, 1908).
—— *A textbook of Roman law from Augustus to Justinian* (Cambridge, 1921).
CALDERINI, A., *Aquileia Romana* (Milan, 1930).
CARCOPINO, J., *Vie quotidienne à Rome à l'apogée de l'empire* (Paris, 1939); English edition, *Daily Life in Ancient Rome*, ed. Rowell, H. T., tr. Lorimer, E. O. (London, 1941).
—— *Les Secrets de la correspondance de Cicéron* (Paris, 1947); English edition, *Cicero: The secrets of his correspondence*, tr. Lorimer, E. O. (London, 1951).
CHARLESTON, R. J., *Roman pottery* (London, 1955).
CHASE, G. H., *Catalogue of Arretine pottery* (Boston, 1916).
CICHORIUS, C., *Rom und Mytilene* (Leipzig, 1888).
—— *Römischen Studien* (Leipzig, 1922).
CLARKE, M. L., *Rhetoric at Rome. A historical survey* (London, 1953).
COHN, MAX, *Zum römischen Vereinsrecht* (Berlin, 1875).
CORBETT, P. E., *The Roman law of marriage* (Oxford, 1930).
COSENTINI, C., *Studi sui liberti, contributo allo studio della condizione giuridica dei liberti cittadini*, i and ii (Catania, 1948, 1950).
CRAMER, F. H., *Astrology in Roman law and politics* (Philadelphia, 1954).
CROOK, J. A., *Law and life of Rome* (London, 1967).
CUMONT, F., *Les Religions orientales dans le paganisme romain* (4th edition, Paris, 1929).
DAUBE, D., 'Two early patterns of manumission', *JRS* 36 (1946), 57 ff.
—— 'Generalizations in D. 18 1. *de contrahenda emptione*', *Studi Arangio-Ruiz*, i (Naples, 1953), 185 ff.
DOER, B., *Die römische Namengebung* (Stuttgart, 1937).
DRUMANN, W., and GROEBE, P., *Geschichte Roms in seinem Übergange von der republikanischen zur monarchischen Verfassung*, vi (Leipzig, 1929).

DUFF, A. M., *Freedmen in the early Roman Empire* (Oxford, 1928; reprinted Cambridge, 1958).

FORBES, C. A., 'The education and training of slaves in antiquity', *TAPA* 86 (1955), 321 ff.

FOWLER, W. WARDE, *Social life at Rome in the age of Cicero* (London, 1908).

FRACCARO, P., 'La riforma dell'ordinamento centuriato', *Studi P. Bonfante* (i, Milan, 1930), 103 ff.

—— *Opuscula*, ii (Pavia, 1957): 'Tribules ed Aerarii', pp. 149 ff.; 'Scauriana', pp. 125 ff.

FRAENKEL, E., *Horace* (Oxford, 1957).

FRANK, TENNEY, 'Race mixture in the Roman Empire', *AHR* 21 (1917), 689 ff.

—— 'The sacred treasure and the rate of manumission', *AJP* 53 (1932), 360 ff.

—— 'On Suetonius' Life of Terence', *AJP* 54 (1933), 268 ff.

FREDERIKSEN, M. 'Republican Capua: a social and economic study', *PBSR* N.S. 14 (1959), 80 ff.

FRIEDLÄNDER, L., *Darstellungen aus der Sittengeschichte Roms* (Leipzig, 1923); English tr., *Roman life and manners*, tr. Gough, A. B. (London and New York, 1913).

FROVA, A., *L'arte di Roma e del mondo romano* (*Storia universale dell'arte*, ii) (Turin, 1961).

GABBA, E., 'Ricerche sull'esercito professionale romano da Mario ad Augusto', *Athen.* N.S. 29 (1951), 171 ff.

—— 'Politica e cultura a Roma agli inizi del primo secolo a. C.', *Athen.* N.S. 31 (1953), 259 ff.

—— 'Studi su Dionigi da Alicarnasso, ii. Il regno di Servio Tullio', *Athen.* N.S. 39 (1961), 98 ff.

GARTON, C., 'A republican mime-actress?' *CR* N.S. 14 (1964), 238 f.

GARZETTI, A., 'Appio Claudio Cieco nella storia politica del suo tempo', *Athen.* N.S. 25 (1947), 175 ff.

GORDON, M. L., 'The nationality of slaves under the early Roman Empire', *JRS* 14 (1924), 93 ff. Reprinted in Finley, M. I. *Slavery in classical antiquity. Views and controversies* (Cambridge, 1960), 171 ff.

—— 'The freedman's son in municipal life', *JRS* 21 (1931), 65 ff.

GRUEN, E. S., 'Political prosecutions in the 90's B.C.', *Hist.* 15 (1966), 32 ff.

GWYNN, A., *Roman education from Cicero to Quintilian* (Oxford, 1926).

HADAS, M., *Sextus Pompey* (New York, 1930).

HALKIN, L., 'Le Père d'Horace a-t-il été esclave public?' *Ant. Class.* 4 (1935), 125 ff.

HATZFELD, J., Les Italiens résidants à Délos mentionnés dans les inscriptions de l'île', *BCH* 1912, 1 ff.

―― *Les Trafiquants italiens dans l'Orient hellénique* (Paris, 1919).

HAYWOOD, R. M., 'Some traces of serfdom in Cicero's day', *AJP* 54 (1933), 145 ff.

HENDERSON, M. I., 'The establishment of the *equester ordo*', *JRS* 53 (1963), 61 ff.

HENDRICKSON, G. L., 'Horace and Valerius Cato', *CP* 11 (1916), 249 ff.

HILLSCHER, A., *Hominum litteratorum Graecorum ante Tiberii mortem in urbe Roma commoratorum historia critica* (Diss. Leipzig, 1891).

HOPKINS, M. K., 'Contraception in the Roman Empire', *Comparative Studies in Society and History*, 8 (1965), 124 ff.

JOHNSON, JOTHAM, *Excavations at Minturnae*, ii. *Inscriptions* Part I. *Republican* magistri (Philadelphia, 1933).

JONES, A. H. M., *The Greek city from Alexander to Justinian* (Oxford, 1926, reissued 1966).

―― *Studies in Roman government and law* (Oxford, 1960).

JÖRS, P., *Über das Verhältniß der Lex Julia de mar. ord. zur Lex Papia Poppaea* (Bonn, 1882).

KARLOWA, O., *Römische Rechtsgeschichte*, ii (Leipzig, 1901).

KASER, M., *Das Römische Privatrecht* (Munich 1935, 1939).

―― Review of Cosentini, C., *Studi sui liberti, ZSS* 68 (1951), 576 ff.

KÖSER, E., *De captivis Romanorum* (Giessen, 1904).

KÜHN, G., *De opificum Romanorum condicione privata quaestiones* (Halle, 1910).

LAMBERT, JACQUES, *Les* operae liberti. *Contribution à l'histoire des droits de patronat* (Diss. Paris, 1934).

LAST, HUGH, Review of Taylor, L. R., *Party politics in the age of Caesar, Gnomon* 22 (1950), 360 ff.

LEJAY, P., 'Appius Claudius Caecus', *Rev. Phil.* 44 (1920), 92 ff.

LESLIE, R., *The Epicureanism of Titus Pomponius Atticus* (Diss. Philadelphia, 1950).

LÉVY-BRUHL, H., *Quelques problèmes du très ancien droit romain* (Paris, 1934) = 'L'Affranchissement par la vindicte', pp. 56 ff.

LEWIS, R. G., 'Pompeius' freedman biographer: Suetonius, *De Gramm, et Rhet.* 27 (3)'. *CR* N.S. 16 (1966), 271 ff.

LOANE, H. J., *Industry and commerce of the city of Rome 50 B.C.–A.D. 200* (Diss. Baltimore, 1938).

MCDONALD, A. H., 'History of Rome and Italy in the 2nd century B.C.', *Cambridge Historical Journal*, 6 (1939), 124 ff.

MAIER, F. G., 'Römische Bevölkerungsgeschichte und Inschriftenstatistik', *Hist.* 12 (1953-4), 318 ff.

MARQUARDT, J., *Römische Staatsverwaltung* (Darmstadt, 1957).

MARROU, H. I., *Histoire de l'education dans l'antiquité* (Paris, 1948).

MATTINGLEY, H. B., 'The date of Livius Andronicus', *CQ* N.S. 7 (1957), 159 ff.

MAXEY, M., *Occupations of the lower classes in Roman society* (Diss. Chicago, 1938).

MOHLER, S., 'Slave education in the Roman Empire', *TAPA* 17 (1940), 262 ff.

MOMMSEN, T., *De Collegiis et Sodaliciis Romanorum* (Kiel, 1843).

—— *Römisches Staatsrecht*, iii 1 (3rd edition, Leipzig, 1887).

—— *Gesammelte Schriften* (Berlin, 1907).

—— *Römisches Strafrecht* (Darmstadt, 1955).

NICOLET, C., *L'Ordre équestre à l'époque républicaine*, i (Paris, 1966).

ORS, A. D', *Epigrafía jurídica d. España romana* (Madrid, 1953).

OXE, A., 'Zur alteren Nomenklatur der römischen Sklaven', *Rhein. Mus.* 59 (1904), 108 ff.

PARK, M. E., *The plebs in Cicero's day* (Diss. Cambridge, Mass. 1918).

PFLAUM, H. G., *Les procurateurs équestres sous le haut empire romain* (Paris, 1950).

PLATNER, S. B., *The topography and monuments of ancient Rome* (2nd edition, Boston, 1911).

RAWSON, B., 'Family life among the lower classes in Rome in the first two centuries of the empire', *CP* 61 (1966), 70 ff.

REID, J. S., *The municipalities of the Roman Empire* (Cambridge, Mass., 1913).

ROBERTIS, F. M. DE, *Il diritto associativo romano dai collegi della reppublica alle corporazioni del basso impero* (Bari, 1938).

—— *Lavoro e lavoratori nel mondo romano* (Bari, 1967).

ROBSON, D. O., 'The Nationality of the poet Caecilius Statius', *AJP* 59 (1938), 301 ff.

ROSENBERG, A., *Untersuchungen zur römischen Zenturienverfassung* (Berlin, 1911).

ROSTOVTZEFF, M., *Social and economic history of the Hellenistic world* (Oxford, 1941).

—— *Social and economic history of the Roman Empire* (revised edition, Oxford, 1957).

SCHTAJERMAN (in Russian, Shtaerman), E. M., *Die Krise der Sklavenhalterordnung im Westen des römischen Reiches*, ed. and tr. Seyforth, W. (Berlin, 1964).

SCHULZ, F., *Principles of Roman law* (Oxford, 1936).

—— *Classical Roman law* (Oxford, 1951).

BIBLIOGRAPHY

SCULLARD, H. H., *Roman politics 220–150 B.C.* (Oxford, 1951).
SHACKLETON BAILEY, D. R., *Cicero's Letters to Atticus* i (Cambridge, 1965).
STAVELEY, E. S., 'The political aims of Appius Claudius Caecus', *Hist.* 8 (1959), 410 ff.
SYME, R., 'Who was Decidius Saxa?' *JRS* 27 (1937), 127 ff.
—— 'Caesar, the Senate and Italy', *PBSR* N.S. 1 (1938), 1 ff.
—— *The Roman revolution* (Oxford, 1939. Corrected reprint 1952).
—— 'Missing senators', *Hist.* 4 (1955), 52 ff.
—— *Tacitus* (Oxford, 1958).
—— 'Sabinus the Muleteer', *Latomus* 7 (1958), 73 ff.
—— 'Who was Vedius Pollio?' *JRS* 51 (1961), 23 ff.
TAYLOR L. R., 'Horace's equestrian career', *AJP* 46 (1925), 161 ff.
—— *Party politics in the age of Caesar* (Berkeley and Los Angeles, 1949).
—— *The voting districts of the Roman Republic* (Papers and Monographs of the American Academy in Rome, Rome, 1960).
—— 'Freedmen and freeborn in the epitaphs of imperial Rome', *AJP* 82 (1961), 113 ff.
THIEL, J. H., *Studies on the history of Roman sea-power in republican times* (Amsterdam, 1946).
TONDO, S., *Aspetti simbolici e magici nella struttura giuridica della manumissio vindicta* (Milan, 1967).
TYRRELL, R. Y., and PURSER, L. P., *The correspondence of M. Tullius Cicero*, vol. i 3rd ed., vols. ii–vi 2nd ed. (Dublin and London, 1904–33).
ULLMAN, B. L., 'Horace, Catullus and Tigellius', *CP* 10 (1915), 270 ff.
VOGT, J., *Sklaverei und Humanitat: Studien zur antiken Sklaverei und ihrer Forschung* (*Historia*, Einzelschriften 8, Wiesbaden 1965).
WALTZING, J. P., *Étude historique sur les corporations professionelles chez les romains jusqu'à la chute de l'Empire d'Occident* (Louvain, 1895–6).
WATSON, ALAN, *The law of persons in the later Roman Republic* (Oxford, 1967).
—— 'Morality, slavery and the jurists in the later Roman Republic', *Tulane Law Review* 42 (1968), 289 ff.
WEAVER, P. R. C., 'Cognomina ingenua: A note', *CQ* N.S. 14 (1964), 311 ff.
WESTERMANN, W. L., *The slave systems of Greek and Roman antiquity* (The American Philosophical Society, Philadelphia, 1955).
WILLEMS, P., *Le Sénat de la république romaine: sa composition et ses attributions* (Louvain, 1878–83).
—— *Le Droit public romain* (Louvain, 1883.)
WILSON, A. J. N., *Emigration from Italy in the republican age of Rome* (Manchester, 1966).

WISSOWA, G., *Religion und Cultus der Römer* (in Müller, I. von, *Handbuch der Klassischen Altertumswissenschaft* v. 4, Munich, 1912).

WLASSAK, M., 'Die prätorischen Freilassungen', *ZSS* 26 (1905), 367 ff.

—— 'Der Gerichtsmagistrat im gesetzlichen Spruchverfahren', *ZSS* 28 (1907), 1 ff.

YAVETZ, Z., 'The living conditions of the urban plebs in republican Rome', *Latomus*, 17 (1958), 500 ff.

INDEX I

GENERAL INDEX

Acastus, slave of M. Cicero, 252 n. 3, 253.
Accensi, **154** f., 157 f., 159.
Accountants, 150.
Accusatio ingrati liberti, 69, 73 f.
Actors, 76 f., 78 n. 6, 83, **138** ff., 202, 225.
Adsertor libertatis, **21** ff.
Aeditui, 195.
L. Aelius Praeconinus, 113.
M. Aemilius Avianius, 135 f.
M. Aemilius Lepidus (censor 179), 44 f.
M. Aemilius Scaurus (*cos*. 115), 47 ff., 114.
Aesopus' son, 233.
Agriculture, 9, 104, **106** ff.
Alapa, 24.
Alumni, **2**, 11, 260.
Amicitia, **220** f., 262 n. 5.
Anagnostae (readers), 148.
Ancillae, 88.
Anteros, slave or freedman probably of Atticus, 252 n. 3, 253 n. 10.
Antiochus of Ascalon, 228.
Antistius, a doctor, 129.
M. Antonius, social relations with freedmen, 123, 140, 225 n. 5; and his own freedmen, 131, 182 f., 187, 190.
Amulus aureus, **66** f., 131, 272.
Apparitores, 153 f., 157 f.
Q. Apronius, possibly a freedman, 105 n. 1, 266 n. 1.
Architects, 76, **132** ff., 254 f.
Aristocritus, slave or freedman of M. Cicero, 252 n. 3, 253, **255**.
Artemidorus of Perga, 130.
Artifices, 95 ff.
Artists, 76, 135 ff.
M. Artorius Asclepiades, 129.
Asclepiades, 129.
Asians, 2, 8, 10, 163, 241.
C. Asinius Pollio (*cos*. 40), 122, 123, 223.
Astronomers, 127 f.

Atargatis, 204.
Attendants, 145 f.
Auctioneers, **99** ff.
Augustus, 227; his policy towards freedmen, 16, 64, 73 ff., 244 f.; restricts manumission, 15, 30; grants privileges to certain freedmen, 65 f.; regulates marriage with freed persons, 82 ff., 211; and his own freedmen, 73, 187 ff.; and Caesar's freedmen, 187; patronage, 123 ff.; social relationships, 186, **223** ff.; his policy towards the Jews in Rome, 206; and Vedius Pollio, 233 f.
M. Aurelius Cottanus, 64.

Bakers (*pistores*), 72, 96, 143.
Balneatores, 99.
Barbarius Philippus, 62.
Benevolentia, 217, 221.
Bequests, to freedmen, 14, 28, **216** f., **239**; by freedmen, **78** ff., 134.
Biographers, 114, 118, 121, 123.
Bodyguards, 146.
Bona Dea, 203.
Builders, 90 n. 4, 99, 169.
Burial clubs, 202 f.
Businessmen, 88, 264.
Butchers, 89, 95 f., 202.
P. Buxurius P. f., 133 n. 7.

T. Caecilius Atticus, 11, 108, 119.
Calatores, 154; to priests, 194.
Cantores, 141, 143.
Capital, 94; from patrons, 93, 103, 105 f., 160, 239 f.; lack of, 105, 107; of sons of freedmen, 67, 233.
Cappadocians, 9.
Caps of liberty, 14.
Captivi, **3**, **4** f., 8 f., 122, 124.
Capua, 36, 105, 273.
Capuan boards, 197 f., 201, 220.
Carthaginians, 3, 8.
A. Castricius Myrio Talenti f., 196 n. 6, 197.

INDEX I

Cattle dealers, 105 n. 3, 202.
Causa liberalis, 21.
Censors, 38 ff., 59 ff.
Children of freedmen, 15, 43 ff., 68, 78 f., 209, **212** ff.
Chilon, slave of the Elder Cato, 115.
Christianity, 205.
Cilicians, 3, 9.
Cillo, a slave, 99, 255 n. 3.
Cimbri, 3, 9.
Cisiarii, 99.
Citizenship, see *civitas*.
Civil servants, 153 ff.
Civitas, **37** ff., 102, 162, 201; linked with *libertas*, 1, 19, 20, 24, **237**.
Class-consciousness, 14, 37, 215, 219, 220, 226, 229 ff., 235, 263.
Claudius (the emperor), 53 ff.
C. Claudius C. f. Pal., 156 n. 14.
Ap. Claudius Caecus, **38** ff., **53** ff., 165, 167, 243.
M. Claudius Glycias (dictator 249), 57, 129 n. 4, 232.
Ap. Claudius Pulcher (censor 50), 60 f.
C. Claudius Pulcher (censor 169), 43 ff.
P. Claudius Pulcher (*cos*. 249), 57.
Clerks, 148 ff.
Clientela, among the *humiles* in general, of Ap. Claudius Caecus, 38 ff., 165, 167; of Scipio Aemilianus, 156, 167; of Clodius, 168 f., 172 ff.; of Catiline, 168 f., 172; of Crassus, 173, 175; among freedmen of other patrons, 243 f.; of Sulpicius Rufus, 49, 165; of Cicero, 166; of Caesar, 167; of Clodius, 223 f.; Chrysogonus allegedly had his own clients, 183.
Clodius, son of Aesopus, 233.
Clodius Philhetaerus, 252, 254 f.
P. Clodius Pulcher, his gangs, 35, 95, 168, **172** ff., 220, 245, 265; his law on freedmen, 50, 265.
Sex. Cloelius, 170.
Cluatius, 133 n. 7, 255 n. 3.
Coactores, 101.
Cognomina, 6 f., 57, 100, 114 n. 10, 122 n. 10, 139, 142, **250** f., 267, 273; foreign names not a safe guide to original nationality, **6** ff., 231; or to freed status, 191, 231, 234, 254; but certain names commonly servile, 111, 187 n. 5; omitted to conceal freed status, 7, 155, 270; second *cognomina*, 114, 124, 188, 232.
Collegia, trade guilds, 51, 105, 164, **168** ff., 220; religious boards and guilds, **194** ff., 220.
Collina, 42, 177 n. 1.
Coloniae, 63 f., 237, 244 f.
Columbaria, 6.
Comitia Centuriata, 45, **51** f., 163 f., **166** f., 177 f.
Comitia Tributa, **37** ff., 167, 174.
Concilium Plebis, 167, 174.
Concordia, 203.
Concubines, 16, 84 n. 5, 211 f.
Conducticii, 90, **98** ff.
Congiaria, see Corn dole.
Conliberti, often married, 15 f., 210; worked together, 97, 102 f., 105; social relationship, 216, 226.
Contractors, 99, 104.
Contubernales, 15, **209** f.
Contubernium, 15, **209** f., 212.
Conubium, 72 ff.
Cooks, 143, 202, 223.
Copyists, see *Librarii*.
Coqui, 143, 202.
Corn-dealers, 105.
Corn dole, 16, 28, 30, 34 n. 2.
L. Cornelius Balbus, 52, 184.
L. Cornelius Cinna (*cos*. 87), 50.
C. Cornelius Gallus, 123, 223, 224.
P. Cornelius Scipio Aemilianus, 112; his remarks on the plebs in 131, 1, **8**, 34, 163; his supporters in 142 probably included freedmen, 156, 167.
L. Cornelius Sulla, 227; enslavement of many Asians as a result of his settlement in 84–5, 2; annuls Sulpicius' distribution bill, 49; his new senators, 60; his own freedmen, 114, **181** ff.; his low friends, 140, 225 n. 2.
Coronarii, 110.
Corumbus, a slave, 133 n. 9.
D. Cossutius, 133, 138.
Craftsmen, 5, 10, 33, 38, 89, **95** ff., **172** ff.
Crates of Mallos, 113.

Daughters of freedmen, 235; *ingenuae*, 113, 214; *libertinae*, 213.

GENERAL INDEX

Decumani, 104 f.
Dediticii, 236 f.
Delos, 2, 102, 104 f., 152; Competeliasts, 199; other cult colleges, 200 f.
Delphi, 2, 32.
Demea, slave or freedman probably of Atticus, 252 n. 3, 253 n. 10.
Dexippus, slave or freedman of M. Cicero, 252 n. 3, 253, **255**.
Diana, 203.
Dionysius, slave of M. Cicero, 252 nn. 2, 3, 253, **255**.
Dispensatores, **143** f., 254, 263.
Doctors, 76 f., **129** ff., 146, 147 f., 254 f.
Domestics, 143.
Domicile, in patron's house, 71; in house of another *ingenuus*, 222 f.

Edicts affecting freedmen, 69 ff., 79 f.
Education of freedmen, 156, 160 f., 164, 192; more likelihood of freedom for the educated, 11; specially trained by the patron, 87, 111, 112 f., 130, 133, 146, 260 f.; educated before enslavement, 111, 132; usually better educated than humble *ingenui*, 153.
Egyptians, 7, 205, 226, 246.
Equites, 59 (Furius), 64 ff., 88, 157, 239, 271 f.
L. Equitius (*tr. pl.* 99), 58 f., 129 n. 4, 230.
Eros, an official in Egypt, possibly a freedman, **191** f., 240.
Esquilina, 42, 46 f.
Ethiopians, 9.
Eunus, 3.

Fabri, 90 n. 1, 172.
Factory owners, 91 ff.
Fadia, 235.
Farmers, 90, 108 f.
Favor libertatis, 28 f.
Festuca, 23.
Fidelitas, 217.
Fides, 80 f., 120 n. 14, 217, 221, 229, 235.
Financial standing of freedmen, 44, 88, 95, 98 n. 7, 108, 109, 113; *see also* Rich freedmen, Poor freedmen, Pay.
Cn. Flavius Anni f., his political career, 42, **56** ff., 167, 212 n. 7, 229, 233; as *scriba*, 154; dropped or did not have a *cognomen*, 232.
Florists, 110, 202.
Foremen, 92 ff., 99 n. 8, 100, 106, 146.
Fortune, 202.
Frumentarii, 105.
'Fugitivus', used of freedmen, 271, cf. 59.
Fullers (*fullones*), 99, 144, 202.
M. Fulvius Nobilior (censor 179), 44 f.
P. Furius (*tr. pl.* 99), **58** f., 64, 212 n. 7, 229, 232.

A. Gabinius (*tr. pl.* 139), 58, 234.
Gardeners, 96 n. 9, 109 f.
Gauls, 3, 9 f., 190, 192.
M. Gellius, 61 n. 1, 230.
L. Gellius Poplicola, 84, 211.
Gens, 81 f.
Geographers, 124, 128.
Gladiators, 87, 141 f.
Grammatici, **111** ff., 147.
Q. Granius, *praeco*, 100.
Greeks, proportion of Greeks among slaves and freedmen, 5 ff., 8, 10; superiority of free Greeks in learned professions, 90, 117 f., 129 f.; conjectured Greek influence on Roman industry, 93 f., and certain influence on education and literature, 110 f., 117 f., 125 f., 205, medicine, 131, religion, 241; vocal in *contiones*, 8, 163; Greek freedmen working in the East, 192; Greek *cognomina* not evidence necessarily for freed extraction, 231 f.

Haruspices, 154, 156, **195**.
Helvius Mancia, 232.
Hercules, 203.
Hermia, slave or freedman of M. Cicero, 252 n. 3, 253.
Hermodorus of Salamis, 133.
Historians, 119, 124.
Histriones, 139, 225.
Holitores, 96 n. 9, 109 f.
Honos, 203.
Q. Horatius Flaccus, philosophical ideas on slavery, 12 f.; on freedmen's sons in politics, 60 f.; as *tribunus militum*, 64 f.; could have been an auctioneer, 100; his *vilicus*,

INDEX I

Q. Horatius Flaccus (*cont.*):
108; on a parvenu, 109, 226; Musa, 131; as *scriba*, 154; relationship with his father, 208, 233, **234** f.; on affairs with freedwomen, 212; and Maecenas, 225; on the social difficulties of a freedman's son, **232**; on Sarmentus, 271 f.
C. Hostius C. l. Pamphilus, 131 n. 10.
Husbands, 15 f., 209 ff.; often patron of wife, 209 ff.

Iaia of Cyricus, 135.
Ingenui, wrongfully enslaved, 4 n. 5, 5, 62, 115, 122, 248; relationship to freedmen in law, 81 ff.; marriage, 82 ff., 210 f.; work, 87 ff.; politics, 163 ff.; religion, 194 ff.; social life, 220 ff.; moral nature of the *ingenuus*, 242.
Interpreters, 154.
Isis, 204 f., 206.
Italians, 10, 55, 122, 203, 248 f., 272.

Jewellers, 98 n. 7.
Jews, 2 n. 6, 8, 163, **205** ff., 226, 241, 249.
C. Julius Caesar, his Gallic captives, 3, 9 f.; Licinus, 10; colonies, 35, 244 f.; new senators, 61; his own freedmen, 72 f., 105, 224; relations with other freedmen, 115 (Gnipho), 116 (Tyrannio), 121, 223 (Apollonius), 186 (Tigellius); his encouragement of doctors, 129 f.; his noted attention to slaves and freedmen for political purposes, 167; reactions of the lower classes to his death, 168, 206; he probably used his freedmen less than some politicians, 185 f.
Julius Rufio/Rufinus, **64** f., 185 f., 212 n. 7, 233.
Juno *Sospes*, 203.
Jurors, 63, **66** f., 229.
Jus commercii, 82.
Jus conubii, 82 ff.
Jus vitae necisque, 71 f., 74.

Kidnapping, 2.

Land-owning freedmen, 39, 43 ff., 108 f.
Lanii, 89, 95 f., 202.

Larcius Rufus, son of freedman, 232.
Lares, 198 ff., 203.
Latifundia, 9.
Lecticarii (litter-bearers), 143, 223.
Letter-carriers, 145, 253.
Lex Aelia Sentia, 15, 69, 73, 76, 209 n. 7, 211.
Lex Cincia, 265.
Lex Cornelia de xx quaestoribus, 154.
Lex Julia de Maritandis Ordinibus, 83 ff.
Lex Julia Municipalis, 63, 100 n. 3.
Lex Junia, 29, 236.
Lex Licinia de sodaliciis, 176 f.
Lex Malacitana, 64 n. 1.
Lex Papia, 83 ff.
Lex Pompeia de parricidiis, 80.
Lex Salpensana, 31.
Lex Tabellaria (139 B.C.), 164 f.
Lex Terentia (189 B.C.), 68 n. 8, 129 n. 2.
Liberalitas, 14.
Libertae, 79 f.
Libertas, 12 ff., 230, 242; linked with *civitas*, 1, 19, 20, 24, 230, 237; the deity, 203.
Liberti, definition, 37 n. 5, **53**; word also used for freed serfs, 195 n. 8.
Libertinae, 76 n. 4, 83 ff., 97 ff., 144 f., 209 ff., 224 f.
Libertini, definition, 37 n. 5, **52** f., 229; synagogue of, 207.
Librarians, 124 f., 148 f., 226.
Librarii, 78 n. 6, **148** f., 257.
L. Licinius Lucullus (*cos.* 74), 116, 182.
Lictors, 154, **156**, 159; to priests, 194.
Lintiones, 99.
Litigation by freedmen, 104, 217.
M. Livius Drusus, 22 f., 75.
Ludi compitalicii, 170, 173 f., 198 f.
Luperci, 155 n. 5, 157, **195** f.
Q. Lutatius Catulus (*cos.* 101), 114.

P. Maenius, 72.
Magistri Capitolini, 196 f.
Magistri of trade colleges, 202.
Magistri vicorum, 198 ff.
Magna Mater, 204.
Maids, 88, 144 f.
L. Mamilius, 258 n. 8.
Managers, 92 ff., 96, 98, 101, 610.
C. Manilius (*tr. pl.* 66), 50.
Manumissio apud IIviros, 31.

GENERAL INDEX

Manumissio censu, 20 f., **25** ff., 31, 41.
Manumissio sacrorum causa, 31.
Manumissio testamento, 14, **20** f., 31, 41.
Manumissio vindicta, **20** ff., 30, 31, 38, 41, 257 f., 261.
Manumission, **11** ff.; rare for certain slaves, 9, 11; master's motives for, 11 ff.; purchased by slave, 16 f.; by public bodies, **18** f., 203; votive offerings for, 203; of *contubernales*, 209 f.; by Cicero, 255 f., 260 f.
Manumission by adoption, 31.
Manumission, informal, 16, 18 n. 3, **29** ff., 72 n. 5.
Manus iniectio, 71 f., 74.
Marcilius, 156 n. 14.
Margaritarii, 98 n. 7.
Mario, slave or freedman of M. Cicero, 252 n. 3, 253, **255**.
C. Marius, 49, 58.
Market-gardeners, 96 n. 9, 119 f.
Marriage, of freedmen, 15 f., **82** ff., **208** ff., 220; of descendants of freedmen, 157.
Maximus, 61 f.
Menander, slave or freedman of M. Cicero, 252 n. 3, 253, **255**.
Mens Bona, 202.
Mensores, 99, 133, 154.
Mercatores, 89, **102** ff., 201; *Pecuarii*, 105 n. 3; *Retiarii*, 105 n. 3.
Mercenarii, 89, **98** ff., 107.
Merchants, 89, **102** ff., 201.
Meretrices, 140, **142**, 214, 225.
Military service, 35, **67** f.
Mimi and *mimae*, **139** ff., 225.
Minerva, 202.
Mines, 9.
Minturnae, 63, 105, 199 n. 2, 201, 273.
Mithras, 205.
Moral effects of *libertini*, 236 ff.
C. Mucius, 133 n. 7.
Municipia, 33, 63.
Musicians, 141, 143, 195.

Sex. Naevius, 100, **230**.
P. Naevius Turpio, possibly a freedman, 105 n. 1, 266 n. 1.
Names, see *nomina*, *praenomina*, *cognomina*.
Negotiatores, 88, **102** ff., 201.
Net-makers, 105 n. 3.

Nicias of Cos, 227.
Nicomedes II of Bithynia, 3.
Nomenclatores, 78 n. 6.
Nomina, 7, 41, 139, **250** f., 267, 273.
Numisius, 133 n. 7.

Obsequium, **69** ff., 81.
Officium, 15, 80, 215, 217, 221.
Operae, 16 f., 69 ff., **75** ff., 81, 116, 142, 146, 222, 258.
Opifices, 68, 89 ff., **95** ff.; in politics, 167, 169, **172** ff.; religion, 205; social life, 218.
Optimate freedmen, 102, **166** ff., 177 f., 245.
L. Orbilius Pupillus, 111 nn. 2, 3, 113.
'*Ordo libertinus*', 37, 59, **162** ff.
Orpheus, slave of Terentia, 15 n. 2, 252.
Ovid, 124, 224.

Paedagogi, 110 f., 147.
Painters (*pictores*), 78 n. 6, 135 ff.
Palatina, 42, 167, 251.
Panurgus, slave actor, 139.
Partnership with patron, 105 n. 7.
Pasiteles, sculptor, 135.
Patronae, 76 n. 4, **78** f., 250.
Patroni, often made bequests to freedmen, 28, 216 f.; patron substitutes *pater*, 48 n. 4; rights of, 66, **68** ff.; inheritance of patronal rights, 76, 78, 187 (Octavian), 188 (Sex. Pompeius); as employers, **87** f., **142** ff.; freedmen could be approached through patron, 164; patron's repute enhanced by freedmen's reports, 166; political use of *liberti*, 168 f., 171, 175 n. 5, **177** ff.; patron assumed to be implicated in actions of freedmen, 183 f., 256; patron could be approached through freedmen, 184; freedmen could have patrons other than their ex-masters, 185 n. 5, 217 n. 1, **223** f.; difficult to determine manumitter when son inherited patronal rights, 188, 190 n. 5; husband patron of wife, 209 f.; father patron of child, 212; social relationship with freedmen, 215 ff.; patrons who were themselves freedmen, 216, 219; approval of freedmen, 217 f.; furthered careers of freedmen's children, 233.

INDEX I

Pay, 87, 124, 140, 146 f.
Peculium, 12, 17, 30, 106, 107, 144, 209.
Pedisequi, 145 f.
Pelops of Byzantium, 252.
Peregrini, 117, 126 f., 129 ff., 133 ff., 139 n. 9, 163, 184, 196 n. 6, 227, 247 n. 1, 254, 269.
M. Perennius Tigranus, 92 n. 4, 93.
Perfumers, 95 f., 97 f., 216, 267.
Pescennius, 252.
Philosophers, 114, **125** ff.
Philotas of Amphissa, 130.
Phrygians, 9, 204.
Pistores, 72, 96, 143.
M. Plautius, artist, 135.
Plebs frumentaria, 34 n. 2, 35, 88, 101.
L. Plotius Gallus, 117.
Poets, 111 ff., 114, 115, 119, 122 f., 125, 241 ff.
Pollex, slave of M. Cicero, 252 n. 3, 253, **255**.
Sex. Pompeius, 65, **187** ff., 266.
Cn. Pompeius Magnus, 118 f., 182, 184 f., 188, 217, 224.
Cn. Pompeius Theophanes, 184, 228.
Pompeius Trogus, 150 n. 2.
T. Pomponius Atticus (for his freedmen *see also under* Caecilius), his staff, 107 f., 146, 148 f., 151 f.
M. Pomponius Marcellus, 113.
Poor freedmen, 88, 95, 98 n. 7, 161, 193.
P. Popilius (senator), **59** f., 212 n. 7, 229, 232.
Population of Rome, **32** ff., 162 ff., 165 f.
Potters, 14, **91** ff.
Praecones, auctioneers, **99** ff.; criers, 154.
Praenomina, 7, 250 f., 267.
Priests, 194.
Procurators, 65 f.; private, 104, 144, **150** ff.; public, 123.
Promissio iurata liberti, 22 f., **75** f.
Prostitutes, 85, 142, 214, 225.
Provocatio, 164.
Public freedmen, **18** f.
Publicani, 88, 103, 104.
Pullarii, 194 f.
Purpurarii, 95 ff.

Race mixture, 1; extent of, 5 ff., 32 ff., 163; effect on morals? 162 f., **236** ff.
Ratiocinatores, 150, 256.
Relegatio, 73 f.
Remmius Palaemon, 109.
Rhetores, 117 f., 121, 123, 124.
Rich freedmen, 44, 67, 88, 109, **157**, 160, 182, 185, 187, 193, 196, **233**, **239** f.; mainly of prominent patrons, 164, 167, 177 f.; in the *Centuriata*, 166 f., 177 f.
Q. Roscius Gallus, **139**.
T. Rufrenus, 92.
A. Rupilius, a doctor, 129.
P. Rutilius Rufus (*cos.* 105), 69 ff., 81, 114.

Sallust, 122.
Sallustius, 252.
Sardinians, 3, 10, 45 n. 4, 269.
Schoolmasters, see *Grammatici*.
Scribae, 56 (Flavius), **153** f., 157 f., 159, 202, 258 f. (Tullius), 271 f. (Sarmentus).
Sculptors, 135 ff.
Secretaries, 149 f., 261 f. (Tiro).
C. Sempronius Gracchus, 48.
Ti. Sempronius Gracchus (censor 169), 34 n. 3, **43** ff.
Senators, freedmen's sons, **52** ff., 157; descendants, 58, 215.
Senatusconsulta, on illegal enslavement, 3; against clubs, 169 ff., 175 f., 198.
Senatusconsultum de Bacchanalibus, 169.
Serfs and freed serfs, 195 n. 8.
L. Sergius, 258 n. 8.
Servius Clodius, 113.
Servius Tullius, 25, **37**, 54 n. 1, 199 n. 5.
'Servus', used to describe freedmen, **172** ff., 229 f., 259, **265** f., 271; used probably of freedmen's sons, 230.
Sevirate, 64, **199**.
Shopkeepers, 33, 89 f., **95** ff.
Singers, 141, 143, 203.
Slave-dealers, 3, 9, 88, 105 n. 7, 106.
Slavery, how freedmen had become slaves, **1** ff.; moral views on slavery, 2, 12, **241** ff.; slave revolts, 3; how freedmen were released from slavery, **11** ff.

GENERAL INDEX

Social distinctions between freedmen, 226.
Societas Cantorum Graecorum, 141, 203, 247.
Sodalicia/sodalitates, 169, **175** ff.; religious boards, 194 ff.
Sons of freedmen, 35, 43 ff., 68, **229** ff.; legal position, 52 ff., 64 f., 67; marrying freedwomen, 86, 211; their rise in society, 157; themselves freedmen, 213; clients of father's patron, 229, 233.
Sositheus, slave of Cicero, 148 and n. 6, 252 n. 3, 253, **255**.
Spaniards, 8 f., 247.
Spartacus, 9.
Spintharus, slave or freedman of M. Cicero, 252 n. 3, 253.
C. and M. Stallii, 133.
Stewards, 143 f.
Stipulatio, 70 f., 73, 74, 77, 81.
Stoicism, 12.
Suburana, 42.
'Sulla litterator', 114 n. 10.
P. Sulpicius Rufus (*tr. pl.* 88), 49, 165.
Surveyors, 99, 133, 154.
Syrians, 2f., 8f., 10, 115, 125, 204f., 249.

Tabellarii, **145**; of Cicero, 253.
Tabernarii, 89 f., 95 ff.; in politics, 167, 169, 172 ff.; social life, 218.
Tasters (*gustatores*), 107.
Teachers, **110** ff., 146, 147, 254 f.
Tectores, 99.
Terentia, wife of Cicero, 125, 252, 253, 263 f.
Testamenti factio, 76, **78** ff., 82.
L. Tettius Samia, 92 n. 4.
Teutones, 3, 9.
Theopompus, secretary to Q. Cicero, 149 n. 11.
C. T(h)oranius (*tr. pl.* 25 B.C.), 62, 212 n. 7, 229, 232.
Thracians, 9, 125, 247.
Thurarii, 97 f., 267.
Tibicines, 141, 143, 195, 269 n. 4.
Timomachus of Byzantium, 135.
Tlepolemus of Cibyra, 136.
Tombs, 4, 32 n. 4, 33, 95, 161, 202, 215 f., 240.

Tribes, 34, **39** ff., 163, 165, 166, 167, 243 f.
Tribuni militum, sons of freedmen, **65**, 157.
L. Tuccius, a doctor, 129.
M. Tullius Cicero, views on manumission, 12 f., 17, 18 f.; on the Clodian law, 50; on the duties of freedmen, 80; on *opifices*, 89, 100; on freedmen in politics, 162 ff.; on the Clodian gangs, 173 ff., 265 f.; relations with own freedmen, 22 f., 73, 218, **252** ff.; relations with other freedmen, 104, 115 f., 119, 121, 134, 136 f., 154 f., 196, 216 ff.; employees, 145 ff., **252** ff.; on Sex. Naevius, 230; on Tigellius, 269 f.
Q. Tullius Cicero, 145; dependence on Statius, 153, 158, 181, 218; comment on Tiro's manumission, 218; and Tiro, 219.
Tutela, 79 f., 84.
Tutors, 62, 110 f.
Twelve Tables, 78.

Ummius (possibly a freedman), 143 n. 7, 254.
Ungrateful freedmen, 69, 73 f.
Unguentarii, 95 f., 216.

Valerius of Ostia, 133 n. 7.
M. Valerius Probus, 113.
P. Vedius Pollio, 13, 190 f., 232, **233** f.
Vernae, **2**, 4 f. 11, 132, 203, 212, 248, 272.
C. Verres, 102, 130, 136, 155, 156 n. 14, 159, 230 n. 2, 266.
Vestals, 194.
Vestiarii, 78 n. 6.
Viatores, 57, **154**, 157; to priests, 194.
Vicesima libertatis, 17, 27, 31, 38.
Victimarii, 194 f.
Vilici, 106 n. 6, **107** f., 144.
Volones, 19, 68 n. 2, 203.
P. Volumnius Eutrapelus, 140.

Weavers, 99.
Weight-makers, 99.
Wives, 15 f., 78 f., **208** ff.

INDEX II
FREEDMEN AND PROBABLE FREEDMEN

Freedmen are listed under *nomen* when it is known. The patron is named in brackets when his identity is reasonably certain but not attested; with a question mark where it is dubious.

Achilles, presumably freedman of Brutus, 210.
Acilius Sthenelus, either freedman or descendant of freedman, 109.
Aegypta, *see* Tullius.
L. Aelius, 217.
Aemilia Aemiliae Tertiae l., 145 n. 1.
Aemilius, *praeco*, probably freedman, 156, 167 n. 2.
? Aemilius ? Lepidi l. Apella, 187.
M. Aemilius Lepidi l. Philemon, 221 f.
Aeserninus, gladiator, perhaps a freedman, 142.
Aesopus, *see* Clodius.
Agonis, *liberta* (i.e. freed serf) of Venus Erycina, 195 n. 8.
Alexio, doctor to Cicero, possibly a freedman, 130 n. 6, 222, 252 n. 3, 254.
Amphio, *see* Lutatius.
Antaeus, freedman or slave of Atticus, 149 n. 1.
Anteros, freedman or slave probably of Atticus, 252 n. 3, 253 n. 10.
Antiochus, *see* Gabinius.
Antiochus, freedman or slave of Atticus, 149 n. 2.
Antipho, an actor, 139.
Antonius M. l. Callias, 187.
Antonius Castor, 110.
(Antonius) Euphorbus, 131, 248.
M. Antonius Gnipho, a Gaul, 5, 246; his *cognomen*, 6; his life and career as a *grammaticus*, 114 f., 122, 146.
Antonius M. l. Hipparchus, 182 f., 213, 248.
Antonius Musa, 129; given the *anulus aureus*, 66; doctor to Augustus, 130 f.; perhaps freed by M. Antonius, 131; possibly a *verna*, 248.

Antonius M. l. Theophilus, 66 n. 1, 190, 213.
Apella, presumably freedman of Lepidus, 187.
Apollonius, *see* Licinius.
Q. Apronius, possibly a freedman, 105 n. 1.
Arbuscula, probably a freedwoman, 140.
Aristocritus, freedman or slave of M. Cicero, 252 n. 3, 253, 255.
Asuvii, 217.
L. Ateius Philologus Praetextatus, 4, 121 f., 251.
C. Atilius Serrani l. Euhodus, 98 n. 7.
L. Aurelius Cottae l. Philostra, 210.
M. Aurelius Cottae Maximi l. Zosimus, 103 n. 1, 147, **157**, **214**, 233.
Aurelius Opilius, **114**, 127.
L. Aurelius L. l. Philo, 247.
C. Avianius M. l. Evander, 136 f.
C. Avianius M. l. Hammonius, procurator, 104, 137, 151; his kindness to Cicero, 221.

Bacchis, a *mima*, probably a freedwoman, 140.
Bardyaei, 178.
Bathyllus, *see* Cilnius.
Billienus, presumably a freedman, 248.
Brutia Q. l. Rufa, 211.
Burbuleius, an actor, possibly a freedman, 139 n. 4.

? Caecilius Attici ? l. Alexio, probably a freedman, not a slave, 108 n. 1, 152 n. 1.
? Caecilius Attici ? l. Alexis, probably a freedman, not a slave, 149, 222.

FREEDMEN AND PROBABLE FREEDMEN

? Caecilius Attici ? l. Areus, probably a freedman, 108 n. 1, 152 n. 1.
Q. Caecilius Attici l. Epirota, *verna*, 11, 248; *grammaticus*, 123; relationship with Gallus, 248.
? Caecilius Attici ? l. Eros, probably a freedman, 253.
Caecilius Attici l. Eutychides, 108 n. 1, 152 n. 1.
C. Caecilius C. l. Isidorus, 13, 109, 239 f.
(Caecilius) Attici l. Philogenes, 152 n. 1.
Caecilius Statius, probably a freedman, 111 f., 248.
M. Caelius M. l. Phileros, 155, 157, 239 f.
Caninia, Caninius, 209.
Cassius C. l. Pindarus, 146.
Cato, *see* Valerius.
C. Causinius Sc(h)olae l. Spinter, 210 n. 8.
Chelido, a courtesan, possibly a freedwoman, 142.
Chrysippus, *see* Tullius, Vettius.
Chrysogonus, *see* Cornelius.
Cilix, *see* Claudius.
Cilnius Maecenatis l. Bathyllus, 140 f., 246.
Cilnius Maecenatis l. Melissus, 5 f., 124 f., 226, 248.
? Cilnius ? Maecenatis l. Sarmentus, probably a freedman, 154, 225, 226, 271 f.
Claudius Ap. l. Cilix, 7, 145, 179 f.
Claudius Ap. l. Phania, 145, 179 f.
Cleophantus, a doctor, freed or peregrine, 131 n. 11.
Clesippus, *see* Geganius.
Clodius Aesopus, the actor, probably a freedman, 139, 225 n. 2.
Clodius P. l. Damio, 175 n. 5, 178.
Q. Considius Q. l. Eros, 155 f., 157, 196.
Corellius Tereus, 110.
Cornelii L. Sullae *liberti*, ex-slaves of the proscribed, 35, 178, 183 n. 1; probably formed a college, 171.
Q. Cornelius *scriba*, possibly a freedman, 61 n. 5, 154, 184 n. 3.
Cornelius (Lentuli l.) Alexander Polyhistor, of Miletus, 4, 246; a teacher, 124.

L. Cornelius L. Sullae l. Chrysogonus, 260 n. 6, 265; his extravagance, 143, 182, 240; money-making, 146, 182, 239; in Sulla's confidence, 181; his power, 182 ff.; and Roscius, 183.
Cornelius L. Sullae l. Epicadus, 114, 147.
Cornelius P. Lentuli l. Pausanias, *accensus*, 155 f., 180.
L. Cossinius L. l. Anchialus, 104, 221.
M. Cossutius M. ? l. Cerdo, 138.
M. Cossutius Menelaus, probably a freedman, 138.
L. Crassicius Pasicles Pansa, 124, 232 n. 2, 248, 251.
Craterus, a doctor, perhaps a freedman, 131 n. 11.
C. Curtius Postumi l. Helenus, 196.
C. Curtius Postumi l. Mithres, 104, 105, 221.
Cyrus, the architect, *see* Vettius Cyrus.
Cytheris, *see* Volumnia.

Damasippus, an art-dealer, perhaps a freedman, 105 n. 7.
Damio, *see* Clodius.
Daphnis, *see* Lutatius.
Demea, freedman or slave probably of Atticus, 253 n. 10.
Demetrius, *see* Julius, Pompeius.
Demochares, *see* Pompeius.
Democritus, perhaps a freedman of Atticus, 152 n. 1.
Dexippus, freedman or slave of M. Cicero, 252 n. 3, 253, 255.
Dionysia, *mima*, 140.
Dionysius, *see* Pomponius.
Diphilus, possibly a freedman, 255 n. 3.

Epicadus, *see* Cornelius.
L. Eprius Chilo, probably a freedman, 156.
Eros, *see* Caecilius, Considius, Julius, Plutius, Staberius, Turius, Tullius, Vergilius.
Eros, an actor, probably a freedman, 139.
Eros, an official in Egypt, possibly a freedman, 191 f., 240.
Eucharis, *see* Licinia.
Euphorbus, 131, 248.
Eurysaces, *see* Vergilius.
Evander, *see* Avianius.

INDEX II

Q. Fabius Africani l. Cytisus, **157**.
Q. Fadius, 235.
Fecenia Hispala, **84** f., 142, 204.
Flora, probably a freedwoman, 214.
Fufius, an actor, probably a freedman, 139 n. 4.
C. Furius Chresimus, 109.

Gabinius A. l. Antiochus, 136, **155**, 159 n. 6.
Galeria Copiola, *mima*, 140.
Geganius Ɔ. l. Clesippus, 240, 251; *viator*, 156; religious offices, 196; inherited from patroness, 239.
Glyco, a doctor, perhaps a freedman, 131 n. 11, 210.
Gnipho, *see* Antonius.
A. Granius M. l. Stabilio, 100.

Hammonius, *see* Avianius.
Herennia T. l., 248.
Hermia, freedman or slave of M. Cicero, 252 n. 3, 253.
Herophilus, an oculist, perhaps a freedman, 131 n. 11.
Herus, perhaps a freedman, 143 n. 7.
Hilarus, *see* Tullius.
Hipparchus, *see* Antonius.
Hispala, *see* Fecenia.
Horaea, *see* Larcia.
Horatius, *coactor*, 101; financial position, 108; and his son Horace, 232, **234** f.; his character, 240.
Hyginus, *see* Julius.
Hylas, *mimus*, 141.

Isidorus, *see* Caecilius.

Julia Ɔ. l. Phoebe, 145.
C. Julii Caesaris *liberti*, support for Octavian, 187; wealth, 239.
Julius (Aug.) l. Celadus, 191.
Julius Caesaris l. Demetrius, 65, 190.
Julius Caesaris l. Diochares, 145.
Julius Aug. l. Epaphroditus, 187.
C. Julius Aug. *liberti* l. Eros, 96 n. 8.
Julius (Aug.) l. Helenus, 187.
Julius Aug. l. Hilarion, 149.
C. Julius Aug. l. Hyginus, *captivus*, 4, 247; his career, 124; his friends, 224, 226.
Julius Caes. l. Licinus, 226, 227, 232 239 ff.; a Gaul, 5, 10, 248; procurator in Gaul, 65, **190** f.

Julius Aug. l. Marathus, 149.
Julius Hygini l. Modestus, 146.
Julius Aug. l. Phaedrus, **125**, **242**, 247.
Julius (Aug.) l. Philadelphus, 187.
Julius (Aug.) l. Polus, 73.
Julius Aug. l. Polybius, 149.
Julius Aug. l. Pylades, 140 f., 147.
C. Julius Caes. l. Salvius, in the civil service, 155, 156, 157; as *Lupercus*, 196.
Julius Aug. l. Sphaerus, 147.
Julius Aug. l. Thyrsus, 187.

Laelius Archelaus, possibly a freedman, 113 n. 5.
Larcia P. Ɔ. l. Horaea, 16, 213.
Larcius Nicia, 232.
Laurea, *see* Tullius.
Lenaeus, *see* Pompeius.
Licinia Ɔ. l. Eucharis, 139 f.
Licinius P. Crassi l. Apollonius, **121**, 147, 149, 223, 228 f.
Licinius L. Luculli l. Callisthenes, 182 n. 3.
Licinius L. Luculli l. *Hector, 182.
Licinius L. Murenae l. Tyrannio, 188, 220, 227 f.; *captivus*, 4, 246; his manumission, 13; work in Rome, 116, 128; relations with Cicero, 116, **254**, 255.
Licinius Philonicus, possibly a freedman, 167 n. 2.
Licinus, *see* Julius.
Livia Drusillae l. Galatea, 210.
L. Livineius Reguli l. Trypho, 221.
M. Livius M. l., 151.
L. Livius Salinatoris l. Andronicus, 111, 248.
Lutatius Q. Catuli l. Amphio, 182.
Lutatius Q. Catuli l. Daphnis, 13, **113**, 147.
L. Lutatius Paccius, probably a freedman, 98, 247, **267** f.

Mallius Glaucia, 223.
Manilius, an astronomer, 5, 115, **127**, 146.
L. Manneius Menecrates, perhaps a freedman, 131 f., 147.
Marcius Sotericus, 240.
Mario, freedman or slave of M. Cicero, 252 n. 3, 253, **255**.

FREEDMEN AND PROBABLE FREEDMEN

Melissus, *see* Cilnius.
Menander, *see* Publicius.
Menander, freedman or slave of M. Cicero, 252 n. 3, 253, **255**.
Menas/Menodorus, *see* Pompeius.
Menecrates, *see* Pompeius.
Metrobius, *mimus*, probably a freedman, 140.
Metrodorus, a doctor, perhaps a freedman, 131 n. 11, 252 n. 3, 254.
Mithres, *see* Curtius.
Musa, *see* Antonius.

N. Naevius Hilarus, 93 n. 2.
P. Naevius Turpio, possibly a freedman, 105 n. 1.
Nicephorus, bailiff of Q. Cicero, perhaps a freedman, 107.
L. Nostius Zoilus, 216 f.

M'. Obellius Acastus *aurifex*, probably a freedman, 98 n. 3.
M. Ocratius M. l., 151.
C. Octavius Octaviae Augusti sororis l. Auctus, 154.
Opilius, *see* Aurelius.
Optatus, 212.
M'. Otacilius Pitholaus, *see* Voltacilius Plotus.

Paccius, *see* Lutatius.
Pansa, *see* Crassicius.
Papias, *see* Pompeius Demochares.
Pasicles, *see* Crassicius.
Pausanias, *see* Cornelius.
Phaedrus, **125, 242,** 247.
Phaetho, *see* Tullius.
Phamea, Sardinian, probably a freedman, his personal political influence, 176; his quarrel with Cicero, 186; influential friends, **186,** 224; his wealth, 240; his origin, 247, and status, **269** f.
Pharnaces, freedman or slave of Atticus, 149 n. 1.
Philargyrus, probably freedman of A. Torquatus, 179 n. 5; not likely to have been a slave or freedman of Cicero, 252 n. 3.
Philargyrus (C. l.), 14.
Phileros, *see* Caelius.
Philologus, *see* Ateius, Tullius.
Philotimus, *see* Terentius.

Plotia T. l., 248.
Plotus, *see* Voltacilius.
Plutia L. l. Auge, 97.
L. Plutius L. l. Eros, 97.
Polyhistor, *see* Cornelius Alexander Polyhistor.
Pompeia Demetri l. Auge, 182.
Pompeius ? Sex. l. Apollophanes, 188.
Cn. Pompeius Cn. l. Demetrius, of Gadara, 5, 246; his influence with Pompey, 182 f., **185,** 224, 226; he kept his links with Gadara, 185, 227; his wealth, 185, 239; perhaps manumitted quickly, 188; not to be identified with an Antonian Demetrius, 190 n. 2.
Pompeius ? Sex. l. Demochares/Demochas/Papias, 188.
Pompeius Cn. l. Lenaeus, origin disputed, 4, 247, 248; as a scholar and Pompeian, **119,** 147, 219 n. 11.
Pompeius Cn. l. Menas Menodorus, 224, 226, 241; held posts normally equestrian and received *anulus aureus*, 65 f.; his success notorious, 182 f.; possibly an ex-pirate freed by Pompey, 188; fought for Sex. Pompeius and Octavian, **189**.
Pompeius Cn. l. Menecrates, 182 f., **188** f.
Pompeius ? Sex. l. Philo, 187 and n. 3.
Q. Pompeius Bithynici l. Sosus, 210 n. 8, 213.
Pompeius Vindullus, probably a freedman of Magnus, 104, 221.
T. Pomponi Attici *liberti*, *see* Antaeus, Antiochus, Anteros, Caecilii, Demea, Democritus, Pharnaces, Pomponius, Salvius, Satyrus, Syrus.
M. Pomponius Attici l. Dionysius, 73, 147, 151; his work for Cicero, **119** ff., 149, 180, 254, 255; Cicero's opinion of him fluctuated, **119** ff., 222; his manumission, 119 f.; named after Cicero, 120, 224, 250.
Porcius Catonis l. Butas, **178**.
Porcius Catonis l. Cleanthes, 130, 148.
Protogenes, freedman or slave of M. Marius, 148 n. 7.
Publicius, Pompey's double, 18 n. 7.
Cn. Publicius Menander, 18, 147, 156.

INDEX II

Publilius the Syrian, his origin, 5, 115, 246; his literary career, 122 f.; he was specially educated, 122, 146; his views on slavery, 242.
Pylades, *see* Julius.

C. Quinctilius C. l. Pamphilus, 98, 267 f.

Rabirius Postumus Hermodorus, probably a freedman, 205.
Q. Remmius Ɔ. l. Palaemon, 109.
Rufio, *see* Julius, Trebatius.
Rupa, probably a freedman, 152 n. 4.

M. Saevius M. l. Nicanor-Postumius, **114**, 251.
Salvius, freedman or slave of Atticus, 148 n. 7.
Sarmentus, probably a freedman, 154, 225, 226, **271** f.
Satyrus, freedman or slave of Atticus, 149 n. 2.
Sceptius, 110.
Scribonius Ɔ. l. Aphrodisius, 124.
Scribonius Libonis l. Hilarus, 187 and n. 3.
? Scribonius ? Curionis ? l. Rupa, 152 n. 4.
Seius, *scriba*, 154.
Sergius, *mimus*, 140.
L. Sergius, probably a freedman of Catiline, 172.
Sorex, probably a freedman, 140.
Spintharus, freedman or slave of M. Cicero, 252 n. 3, 253.
Staberius Eros, 5, 14, **115** f., 246.
Statius, *see* Caecilius, Tullius.
Stephanio, probably a freedman, 139.
Syrus, freedman or slave of Atticus, 149 n. 2.

P. Terentius Lucani l. Afer, his career, 112 f., 244; education, 112 f., 146; his friends, 224; he displays no special feeling about slavery, 241 f.; his origin, 112, 247.
Terentius Ɔ. l. Diocles Tyrannio, 125, 146.
Terentius Ɔ. l. Philotimus, 196 n. 1; had business interests, 104, 105, **264**; steward to Cicero, 144, 150, 253, 262, **263** f.; other work for Cicero, 145, **263** f.; as procurator, 152, 263 f.; Optimate views, 153 n. 3, 179, 263 f.
P. Tettius, possibly a freedman, 155.
Theodorus of Gadara, **123** f., **191**, 246, 248.
Theudas, 179 n. 5.
Tigellius, Sardinian, perhaps a freedman, 143, 226, 247; a singer, 141, 186, 269; his social importance, 184, **186**, 225; perhaps a freedman, 186, **269** f.; may have had political influence, 186.
Timagenes of Alexandria, 5, **123**, 223, 246.
Timarchides Verris l., 155, 159.
Tiro, *see* Tullius.
Tityrus, 17, 107, 209.
C. Trebatius ? Testae ? l. Rufio, 133 n. 9, 148.
? Trebianus ? Trebiani l. Theudas, 179 n. 5.
Trebonii, *thurarii*, **97** f.
P. Trebonius P. l., 216 f.
Truttedia P. Amphionis l. Appia, 250 n. 9.
Trypho, 179 n. 5.
M. Tulli Ciceronis *liberti*, 252 ff.
M. Tullius M. Ciceronis l. *scriba*, 89 n. 5, 156, 252, 253; *cognomen* unknown, 7, 232 n. 4, 258; *scriba* in Cilicia, 154, 180, 258; his manumission, 258; his career, **258** f.; relationship with Cicero, 255, **258** f., 264.
Tullius M. Ciceronis l. Aegypta, 252, 253, 255; his *cognomen*, 7; as a *tabellarius*, 258; his character, 258.
Tullius M. Ciceronis l. Chrysippus, 75 n. 1, 252, 253; in Cilicia, 180; education, 218; relationship with Cicero, 218, **257** f.; his defection, 218, **257** f.
Tullius M. Ciceronis l. Eros, 252, 253, **259**.
Tullius M. Ciceronis l. Hilarus, 252, 253, 264; activities in Macedonia, 73, 256 f.; an accountant, 150; client of Atticus, 223.
Tullius M. Ciceronis l. Laurea, 252, 253; a poet, 119, 259; loyal to Cicero, 219 n. 11, 259; no evidence for identification with M. Tullius *scriba*, 259.
Tullius M. or Q. Ciceronis l. Phaetho,

FREEDMEN AND PROBABLE FREEDMEN

252, 253; known only as a *tabellarius*, 257.
Tullius Q. Ciceronis l. Philologus, 119.
Tullius Q. Ciceronis l. Statius, his manumission, 21; his secretarial work, 149; in Quintus' confidence, 153, 158, **181**; perhaps not *accensus* in Asia, 158; work in Asia, 181; his notoriety, 181, 184; his importance, 193; probably not *Lupercus*, 196; relationship with Quintus, 218.
M. Tullius M. Ciceronis l. Tiro, 251, 252, 253, **259** ff.; his origin uncertain, 11, 260; his manumission, 13, 15, **261**; feelings of the Cicerones towards him, 13, **218** f., **261** ff.; business interests, 104, 108, 262; financial position, 146 f.; education, 146, 260 f.; secretarial work, 149, 261 f.; other employment, 152, 261 f.; political views, 153 n. 3, 179, 262; in Cilicia, 180; relationship with *ingenui*, 208, 222; unmarried, 214; loyalty to Cicero, 218 f.; his dates, 259 f.; scholarship, 262 f.
Turius Q. Turi l. Eros, 152 n. 4.
Tyrannio, *see* Licinius, Terentius.

P. Umbrenus, 102 n. 4, 103 n. 5.
Ummius, possibly a freedman, 143 n. 7, 254.

M. Vaccius M. l. Theophilus, 247.

Valerius, *praeco*, perhaps a freedman, 156.
Valerius Cato, 5, **122**, 248.
M. Vergilius Eurysaces, *pistor*, **96**, 100, 239.
Vergilius Vergili l. Eros, 149.
(Verres) C. l. Timarchides, 155, 159.
M. Verrius Flaccus, 124.
Vettius Cyri l. Chrysippus, 258 n. 2; freedman of Cyrus, 134, 146, 148; worked for Cicero, 134, 222 f., 254; worked for Caesar, 134.
(Vettius) Cyrus, the architect, perhaps a freedman, 133, 254.
Vettius Philocomus, possibly a freedman, 113 n. 5.
Vetulenus Aegialus, 109.
Veturii, 97.
Q. Vibius Q. l. Simius, 247.
Vindicius, 24 f.
Vindullus, *see* Pompeius.
T. Vinius Philopoemen, 66.
Voltacilius Plotus, *rhetor*, 14, 144, 146, 147; name dubious, 118; taught Pompey, 118; wrote history, 119.
L. Volteius, possibly a freedman, 155.
Volumnia Eutrapeli l. Cytheris, **140**, 142, 224 f.
Vulteius Mena, Horatian character, probably a freedman, 100 f., 109.

Zoilus, *see* Nostius; 208.
Zosimus, *see* Aurelius.